CADOGAN GUIDES

"Cadogan Guides are mini-encyclopaedic ... they give the explorer, the intellectual or culture buff—indeed, any visitor—all they need to know to get the best from their visit ... a good read too by the many inveterate armchair travellers.'
—The Book Journal

"The quality of writing in this British series is exceptional ... From practical facts to history, customs, sightseeing, food and lodging, the Cadogan Series can be counted on for interesting detail and informed recommendations."
—Going Places (US)

"Standouts these days are the Cadogan Guides ... sophisticated, beautifully written books."
—American Bookseller Magazine

"Entertaining companions, with sharp insights, local gossip and far more of a feeling of a living author ... The series has received plaudits worldwide for intelligence, originality and a slightly irreverent sense of fun."
—The Daily Telegraph

Other titles in the Cadogan Guides series:

AUSTRALIA
BALI
BERLIN
THE CARIBBEAN
ECUADOR,
   THE GALÁPAGOS
   & COLOMBIA
GREEK ISLANDS
INDIA
IRELAND
ITALIAN ISLANDS
ITALY
MEXICO
MOROCCO
NEW YORK
NORTHEAST ITALY
NORTHWEST ITALY
PORTUGAL
PRAGUE
ROME

SCOTLAND
SOUTH ITALY
SOUTHERN SPAIN
SOUTH OF FRANCE—Provence,
   Côte d'Azur & Lanquedoc-Roussillon
SPAIN
TUNISIA
TURKEY
TUSCANY, UMBRIA &
   THE MARCHES
VENICE

Forthcoming:
AMSTERDAM
CENTRAL AMERICA
CZECHOSLAVAKIA
GERMANY
JAPAN
MOSCOW & LENINGRAD
PARIS

ABOUT THE AUTHOR

Frank Kusy is a professional travel writer. Born in England, the son of Polish-Hungarian immigrants, he first travelled abroad at the age of four and has been wandering ever since. He left Cardiff University for a career in journalism and worked for a while with the *Financial Times*. He has also written a successful guidebook to India in the Cadogan Guides Series.

CADOGAN GUIDES

THAILAND

FRANK KUSY

CADOGAN BOOKS
London

THE GLOBE PEQUOT PRESS
Chester, Connecticut

Cadogan Books Ltd
Mercury House, 195 Knightsbridge, London SW7 IRE

The Globe Pequot Press
138 West Main Street, Chester, Connecticut 06412, USA

Cover design by Keith Pointing
Cover illustration by Povl Webb
Maps by Thames Cartographic Services Ltd

Editor: Victoria Ingle
Series Editor: Rachel Fielding
Updaters: Michael Davidson and Brian Walsh
Indexer: Valerie Elliston

First published 1988, with Burma guide.
Second edition October 1991, updated and revised.

A Catalogue record for this book is available from the British Library
ISBN 0–947754–45–8

Library of Congress Data available
ISBN 0–87106–154–6

Photoset in Ehrhardt on a Linotron 202
Printed and bound in Great Britain by
Redwood Press Limited, Melksham, Wiltshire

To my grandfather, László Hunor, with gratitude.
Nam-myoho-renge-kyo.

ACKNOWLEDGEMENTS

It is impossible to mention everybody who has contributed to this guide, but special thanks go to: Trailfinders (especially Gail Randall and Beth Hooson); Ian Pollack and 'Swit' Prasertpont (Chiang Mai); Sukhum, Mongkon and T T Guest House (Bangkok); Mr Virat, K. Kultida and Korakoat Jitrapiriom (Bangkok); Poo & Tangsukjai restaurant (Chiang Mai); Vanna and Yoothapong Kunateerachadalai (UK); Miss Tassanee Bhikul (Songkhla National Museum); Sue Wild and Toss Putsorn (Koh Samet); Dr Sally Meecham-Jones, Anne Edwards and Bridget Crampton (UK); Dave Glynn-Thomas (Canada); Stephen ('Wherever I lay my hat, that's my home...') Merchant, Rosie Targett, Anna Donovan, Georgia and Tony; to Jessica Kent (who was there when it all began), and to my parents.

For cordial service, friendly assistance and lots of information, I should like to thank TAT (Tourism Authority of Thailand), especially offices in London, Bangkok, Phuket, Pattaya, Hua Hin, Kanchanaburi and Chiang Mai.

Finally, a special *sabai! sabai!* to the following, for sharing the joys of Thailand with me: BANGKOK: John Runcie, Kate Burton (UK); Romy de Weerdt (Belgium); Lynn Cote (Canada); Anek Chitrbandh, 'Froggy' and Roof Garden Guest House. CHIANG MAI: Jill and Jane (NZ), Poo and Boon Tean; BAN CHIANG: Thadsanee Kanyarat (and National Museum); CHIANG RAI: 'Chat'; HAT YAI: Adrian Dale, Tim and Tracey (UK), Alfred and Stefano (US); HUA HIN: Tipawan Thampusana (TAT); KAN-CHANABURI: Jos Aarts (Holland), John Richards, Tina and Jill (UK), Berni Koppe (Canada), Sunya Koohamongkol; KHAO YAI: 'Po'; KOH PHI PHI: Leonard, Johann, Anna and Katrina (Sweden); Clare and Fiona (UK), Ann and Herb (US), Donna (NZ) and Ann (Canada); KOH PHANGAN: Alistair and Debbie (UK); KOH SAMET: Janine and Jenny (Australia), Anya (Germany); Eileen and Katrina (UK); Judy & Nuan Kitchen; KOH SAMUI: Raewyn Annas, Karen and Pete Lloyd (NZ), Karen and Frank (Australia), Dominic and Colin (UK), Poh, Sak, Kai and Moon Bungalow; KOH SI CHANG: Toom & Tiewpai Hotel, Alison Campbell (UK), Andrea Nidhof (Germany); KRABI: Jate and PP Guest House, Hans Carlsson (Sweden); Erica (UK), Mark (Switzerland), Philip and Larry, Mary and Joom; LAMPHUN: Duang Chan Longlai; MAE HONG SON: Helmut and Julia (Germany), Caroline Lander (UK), Florence and Michelle (France), and 'Nok' Anan; MAE SARIANG: Peter Charlesworth (UK), Pai Toon; NAKHON PATHOM: Boon Khong Luksapol, Siammit and Supap; NAK-HON RATCHASIMA: Nikki & 'La Ploy'; NONG KHAI: Wolfgang Marik (Germany); and Boonthom ('Prem') Natenee; PAI: Willi (Switzerland), Duang, Kim and 'Jungle Joe'; PATTAYA: Scott Fisher (Australia); PHANG NGA: Sayan Tamtopol; PHUKET: Didden Alex (Belgium); SOPPONG: Albert (Malaysia), Elbe, Rob and Tracy (UK); SUK-HOTHAI: Lakana & Chinawat Hotal.

The updaters would like to thank the following people for their assistance: Amanda and Pathei, Rachel (Koh Samet), Oliver (Pattaya), Sanong Pamueng (Bangkok), Jack Stauff, all the TAT staff and Antony Aikman. Particular thanks go to Susan, Joe, Barbara, Keeley, Jennifer, Pat and George for their kind help, humour and hospitality.

CONTENTS

Part V: Bangkok *Pages 48–87*

Part VI: Around Bangkok *Pages 88–127*

Part VII: The North *Pages 128–85*

Part VIII: The Northeast *Pages 186–202*

Part IX: The South *Pages 203–55*

Language *Pages 256–60*

Index *Pages 261–6*

LIST OF MAPS

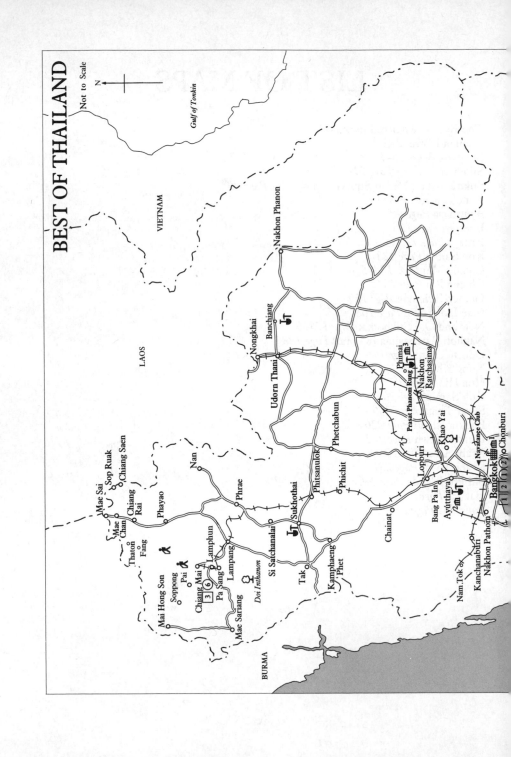

BEST OF THAILAND

Not to Scale

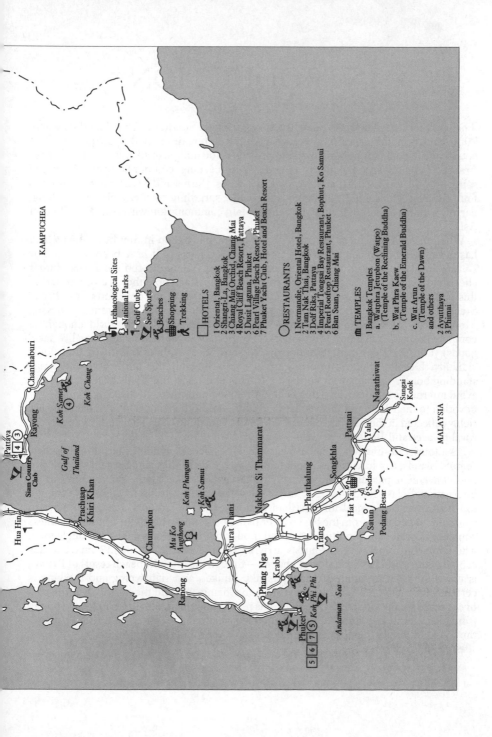

INTRODUCTION

Thailand, formerly known as Siam, is a small, friendly Southeast Asian kingdom where 20th-century modernity exists alongside a unique culture developed over 700 years. The country has a population about the same as the UK (60 million in an area about the size of France, 500,000 sq km), and is bounded—proceeding counterclockwise from the south—by the Gulf of Thailand, Kampuchea, Laos, Burma and Malaysia. It divides into four distinct regions—the mountainous north, the sprawling northeast plateau, the long, narrow isthmus of the south, and the central plain commonly known as the 'Rice Bowl of Asia'.

What makes Thailand so special is that it is the only nation in Southeast Asia which has never really been colonized by a foreign power. Parts of it have been occupied by Burma and Laos, or lost outright, but never for long enough to rob the Thais of their cherished national character, customs or traditions. As a people they are very proud of this fact, and commonly refer to their country as 'Muang Thai' or 'Land of the Free'. Steered into the 20th century by a remarkable succession of kings—beginning with King Mongkut (of *The King and I* fame)—Thais today remain Third World enough to compete favourably in Third World markets (especially in fabrics and high-quality 'fake' goods) yet progressive enough to borrow Western ideas without sacrificing their individuality. Despite great poverty in certain areas—notably the northeast—and long-standing border disputes with bordering Burma and Laos, the Thais have managed to avoid internal revolution. Two things hold them together through thick and thin—their devotion to their king and their belief in Buddhism. Both symbols of national unity are richly reflected in their art and culture. More than anything else, Thailand is a country of royal palaces and Buddhist temples—thousands of them.

As a tourist destination, Thailand has much to offer. It combines beautiful beaches, remote islands, tropical jungles, mountain valleys, ancient sites, and bargain shopping in one convenient package. And it's still remarkably cheap. Here you can stay in an international-class hotel for £30, buy a new fashion wardrobe for £50 and enjoy a top-quality gourmet meal for less than £10 a head. The country appeals to a broad spectrum of people—from the backpacker living on a shoestring to the affluent business couple who prefer air-conditioning and all mod-cons. It especially appeals to single men, who comprise some 70% of tourists arriving in the country. Thailand's image as sex capital of the world has been slow to change—though the raunchy beach resort of Pattaya is now losing out to family-style resorts like Phuket, and sightseeing and trekking is certainly the main preoccupation of visitors to Chiang Mai and the north. Over the past five years or so, the kind of traveller here has perceptibly changed—from hippy to yuppie, from beach-bum to culture-vulture, from backpacker to package tourist. But Thailand, the 'Land of Smiles', happily accommodates everyone and there is now only one tourist season—all year round.

Part I
GENERAL INFORMATION

A tuk-tuk

Preparing to Go

Thailand has a lot more to offer than shopping in Bangkok, trekking in Chiang Mai, beachcombing on Phuket, or 'entertainment' at Pattaya. If these increasingly touristy attractions are all you want or have time for, then a number of good package-tour companies will be delighted to plan your trip for you. If, however, you want a holiday away from the tourist centres, and can make the time to explore the country properly, travel independently and plan your own itinerary. While the ideal length of stay—for a comprehensive tour of Thailand—would be around 3 months, you could cover most of its highlights in just 8 weeks. This would allow two weeks in and around Bangkok, two weeks in the north, three weeks in the south, and a week exploring the neglected northeast.

There is no 'traveller's trail', as such, in Thailand. Most travellers arrive by air in Bangkok, from where they generally head north to Chiang Mai or south to the beaches. People entering the country overland from Malaysia have a straight run up the southern isthmus to Bangkok, while those entering overland from India or Nepal drift down to the capital from the far north. In general, the best way to plan your Thailand holiday is to decide what it is you want—and then choose two or three centres which fit the bill. To help you, Bangkok and Chiang Mai have the best shopping and sightseeing, Phuket and Pattaya the best water-sports and 'upmarket' beach resort facilities, Koh Samui and

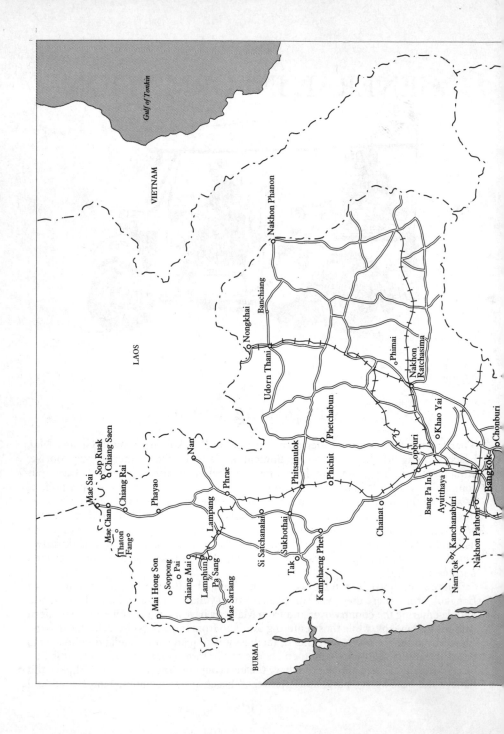

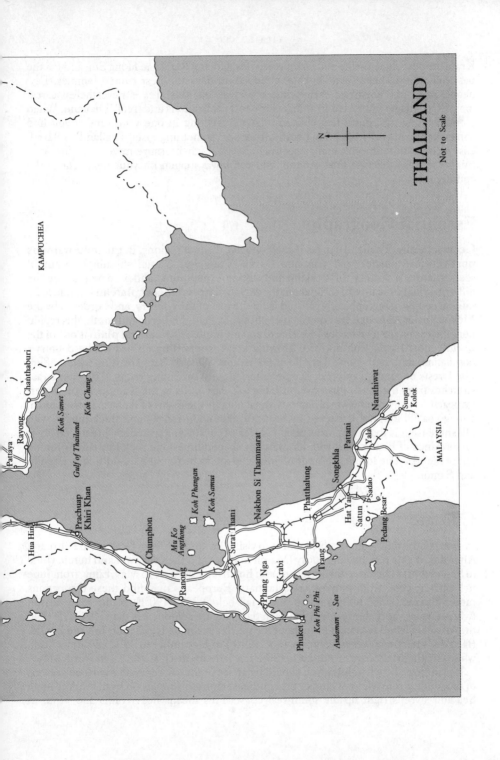

Krabi the best coral-diving and offshore islands, Chiang Rai, Mae Hong Son and Pai the best hill-tribe trekking, and Sukhothai and Ayutthaya the best ruined temples. Few people make the northeast their prime objective, but this area is nevertheless a real magnet to anyone interested in archaeology, lost civilizations and 'real' Thailand. When planning your trip, don't feel obliged to see everything in one visit—and if you find somewhere you really like, don't rush off to 'see' something else. Thailand's relaxed, easy-going nature doesn't really encourage hectic, high-pressure travel. Besides, anything you miss the first time around, you can always catch on your next visit to the country.

Essential Geography

Geographically, Thailand can be divided into five distinct regions. In **the mountainous north**, whose jungles spill over into Burma, Laos and China, stunningly beautiful scenery attracts visitors for trekking and rafting expeditions, and a chance to see the hill-tribe villages scattered throughout the region. **The northeast plateau** is home to 20 million people, geographically isolated from the rest of the country, and bordered by the Mekong river. Although less spectacular physically than the north and south, this region nonetheless has its own backwoods charm and mystique. **The central plain** is one of the world's most fertile fruit and rice growing areas, supporting a third of the country's population, and the historical cradle of the nation. West of Bangkok, this region offers vast forests of bamboo and teak, scenic waterfalls and cascading rivers. **The east coast** stretches from the Chao Phya river at Bangkok, eastwards to the Kampuchean border. Its beaches have become world-famous, most notably the resort of Pattaya. In **the south**, a long coastal lowland is backed by beautiful mountain ranges and thick jungle, with off-shore islands that meet many people's idea of paradise. Particularly breath-taking is the province of Phang Nga, with its strangely shaped limestone rock formations jutting out of the sea. The loveliest islands of Thailand are to be found here—Phuket, Phi-Phi and Samui.

Climate

In general, the most comfortable months to visit Thailand are from October to February. After this, it gets very hot and sticky (March to June) and then very wet and humid (June to September). The three main seasons are: hot, from February to May; rainy, from June to October; cool, from November to January. Europeans may find these distinctions rather blurred, since temperatures rarely fall below 33°C (90°F) in the rainy season (when several short showers may fall each day) and are seldom less than 24°C (75°F) in the so-called 'cool' season. Throughout the year, the climate is generally hot and humid. Bangkok's temperatures range from 16°C (62°F) in December to 35°C (96°F) in April, while Chiang Mai ranges from 20°C (68°F) in January to 28°C (82°F) in April/May.

If planning a beach holiday, you should be aware of the *two* separate monsoon seasons of the south. From May to October the southeast monsoon comes up from the Andaman Sea and sweeps right up the southwest coast. This means heavy rains and winds at

4

Phuket, Krabi, Phi Phi and Phang Nga. From November to February, the northeast monsoon comes over from Kampuchea and hits the southeast coast of the isthmus affecting resorts like Samui and Songkhla. Sometimes these monsoons come early, sometimes late, but the good thing about them is that they rarely hit both coastlines at the same time. Thus, if the weather breaks down at Samui, you'll often find it perfect at Krabi, a relatively short bus ride away, or vice versa. I've only ever met one couple who got the worst of both worlds—they arrived at Koh Phangan when monsoons were raging on both sides of the peninsula. All the beaches are best visited a month or two *after* the rains, when infestations of sandfleas and mosquitoes have died down. March and April are nice practically everywhere, which is why the Thais have their school holidays then. Thailand in general is busiest between November and April, which is its high tourist season. Visiting in September and October, when rains are only intermittent, can be a good idea—fewer tourists, more empty beaches, and discounts on many hotels.

Getting to Thailand

From the UK

There are direct flights to Bangkok from London on **Thai Airways, British Airways** and **Qantas**. Scheduled fares are in the range of £730–840, but naturally it's cheaper to go through a travel agent. Booking through a cheap flight specialist like **Trailfinders** (tel 071 603 1515) or **STA** (tel 071 937 9962), you can get low-season discount return fares of £400–470 (with Thai Airways International). If you don't mind a change of planes, then cheap low-season returns can be obtained—from **KLM, Lufthansa, Swissair, Philippine Airlines, Cathay Pacific, Gulf Air** and **Royal Jordanian**, starting at around £495.

If you buy a **one-way ticket** from London to Bangkok (currently around £200–250 from bucket-shop agencies), you'll almost certainly be able to pick up a cheap return flight in Bangkok (cf. Banglampoo/Soi Ngam Dupli, Bangkok section).

Since cheap flights out of London are often heavily booked (especially from July to December), it's advisable to book two months before your intended departure date. Check travel sections of magazines like *Time Out, LAM* and *TNT* for current cheap fare deals.

From the US

Thai International, Korean Airlines, Canadian Airlines and **China Airlines** all offer budget or 'Super Apex' flights to Bangkok from US$1000 to US$1200 round-trip (from Los Angeles and San Francisco), from US$1200 to US$1400 (from New York). While New Yorkers often find it cheaper to fly to London and pick up onward tickets there, it's always worth contacting **Access International**, 101 W 31st St, 1104 New York, NY 10001 (tel 333 7280) to see if they have any last-minute specials.

From Canada

Canadian Airlines operates direct-flight services to Bangkok from Toronto and Vancouver for C$1900, but it's still **Korean Airlines** that have the best budget deals—their popular round-trip 'milk run' ticket from Vancouver to Bangkok via Seoul costs C$1440–1650; low-season one-way tickets are C$971, high season C$1133.

From Australia

Flying to Bangkok, one-way economy tickets cost around AUS$1100 from Sydney/ Melbourne, around AUS$1000 from Perth. Buying advance-purchase tickets (must be booked and paid for 21 days before departure date), one-way fares are only AUS$600– 700 from Sydney/Melbourne (AUS$1000–1400 return) and around AUS$500 from Perth (AUS$900–1000 return). Further reductions may be obtained by shopping around at cheap-flight specialists in Sydney like **Travel Specialists**, 7 Piccadilly Arcade, 222 Pitt St (tel 2679122) and **Student Travel Australia**, 1a Lee St, Railway Square (tel 2126744).

Many Australians are now entering Thailand on the overland route from Bali or Singapore (around AUS$500 from Sydney) or via Denpasar (about AUS$250–300 from Darwin).

Package Holidays

These are best booked in the UK, where several tour companies are now offering Thailand at very competitive prices. A good example is **Jetset Tours**, 74 Oxford Street, London WC1 (tel 071 631 0501)—10 days in Bangkok at just £600 (little more than a return fare), and a 17-day *Thailand Discovery* tour at around £1000, taking in Bangkok, Kanchanaburi, Chiang Mai and Pattaya. Several other operators include **Cox and King's Travel**, St James Court, 45 Buckingham Gate, London SW1E 6AF (tel 071 834 7472), who do temple, cultural and wildlife tours; **Poundstretcher**, Hazelwick Ave, Three Bridges, Crawley (tel 0293 518060), who offer three-weeks-for-the-price-of-two deals; and **Kuoni**, Kuoni House, Dorking, Surrey (tel 0306 885044), who feature Thailand in both their Worldwide and Kuoni 3 programmes—13 to 19 day packages in Bangkok and Pattaya from £650–800. **Exodus Expeditions**, 9 Weir Road, London SW12 OLT (tel 081 675 5550) and **The Travel Alternative**, 27 Park End St, Oxford OX1 4HU (tel 0865 791636) both specialize in explorer and adventure holidays.

In general, the more you pay for a package tour, the more 'plastic' is the environment. Also, while sightseeing trips with English-speaking guides are often laid on, they are not included in the price. You have to pay for these yourself.

Of the many companies who offer semi-organized tours geared to the budget-conscious independent traveller, the best is **Trailfinders**, 42–50 Earls Court Rd (tel 071 938 3366). They provide a complete travel service—insurance, inoculations, information, visas and cut-price air tickets. They also offer a number of tours in Thailand, with optional possible combinations of Malaysia, Singapore and Indonesia. Another company offering the same kind of tours and services is **Topdeck Travel**, 133 Earls Court Rd, London W8 (tel 071 373 8406).

Passports and Visas

A valid passport and a **visa** is required by all foreign nationals arriving in Thailand. However, transit passengers with confirmed onward air tickets are allowed to stay in

Thailand for up to 15 days without visas. Staying longer than 15 days, you've a choice of three kinds of visa: a 30-day **transit visa** (£5.50 or US$9), a 60-day **tourist visa** (£8 or US$13), or a 90-day **non-immigrant visa** (£13.50 or US$21). All visa applications should be accompanied by two passport photos, and (in the case of the non-immigrant visa) by a letter of financial guarantee from a reliable referee (e.g. bank manager). Visas are obtainable from all Thai embassies and consulates. In the UK, apply to the Thai Embassy, 30 Queen's Gate, London SW7 (tel 071 1589 0173) between 9.30 am and 12.30 pm, Mon–Fri. Collect visa (and passport) 2 days later, before 1.

All visas of entry into Thailand are valid for 90 days from the date of issue. Visas are officially non-extendable (as my embassy quipped: 'Thailand is the land of the lotus eaters—who wants to leave?'), but the Thai immigration office at Soi Suan Phlu, Sathorn Tai Rd, Bangkok, sometimes grants extensions—here, it helps to have a big smile on your face and a very good reason for staying. Possibly the best place to extend visas is on Koh Samui (cf. p. 208), where you can get a 30-day extension on a tourist visa with no problem, but it's highly unlikely you'll get more than 15 days extension on a transit visa.

If you want to stay over 60 days in Thailand—and don't want the hassle involved in getting a non-immigrant visa, or of extending a transit or tourist visa—then your best bet is to buy a **two-entry tourist visa** (£16 or US$26). This gives you two lots of 60 days in the country. To claim the second lot, you've got to go out of the country and come back in again. The simplest place to do this is Pedang Besar (cf. Hat Yai, Getting There) just across the Malaysian border. You can also get a **dual-entry non-immigrant visa** (£27 or US$42), which allows a stay of 120 days—again, provided you leave and re-enter the country.

Customs

You can bring into Thailand 200 cigarettes (or 250 grams of tobacco), a quart of wine or alcohol, and up to 2000B in Thai currency. You can't bring in any drugs or pornographic literature. You can take out up to 500B in Thai currency, and any amount of gems and jewellery. You can't take out any Buddha images (except pocket-size ones), antiques or art objects, unless you've got permission from the Fine Arts Department (ring Bangkok National Museum on 224–1370 for further details). Visitors leaving Thailand are also prohibited from taking out over US$10,000, unless declared on arrival, or granted permission by the Bank of Thailand.

Jabs and Tabs

No vaccinations are required for Thailand, unless you are coming from a contaminated area. This said, jabs are strongly recommended against cholera, typhoid, tetanus, polio and infective hepatitis. A single dose of Hepatitis A vaccine will give you 60–70% protection only, so it's still wise to stick to bottled or purified water in Thailand.

Malaria pills are essential. You'll need to start taking these a week before you set off, and to keep on taking them for four weeks after your return. Since certain brands can cause unpleasant side-effects (nausea, vomiting, etc), it's wise to order them from your doctor a good two weeks before your departure—that way you've got time to change your prescription if they don't agree with you. It's worth ringing up the London Hospital of Tropical Diseases (tel 071 387 4411) for up-to-date information, or contacting Trailfinders' excellent medical centre.

Diarrhoea tablets are also recommended for 'emergencies'. The most widely prescribed are Imodium and Lomotil (Codeine-Phosphate is also okay, but can be toxic). In general, diarrhoea is best left to remedy itself. Use tablets only if you're on a busy schedule, and simply can't afford to be sick.

An excellent guide to health abroad—both readable and informative—is Dr Richard Dawood's *Travellers' Health* (Oxford University Press, UK). It's also available in the States, published by Viking under the title *How to Stay Healthy Abroad*. Also worth obtaining (UK only) are the DHSS leaflets SA35 (Protect your Health Abroad) and SA30 (Medical Costs Abroad). Your doctor should stock these.

Money

Prices are rising all the time, but Thailand is still a fairly cheap place to live. The cost of a two-week holiday—including food, accommodation, transport, tours and entertainment (but excluding shopping!) is currently around £300 (on a shoestring), £450 (mid-range comfort) and £800–1000 (living in style). Cutting out alcoholic drinks and staying away from expensive tourist centres will reduce the above estimates substantially.

Travellers' Cheques are the safest means of carrying your money. They normally have automatic insurance and are easy to replace. Since Thailand has no currency black market (unlike say, India or Burma), there is no advantage in taking lots of cash, especially since travellers' cheques command a better exchange rate at Thai banks than hard currency. For safety, order your cheques in small denominations, keep them separate from your sales receipt (record of purchase), and keep a note of the refunding agent's address in Thailand (vendor should supply this) in a safe place.

Major **credit cards** such as American Express, Visa, Diners Club, Carte Blanche and Master Charge are accepted in many large hotels, restaurants and department stores. A credit card can be a lifesaver if, for any reason, your travellers' cheques and money go missing. It's also very handy for shopping, especially when a bargain silk sale comes up on your last day in Bangkok and you're clean out of cash.

Travel insurance is essential. If your bank or travel company can't suggest a good policy, check out the comprehensive schemes offered by Trailfinders or Topdeck Travel (cf Package Tours). Your policy should cover lost luggage, money and valuables, personal liability and travel delay. It should also supply a 24-hour number to contact in the case of a medical emergency.

For currency exchange see 'Changing Money' on p. 24.

What to Take

In general, the less you take the better. You can buy all you need—clothes, baggage, toiletries etc—in Bangkok, and often a good deal cheaper than at home. But don't bring

8

too little! I've seen smug repeat visitors arriving in Thailand with nothing but the clothes they stand up in. They stop smiling when they have to spend their first day in Bangkok's extreme heat, shopping for basics like toothpaste and sun-cream. The message is travel light but bring all essentials. Make up a short but comprehensive shopping list, and leave a copy at home with someone reliable—this will assist insurance claims should your luggage be lost or stolen.

Luggage

Don't take more luggage than you can easily carry—toting heavy bags around in Thailand's humid heat can be exhausting, to say the least. Try and pack everything in one large soft bag, or in a frameless rucksack with top carrying-handle and plenty of pockets. All small items—camera, newspaper, books, etc—can go in a small shoulder bag or day-pack—useful not only for travelling on the plane, but also for sightseeing and day-outings within Thailand. Inside the country, it's a good idea to wear shoulder bags diagonally across the body—this prevents theft. If you're going to be doing a lot of travelling between towns, consider leaving the inevitable accumulation of presents and souvenirs in store—most of the larger hotels and major rail/bus stations have left-luggage rooms. This leaves you free to get around without the encumbrance of excess luggage. Check with your airline regarding luggage allowance—if it looks like you're going to go seriously overweight on your return flight (and this is *very* common), consider freighting a few kilos home prior to departure, or posting parcels home by sea or air-mail. The main Bangkok post offices have an excellent packing service.

Clothing

Cool, cotton clothes are your best bet—and you should pack at least one smart, casual outfit. The Thais are smooth dressers. Nobody can look cooler than the hip young Thai leaning lazily on his Japanese motorbike in his designer disco-jacket, his personalized cufflinks, his Levi jeans, and his custom-made shoes. Even ordinary Thai housewives are decked out like fashion models. While you can kit yourself out in the latest styles at Bangkok's numerous department stores and boutiques, it's worth bringing a jacket and tie if you're going to be staying at a plush hotel, or intend visiting high-class restaurants or nightclubs.

For the rest, you can get away with just two T-shirts (or cotton shirts), a pair of trousers or jeans, a skirt or dress, two sets of socks and underwear, a comfy pair of flat shoes, swimwear, a towel, a sun hat, a pair of shorts and perhaps a pair of sandals (or thongs/flip-flops). If you're going during the rainy months, also include a light water-proof, and a small, folding umbrella. If you're visiting northern Thailand from November to January, when it gets quite cold at night, take a warm sweater and a sleeping bag.

Because clothes tend to dry quickly, bring only a few and wash them regularly. Many hotels and guest houses, for a modest fee, will wash them for you, or will be able to recommend a laundry service nearby.

Equipment

Things worth taking are a money-belt (or security wallet), sunglasses and suncream, a small torch and spare batteries, a roll of toilet paper, a water bottle and some water-purification tablets (Puritabs are best), personal toiletries (including a mirror and a sewing kit), a washing line and soap powder, a penknife with openers (useful for peeling fruit), a personal medical kit (should include mosquito repellant, antiseptic mouth-wash etc), reading and writing matter, playing cards or travel-scrabble (good for whiling away long train journeys), perhaps a walkman (pirate cassettes are very cheap in Bangkok and Chiang Mai), a camera and lots of film. You can buy film in Thailand, but it can be a little pricey, and you need to check the expiry date before purchasing.

Other useful inclusions are a small alarm clock (for catching early trains), a combination padlock (for securing baggage etc), snorkelling equipment (the stuff hired out on Thai beaches is seldom good quality), a half-sheet with attached pillowcase (for budget lodges with dirty linen, or trek huts with no linen at all) and, of course, a mosquito net (as big as possible—most Thai accommodation has vast beds). An inflatable pillow always comes in handy, especially on long and arduous bus journeys. Spectacle and contact lens wearers should take spare glasses/lenses, and should have their prescriptions noted down somewhere safe, in case replacements are required. Finally, consider taking along a few small presents for the Thai friends you'll be making along the way. Photos of yourself and your family go down well. So do postcards of your home town or of the English royal family; Thais particularly like those of the Queen on horseback. Small foreign coins make good gifts for children, while Thai women like Max Factor make-up. It's difficult to know what to give Thai men, though a bottle of Scotch generally goes down well, as do English or American cigarettes. When presenting gifts to Thais, remember to do so with both hands, giving a slight bow called a *wai*.

Books and Information

The more you read about Thailand, both before going and whilst there, the more you're likely to enjoy the country. Visit your local library, scout around the larger bookshops and (if in the UK) drop in on Trailfinders, who issue free handouts on Bangkok, Thailand and Southeast Asia. They also have an excellent little reference library, full of useful guides, maps and travel mags.

Tourist Information

For general information, plus a decent map of Thailand, visit your nearest TAT (Tourism Authority of Thailand) office. TAT has overseas offices at:

Australia: 12th Floor, Royal Exchange Bldg., 56 Pitt Street, Sydney NSW 2000 (tel 277540).

France: 90 Avenues des Champs Élysées, 75008 Paris (tel 45 62 86 56).

Japan: Hibiya Mitsui Bldg., 1–2 Yurakucho 1-Chome, Chiyoda-ku, Tokyo 100 (tel 58 06 776).

UK: 49 Albemarle St, London W1 (tel 071 499 7679).

USA (East): 5 World Trade Center, Suite 2449, New York, NY 10048 (tel 43 20 433).

USA (West): 3340 Wilshire Blvd., Suite 1101, Los Angeles, California 90010 (tel 38 22 353).

In Thailand, TAT has its head office in Bangkok, and local offices at Kanchanaburi and Pattaya (central), at Chiang Mai and Phitsanulok (north), Nakhon Ratchasima (northeast), and Phuket, Surat Thani, Hat Yai and Songkhla (south). All are helpful, efficient and hand out useful material.

Maps

Two good country maps of Thailand, published by APA and Nelles, are sold in the UK, but it is best to wait till you get to Bangkok (e.g. The Bookseller, Patpong), where you can pick them up at a quarter of the price. If you're into serious map-reading, visit Bangkok's TAT head office on Ratchadamnoen Nok—this offers a remarkably detailed 4-map set, covering central, northeast, north and south regions, for 75B.

City maps of Bangkok and Chiang Mai, compiled by Nancy Chandler, sell both in Thailand (65B) and at major travel bookshops abroad. Packed with useful information, these are actually better city guides than maps. TAT do a reasonable map of Bangkok (free), and their provincial offices issue complimentary town/city maps. Most bookstores in Bangkok sell the essential 'bus map' (40B), which is a bus map, an excellent city map, and a country map all rolled into one.

Books

Western bookshops don't tend to stock many books on Thailand, and you may be better off waiting till you get to Bangkok and Chiang Mai. Here you can pick up some excellent titles, including Carol Hollinger's *Mai Pen Rai means Never Mind* (Asia Book Co.), a wry, witty and well-observed account of Thai manners and cultural conflicts; the perceptive *Siam in Crisis* by Sulak Sivaraksa (DK Books); and the absorbing *Everyday Life in Thailand—an Interpretation* by Dr Niels Mulder (DK Books), a first-class analysis of Thai customs, society and religion.

If you want to know more about Buddhism, and don't want to wade through vast tomes on the subject, look out for *Understanding Thai Buddhism*, a short, readable study of M. L. Manich Jumsai (DK), or *A Meditator's Diary* by Jane Hamilton-Merritt (Pelican, UK), an interesting account of one Western woman's experiences in Thai monasteries.

For history and archaeology, there's still nothing to touch A. Clerac's *A Guide to Thailand* (OUP, UK). The author was French ambassador to Thailand, travelled the country by limo, and is generally spot on. Also worth a read is *Thailand, a Short History* by David K. Wyatt (Yale University Press, London). Two good introductions to the northern hill-tribes of Thailand are *Peoples of the Golden Triangle* by Paul and Elaine Lewis (Thames and Hudson, UK), and *People of the Hills* by Preecha Chaturabhand (DK Books). A few modern Thai novels have recently appeared in English translation. Two recommended ones are *Rice without Rain* (Andre Deutsch) by Min Fong Ho, a racy little story about the City of Angels, Bangkok, and *A Child of the North East* by Kampoon Boon Tawee (DK Books), an award-winning novel about a year in the life of a northeastern village in the 1930s. If you want to know more about Thai food, *Thai Cooking* by Jennifer Brennan (Futura, McDonald and Co, Sydney) is probably the best all-round introduction; also *Cooking Thai Food in American Kitchens* by Malulee Pinsuvana, full of well-illustrated recipes.

Further Reading
Shaw, J.C., *Thai Ceramic*
Petchsingh, Trirat, *The Third Encounter*
Bowring, John, *Kingdom and People of Siam*
Chuawiwat, Tom, *The Life of Lord Buddha*
Hoebel, R. and Rolwick, H., *The Sun Blessed Land*
Hoskin, John, and Lapin, Lindie, *Siamese Ruby*
Warren, William, and Lloyd, Ian, *Bangkok*.

Newspapers

Bangkok has two morning papers, the *Bangkok Post* and the *Nation*, and one in the afternoon called *Bangkok World*. Most travellers favour the *Bangkok Post*. It's a real gossip rag, with all kinds of wry, humorous pokes at life in Thailand and in Europe. It goes in for sensational headlines like 'Monk gored to death by rogue elephant', and it prints some really outrageous letters from foreign tourists. Half of these, I'm convinced, are fictitious.

On Arrival

Orientation

Most visitors enter Thailand via Bangkok, and have few problems adapting to the capital city's busy, yet relaxed, modernism. Much of the rest of the country isn't anything like as developed, but wherever you go the people are just the same—easygoing, friendly and hospitable. Unlike many Asian countries, Thailand has no history of Western colonialism. It's a poor country, yet proud and independent. The Thai people aren't into hassling tourists for money, gifts or favours. Instead, they aim to make foreign guests feel relaxed and at ease. This they do as a matter of courtesy, with no expectation of reward. What they do expect however, is that you show the same kind of respect yourself—particularly to their king, their religion and their customs. Wandering around like a colonial overlord, treating the Thais like second-class citizens, won't win you any friends. Unless you're polite, respectful and ask for things nicely, you'll certainly run up against *mai pen rai* (no worry, no hurry) in its severest form. The Thais can be remarkably slow, forgetful and awkward when they've a mind to be. In recent years, as they've witnessed tourists skinny-dipping on their beaches, scaling sacred monuments for photographs, and displaying physical affection in public places, they've lost quite a lot of respect for Europeans. The tendency of a growing minority of Thais is to take grasping foreigners—especially those who are here for sex and sin—for as much money as they can.

Getting along with the Thais is easy, just as long as you observe a few *dos* and *don'ts*: *do* dress neatly when visiting temples and religious shrines (i.e. no shorts, sarongs, or sleeveless tops); *do* remove shoes when entering Thai houses, temple chapels and mosques, and *do* smile a lot and learn a few Thai courtesy phrases; *don't* insult the royal family—unless you want a bad accident; *don't* get caught with drugs—unless you want a long spell in prison; *don't* touch Thai adults on the head (the most sacred part of the body) or slap them heartily on the back—unless you fancy being slapped about in return. You *don't* have to *wai* (bow, with hands together in prayer, the standard Thai greeting) to younger people, only to elders or important people. The Thais *don't* go in for open, lavish displays of affection (except to children), and frown on foreigners groping each other out of doors. Thai guys *don't* kiss with the mouth (kissing with the nose is the custom!). A very big *don't* is pointing your feet at people (or Buddha images)—the sole of the foot, being in contact with the earth, is considered the most degraded part of the body. In Thai temples or houses, either kneel or sit cross-legged, or perfect the 'Asian squat'. Anything will do, just so long as your feet are tucked out of sight. The biggest *don't* of all is to lose your temper. Normally, the Thais are the nicest, smiliest people you can imagine. You can kid around with them, and they'll always pick up on it. The Thais have a good sense of joy, but if provoked they also have a less noble side, which you should be aware of (but not to the point of paranoia). The Thais may not often show anger ('they don't have the energy', was one wry comment, 'it's too hot!')—but when they get mad, they get *very* mad.

TAT publish a short guide to *Dos* and *Don'ts* in Thailand, which is well worth picking up from their airport desk, on arrival in Bangkok.

Thailand must be one of the few countries in the world where it's more hassle to travel as a man than as a woman. Okay, women travellers have to fend off the occasional over-amorous trek guide or monk, but in general they are treated with the highest respect by Thai men. Over-familiarity, however, can be misinterpreted as a come-on, and as a woman on your own you'll have to be careful about how open and friendly you are. As one girl reported:

> I received three separate offers of marriage from Thai men. They
> thought I must be rich and would be able to support them. Thai guys
> have a definite thing about Western women—they want to marry them
> and come to the West.

Male travellers don't get off so easy. Thailand is essentially a country for men, and a foreign man on his own is a prime target for enterprising Thai prostitutes. Sometimes it's impossible to get a quiet cup of tea, without an endless procession of touts turning up to offer 'big boy' massages or short-time rental of their daughter, sister or even grand-mother. The main 'hit' spots are Bangkok, Pattaya and Koh Samui. Here, as one guy related, prostitutes are now ensnaring travellers by the most ingenious means:

> I'd been down to Koh Samui, and my ears were blocked up from
> swimming. So I decided to visit a local doctor and have them syringed.
> Well, I was waiting at the bus-stop and a very smart-looking Thai lady
> beckoned me over. She had a map of Bangkok, and wanted me to
> recommend a good hotel since she was from Malaysia (she said) and
> would be quite lost in the busy capital. We chatted for a bit, and then I
> happened to mention that I was off to the doctor to have my ears
> syringed. 'What luck!' she announced, '*I'm* a doctor actually!' I looked at
> her sideways and said 'Oh *are* you?' And she replied, 'Yes, I could make
> you feel *much* better!!'

Getting Around

Thailand is a very easy country to travel around. Air, rail and bus services are modern and efficient—everything usually runs on time. Out of Bangkok, most towns are fairly small and manageable, which makes sightseeing easy. In town, you often have a choice of local transport—usually *tuk-tuks* and *songthaews*, sometimes taxis and buses too. Some beach resorts are conveniently explored by motorbike, and some ancient temple towns are best toured by bicycle, or even on foot. In a few places (e.g Krabi, Sukhothai) air-conditioned minibus tours are an excellent way of getting round the sights.

By Air

Thai Airways flies to all major centres in Thailand. Fares are very cheap—with 20% discounts on certain night flights—and some examples are as follows:

From Bangkok to		
	Chiang Mai	1650B
	Chiang Rai	1855B
	Hat Yai	2300B
	Lampang	1395B
	Nakhon Ratchasima	540B
	Phitsanulok	920B
	Phuket	2000B
	Surat Thani	1710
	Udorn Thani	1260B
From Chiang Mai to	Chiang Rai	420B
	Hat Yai	4150B
	Phitsanulok	650B
	Phuket	3755B
	Surat Thani	2970B
	Udorn Thani	2815B

Addresses of Thai Airways offices are:

Bangkok: Head Office, 6 Larn Luang Rd (tel 2800090–110); Reservations (tel 2800070–80); Don Muang Airport (tel 5238271–3); also at 89 Vibhavadi Rangsit Rd (tel 5130121).

Chiang Mai	240 Prapokklao Rd	(tel 211541, 210042)
Chiang Rai	870 Phaholyotin Rd	(tel 711179, 713663)
Hat Yai	166/4 Niphat Uthit 2 Rd	(tel 245851, 243711)
Khon Kaen	183/6 Maliwan Rd	(tel 236523, 239011)
Lampang	314 Sanambin Rd	(tel 217078, 218199)
Mae Hong Son	71 Sinhanatbamrung Rd	(tel 611297, 611194)
Nan	34 Mahaprom Rd	(tel 710377, 710498)
Nongkhai	453 Prachak Rd	(tel 441530)
Pattani	9 Preeda Rd	(tel 394146)
Phitsanulok	209/26–28 Bromtrailoknart Rd	(tel 258020, 251671)
Phrae	42–44 Rasdamnern Rd	(tel 511123, 511977)
Phuket	78 Ranong Rd	(tel 211195, 212499)
	41/33 Montree Rd	(tel 212400, 212644)
Songkhla	2 Soi 4, Saiburi Rd	(tel 311012, 314007)
Surat Thani	3/27–28 Karoonat Rd	(tel 272610, 273355)

Trang	199/2 Viseskul Rd	(tel 218066, 210863)
Ubon	292/9 Chayanggoon Rd	(tel 254431, 255894)
Udorn	60 Makkang Rd	(tel 211004, 243222)

By Train

Thailand's State Railway has four trunk routes, running to the north, northeast, east and south. All long-distance trains have sleeping cars and/or air-conditioned coaches. Train reservations can be made at the Advance Booking Office of Bangkok's Hualamphong station (tel 2233762, 2247788) from 8.30 am to 6 weekdays, 8.30 am to 12 noon weekends. Schedules and fares are available from the State Railways of Thailand (tel 2230341, 2237010, 2237020). In addition to the regular passenger fares quoted throughout this guide (cf. Getting There sections), there are surcharges for Rapid (20B) and Express (30B) trains, for sleeping berths (1st class air-con, 210B; 1st class non air-con, 130B; 2nd class air-con, upper berth 150B, lower berth 180B; 2nd class non air-con, upper berth 70B, lower berth 100B), and for air-con 2nd class coaches (40B).

Trains are usually a little slower than buses, but they compensate by being safer and a lot more comfortable. I would recommend them for all long-distance travel. Unlike in a bus, where you're pinned to your seat, you can stroll around and stretch your legs. If you buy a sleeping berth on an overnight train to Chiang Mai or to Surat Thani (for Samui) from Bangkok, you'll arrive refreshed and relaxed—not (as on a bus) a limp rag. The Express trains are the quickest form of rail transport—they reach destinations a lot quicker than Rapid trains (not rapid at all) or languishing Ordinary trains. Travelling 3rd class is okay on short journeys (say, up to 3–4 hours), but I wouldn't suggest it for long overnight trips. One person, travelling south from Hua Hin to Surat Thani, reported 3rd class compartments so crowded that people were sleeping under seats and even in hammocks strung up between luggage racks. I believe it—one journey I made from Nong Khai down to Bangkok was a 3rd class nightmare. A whole family occupied my seat while I was in the toilet. I hadn't the heart to kick them out, and spent 14 hours eating peanuts and tossing back Mekong whisky in the gangway with local youths. Most of the Thai language I ever learnt, I picked up that night. Overnight trains like this always serve meals and drinks. The vendors are often young boys, who eat, sleep and live on these trains. 'Where is your home?' I asked one of these lads. 'Train 41 to Chiang Mai!' was the bright response. And then, as an afterthought, 'Oh, and on train 42, going back to Bangkok!' His name was Vishu, and he earned just 10B (25p) for each 12-hour journey he made—plus 10% commission on every beer he sold. His father, his two uncles, and his ten brothers and sisters also lived on trains.

By Bus

Here you have a choice between public state-run buses and private 'tour' buses. Both are cheap, uncomfortable and subject to accidents—which is why many drivers wear Buddha amulets and charms. Government buses are cheap, and travel throughout the country. Private buses run mainly between major tourist centres like Bangkok, Pattaya, Phuket, Koh Samui and Koh Samet. They are a little more expensive, but offer 'civilized' comforts like free meals, pillows and blankets (for overnight journeys) and, more ominously, videos. I once travelled up to Bangkok from Hua Hin on one of these

15

'video' buses—never again! The only functional speaker in the bus was directly above my head, and I had to strap my sleeping bag over it in order to block out the loud orgasmic moans of 'Lovely Young Tracey', an awesomely explicit pornographic film which somehow lulled every Thai passenger aboard to sleep.

On the whole, I would recommend ordinary (non air-con) buses for short point-to-point trips of 4 hours or less. For anything over that, it's worth paying a little extra for an air-con bus. If you've got long legs, either sit right at the front, or in the conductor's seat by the rear entrance (he won't mind sharing). Overnight bus journeys have a bad reputation for theft—I've even heard of whole busloads of people being ripped off, after phoney 'waitresses' put them to sleep with drugged drinks. The introduction of video cameras onto prime-risk routes (like Bangkok–Chiang Mai and Bangkok–Surat Thani) has reduced such incidents dramatically, but you should still never accept food, drinks or sweets from strangers. Buy your own food on buses—there's no shortage of it. At each stop (and there are several), an endless procession of baseball-hatted youths mount the bus hawking bottles of Fanta and Coke, boiled eggs in a basket, Chinese dim-sums, barbecued chicken on sticks, iced drinks in plastic bags, carved pineapples, trays of sweets and even girlie mags. Round and round they go, entering the bus at one exit and leaving by the other, rather like a continually revolving mobile restaurant. As often as not, the bus only leaves this scene of culinary delights at all because a biblical plague of wasps, drawn by the sweet and sticky food within, has spurred the driver into action—and when he gets going, watch out.

Local Buses
These operate in many larger cities, notably Bangkok and Chiang Mai, and are very cheap. They can also be very slow. You'll need a town map or English-speaking assistance to use local buses as their destinations are usually posted only in Thai.

Taxis and Tuk-Tuks

You'll find taxis and motorized *tuk-tuks* (the noisy 3-wheeled vehicles locally known as *samlors*) in Bangkok and several regional centres. Neither use meters, and both have a 'local' and a 'tourist' price. If a local TAT office tells you that the in-town *tuk-tuk* fare is 10B, that will be the price for locals. As a tourist, you'll be charged 30B. If you bargain hard, and this is essential, you should arrive at a mutually satisfactory fare of 15–20B. Fares differ from town to town, but since taxis are air-conditioned, they charge 10–20B more than *tuk-tuks*. If you're not sure what the fare should be, ask a local person. *Never* set off in a taxi or a *tuk-tuk* without agreeing the cost of your journey in advance. And *always* insist that they take you to the hotel or guest house of your choice, not to one of their 'recommendations'. Some *tuk-tuk* drivers will charge you a lower price if you agree to go through the motions of looking around in a jewellery shop of their choice. They have a deal with the owner, who gives them petrol coupons for bringing in *farangs*. If you don't want this hassle, state your destination, agree on a price, and add 'no looking, no shopping, no massage', and remember to smile. Outside of Bangkok, you'll often come across bicycle *samlors*, similar to the 3-wheeled cycle rickshaws found elsewhere in Asia, which are a slow but relaxing way of getting around town. You should hardly ever have to pay more than 10B on one of these.

16

Songthaews

These small pick-up trucks have two rows (*songthaews*) of seats, and pursue a more or less fixed route round Chiang Mai and other regional centres. They are sometimes known as *bemos* (in the Indonesian fashion) and have established themselves as the main form of transport on islands like Phuket and Koh Samui. You flag them down as you would a taxi, and pay 5–10B to go anywhere on their route. If you don't like their route, you can hire out the whole vehicle. Late at night, when other forms of transport may be off the road, this can be a very good idea, and in a group, quite cheap.

Cars and Motorbikes

Driving a **car** in Bangkok's mad traffic is strictly for the brave. The experience is only recommended to people who've had a full, rich life and don't mind leaving it behind. Cars can be rented from agencies like Hertz (Bangkok, tel 2524903; Chiang Mai, tel 235496) or Avis (Bangkok, tel 2330397; Chiang Mai, tel 222013). Many top hotels at major centres can also arrange car rentals.

Motorbikes are very popular as a means of touring Chiang Mai and island resorts like Phuket and Koh Samui. In general, you're much safer on a solid road-bike (250–500B a day) than on a rickety moped (100–200B a day). When hiring, don't be fooled by bike-shop signs like: 'Please give us serve you! With responsibility prices and free for helmet!' None of them will insure against breakdown or accidents, so you should check your machine very carefully before signing any hirer's agreement. In many cases, if the bike packs up, you may be liable for full repair costs. Many people prefer to hire **bicycles**, which are available at several tourist centres. The average daily hire rate is 40B.

You're supposed to have an international driver's licence to use cars, motorbikes and jeeps in Thailand. Personally I've never been asked to produce one, but I have heard of unlicensed travellers being stopped by the police and charged exorbitant fees for so-called 'temporary' licences.

Where to Stay

There's a wide range of accommodation in Thailand, from opulent super-luxury hotels to simple beach bungalows on remote islands. Places to stay are most abundant in Bangkok, Chiang Mai, Pattaya, Phuket and Koh Samui, where the tourist boom has produced an excess of hotels offering attractive discounts in low season. The 'Where to Stay' sections in this book are divided into four categories, where applicable—**Luxury, Expensive, Moderate** and **Inexpensive**.

Luxury hotels cost around 2000B for a single room, and 3000B or more for a double. **Expensive** hotels charge 1000–2000B. Hotels in these categories are air-conditioned, and have swimming pools, bars, restaurants, coffee shops and various recreations. Some offer sporting facilities, entertainment (e.g. a Thai dinner-dance show) and a night-club/disco. Service is generally excellent, and the 10% service charge (and 11% government tax) which is politely added to your bill is usually worth it. Many hotels will often give 20% discounts between May and September. Sometimes, if you book through the hotel's travel agency, you get another 20% off your bill.

17

Moderate hotels have single rooms for about 350–500B, doubles for 400–1000B, and are generally very good value. You get the same deal as at a luxury hotel, though there will be far fewer facilities. Several of these hotels offer 50% discounts in the low season. From November to February (high season), it's wise to book in advance—they're often full at this time of year.

The **Inexpensive** Thai-style hotels generally offer a choice between air-conditioned (300–400B) and fan-cooled (180–300B) rooms. Because of the humidity, many travellers pay the extra for air-con comfort, and in the hot season only masochists take rooms with no fans at all. There's often a party going on next door to cheap 'fan' rooms, which means your sleep may suffer, and they sometimes have a few resident cockroaches. Rooms without a bathroom (and no roaches) cost in the region of 100–150B. Cheap budget accommodation is found mainly in guest houses, some with meals and laundry services, which charge around 80–120B per person. Rooms are fairly basic, but have a fan, a shower and a toilet, and are perfectly adequate. There are also a few **Youth Hostels**—in Bangkok, Chiang Mai, Kanchanaburi, Lopburi, Nakhon Pathom and Phitsanulok. On the beach, you normally have a choice between cheap bamboo huts (60–90B per person) and swanky bungalows with modern comforts (350–800B).

If travelling alone, it's a good idea to make a friend with whom you can share accommodation costs. This is because most places to stay cater primarily for couples, and charge more or less the same for one as for two people. Single rooms often have two beds. In cheaper hotels and guest houses, you should check a) toilets and waste bins for cockroaches; b) bed-linen for cleanliness; c) under mattresses for bedbugs; d) mosquito-netting on windows for holes; e) door-locks for security; f) fans and air-conditioning units for controllability (some have only one speed—very fast or very cold). Finally, you need offer tips only to staff of major hotels—10 or 15B should cover most individual services, including porterage.

Eating Out

Food

There's a standing joke about the Thais, that they only have one meal a day—it starts at 8 am and finishes at 8 pm. This may be an exaggeration, but Thai people certainly love their food, and they prefer to pick at things (a bowl of this, a bag of that) all day long, rather than sit down to a 'proper' meal in the Western sense. No foreign visitor need ever worry about going short on food here—it's on offer practically around the clock. As a friend of mine, a Dutch restaurateur in Bangkok, said:

> Finding places to eat is never a problem, because half of Thailand is constantly cooking for the other half! If you're hungry, you can close your eyes, wander a minute or so in any direction, and be pretty sure of walking into some good, hot food. I've friends here in Bangkok who go out every night, and who—in two or three years—have never yet dined at the same place twice. That's quite something, isn't it? And the quality of

food in Thailand is just superb. Every street vendor throughout the country is sold out of what he has cooked every day. Again, quite amazing.

Thai cuisine—a cross between Indian and Chinese food, with a dash of inspiration from Portugal, Indonesia and France—is hot and spicy, yet delicate, encompassing a whole spectrum of flavours. A typical Thai meal uses fresh coriander (the soul of Thai cookery), garlic and chilli as springboards for a carnival of tastes. Other characteristic flavourings are tamarind juice, ginger, coconut milk and lemon grass, called *makroot*. The hottest, most lethal ingredient is *phrik kii noo*, a small green chilli pepper which has foreigners diving for water and beer when they should be reaching for a far better antidote—rice. If you don't want fiery food, then ask for something *mai pet* (not hot) or stick to readily available Chinese food, which is often less spicy. Traditionally, the Thai dinner comprises five dishes—including curries, soups, salads and vegetables, served around a central bowl of rice. It is accompanied by a hot, pungent sauce known as *nam phrik*, and by a fish sauce called *nam plaa*, made from anchovies or shrimp paste, which is used in the place of salt. The meal is washed down with whisky or brandy (by the men) or with fruit juice or iced jasmine tea (by the women). Thai food is for most *farangs* (foreigners) an acquired taste. An easier introduction is in the north, where the cuisine is fairly mild, or in the south, which is famous for its tasty seafood and its Muslim-style sweet and mild curries. It's hardest to acquire in the northeast, notorious for its incandescent 'specialities' and salads.

Local fare ('street food') can be sampled at the numerous noodle shops, night markets and pavement food-stalls found in most tourist centres. Most dishes are around 15B, and include *tom yum* (a spicy soup flavoured with lemon grass, lime juice, shrimp, chicken or pork), *tom yam kung* (the standard Thai soup, with shrimp, lemon grass and mushrooms), *pat thai* (fried noodles with onions, peanuts, vegetables and egg), *mee krob* (fried noodles plus anything the cook has on hand), *hor mok* (fish in chilli, onion and garlic sauce), *kai yang* (spicy barbecued chicken), *kang kiew wan kai/nua* (chicken/beef curry), *kao pat* (fried rice with onions, vegetables, sometimes an egg), and *kao pat kai/mui/gung* (chicken/pork/shrimp fried rice). If you want something else, look to see what the locals are eating and, if it looks edible, point to it. Street food is safe enough, just so long as you can see it's been freshly cooked. Stir-fried vegetables, seafood omelettes, and anything that comes out of a sizzling wok are all things you just can't go wrong with.

When eating out in restaurants, it's best to go in a group and to order as a 'family' rather than as individuals—the Thais are used to communal eating. A good restaurant meal can be had for around 150B a head, including a drink. Normally, each Thai restaurant has its own specialities, and it's a good idea to ask the waiter 'What's special?' (*Mee arai phe set?*). Outside of Bangkok, you may have no other option, since fewer restaurants will have English menus. Mind you, the tourist boom has produced some marvellous attempts to make Thai dishes intelligible to the *farang* diner. While you're waiting for your meal (it won't be long), puzzle over items like 'Pog leg in gravy sauce, with Bread as side order', or 'Bean curd with Hom's Bowel Soup', or 'Pig Legs in Hot and Sour soup'. The beach restaurants of Koh Samui proudly advertise 'Barbecued Crap', while the floating restaurants of Kanchanaburi tempt travellers with 'Yum Bean', 'Pork Stomach with Salted Butter soup', and 'Bucket of Ice'. Pee Pee islands have their 'Two choices of fried egg—one sunny side up, two over easy', and Pattaya offers something very special—'Horse Balls'! Thais are also very fond of skinned frogs, crunchy insects, serpents' heads and (a Chinese delicacy) birds' nests. Don't be alarmed—there's some really good stuff in there, if you're prepared to experiment. If you want to play safe, stick to favourite Thai dishes like *kai ho bai toei* (seasoned fried chicken in leaf wrappers), *pla brio wan* (snapper fish, with ginger and garlic sauce), *thotman plak rai/kung* (Thai-style fish/shrimp balls), *gaeng mussaman* (Thai Muslim curry), various kinds of *yam* (Thai salad), or curry and *nam phrik* dipping sauce, with fresh vegetables. Delicious sticks of satay and fat omelettes stuffed with pork and stir-fried vegetables also appeal to the Western palate.

Thai restaurants don't do much in the way of desserts—unless you like sweet, sticky coconut items—but there's a vast choice of fruits. For your fruit salad, there are mangoes, pineapples, watermelons, papayas (great for upset stomachs), pomegranates, oranges, jackfruits, durians (okay, if you can bear the smell!), lychee-like rambutan (jokingly referred to by Thais as 'white man's balls'), longans (similar to lychees, but without a prickly skin), strawberries and over 20 varieties of banana. If you're into ice-cream, look out for the Foremost ice-cream parlours, in Bangkok and some provincial towns.

To get service in a Thai restaurant, beckon waiters with a wave of the hand (preferably as the locals do, with fingers waving downwards, in towards the palm). Clapping, hissing, and snapping fingers is bad manners, and a sure way of being left to starve. Only waiters in middle to high-class restaurants expect a tip, which should be around 15–25B, or 10% of the bill. If you want a change from Thai/Chinese food, larger hotels and coffee shops serve an approximation of European food, and all the major beach resorts and tourist centres are now gearing themselves to Western gourmets. In Bangkok and Chiang Mai, you can now choose from around a dozen international cuisines, and yes, there is a Mcdonald's.

In the 'Eating Out' sections of this book, prices given are for a full meal with beer included, but no wine.

Drinks

Thai-style coffee is unpalatably sweet to most Westerners. It's heavily laced with sticky condensed milk, which lurks like treacle at the bottom of the glass, and is best left there. If you don't want milk/sugar, ask for your coffee *mai sai nom* or *mai sai naam taan*. Alternatively, ask for *Nescafé*, which comes with little packets of Coffeemate—very civilized. There's just no pleasing some people: one coffee connoisseur travelled the length and breadth of the country, before discovering that 'Thai Airways do just about the only drinkable coffee in Thailand'. Thai coffee, whether good, bad or indifferent, is often accompanied by a weak, but refreshing, glass of free Chinese tea. Coffee shops are very popular in Thailand—especially among young 'groovy' Thais, who hang around them much in the same way that pre-Beatles teenagers in the West used to patronize 'milk bars'. Several coffee shops style themselves 'disco cafés', and have entertainments ranging from live music and talent shows, to transvestite cabarets (in Trat) and can-can dancers (in Krabi). They constitute a whole new sub-culture in Thai society, and deserve a book all to themselves.

The brand of whisky favoured by most Thais is *Mekong*. This local firewater is very cheap (90–120B a bottle) and fairly strong. Taken with Coke, it tastes pleasantly like Bacardi rum; taken in excess it produces a violent hangover. It's worth paying a little extra (120–150B a bottle) for *Sangsom* whisky, which is far smoother. Thai beer is strong but pleasant. It reminds many Westerners of good quality German lager. The two main brands are *Singha* ('Happiness you can drink') and *Kloster*. Of the two, *Kloster* is better regarded by *farangs* who know their beer. In a restaurant, *Singha* goes from 40B (small) to 70B (large); *Kloster* costs 10–15B more.

Bottled soft drinks can be even sweeter than coffee. Thais are especially fond of 'fortified' drinks with healthy names like 'Lipo-Vitan E' and 'Electrolyte Beverage'. These drinks abound in northern trekking areas, where people often need all the fortification they can get. Sample delicious milkshakes, *lassis* and fruit juices at ice-cream parlours or cheap guest-house restaurants in Bangkok or Chiang Mai. But don't drink local tap water, unless boiled. Bottled mineral water—usually *Polaris* ('ozonated artesian well-water')—is cheap and widely available.

Health

People can get sick in Thailand although it's a very clean country, and food is generally freshly cooked on the spot. The sudden change in diet can sometimes cause tummy problems ('Bangkok Boogie') and it's wise to avoid spicy food, raw vegetables and ice for the first few days of your stay. Thereafter you can avoid sickness by drinking only boiled or bottled water, and by eating only peeled fruit. If you do get a stomach upset, the best cure is bland food (boiled rice, bananas, etc) and warm tea. To prevent dehydration and dizziness, drink plenty of fluids and take extra salt with food. Also, ease slowly into the heat—the most common affliction amongst European visitors to Thailand is sunburn. Use sun-cream for protection, and don't doze off at the swimming pool.

There are so many stray dogs in the country, especially around temples, that rabies is a risk. In certain areas (e.g. Pai, Mae Sariang) it's highly inadvisable to go strolling around at night on your own. When Siamese dogs take it into their heads to attack, they mean business. If bitten, whether by a dog or rat, wash the wound immediately with clean water or alcohol, soap or detergent, and head immediately to the nearest doctor or hospital (your hotel will know where the nearest is). You may need a rabies shot.

Malarial mosquitoes inhabit beach resorts like Koh Samet and the hilly, forested areas of northern Thailand. If, following visits to these regions, you develop a fever, get an immediate blood check. If there isn't a local malaria centre, head straight for the Hospital of Tropical Medicine in Bangkok, or ring Bangkok's Malarial Division (2816650) for advice.

While it's worth visiting your dentist and optician for a check-up before coming to Thailand, you can get excellent (and often cheaper) dental/optical services in Bangkok and Chiang Mai. The cost of a pair of smart, fashion spectacles—at a reliable optician like Universal Optical, 138 New Rd, Bangkok—is just £35–45, inclusive of lenses. An hour of private dental work in Chiang Mai could cost you as little as 60B. People with contact lenses will be pleased to learn that Thailand's high humidity makes lens wear extremely comfortable.

Hospitals

In Bangkok:	Ramathibodi Hospital, Rama IV Rd (tel 2460024; 2811364; 2819110).
	Bangkok Christian Hospital, 124 Silom Rd (tel 2336981).
	Chulalongkorn Hospital (tel 2528181).
	Samitivej Hospital, Soi 49, Sukhumvit Rd (tel 3920011–9).
In Chiang Mai:	McCormick Hospital, Nawarat Rd.
	Ariawongse Clinic, Changmoi Rd.
	Chiang Mai Hospital, Suan Dawk Rd.

For a complete list of hospitals and clinics, check in the English language Yellow Pages, assuming you have time.

Security

Thailand is a relatively safe country—most of the population are good Buddhists, to whom the thought of theft or violence on foreign guests is alien. But some visitors do let their guard down, lulled into a false sense of security by Thai friendliness, and there are always a few horror stories doing the rounds from travellers who've been ripped off, doped on buses, or stuck with huge bills in restaurants. Even a good barrel like Thailand has a few rotten apples. As anywhere, your best security is yourself. Wandering around with an exposed money belt bulging with cash is like wearing a sign saying 'Please rob me!' If you must wear a belt, keep it out of sight under your shirt or skirt, and take note that, especially on crowded Bangkok buses, many belts have been slit open by expert razor-thieves. Surplus cash and all valuables should be stored in hotel safe deposits, but never leave your credit card in a hotel safe (cf. Chiang Mai, Trekking)—it may be copied during your absence. In transit, i.e. when travelling from town to town, *never* leave your bags unattended. And, as one experienced tour leader suggested, always keep 1000B handy, to give someone if you happen to be held up—they'll usually take it and run, without checking you for the rest. Be aware of pick-pockets and street touts, who often pose as friendly 'students'. These 'students' say they want to practise their English with you, then invite you to an expensive restaurant, nightclub or 'government shop'. One couple accepted such an offer from a 'nice young man' outside the Grand Palace, Bangkok. They had to pay a horrendous 1400B lunch tab after their host 'went to the toilet' and never came back.

If dark streets, crowded markets and public buses are prime risk areas for theft, you can at least relax in your room. Apart from beach bungalows, most places in Thailand, even the cheapest guest houses, have their rooms secured by the same push-button door-lock, which locks from the inside; but bring a combination lock anyway—for your bags and for insecure beach huts. Though rooms are generally safe, don't leave cash or valuables in them.

If travelling on your own, take extra care, especially when you find yourself booked into a seat right at the back of a night bus. In the course of the long, long journey, you may well be offered food, drinks or sweets by 'kindly' strangers. Don't accept them—there's a good chance they are drugged. One guy spent hours of friendly travel with a charming old man, who appeared totally incapable of deceit, before accepting a cigarette. He woke up on the boat pier at Surat Thani with the rest of the cigarette pack, and nothing else.

In the case of theft or loss, you can report to the **Tourist Police** (phone numbers are posted at all hotels, and at the airport) or dial 195 for TAT's English-speaking assistance service, but don't expect bags of sympathy. This is, remember, a Buddhist country, and therefore your safety and security are considered to be your own individual responsibility. So, if you have your own ways of protecting your interests, stick to them. Don't, as one poor traveller did, break the habits of a lifetime and stick all your money under your pillow at night. He was halfway to a different city before he remembered about it.

Drugs

Up until quite recently, Thailand was a major narcotics centre and a favourite 'hippy hangout'. But then came international pressure against heroin production, large-scale package tourism, and the 1987 Visit Thailand Year, all of which convinced the Thai government that it was time for a big clean-up. Stiff new drug laws were introduced, making possession and sale of narcotics punishable by hefty fines and severe prison terms.

There are some 700 *farangs* languishing in Thai jails on drugs-related charges. Many of them are there on the evidence of local street-dealers who turned out to be police informers. Few of them receive any other visitors except the few sympathetic backpackers who respond to guest-house notices in Bangkok's Banglampoo district. None of them have been able to afford to 'buy' themselves out of trouble. Fines are so high that one guy, caught with just three sticks of dope, had to fork out 22,000B (£500) to escape a minor possession charge which could have imprisoned him for *five years*.

The simple message with drugs is—*don't*. Be especially careful with 'fun drugs' on Koh Samui—there are no measurements involved, you don't know how much you're taking, and what you expect to be an hour or two of harmless fun can well turn out to be 12 hours of unmitigated hell which you'll just have to sit out patiently. Anyone crossing the border from Thailand to Malaysia should watch their bags in case 'extra luggage' is smuggled into them by drug-dealers looking for innocent tourists to take on their risk. Importation of drugs into Malaysia carries the death penalty. Finally, even if you're sensible about drugs, never travel with someone who isn't. Be warned that you only have to *accompany* someone possessing narcotics to be implicated yourself.

Communications

Postal Services
Postal services in Thailand are excellent. Bangkok's **Central GPO** in New Road, Silom, is open 8 am–8 pm, Mon–Fri, 9 am–1 pm at weekends. It has a **24-hour telegram service** and a **parcel-packaging** counter. Outside Bangkok, most post offices are closed at weekends, and are open only until 4.30 pm during the week. The **Poste Restante** service is generally very reliable, though you'll need to insist that friends and

family writing to you print your surname in block capitals, and underline it. This ensures that a letter to say, Joe E. *Bloggs* is correctly filed under 'B'. Anything carelessly addressed to Joe E Bloggs, on the other hand, could well be filed under 'J', or even 'E'. You'll generally be charged 2B for every letter or postcard you collect.

Phone Services

Phone services, in the cities at least, can be amazingly efficient. In general, it's best to make international phone calls from large hotels—it costs more (about 80B per minute, to anywhere in the world) but is really worth it. One traveller, used to the vagaries of Asian phones, requested an overseas call at the Oberoi Hotel, Bangkok, and then sat down to plough through *Gone with the Wind*. To her astonishment, she was connected in two minutes flat. Bangkok and Chiang Mai post offices have international call facilities too, and you can either dial direct or get an operator to dial for you. If phoning overseas yourself, just pick up the receiver, ask the operator for your number, put down the phone, and wait a few minutes for it to ring. This means you've been connected. Local (in town) calls cost 5B, and you can phone from most hotels and many guest houses. If using the domestic phone service to call from town-to-town (i.e. from Bangkok to Chiang Mai), you'll often get better results by asking hotel operators to dial for you. Most provincial towns have local telephone exchanges, but their service isn't all that good.

Electricity

Electricity is 50 cycle, 220 volt AC, in Bangkok and most of Thailand. The better hotels supply their guests with adaptors for electrical appliances.

Time

Time in Thailand is 7 hours ahead of London GMT, 12 ahead of New York and 3 behind Sydney. Bear this in mind when making long-distance telephone calls.

Changing Money

The Thai Baht (B) divides into 100 Satang, which have all but disappeared. Notes are 10B (brown), 20B (green), 50B (blue), 100B (red) and 500B (purple). Coins are 5B, 2B and 1B (silver). The new 5B coins, worth noting, have a copper edge—this is the only way of telling them apart from the near-identical 1B coin. The approximate exchange rates at time of writing are:

$$£1 \quad = 44B$$
$$\$1 \quad = 25B$$
$$AUS\$1 = 20B$$

It's not necessary to change any foreign currency prior to arrival. Exchange facilities are readily available on a 24-hour basis at Bangkok airport—rates here are often better than rates quoted abroad. In Thailand you can exchange foreign currencies at banks (open 8.30 am–8.30 pm, Mon–Fri), currency-exchange counters at main banks (open

8.30 am–10 pm daily) and authorized money-changers (24-hour service, daily). Use hotels only to change money in emergencies, as their rates are usually poor.

Embassies

Most Bangkok embassies receive visa applications between 8 am and 12 noon only, and may require your passport overnight. If you need a visa for India, Burma or Nepal, you don't have to apply yourself—you can get a travel agent (see General Information, Bangkok) to do it for you. Addresses of major embassies are as follows:

ARGENTINA	20/85 Prommitr Villa, off Sukhumvit 49/1. Tel 2590401–2.
AUSTRALIA	37 Sathon Tai Rd. Tel 2872680.
AUSTRIA	14 Soi Nantha, Sathon Tai Rd. Tel 2863011, 2863019, 2863037.
BELGIUM	44 Soi Phraya Phiphat, off Silom Rd. Tel 2360150–, 2367876.
BRUNEI	14th Fl, Orakarn Bldg, Soi Chitlom, Phloenchit Rd. Tel 2539126–4.
BURMA	132 Sathon Nua Rd. Tel 2332237.
CANADA	11th and 12th Fl, Boonmitr Bldg, 138 Silom Rd. Tel 2341561–8.
CHILE	15 Soi 61, Sukhumvit Rd. Tel 3918443, 3914858.
CHINA	57 Ratchadaphisek Rd. Tel 2457030–44.
CZECHOSLOVAKIA	197/1 Silom Bldg, 7th Flr, Silom Rd. Tel 2334535, 2341922.
DENMARK	10 Soi Atthakan Prasit, Sathon Tai Rd. Tel 2863930, 2863942–4.
EGYPT	49 Soi Ruam Ruedi, Phloenchit Rd. Tel 2530161.
FRANCE	35 Customs House Lane, Off New Rd. Tel 2340950–6.
GERMANY	9 Sathon Tai Rd. Tel 2132331–6.
HUNGARY	28 Soi Sukchai, off Sukhumvit 42. Tel 3917906, 3912002–3.
INDIA	46 Soi Prasanmit, Sukhumvit Rd. Tel 2580300–6.
INDONESIA	600–602 Phetburi Rd. Tel 2523135–40.

IRAN	602 Sukhumvit Rd (between Soi 22 and 24). Tel 2590611–3.
IRAQ	47 Pradiphat Rd, Phayathai. Tel 2785335–8.
ISRAEL	31 Soi Lang Suan, Phloenchit Rd. Tel 2523131–4.
ITALY	399 Nang Linchi Rd. Tel 2872054–7.
JAPAN	1674 New Phetburi Rd. Tel 2526151–9.
KOREA (S)	Sathorn Thani Bldg., 90 Sathon Nua Rd. Tel 2340723–6.
LAOS	193 Sathon Tai Rd. Tel 2860010
MALAYSIA	35 Sathon Tai Rd. Tel 2861390–2.
NEPAL	189 Sukhumvit Soi 71. Tel 3917240.
NETHERLANDS	106 Wireless Rd. Tel 2547701–5.
NEW ZEALAND	93 Wireless Rd. Tel 2518165.
NORWAY	20th Flr, Chokchai Bldg, 690 Sukhumvit Rd. Tel 2580531–3.
PAKISTAN	31 Soi Nana Nua, Sukhumvit Rd. Tel 25302888.
PHILIPPINES	760 Sukhumvit Rd. Tel 2590139–40.
POLAND	61 Soi Prasanmit, Sukhumvit Rd. Tel 2584112–3.
PORTUGAL	26 Captain Bush Lane, Si Phaya Rd. Tel 2340372.
SAUDI ARABIA	10th Fl, Sathorn Thani Bldg, 90 Sathon Nua Rd. Tel 2350875–8.
SINGAPORE	129 Sathon Tai Rd. Tel 2862111, 2861434.
SPAIN	104 Wireless Rd. Tel 2526112, 2528368.
SRI LANKA	48/3 Sukhumvit 1. Tel 2512789.
SWEDEN	11th Flr Boonmitr Bldg, 138 Silom Rd. Tel 2343891–2, 2330295.
SWITZERLAND	35 Wireless Rd. Tel 2530156–60.
TURKEY	153/2 Soi Mahadlek Luang 1, Ratchadamri Rd. Tel 2512987–8.

UNITED KINGDOM	Wireless Rd.
	Tel 2530191–9.
U.S.A.	95 Wireless Rd.
	Tel 2525040–9, 2525171–9.
U.S.S.R.	108 Sathon Nua Rd.
	Tel 2349824, 2342012.
VIETNAM	83/1 Wireless Rd.
	Tel 2515835–8.
YUGOSLAVIA	28 Soi 61, Sukhumvit Rd.
	Tel 3919090–1.

Shopping

Thailand is a shopper's paradise, full of temptingly cheap bargains. There's quality silk, jewellery, antiques, bronzeware, nielloware (silver inlaid with black alloy), copy designer goods and modern fashion clothes in Bangkok. There are ethnic hill-tribe crafts and silver in Chiang Mai. There's *mudmee* tie-and-dye silk at Pakchongchai; precious gems at Chanthaburi and Kanchanaburi; cultured pearls at Phuket; beautiful cotton fabrics at Hua Hin, Songkhla and Nong Khai; and even cheap hi-fi equipment (mostly smuggled in from Singapore) at Hat Yai. The list of attractions is endless—nearly every Thai centre has some 'local' speciality worth buying, and throughout the country shopping is so very convenient. If there's one shop selling leather boots, there will be a whole cluster of shops selling boots all around it. So, not only can you do all your shopping in one place, but you can wander easily from one shop to another, comparing prices and quality. If a shop hasn't got just what you want in stock, it can generally produce it for you overnight. The same goes for tailors, who can run up any garment to your specifications within 24 hours. Bulky purchases, such as teakwood furniture or heavy antiques, can be shipped home for you. Expensive jewellery can be verified at Bangkok's reliable gem-testing laboratory. Large hotels have their shopping emporia, and Bangkok department stores have their fashion boutiques. These are the places to shop in air-conditioned comfort. Outside, on the streets, there's invariably a market in full swing, offering a wide variety of fabulous goods at knock-down prices. The markets, and various smaller shops, often stay open till late evening (including weekends). Most tourist shops, however, are open Mon–Fri only, from 8 am to 9 pm, and department stores from 10 am to 7 pm. For an idea of what's available, and how much it should cost, pick up the TAT's *Official Shopping Guide* from their airport desk, on arrival. This handy publication lists some 200 shops in Bangkok, Phuket, Chiang Mai and Pattaya where the quality of goods (mainly silk, leather, jewellery and handicrafts) is guaranteed. These shops display the TAT-approved sticker—the logo is a woman hawker with carrier baskets.

All prices quoted throughout this guide are the result of hard bargaining, an integral part of shopping in Thailand. The Thais love bargaining, especially if you show you're enjoying it too. Smile a lot while haggling, and never lose your cool. If the first price asked is too high (it nearly always is), use some local lingo to bring it down. Say *Mai! Ma dai!* (No! Too much!) and make some absurdly low counter-offer. Now it's their turn to cry *Ma dai! Ma dai!* (No way, José!). Let them calm down, and then offer 30–50% of the first

27

Flower Festival Float

asking price—they'll generally accept it. As a rule, the longer you bargain for something, the cheaper it gets. I once met a girl in Chiang Mai who'd spent six days negotiating over a beautiful hill-tribe coat—she got the price down from 2000B to 850B. But the good old 'walkaway' technique only works if you've lots of time to spare, and don't mind if the article is sold in the meantime to someone else. Besides which, the Thais have got wise to tourists—they just know if you really want something. You can walk away as far as you like, and it won't bother them; they know you'll be back soon. On the other hand, they're not unreasonable. Just as soon as you've given them a good battle, they'll give you a decent price. Finally, I wouldn't suggest doing all your shopping in one or two cities. Shop around, and try to buy at source. Looking for, say northeastern silk (the best in Thailand) at Khorat, or blue sapphires (from the local mines) at Kanchanaburi, you'll not only get a better choice of produce, but often better prices too.

Festivals

Thai festivals are a combination of joyful, colourful merriment and solemn religious ritual. The temples are the focal points of all local celebrations, which are connected either with Buddhism, animals, the crops or honouring past kings. Many events feature folk/classical dancing, percussion music, competitions, beauty contests, fireworks and Thai boxing. There are festivals throughout the year, primarily in the early summer (before it gets too hot to celebrate anything), in the early autumn (just after the rains), and at year-end. There are no fixed dates for many festivals (the timing of which varies from year to year, in accordance with the lunar calendar) though by October, TAT has usually published its annual listing of events for the forthcoming year (with dates), and you can pick this up from your nearest tourist office. Major festivals include:

January

1
 Public holiday.
 Chiang Mai, *Winter Fair* (one week).

10–11
 Chaiyaphum elephant round-up, re-enactment of medieval warfare and demonstration of skills.

February
 Nationwide *Magha Puja* (Full Moon day). Commemorates the 'spontaneous' gathering of 1250 of Buddha's disciples.
 Chiang Mai, *Flower Festival* (three days).

March
 Phuket, *Seafood Festival* (two weeks).

April

6
 Chakri Day, public holiday. Commemorates Rama I, founder of the Chakri dynasty.

12–15
 Songkran Festival, nationwide. Celebrates the lunar New Year. Much liberation of birds and fish, lots of water-throwing. Everybody gets very wet—great fun.
 Ayutthaya, *Glory of Ayutthaya* (ten days). Spectacular sound and light show.

May

5
 Coronation Day, nationwide. Best in Bangkok, where the King and Queen commemorate their 1946 coronation at Wat Phra Keo.
 Visakha Puja (Full Moon) nationwide. Wat-based celebrations, commemorating the date of Buddha's birth, death and enlightenment.

July
 Asalha Puja (Full Moon), nationwide. Held in remembrance of Buddha's first sermon.

August

12
 Queen's Birthday. Public holiday for Queen Sikrit's birthday.

October
 Phuket, *Vegetarian Festival* (nine days).

23
 Chulalongkorn Day. Public holiday in honour of King Chulalongkorn (Rama V).

October/November
 Tod Kathin (one month). Marks the 'official' end of the rainy season. King presents robes to the monks of the Temple of Dawn, Bangkok. Monks nationwide receive new robes. Spectacular royal barge procession (Bangkok).

29

November

Loi Krathong (Full Moon), nationwide, but best in **Sukhothai** and **Chiang Mai**. Myriad banana-leaf boats, prettily illuminated by candles, are floated on rivers, lakes and canals. Perhaps the most 'typically Thai' festival—masses of happy-happy people, lots of spectacle and atmosphere.

Surin, *Elephant Round-up* (two days). Up to 200 elephants playing soccer and tug o' war, 'walking over men in the ground', and parading in 'full battle dress'. Touristy, but photogenic.

November/December
Nov 28–Dec 5

Kanchanaburi, *River Kwai Bridge Week.* Historical exhibitions, folk performances and amazing sound-and-light show nightly.

December
5

King's Birthday nationwide, but best in **Bangkok**. Boat races, illuminations and royal troops parade.

Itineraries

Six possible itineraries for a one-month stay:

Sun and Fun
3 days Bangkok – 1 week Pattaya – 3 days Koh Samet – 1 day Bangkok – 2 weeks Phuket.

A Bit of Everything
3 days Bangkok – 2 days Chiang Mai – 4 days trekking/rafting near Chiang Mai – 1 day Sukhothai – 1 day Bangkok – 4 days Phuket – 3 days around Krabi – 2 days Koh Samui – 2 days Hat Yai – overnight train to Bangkok – 1 day Bangkok – 2 days Pattaya – 2 days Koh Samet – 1 day Bangkok.

Seeing the Country
3 days Bangkok – 2 days Chiang Mai – 2 days Mae Hong Son – 3 days Chiang Rai, including The Golden Triangle – 3 days Sukhothai/Phitsanulok – 2 days Udorn Thani – 2 days Nakhon Ratchasima – 1 day Bangkok – 1 day Kanchanaburi (River Kwai Bridge) – 1 day Hua Hin – 3 days Phuket – 2 days Krabi – 2 days Koh Samui – 2 days Hat Yai.

Beach and Sea Sports
3 days Bangkok – 4 days Pattaya – 3 days Koh Samet – 1 day Bangkok – 1 week Phuket – 3 days Phi Phi Islands – 4 days Krabi area – 3 days Koh Samui.

Classical Tour
1 week Bangkok – 3 days Ayutthaya – 1 day Lopburi – 3 days Chiang Mai – 1 day Lamphun – 3 days Sukhothai – 2 days Nakhon Ratchasima/Phimai – 1 day Ban Chiang – 2 days Nong Khai – 1 day Bangkok – 2 days Songkhla.

Away from it All
2 days Bangkok – 4 days Koh Samet – 1 week Koh Chang – 1 week Krabi area – 1 week Koh Phangan/Koh Tae Nai.

Part II

TOPICS

People and Society

Thailand is a synthesis of numerous different racial and ethnic groups—mainly Thai, Chinese, Mon, Khmer, Lao, Malay, Indian and Persian—who have either been assimilated by right of conquest, or who have arrived as migrants. If Thailand has an indigenous people at all, it's probably the old Mon-Khmer stock who inhabited the country before the Thais arrived, though even before them there was an aboriginal negroid population, all traces of whom have now disappeared.

While there is no 'typical' Thai physiognomy or physique, the Thai people—especially the women—are generally considered the most attractive in Southeast Asia. This probably has less to do with their physical attributes than with their disarmingly charming national temperament. Thai society places great value on polite speech and polite smiles. The Thais have got smiling down to a fine art; it has been said that they have a smile for every emotion. They are also masters of relaxation, with a national motto of *mai pen rai* which loosely translates as 'no hurry, no worry'. On the surface, they appear a happy, optimistic people who—having maintained their independence and freedom through several centuries—exude a self-confidence and a deep trust in their own ways which enables them to tolerate other people, and to get along with each other with the minimum of overt conflict. All of which makes Thailand one of the easiest, most pleasant countries in the world to travel around.

The 'land of smiles' is, on the whole, a land of genuine smiles—smiling makes everyone feel comfortable, secure and welcome. Behind the smiles however, Thailand

32

has one of the highest murder rates of any country, as well as escalating drug addiction and some one million prostitutes. The Thai character is enigmatic, and highly unpredictable: because there is no allowance for criticism or for resolution of negative feelings through discussion, when anger comes to the fore, it often does so very suddenly and often very violently.

Such violence, in a general sense, lies at the heart of current social problems in the country, and it derives much from the impact of modernity. The Thais are fundamentally a conservative people who have raced into the modern age at breakneck speed. During the 1932 revolution, the power of the nobility transferred overnight to a new class of educated commoners. Suddenly, money and power—two things that the Thais greatly respect—came within the reach of the general population. A mass migration began to provincial centres like Bangkok and Chiang Mai, swelling these capitals with a multitude of peasants looking for money and work. Few of them found what they came for. But even fewer return to certain poverty in the fields.

Today, while roughly half of Thailand's population—mainly the new class of provincial capitalists and those living off tourism—can now make ends meet, the remainder still live a hand-to-mouth existence. A consequence of this has been the alarming growth of prostitution amongst girls from the poorer rural areas. They migrate to the cities and to the tourist beaches in search of work. The minimum monthly wage for any job stipulated by the government is 2200B a month, but jobs are so scarce they will accept wages of 600B a month or even less. Many of them start out as waitresses, and then, when their friends report getting a month's pay in a day from 'entertaining' rich foreigners, they turn to prostitution themselves. There is no moral stigma attached to this profession. Money is so highly respected that, as long as a prostitute cares for her parents, she can still present herself as a 'good' person and may—after enough cash has been stashed—return home and be accepted as a good marriage bet.

Almost too late, Thailand is waking up to the sobering reality that tourism and 'progress' have their price—time-honoured customs, traditions, folklore, even national identity, are being eroded and undermined. The current trend in Thai society—popularly described as 'modernization without development'—indicates that the brakes have already been applied. But have they been applied too late?

Monarchy

The importance of the king in Thailand cannot be overemphasized. The Sukhothai ideal of the king was as 'father of the people'. The Khmer ideal, adopted by Ayutthaya, was of the king as *devaraja* or 'Lord of Life'. Until quite recent times, Thai monarchs were—at least in theory—the most absolute in the world. They were credited with possessing near-divine powers, and the penalty for touching one (or even whispering during a royal audience) was death. Today, Thailand is the only country in Southeast Asia (apart from Brunei) still to have a hereditary monarch as its head of state. And while King Bhumibol, the present ruler, is only a constitutional monarch, he still remains the spiritual and temporal head of the nation, the lynchpin of Thai unity.

Bhumibol, together with his lovely Queen Sikrit, is a 'working royal' who has earned the respect of other nations and the love (almost worship) of his own subjects through his active sponsorship of innumerable public projects—land reclamation, irrigation, dams, cottage industries and rice cultivation—aimed primarily at helping the poor and under-privileged in remote rural areas of his kingdom. He is, in many respects, a thoroughly modern monarch, and a man of many talents—artist, composer, musician and award-winning sailor.

Even by Thai standards, Bhumibol's popularity is impressive. Every household, every bus and train, every restaurant and hotel, every museum, temple and village hut, has a garlanded or gilt-framed picture of the King (and often his Queen) in a prominent place, usually next to a Buddhist altar or a spirit shrine. And at 6 each evening, when the national anthem blares forth from every tinny tannoy or transistor in the country, everything grinds to a halt as the Thais acknowledge with silent respect their powerful and popular king. Never, it seems, has a Thai monarch been so venerated and so valued by his people. Certainly, this is much to do with Bhumibol himself—a hard-working, gifted and caring man if there ever was one—but is there another reason? I've asked several Thais why they *really* value the king's presence, and the following answer is fairly typical:

> The military has so much power now. If we don't have the king, the
> military is sure to take over the government, and many problems are
> going to happen. The king is so important. He's a really good guy—
> much better than the government!

Creepies and Crawlies

As a hot, humid country, Thailand has its fair share of insects, reptiles and rodents. It also has some pretty weird animals, including the pink dogs of Ayutthaya, painted with antiseptic, and the pink, albino, water-buffaloes of Koh Samui, which are nick-named *farangs* by the islanders because they look so strange and anaemic.

Cockroaches hang out in bathrooms mainly, and are found in all but the best hotels. They're a smaller variety than, say, India's, but they get everywhere. If you're having a shower, they'll pop out of sinks and toilets to join you. If you're lying on your bed feeling lonely, they'll pop up on your shoulder to keep you company. If you really can't stand them, you have a choice of remedies: get a room without an attached bathroom; splash out on a decent hotel; sleep under a mosquito net, or finally, be really mean to the critters and sleep with the light on all night.

Night-time is when the mosquitoes come out to play and eat, and seem to dine exclusively on foreigners. The best preventative is a generous application of *Autan* to arms, ankles and face when going out in the evening. Mozzies are worst during the damp months of June to November. The malarial variety are restricted to certain areas like Koh Samet, Kanchanaburi and Mae Hong Son province. In these places extra precautions are necessary, including sleeping under a mosquito net and spraying your room, remembering to keep all doors and windows shut.

Lizards come in three main varieties—from the small chin-chuck (don't toss these out—they eat mosquitoes) to the medium-size gecko and the large talkay. On Koh Samet, I found a talkay squatting on my bungalow toilet. Later it took up residence in the roof, stomping over the ceiling and clucking to itself all night. Lizards are a chatty, friendly lot—there's one in the grounds of the Hua Hin Railway Hotel that poses and preens itself for the camera—and do nobody any harm.

The same can't always be said for spiders, especially the huge fanged variety found up in the north. Koh Samui has some whoppers too, some the size of dinner plates who lie in wait on your bungalow bed awaiting your return. Mind you, Samui is famous for its wildlife in general. During my stay, I received visits from ants, lizards, baby scorpions and snakes. Apparently I was 'lucky'. A friend of mine had her underwear taken away and eaten by rats, another her toothpaste devoured by a tribe of cockroaches. One couple on Koh Phangan had unwisely left a bunch of bananas out one night. Their bungalow was invaded by a flock of giant bats.

Snakes in Thailand get a really bad press. They deserve it—90% of them are supposed to be poisonous. Don't worry too much, though. Encounters with them are rare, except when trekking in the northern hills, and even then local guides walk on ahead and root them out. The poisonous snakes are usually small and green—the smaller they are, and the less they move, the more lethal they're supposed to be. So, if you come upon a huge, fat, long one, and you're fresh out of snake serum, don't worry—this one will only crush you to death. If that's little comfort, remember that most snakes in this country end up as handbags or cowboy boots, and a select few on restaurant menus.

Siamese Twins

The name is derived from In and Junn (1811–74), twins who developed from the same ovum and lived, fused together, in a small houseboat in the village of Meglong, 60 miles southwest of Bangkok. Destined to become world celebrities, In and Junn were to marry a pair of South American sisters and father 21 children, as well as becoming farmers, landowners and respected members of the community.

Joined at the base of the chest, a little off centre, by an 8-inch-thick ligament 6 inches long, the pair tried, as much as possible, to ignore the deformity and lead 'normal' lives, even participating in sports such as gymnastics and swimming. They maintained two separate households, spending three days with the family of one, followed by three days with the family of the other. They were both quite astute and business-minded: in 1870, Junn's assets from his farm stood at $23,000, and In's at $7,000. They also turned their deformity into financial gain, and were invited all over the world to be viewed by the curiosity-seeking public.

As time went on, their radically different personalities came into conflict, and their relationship began to deteriorate. Junn was moody, volatile and hot-tempered, often drowning his sorrows in heavy drinking bouts, while In was quiet and even-tempered. Tension mounted to such an extent that Junn threatened his brother with a knife, and begged their doctor to separate them whatever the risk. Junn eventually suffered a stroke, which paralysed his right side. Finally, he succumbed to a bout of bronchitis and died whilst in transit from his house to his brother's, in freezing temperatures. His death was, inevitably, followed an hour later by In's.

Part III
HISTORY AND RELIGION

History

For a number of reasons, early Thai history is very obscure. Firstly, the Thais—or Siamese—had no written language until the 13th century, and the little we know of them prior to this time has been gleaned from the journals of various Chinese travellers. Secondly, the high humidity of Thailand's climate has destroyed most of its art treasures and deserted cities, leaving few clues as to the glories of past civilizations. Thirdly, and most disastrously, the powerful Thai capital of Ayutthaya was completely sacked by the Burmese in 1767, and a vast treasurehouse of precious records and archives literally went up in smoke. Painstaking efforts to reassemble pre-Ayutthayan history have only been partially successful. The yawning gaps that remain may never be filled by anything but myth and legend.

Until quite recently, it was believed that the Thai people originated in southern China, Burma and Mongolia, and that they were forced down into present-day northern Thailand following Kublai Khan's capture of Nanchao (their capital in south-central China) in 1253. Recent archaeological discoveries, however, have completely upturned this theory. During the 1960s a series of prehistoric sites was located—at Kanchanaburi, at Mae Hong Son, and finally at Ban Chiang—which suggest that Thailand was probably the home of the world's oldest Bronze Age civilization, dating back some 5000 years. The Thais are very keen to substantiate this—it would mean that their civilization predates that of China, whose own Bronze Age began around 2000 BC. It would also suggest that the original Thais migrated *to* China, rather than—as popularly supposed—the reverse.

36

Sukhothai – Ayutthaya

Whatever, the early 13th century witnessed a large-scale migration of Sino-Thai peoples southward from China, and down into the hill country of present-day northern Burma, Thailand and Laos. In 1238 Thai armies captured the Khmer garrison-town of Sukhothai in north-central Thailand, and the various Thai tribes came together to form their first major kingdom. From this capital, they expanded rapidly outwards to displace the Mons (who'd entered central Thailand from southern Burma, and founded a major empire from the 6th to the 11th centuries) and the Khmers (who'd driven westward into Thailand from present-day Kampuchea). The previous name of Sukhothai ('happy Thai') was Sayam, and it was during this period that Siam became a nation with a culture and character all its own. Well, not *quite* all its own—selective borrowing did take place. For instance, the Sukhothai Thais soon came into contact with the already ancient civilization of India, with enduring effect on their cuisine, calligraphy and complexions.

In 1275 King Ramkhamhaeng, Sukhothai's most notable ruler, began his 40-year reign. The cultural and military *paterfamilias* of the country, he gave the Thais—already united in speech and in customs—their first written language. He borrowed from the Cambodian Khmers to establish the first Thai alphabet. A wise and enlightened ruler, he also abolished slavery, codified the law, and established Buddhism as the national religion. Sukhothai had three more kings after Ramkhamhaeng, but none equalled his talents. The capital was intermittently attacked by the Burmese and was finally abandoned when Ramatibodi, Prince of Utong, captured the Khmer strongholds of Chanthaburi and Lopburi—establishing in 1350 a far safer and more central government at Ayutthaya, 40 miles up the Chao Phya River from modern Bangkok.

Ayutthaya was capital of Siam for more than four centuries. Its power stretched from Luang Prabang in the north all the way to Johore and Singapore, even including (under King Naresuan) the Shan states and Kampuchea. Ramatibodi, considered the first Thai king, was a progressive ruler who devised a new code of laws and received the emissary (Portuguese) from the West in the early 16th century. Soon the city was receiving regular visitors (mainly traders) from Japan, France, Holland, Spain and England. The word *farang*—a corruption of *feringhi*, used by Indian immigrants to denote the French—appeared around this time, and was used by Thais to describe white people in general.

By the end of the 17th century, Ayutthaya had clinched important trade deals with the Dutch and English, and was—at least as far as Europe was concerned—the most consequential capital in Southeast Asia. Then came the wooden horse that was to wreck its fortunes—an ambitious Greek adventurer named Constantine Phaulkon. King Narai first employed him as his interpreter with *farangs*, but it wasn't long before he became the king's Prime Minister. This appointment, and his clear French sympathies, aroused much envy amongst the Thai nobles. In 1688—following his conspiracy to replace Narai with a French-controlled puppet-king—the nobles were forced to unite in self-defence. The French garrison at Bangkok which Phaulkon had helped to establish, was ousted and he was arrested and publicly executed on July 5 1688. For the next 150 years, the Thais kept contact with the West to the barest minimum.

Much of Ayutthaya's history had been spent fighting the Khmers in the east and the

37

Burmese in the west. Under King Narai's successors—a generally poor bunch—the capital became progressively weaker. Burma returned to the attack in 1758, commencing a 9-year siege which ended—in 1767—with the total destruction of Ayutthaya. Ironically, one of the few survivors (albeit brief) of the ensuing holocaust was the debauched King Ekatat—the last of Ayutthaya's rulers—who in true Nero fashion dallied with girls and executed a 'favourite' general while his capital went up in flames. So frustrated were the Burmese conquerors by the city's years of stubborn resistance that it slaughtered or sold into slavery all but 10,000 of its one million inhabitants. Palaces, buildings and even temples were left smoking ruins. The city's precious histories and records were destroyed, and all its treasures taken away as war booty. The effect on the Thai nation has been compared to that of a nuclear bomb.

Thonburi

If the Burmese thought Thai power crushed along with Ayutthaya, they were wrong. Shortly before the capital fell, a brilliant young general called Taksin fled southeast with a few hundred followers to the area of Rayong. Here he reorganized his forces, and returned to the fight. Within a few short months, he had rallied the Thai people, ousted the Burmese from the country, and re-established the Thai kingdom almost to the size it had been before Ayutthaya's capture—a remarkable accomplishment. Taksin proclaimed himself king, and established a new capital farther down the Chao Phya River at Thonburi. After seven years of rule, he decided to stay put in the capital and sent trusted generals out on campaign in his stead. The most notable of these, General Chao Phya Chakri, repelled the Burmese and subdued the Lao kingdoms of Vientiane, Luang Prabang and Chiang Mai. In 1778, Chakri found the legendary Emerald Buddha in Vientiane, and sent it back to Thonburi.

Near the end of his reign, King Taksin developed an anti-social form of megalomania. Convinced that he was a reincarnation of Buddha, he began flogging Buddhist monks, Christians, Chinese and anyone else who crossed him, and put some of his wives to death on trumped-up charges. A revolt broke out in Thonburi, and General Chakri hurried back to the capital to find himself declared the new king by the army and nobility in April 1782. There was some difficulty in knowing what to do with Taksin. In the end, recognizing his many achievements on behalf of the state, his ministers had him tied in a velvet bag and beaten to death with sandalwood clubs. This rather drastic rite—which we are told was 'painless'—had been instituted by King Trailok in 1450 for those of royal descent and avoided the shedding of royal blood. Taksin was the last—perhaps the only—reigning Thai monarch to die in this fashion.

Bangkok

General Chakri, now Rama I, moved his capital across the Chao Phya river from Thonburi to the village of Bangkok. He named the new city Krung Theb Ratanakosin, and supervised its construction with his Grand Palace at the centre. It was Rama I who founded the Chakri dynasty (of which King Bhumibol Aduldej is the ninth and present ruler) which was to transform and modernize the state, both by overhauling Thai forms of government and by borrowing from the West.

Rama I was a broadminded reformer who spent much of his long reign (1782–1809) in governmental consolidation and reconstruction. He devised a new code of law, tightened up the Buddhist priesthood, and did much to recover the religious and secular knowledge lost at Ayutthaya. He is also credited with writing at least part of the *Ramakien*—Thailand's definitive literary masterpiece—which is based on the Indian *Ramayana* epic. Under Rama I, the nation began at last to enter a period of peace and prosperity.

Rama II (1809–24) is chiefly remembered as a poet, but he also made a number of positive legal and administrative reforms. His major shortcoming was in not designating an heir. When he died suddenly, Prince Mongkut—his eldest son by the queen—had just entered the priesthood at the age of 20. The nobles were left with no option but to appoint Prince Chesda—the son of a consort—as Rama III (1824–1851). The new king was a devout Buddhist, who constructed some fine temples (including Wat Arun and additions to Wat Po), as well as supporting the work of Prince Mongkut, who had wisely elected to stay put in the Sangha (the monastic order) out of his brother's way. When Rama III died in 1851, having also failed to designate a successor, the nobles sought out Mongkut in his temple sanctuary and elected him Rama IV.

King Mongkut was a gifted, enlightened ruler who successfully ushered Thailand into the modern world. That he is chiefly remembered as the light-hearted libertine of the film *The King and I*—based on the fanciful recollections of Anna Leonowens, the English governess hired as tutor to his children—is indeed unfortunate. The sybaritic demagogue portrayed in the film bore little resemblance to the austere, venerated monarch who had spent 27 years in a Bangkok monastery. Significantly, the king's voluminous state papers contain just one brief reference to Anna—as an appendix to a shopping list!

Mongkut's domestic achievements were impressive—he restored the beautiful palace at Bang-Pa-In, he reformed the Buddhist priesthood (founding the new ascetic Thammayut sect), he introduced minted coins, and he began to reorganize his army along modern European lines. But it was as an international diplomat that he really excelled. As the other nations of Southeast Asia fell one by one under Western colonial control, losing their culture and traditions in the process, Mongkut took steps to avoid the same fate for Thailand. In 1864, he wrote to his ambassador in France of his dilemma:

> Siam is being harassed by the French on one side, with the British
> colony on the other ... It is for us to decide what we are going to do;
> whether to swim up river to make friends with crocodile or to swim out
> to sea and hang on to the whale.

In the event, by negotiating a series of clever trade treaties with Britain, France and the United States (he once even offered Abraham Lincoln some war-elephants to help him win the American Civil War!), Mongkut kept all these powers at bay and established the principle of Thailand as an independent buffer-state between all the colonial powers in Southeast Asia. A keen astronomer, in 1868 he calculated the time for a total eclipse of the sun, and moved his entire court (plus several Thai and foreign scientists) out to the best viewing point. The eclipse took place exactly as predicted, disproving ancient Thai myths about a giant obscuring the sun, and Mongkut returned home in triumph. Sadly, the spot he'd chosen for his camp contained fever, and he died shortly after of severe malaria.

His able son and successor, King Chulalongkorn (1868–1910) was appointed as Rama V. Despite an inauspicious start to his reign—his first queen fell from a royal barge and drowned—Chulalongkorn went on to become the only king of Thailand to earn the prefix 'the Great'. He finally abolished slavery as well as prostration by Thais before the monarch, he modernized the army and administration, he opened up the land with railways, and he was the first reigning Thai monarch to travel abroad. Above all, he was a great humanitarian and it was he who raised Thailand from a feudal to a modern 20th-century state.

Chulalongkorn's greatest achievement was to preserve Thailand's precarious independence as a 'buffer' between the British (India, Burma, Malaya) and French (Indo-China) colonial states. True, he was forced to make concessions—ceding his claim to Kampuchea and part of Laos to the French in 1904, and four minor Malay states to Britain in 1909—but he nonetheless kept his country free from colonial rule. A much-loved monarch, the date of his death (23rd October 1910) is now a national holiday.

Chulalongkorn was succeeded by his son, King Vajiravudh (1910–25), who became Rama VI. He was a noteworthy poet, who patronized literature and the arts. He is also remembered for launching the Boy Scout movement, and for passing a law requiring all Thais to 'acquire' last names (before 1916, they all had just one name). But the most spectacular act of his reign was to enter World War I, dispatching a token force of Thai troops to support the Allies in France.

Next on the throne was King Prajadhipok, who as Rama VII (1925–32) was the last of Thailand's absolute monarchs. An amiable, cosmopolitan young man, Prajadhipok faced first the international financial depression of the 1920s—which forced him to make a series of unpopular governmental cutbacks—and then growing dissatisfaction from the class of European-educated junior officials, who resented being passed over for senior appointments by 'old guard' princes. On 24th June 1932, a junta of 27 army officers styling themselves the Promoters seized the government in Bangkok in a bloodless 'revolution'. They sent the king an ultimatum demanding he accept constitutional status under their leadership. He agreed so promptly, that they sent a second letter apologizing for the rudeness of the first one!

Shortly after the Promoters (now the People's Party) launched their new constitution (December 10th 1932), King Prajadhipok decided to abdicate (1935) in favour of his ten-year-old nephew, Anan da Mahido, or Rama VIII, who could adapt better to the challenge of a constitutional monarchy. The 'cold *coup d'état*' of 1932 set the scene for a long series of similarly bloodless coups and counter-coups, new constitutions, elections and unsuccessful attempts to overthrow the government by force. It soon became apparent that the Thais didn't care much who actually governed the country, just as long as the king was safe on the throne. The stability of the Crown as a counter-balance to the coup meant that nothing much really changed from one government to the next—especially since each new government since 1932 sought the king's approval. Further, until 1957 at least, those politicos who mounted the successive coups were mainly the same 'Promoters' who had led the first coup group. Bound by a gentlemanly oath of mutual loyalty, they overthrew each other with as little violence as possible—an example not followed by the younger politicians who came after them.

World War II faced Thailand with a major dilemma. When the Japanese arrived on December 7th 1941, the government had little option but to welcome them in. Later, when an Axis victory looked probable, the Thai government even declared war on Britain and the US. In return, it gained from Japan the 'reward' of the four northern provinces of Malaya. But Thailand's involvement with the Japanese was never anything more than tepid—beneath the surface, she remained sufficiently aligned to her Western 'adversaries' to provide them with an active Free Thai underground. Somehow (a diplomatic *tour de force*!) Thailand emerged at the end of the war stronger than before—no longer bound by cumbersome treaties which previously gave foreigners in Thailand special privileges.

In December 1945, King Anan Mahidol returned from his studies in Switzerland to take up the throne as Rama VIII. Just a few months later, on 9th June 1946, he was found shot through the forehead in the Grand Palace. Accident or foul play? Nobody has ever known for certain. His younger brother, King Bhumibol Aduldej, succeeded him in 1950 as Rama IX. Though arriving on the throne under the most difficult circumstances, he has handled the job with commendable skill and diligence.

Political power, meanwhile, was largely in the hands of one man—Field Marshal Pibul Songgram—who held the prime ministership of the country for much of the period before and during World War II. He fended off a number of attempts to unseat him, but was finally toppled in 1957/8 (two successive coups) by Field Marshal Sarit Thanarat. A tough army man, Sarit exercised sole government over the country (which he placed under martial law) until his death in 1963. Stability returned to government, and Thailand entered a period of unprecedented social and material well-being. Sarit's main domestic concern was the impoverished northeastern regions of the country, which he saw as prime targets for Communist propaganda. Despite major electrification and irrigation schemes, aimed at relieving the problems of the drought-stricken northeast, Sarit's successor, Field Marshal Thanom Kittikachorn, soon discovered that the Communists had already got a firm foothold in this region. This (and other reasons) delayed the much-anticipated democratic constitution and the holding of free elections until 1969. Democracy lasted just two years. In late 1971, Marshal Thanom abolished it in a bloodless coup. This did not go down well with Thai students however, and they staged a mass demonstration in October 1973. This devolved into a bloody revolution, resulting in the death of some 100 students at the hands of the military.

In 1975, a free democratic election resulted in a right-wing coalition government led by M. R. Kukrit Pramoj. The following year, following Kukrit's unpopular alignment with Communism (following the collapse of Vietnam and Cambodia), renewed student riots gave the military its required excuse to resume control of the country. The new premier, Thanin Kraivichien was unseated by General Kriangsak in October 1977, and by General Prem in 1980. Each new incumbent has promised the same strong checks on Communism and the same liberalization of the constitution. In recent years, this has resulted in a semi-open political system known as the 'halfway democracy'. This also means a halfway dictatorship, which has turned political parties already plagued by factional struggles into weak organizations. Opposition parties fare poorly whenever they attempt to topple the present government. In fact, they are merely waiting in the wings to join the coalition should there be a reshuffle. However, though Thailand's political situation is still far from clear, it is essentially a stable country, united both by its religion and by its strong and respected king. Even the coup of early 1991 was no more than a ripple on the relatively calm waters of Thai politics and life.

41

Religion

The professed religion of 95% of Thais is *Theravada* Buddhism. The greatest of all Thai institutions, Buddhism is the single most important unifying force in the country. It preserves and perpetuates the Thai nation and its traditions, and it moulds the Thai character and personality. The politeness, modesty and tolerance of the Thai people stem directly from their belief in Buddhism, which extends its influence to every aspect of daily life.

The Buddha

The historical Buddha, known as Gautama or Shakyamuni, lived about 2500 years ago in India. A royal prince, he spent his early life surrounded by wealth and luxury. At the age of 19 (29 according to some sources) he became preoccupied with the questions of birth, old age, sickness and death, and set off on a long quest for the Truth. Finally, at the age of 30 (or 35) he achieved his enlightenment under the Bo tree at Bodhgaya, in North India. The remaining 45 years of his life, he spent teaching his new philosophy to as many people as possible, irrespective of their status. His teaching incorporated the Hindu doctrines of *karma* and reincarnation, but he reinterpreted them in a far more dynamic form. Karma could be changed. Enlightenment could be achieved by anyone, and in this lifetime. It was a simple, optimistic message which spread in time to Sri Lanka, China, Nepal, Tibet, Central Asia, Southeast Asia and Japan. In India, about a century after the Buddha's death, a schism appeared in the *Sangha* (community of monks), causing a division into two major schools. The conservative *Theravada* school (later termed *Hinayana* or 'lesser vehicle') clung to the earlier, provisional teachings of the Buddha, and held that enlightenment was an individual pursuit, achieved by meditation and by self-denial. The progressive *Mahayana* school (or 'greater vehicle') taught that enlightenment was a collective altruistic pursuit with the ultimate aim of bringing all humanity to salvation. This school was based on the Buddha's later teachings—principally, the Lotus Sutra (*Myoho Renge Kyo*) taught by the Buddha in the last eight years of his life, and revealed as his supreme teaching by the 13th-century Japanese monk Nichiren. While the *Theravada* (*Hinayana*) sect always refers to the Buddha in terms of external symbols (e.g. *stupas*, pagodas, temples), the growing realization of the *Mahayana* sect is to look for the Buddha nowhere else but in themselves, and in every living thing.

Buddhism in Thailand

Buddhism arrived in Thailand from India and Ceylon, probably around the 3rd century BC. The country's former religion—animism or spirit worship—was not so much replaced by Buddhism as integrated with it. The same process of integration took place when Brahmanism arrived (also from India) in the 11th century AD. Thai religion then became a fascinating blend of different elements: *Theravada* Buddhist (though with traces of *Mahayana*), Hindu Brahmanist, and animist. Thai Buddhism was, therefore, a form of 'popular Buddhism', which later evolved into an institutionalized 'civic' Buddhism. It is—as evinced by the profusion of Hindu gods and beliefs represented in Buddhist temples, and by the Thai fascination with animistic 'lucky' charms—an extremely flexible religion!

In Thai Buddhism, negative *karma* (present sufferings caused by past errors) is erased, and *nirvana* (perfect enlightenment) made possible, by making merit. A very popular way for ordinary people to make merit is to free captured birds, tortoises and fish. These are often sold outside temples, freed by devout Buddhists, and captured again to give more devotees a chance to make merit. Even kings must make merit, and the present monarch, Bhumibol, made a great deal of merit in 1957 by becoming a monk for 14 days. For a Thai man, becoming a monk is the best possible way of making merit. He not only makes merit for himself (monkhood turns him from a 'raw' into a 'ripe' man, and makes him a suitable marriage prospect), but he also makes merit for his parents. Most Thai men spend at least a few months serving in a Buddhist monastery, and some 350,000 monks, novices and nuns currently support Thailand's 28,000 or so Buddhist temples. Monks make merit because they live an austere life, eating only twice a day (after noon, they can only take drinks), owning nothing but an umbrella, a razor and maybe a few books, wearing simple yellow robes, and sleeping in bare, spartan cells. Each morning around 6 am, they walk the streets collecting their first meal of the day. This gives each Thai family who gives a spoonful of food a chance to make some merit too.

There are two main sects in the general community of monks called the *Sangha*. The *Thammayut*, founded by the ascetic King Mongkut in the mid-19th century, are in the minority. This sect enjoins its monks (*bhikkus*) to spend most of their day studying, to avoid touching even paper money, and to live as austerely as possible. Several *Thammayut* are 'forest-dwelling' monks, who spend their time exclusively in prayer and meditation. The other main sect, the *Mahanikaya*, comprise the vast majority of Thai monks. They are ordained for a period from five days to three months, usually during the rainy season, when all monks stay put inside their monasteries. Most *Mahanikaya* are poor country boys who, having taken advantage of the educational advantages of monkhood (the temple is the traditional intellectual centre of the community), leave the *wat* to become lorry drivers, soldiers, kick-boxers and tourist guides. Only a small percentage of monks stay in the *Sangha* for more than a few years.

Underlying orthodox Buddhism is the pervasive influence of Thai animism. This religious system deals primarily with *phis* or nature spirits, who must be constantly appeased if life is to run smoothly and happily. To gain their favour or protection, Thais commonly wear sacred amulets or holy water, often imbued with 'power' by Buddhist monks. Furthermore, in almost every Thai house compound, there is a 'spirit house' erected to appease the *chao thi* or 'lord of the land'.

As animistic symbols of power continue to multiply—magically gifted monks and charms included—concerned critics within the *Sangha* have begun to argue strongly for a revitalized Buddhism which is relevant to modern times. They point out that temple education—which concentrates much on arid rules and ceremonies, and little on Buddhism's deeper wisdom or goal—prepares its young monks far better for life outside the *Sangha* than for any meaningful contribution within it.

But a growing section of the population just isn't interested in religion any more. Survival, not spiritual growth, now seems to be people's main concern. And while Thailand's minority religions—the Muslims of the far south, the Christians of the north, the Indian Hindus, Chinese Confucianists, Taoists and *Mahayana* Buddhists—have all made a few converts, the new gods of materialism and money look set to claim very many more.

Part IV

ART AND ARCHITECTURE

Thai art and culture is basically a compound of three separate influences—Khmer from the east, Burmese from the north, and Srivijaya from the south—together with selective borrowing from India and China. In historic terms, art in Thailand has been exclusively **religious** art. The main impetus behind the creation of buildings, paintings, sculpture and dance is to create merit, not for self-glorification or personal self-expression, but to create beautiful things—often incorporating Buddhistic and Brahmanic symbols (e.g. the Wheel of Law, the Tree of Enlightenment, Vishnu and Shiva)—to ensure beautiful circumstances in the life to come. So, sculptures are mostly of the Buddha and of the Hindu gods. Architecture is mostly temples and *stupas* (often containing 'relics' of the Buddha) and worshipping places of Brahmanic deities. Paintings are mainly linear-form murals on stucco temple walls (mostly destroyed by Thailand's humid climate), depicting mainly the 547 **Jakarta** stories of Buddha's life or the *Ramayana* epic of Hinduism. Literature follows a uniformly religious theme, and culminated in the Thai version of the *Ramayana*, called the *Ramakien* (most other Thai writings, apart from a few 17th- and 18th-century romantic stories were lost at Ayutthaya in 1767). Music and classical dance drama also has a rich religious and historical heritage, and is still mainly performed in temples, in celebration of the power of Buddha.

Sculpture

As the main artistic impetus in Thailand has been Buddhism, Thai sculptors have concentrated mainly on building Buddha images for worship. All representations of Buddha are strictly stylized. In theory, they are all copies of an 'ideal' image based on portraits made of the Buddha during his lifetime. Sculptors of the Buddha image were

44

not expected to be original or experimental, merely to copy earlier (presumably more authentic) images. The 'ideal' Buddha image is generally tall, slim and willowy, with an asexual body (no muscles, no bones). His eyebrows are like drawn bows, his nose like a parrot's beak, and his chin like a mango stone. Around the 5th–6th century AD, it was decided that Buddha had been born with 33 'extraordinary signs'. These included tightly-curled hair, a topknot (*usnisha*) on the head, and long earlobes (an indication of princely rank; princes wore heavy ear jewellery from birth). Further stylization of these images, which varied in size from the miniature to the colossal, derived from their depiction of Buddha in four prescribed postures or 'attitudes'—standing, sitting, reclining or walking. In the course of time, inevitable variations in style took place, which serve as a guide to the period in which they were composed.

The historical Buddha regarded himself as an ordinary (albeit enlightened) man, and not supernatural or godlike. He did not wish to be worshipped in his lifetime, nor to have images and statues built to him after his death. But all prophets tend to become objects of worship, and around 500 years after the Buddha's death the first image of him appeared in present-day Afghanistan. Influenced by Grecian settlers (remnants of Alexander the Great's army), this prototype image was in the Greco-Roman style, with a halo, classical features and simple, flowing robes. By the 5th century, the art of Buddha-building had spread to India. During the famous Gupta period (the Golden Age of Indian art) images began to acquire their 'extraordinary signs', and to be coated with (or made of) gold—this being the purest metal, symbolic of the Buddha's purity.

The earliest Buddha images fashioned in Thailand appeared in the Mon kingdom of **Dvaravati**, which flourished in central Thailand between the 6th and 11th centuries. This style has an idealized Mon face—broad, with well-formed features, bulging eyes, and a large, sensitive mouth—with the *usnisha* as a round knob. Standing figures usually have hands raised in the gesture of exposition; seated ones (often under a *naga* or sacred serpent) are usually in the attitude of giving the first sermon, or of subduing Mara (symbol of earthly desires). Between the late 7th and 13th centuries, the empire of **Srivijaya** in the south was heavily influenced by India with whom it did a lot of trading. The Srivijaya style of Buddha (and *Mahayana*-type Bodhissatva) images derives from Indian types, mainly Gupta and Pala. Srivijaya figures are typically well-proportioned, naturalistically modelled, and often backed by a backslab or *mandala* surmounted by a parasol.

The **Lopburi** style of the Khmers, who ruled much of northeast and central Thailand between the early 11th and late 13th centuries, continued to portray Buddha as an ascetic. Typical images are small, with realistic proportions and a masculine appearance. Features are gentle, benign and refined, with bulging eyelids, flat nose and thick lips. Figures are usually seated on the *naga* in the attitude of dispelling fear. By the 12th century, the god-king culture of the Khmers led to the creation of Buddhas wearing crowns, jewelled earrings and rather stern, lawgiving expressions.

The **Sukhothai** period, commencing in the 13th century, is considered the Gold Age of Thai art. It re-interpreted traditional models—giving its Buddha images graceful curves, a flamelike *usnisha*, pointed features and an oval face—and it invented the 'walking Buddha', for which there was no prototype. The pre-Ayutthayan style of **King Uthong** favoured the square-faced Buddha with thick lips, smiling mouth, connected eyebrows and cone-shaped *usnisha*, seated on a plain base subduing Mara. During the

Ayutthaya period (14th–18th centuries), early delicacy and craftsmanship deteriorated as the concept of divine kingship inevitably affected religious art. Buddha images became mass-produced and very ornate, often heavily bejewelled and dressed in royal finery. Some say Ayutthaya created a Buddha in its own image—materially rich, spiritually corrupt—which foretold its own ruin.

The present **Bangkok** period has produced little fresh art. After Ayutthaya's destruction, it became practice for sculptors to tour the country resurrecting and renovating old Buddha images, producing nothing new themselves except poor, hackneyed copies of earlier styles. With the loss of Buddhism's vitality at Ayutthaya, religious art went into steep decline. Even today, art students in Bangkok are principally engaged in copying murals from the walls of the Grand Palace. But though some advances have been made in painting and in the minor arts, a definitive Bangkok style of art and architecture has yet to emerge.

Architecture

Architecture is synonymous with temples. These are usually typically Thai, though the larger examples often display Indian-style *stupas*, or Cambodian and Burmese elements. The standard Thai temple is called a **wat**, and contains within its compound various buildings and structures. The most notable are the *bot*, the main chapel and ordination hall containing the temple's main Buddha image; one or more *viharns*, or secondary chapels, used for public worship and housing lesser Buddha images; one or more *chedis* (*stupas*, pagodas), either Thai-style with a bell-shaped dome tapering into a spire, or Khmer-style (*prang*) with an elliptical spire, and often containing relics of the Buddha or of royal personages; and the *sala*, an open-sided rest house or pavilion, used for visitors, and pilgrims.

The most conspicuous architectural feature of Thai temple buildings are their roofs—generally steeply sloping (for quick run-off of rain), many-tiered, and covered with cheerfully coloured glazed tiles. The motifs of the *naga* (holy serpent) and *chopha* (Brahma's carrier, the swan) turn up as horn or beak-shaped finials on the ridge ends of temple roofs. On Chinese temples, the motif is a dragon. Many Thai temples, especially in Bangkok, have a number of stone Chinese figures (usually mandarins or *singha* lions) dotted around their compounds. These were brought into Thailand by Chinese junks, which used them as ballast to weigh down very light cargoes of ceramics. The male variety of the *singha* has a stone ball in its mouth. It is believed that anyone who can remove the ball without damaging the figure or the ball will live for ever. Hindu deities feature prominently in Thai art—notably blue-faced Rama (often bearing a bow and arrow), and the Naga snake (Hindu god of the underworld, said to have saved the Buddha from drowning while he was meditating), which often lead the way up the entrance of temples. Many Thai temples also have a mirrored or reflecting-glass façade, an animist influence designed to deflect or frighten away evil spirits.

Music and Dance

Classical Thai **music** shows influences of Indian, Javanese, Chinese, Burmese, Malay and Khmer musical traditions. It is customarily played by a *piphat* woodwind and percussion band comprising between five and twenty players. The principal woodwind instrument is called a *pi*, and both looks and sounds like an oboe. Percussion instruments are divided between xylophone-like instruments called *ranad* and a semi-circle of gongs called the *gong wong yai* (both of which provide the melody), and an assortment of drums, cymbals and lesser gongs (which provide the rhythm). The intricacies of Thai music, which has defeated transposition by Western bands, arise from its complex musical scale, in which seven full tones (and no semi-tones) separate an eight-note octave. Thai musicians play seated on the floor before their instruments, and they generally perform at festivals, funerals and weddings. 'Modern' Thai music, as played in low-lit jazzy 'disco cafés', leans heavily on '60s R and B, Country and Western, and soulful Western-style ballads. There is either a 'Cliff Richard and the Shadows'-type band with twanging guitars and a stock of summery 'happy-happy' songs; or there is a female vocalist rendering plaintive, wistful Western-copy tunes, with droning, dirge-like accompaniment on keyboards. You'll love it to pieces.

Thai classical **dance** is heavily influenced by Indian temple dancing, on which it is modelled. The two major dance-drama forms are the *khon*, where the performers (originally all men) wear masks, and the *lakhon*, usually performed by women dancing both male and female roles. Both dramas are commonly based upon stories from the *Ramakien*—the Thai version of the Hindu *Ramayana* epic poem. Briefly, this tells of the great prince Rama (a reincarnation of Vishnu) who is sent to earth by Brahma, creator of the world, to destroy the demon king Ravana. He wins the beautiful princess Sita, but is banished by his earthly father, the king of Ayodhya, and wanders around in the forest for 14 years accompanied by Sita and his younger brother Lakshman. Then Ravana, who wants Sita for himself, steals her away and a powerful monkey-king called Hanuman deserts Ravana's army and decides to help out Rama instead. Many battles ensue, before Rama finally kills Ravana, recovers Sita, and returns to Ayodhya to reclaim his throne. It's a long, long story never performed today in its entirety. Most classical dinner-dances at major hotels in Bangkok and most tourist-oriented 'cultural shows' depict only a few selected scenes—a far cry from the marathon performances of the courts of old Siam, which used to run for days on end. Both *khon* and *lakhon* are highly stylized forms of dance, with prescribed hand and feet movements to indicate subtle changes in mood and feeling. Of the two, the *Khon* is more visually striking, with the performers wearing ornate traditional masks and costumes (deep green for Rama, gold for Lakshman, white for Hanuman etc). A third form of Thai drama, the *nang* or **shadow-play** in which the story is told by means of large, elaborate silhouettes cut out of buffalo hide, is little seen nowadays, even in the south where it was once most popular. The dance which tourists are most likely to come across in Thailand is the notorious *Ramwong* or circle-dance. This is one of those embarrassing audience participation affairs where unsuspecting dinner-dance guests are suddenly plucked onto the stage and shuffle around looking horribly ill-at-ease, while their friends take lots of unkind photographs!

Part V

BANGKOK

Royal barge

Despite its trappings of progressive modernism—high-rise hotels, fast-food restaurants and *haute couture* boutiques—Bangkok remains distinctly Thai and is one of the friendliest, liveliest cities in the East. 'It's unique', was one typical comment, 'the kind of place where you can arrive and feel at home right away.' Others say the city is like getting used to a strong cheese—the heat, the noise, the pollution and the mind-numbing traffic may overwhelm you at first, but once you've acquired the taste, all other cities seem dull and bland by comparison. The key to Bangkok's provocative, intriguing Asian mystery is that it has no centre. It's not like a city at all. Rather, it's a country town gone wild—a series of self-contained villages loosely strung together to make up a 'city'. Bangkok's veneer of urban sophistication is never more than paper-thin. One-fifth of its population still live a totally traditional life on its waterways and *klongs* (canals); white-collar company directors still sing happy folk songs on their way to work; barefoot groups of orange-robed monks still tour the grey city pavements each dawn, begging for alms; students still bound up to lost tourists at crowded traffic intersections, offering help; and everybody (I mean everybody) gives you a smile and a cheery *Sawatdee*, no matter how busy they are. It's not just that Bangkokites like tourists (which they do)—they are simply country people, living in a big city.

So, welcome to 'Krungthep Manakhon Bovorn Ratanakosin Mahintharayutthaya Mahadilokpop Noparatratchathani Burirom Udomratchanivetmahasathan Avatarnsathit Sakkathattiya-visnukarmrasit'—or simply 'Krungthep', as the locals call it. This short title means 'City of Angels' (Los Angeles?), and is just one of many sobriquets that Bangkok has earned over the years. Current favourites include 'Venice of the East' (a reference to its many canals), 'Bargain Basement of Asia' (you can save, and spend, a fortune here) and 'Sex Capital of the World' (men, watch out). But the name Bangkok, an abbreviation of Tumbol Bangmakok, simply means 'Village of Wild Plums'—and that's just how it started out.

History

When Rama I moved his capital here from Thonburi in 1782, Bangkok was a tiny mosquito-infested village (with plums), overlooking the Chao Phya River. His vision was to rebuild Ayutthaya, the old capital gutted by the Burmese in 1767, in a new setting. To this end, he used artisans, advisers, and even building materials from the ruined ex-capital, and even cut canals to the eastern side of Bangkok to surround it (like Ayutthaya) with water. For the first century of its life as a capital city, Bangkok's only form of transportation was by water—and when King Mongkut cemented new trade agreements with the West in the late 19th century, the numerous *klongs* fanned out even further to accommodate a large influx of new merchants, traders and shippers. Road transport only became a prominent feature after WW II, and even as recently as the early 1960s, Bangkok was still a charming, leisurely city with sparse motorized traffic and a few tree-lined roads. By this time, it had acquired a skyline of glittering spires and steep orange and green roofs—evidence of its many temples (more than 300). Looking upon this colourful vista from his convalescent bed at the Oriental Hotel, Somerset Maugham expressed his wonderment: 'It makes you laugh with delight to think that anything so fantastic could exist on this sombre earth ... The artists who developed [these temples] step by step from the buildings of the Ancient Khmers had the courage to pursue their fantasy to the limit.'

In 1960, Bangkok had a population of just 1½ million. In 1965, it became a designated venue for American troops on R and R (Rest and Recreation) from Vietnam. The result was a boom in bars, cinemas, hotels, restaurants and massage parlours. The city became a magnet for poor rural people—especially young girls—seeking to escape a life of hopeless poverty in the country provinces. The consequent migration was dramatic. By the early '80s, the lure of employment, money and bright lights had flooded Bangkok with 6 million people—40 times the population of the second largest city, Chiang Mai. One in ten Thais now live in Bangkok, and more than half of these are of Chinese descent. One million of the capital's inhabitants own and drive cars—the result is a traffic nightmare, and the lowest oxygen level of any city in the world. An order has gone out to ban the production of any new *tuk-tuks* (the main offenders) but they just keep on appearing.

Bangkok Today

Despite the frequent clouds of smog, Bangkok maintains an incredibly clean 'front'— waste-bins and street cleaners everywhere. No longer is it a drab, malarial city of canals and waterways—many of these have now been filled in—but a bright, fast-moving and optimistic metropolis of broad, neon-lit avenues, behind which—in a labyrinthine maze of narrow *sois* (streets)—traditional life goes on in hundreds of street markets, floating markets and tiny temple courtyards converted into yet more markets. If one thing holds the jigsaw of Bangkok together, it must be its markets—which seem to have no beginning and no end. And if one place holds the nation together—socially, politically, and commercially—it must be Bangkok. In all respects, it's a city-state—Thailand's only really modern, developed centre. The bewildering contrasts between rich and poor, beauty and ugliness, spirituality and materialism, may unsettle—even shock—you, but Bangkok still has more variety, more charm and more character than any other capital city in the East. A big statement? Well, just spend a few days here and you'll surely agree.

WHEN TO GO

Bangkok is most comfortable from December to February—during these months, humidity is low and temperatures are often comparable to a pleasant English summer. Hotels have their high season from October to April (the big ones are often full, so book in advance) and their low season from May to September (when it is possible to get a discounted 3-star double room for as little as £15).

Festivals

Festivals take place throughout the year, though apart from Lumpini Park and Chao Phya River, there's nowhere really to hold them. The best riverside festival is **Loi Krathong** (October/November), when flotillas of boats put out from the Oriental pier to launch gaily-decorated candlelit floats. Street festivals happen daily in Bangkok, especially in and around the temples. Check out Chinatown—the Chinese really know how to hold a party.

GETTING TO AND FROM BANGKOK

By Air

Perfectly placed for stopover traffic, Bangkok benefits from the ease with which it can be combined with other Asian destinations, such as Hong Kong, Bali, Delhi and Rangoon. It's a great place to pick up cheap airline tickets (especially in the discount centres of Banglampoo and Soi Ngam Dupli) and to obtain visas.

Don Muang Airport, 25 km north of the city, is one of the busiest airports in the world, serving over 30 international airlines. Small, modern and efficient, it has a tourist information centre, a hotel-booking desk, two currency-exchange points, a lost and found baggage service, a left-luggage office (20B a day, per piece) and a Thai International restaurant up on the observation deck (the only place to enjoy a civilized cup of coffee). **The Airport Hotel** (tel 5661020) is directly connected to the airport (very handy), has good rooms from 1900B single, 2500B twin, and offers complimentary transfers from the airport and into town. They also offer short-term rooms if you want to rest before or after your flight, between 8 am and 6; 400B (single), 450B double, maximum stay 3 hours.

From Don Muang, there are several choices of transport into the city:

Air-con limo direct to hotel—the most comfortable option. **Thai Limousine** sells tickets for 300B in the International Lounge, and for only 200B in the Domestic Lounge.

Air-con minibus, dropping off at individual hotels. **Thai Limousine** sells 100B tickets, from 9 am to midnight only.

Private taxi, hired at the airport exit. Bargain hard for the 200B minimum fare.

Public bus, from the street-stop outside the airport. Two useful buses are No. 59, which goes to Victory Monument (continue on No. 39 for Democracy Monument/Banglampoo); and No. 29, which goes to Phetburi Rd (change here for Democracy Monument), Rama I Rd (for Siam Square, change here for Sukhumvit), and Hualamphong station (for Silom-Surawong). The fare is just 5B. Two comfy **air-con buses,** Nos. 4 and 29, head into town from the airport for 15B.

Train, from Don Muang rail station (connected to the airport via Airport Hotel). Trains leave for Hualamphong station every 20 minutes or so, from 3 am to 10. Fare is 5B, 3rd class (add 20B fee for Rapid trains, 30B for Express).

From airport to town takes between 45 minutes (at night) to 1½ hours (at rush hour). If travelling by public transport (i.e. bus or train), keep an eagle eye on your bags and wallet—the airport route is plied by expert thieves.

Airport Tax
When leaving, or flying within the country, have your **Airport Tax** handy—200B for international flights, 20B for domestic flights. If in transit (i.e. if you haven't left the airport building), you don't have to pay this—but you do need to fill in a declaration form.

    Domestic flights on Thai Airways, servicing several destinations within the country, also leave from Don Muang airport—see General Information section.

Airlines with offices in Bangkok are as follows:

International

Aeroflot	Regent House, 183 Ratchadamri Rd	251–1223–5
Air Canada	1053 New Rd	233–5900–9 Ext 11–14
Air France	942/51 Charn Issara Tower, Rama IV Rd	2341333–9
Air India	Amarin Tower, 500 Phloenchit Rd	256–9614–9
Air Lanka	942/51 Charn Issara Tower, Rama IV Rd	236–9292
Alitalia	Boonmitr Bldg, 138 Silom Rd	233–4000–4, 234–5257
American Airline	Maniya Bldg, 518/2 Phloenchit Rd,	251–1393, 252–3520–2
Bangladesh Biman	Chongkolnee Bldg, Suriwong Rd	235–7643–4
British Airways	2nd Fl, Charn Issara Tower, Rama IV Rd	236–8655–8
CAAC (China)	134/1–2 Silom Rd	235–1880–2, 235–6510–1
Canadian Airlines	518/2 Maniya Bldg, Phloenchit Rd	251–4521, 251–1393
Cathay Pacific	5th Fl, Charn Issara Tower, Rama IV Rd	233–6105–9
China Airlines	4th Fl, Peninsula Plaza, Ratchadamri Rd	253–5733–7
Dragonair	Sukhumvit Soi 18	258–1413–6
Egypt Air	120 Silom Rd	231–0503–8, 233–7599
Finnair	518/2 Maniya Bldg, Phloenchit Rd	251–5012, 251–5075
Garuda Indonesia	944/19 Rama IV Rd	233–0981–2, 233–3873–4
Gulf Air	518/5 Maniya Bldg, Phloenchit Rd	254–7935–8
Indian Airlines	2/1–2 Decho Rd	233–3890–2
Iraqi Airways	325–329 A.S.C. Bldg, Silom Rd	235–5950–5
Japan Airlines	Wall Street Tower, 33/33–34 Suriwong Rd	233–2440, 234–9111
KLM	2 Patpong Rd	235–5155–9
Korean Air	Room 306 Dusit Thani Bldg, Rama IV Rd	234–9283–7
Kuwait Airways	159 Ratchadamri Rd	251–5855

Lauda Air	Wall Street Tower, 33/67–68 Suriwong Rd	233–2565, 233–2544
Lot-Polish	485/11–12 Silom Rd	235–2223–7, 235–7092–4
Lufthansa	Bank of America Bldg, Silom Rd	234–1350–9, 255–0370
Malaysian Airlines	98–102 Suriwong Rd	236–4705, 236–5871
Myanmar Airways	48/5 Pun Rd, Silom Rd	233–3052, 234–9692
Northwest Orient	Peninsula Plaza, 153 Ratchadamri Rd	253–4423–5
Pakistan International	52 Suriwong Rd	234–2961–5, 234–2352
Pan Am	518/2 Maniya Bldg, Phloenchit Rd	251–4521, 252–8842
Philippine Airlines	56 Chongkolnee Bldg, Suriwong Rd	233–2350–2, 234–2483
Qantas Airways	942/51 Charn Issara Tower, Rama IV Rd	236–7493–4, 237–6268
Royal Brunei	2nd Fl, Charn Issara Tower, Rama IV Rd	235–4764, 234–0007
Royal Jordanian	56 Yada Bldg, Silom Rd	236–0030
Royal Nepal Airlines	Sivadon Bldg, 1/4 Convent Rd	233–3921–4
Sabena	CCT Bldg, 1 Suriwong Rd	233–2020
SAS	412 Rama I Rd	253–8333
Saudia	CCT Bldg, 109 Suriwong Rd	236–9395–9, 236–0112
Singapore Airlines	Silom Center, 2 Silom Rd	236–0440, 236–0303
Swissair	IBM Bldg, 1 Silom Rd	233–2930–7
Tarom	89/12 Soi Bangkok Bazaar, Ratchadamri Rd	253–1681–5
Thai Airways International	89 Vibhavadi-Rangsit Rd	513–0121
	185 Silom Rd	233–3810, 234–3100
TWA	12th Fl, Charn Issara Tower, Rama IV Rd	233–7290–1
United Airlines	Regent House, 183 Ratchadamri Rd	253–0558–9

Domestic

Bangkok Airways	144 Sukhumvit Rd	253–4014–6, 253–8942–7
Thai Airways	6 Lan Luang Rd	280–0070, 280–0080
	4th Fl, Charn Issara Tower, 942/136 Rama IV Rd	236–7884–5

Airports

Bangkok International Airport	523–6201, 531–0022–59
Bangkok Domestic Airport	523–6201, 523–7222

By Rail

Bangkok's central railway station, **Hualamphong**, is at the western end of Rama IV Rd. It covers all routes north and northeast, plus many southern destinations. The Advance Booking office at Hualamphong (open 8.30 am to 6 pm weekdays, 8.30 am to noon weekends) has a tourist information desk, and hands out rail timetables. Trains for Kanchanaburi leave from Bangkok Noi railway station, across the river.

By Bus

Regular air-conditioned (air-con) and non air-conditioned (non air-con) buses leave for most tourist centres from three main bus-stations in Bangkok. These are the **Northern Bus Terminal**, Phahonyothin Rd (tel 271010), which services Ayutthaya, Chiang Mai, Chiang Rai, Lamphun, Lopburi, Phitsanulok, Sukhothai, Khorat, Nong Khai and Udorn Thani; the **Eastern Bus Terminal**, off Soi 42, Sukhumvit Rd (tel 3912504), which covers Pattaya, Rayong, Si Racha and Chanthaburi; and the **Southern Bus**

Terminal, Charansanitwong Rd (tel 4110511), which runs out to Hat Yai, Hua Hin, Kanchanaburi, Krabi, Nakhon Pathom, Phang Nga, Phuket, Koh Samui and Surat Thani. The Northern and Eastern bus-stations have baggage-deposit facilities (20B per piece)—very useful if you're heading north, and want to fly straight out on your return to Bangkok (the Northern terminal is close to Don Muang airport).

GETTING AROUND BANGKOK

With its high humidity, broken pavements and traffic-choked streets, Bangkok is not a city conducive to walking. Apart from a stroll to the local shops, you'll nearly always have to take some form of transport. This usually means travelling by bus, taxi, *tuk-tuk* or hired car—and a head-on encounter with Bangkok's diabolical traffic. Well, is it really that bad? One of the city's leading newspapers, *The Nation*, evidently thinks so:

> We believe that no system in the world could improve the traffic in
> Bangkok. The reason is simple: there are too many vehicles in the city.
> The conventional wisdom is that if you line up all motor vehicles
> registered in Bangkok Metropolis on the city streets, there will not be
> enough road space for any vehicle to move... Every time it rains the city
> grinds to a halt and many a motorist is ready for the psychiatric ward.

The *Bangkok Post* adds an optimistic footnote:

> Within the next 10 years, the population in Bangkok could well exceed
> 11 million ... You can imagine how chaotic it would be for Bangkok
> traffic without expressways and the sky train which we are going to build.
> If no obstacles arise, the ETA will commence the construction of three
> routes for the 'Sky Train' late next year.

Every major paper ran an editorial ridiculing the new city police chief's promise to 'solve Bangkok's traffic problem' (and as of late 1991 there are still no signs of any preparations for the construction of this monorail system). Everyone knows it's quite insoluble. At rush hour, the highways are jammed solid all the way up from Sukhumvit to Silom, and vendors casually wander from car to car, selling newspapers and puzzle games to keep the drivers from dozing off at the wheel. Traffic is particularly slow from 7.30 to 9.30 am, and between 4 and 7 pm—these are the rush (crush) hours, and you'll need to allow for extra travelling time (especially if you've a plane or train to catch). But traffic jams in Bangkok are never dull. If stuck in a stationary bus or taxi, you'll be constantly entertained by close encounters with mad-cap motorcyclists (their bikes often stacked high with carpets, hi-fi equipment, toilet brushes and—when there's an inch of spare room—a baby or two). And wherever you stop, there'll always be enough colourful street-action to keep you amused, and your camera clicking.

By Bus

Public buses are the cheapest form of transport. They'll take you virtually anywhere in the city for just 3B. But they're often hot and crowded, and have a poor reputation for pickpockets and slit-bag thieves. Every route has at least one air-con option (5B for the first 10 km)—take it if you can. Last bus services are around 11 pm, though a few services run through the night. Check with your hotel regarding route numbers and bus-stops— Thai buses rarely have English-language destination boards. An essential buy is a **Bus**

Map (35B) listing routes and numbers—available from most bookshops and stationers. The two clearest maps (at present) are those printed by M. Suwanchai and K. S. Thaveepholchar.

By Taxi

Taxis are plentiful, air-conditioned, and the easiest way of getting around—especially if you're short on time. Taxis stopped on the street tend to be cheaper than those on standby outside hotels. But none of them use meters. It's essential to agree a fare (40–60B for short journeys, 70–200B for across town) before setting off.

By Tuk-Tuk

Tuk-tuks (motorized *samlors*) are a little cheaper than taxis (i.e. 30–50B short trips, 60–90B long hauls) and are often manned by manic drivers who know every short-cut going in their part of town. Few of them speak or understand English though, and many get lost outside their 'beats'. Ask your hotel to write your destination in Thai, and to give you one of their own cards, so that you can get home again. With *tuk-tuks*, you need to bargain very hard to get a fair price—and this must be agreed *before* you set off.

By Boat

River-transport is the ideal way of beating Bangkok's traffic, and is very cheap. The Chao Phya River snakes through the capital, and not only affords a completely different view of the city, but connects many of its sightseeing attractions. The main form of public river-transport is the *Chao Phya Express* (*rua duan*)—a large, long river-taxi with a red roof, a large number board, and usually a little guy aboard frantically blowing a whistle. You can't miss it.

Express boats are very cheap (from 3B to 7B, depending on distance) and very regular (one every 20 minutes or so, from 6 am to 6 pm). There are about 40 stops on the route, including some really useful ones like the GPO, the Grand Palace, the National Museum, Prannok Rd (for the Southern Bus Terminal) and Banglampoo. Many people take the rewarding one-hour trip all the way up from the Oriental Pier to Nonthaburi, taking lunch at the nice little restaurant (English menu and good local food) 100 yards below the Nonthaburi pier.

Slower **cross-river ferries** (*rua kham fak*) operate from several jetties, and simply go back and forth across the river. **Longtail taxis** (*rua hang yao*) zip up the Chao Phya and through the narrow *klongs* at incredible speeds. They are a good bet if you're in a hurry, or want to travel in style. You can charter one in a group (100B one-way) from the Oriental Hotel to the Grand Palace, or vice versa. For something special, go to Tha Tien pier (behind Wat Po), where share-fare longtail boats leave every half-hour from 6.30 am to 6 pm for the picturesque side-*klong* trip down **Klong Mon**. This outing features canalside temples, fruit orchards, orchid farms, and fascinating scenes of waterborne life. On Sundays, you can hire a whole longtail boat (for a group of up to 20 people) to see all the major temples, the floating market, the royal barges and the *klongs*, for just 400B. This is a 7-hour excursion, offered by **No 1 Siam Tour** (tel 2330581) at Oriental Hotel pier. Any other day, the best deal like this you can get is a short 3-hour speedboat trip (10 persons only) costing 500B. To arrange this, get a small group together and bargain for your own boat. If there's only one or two of you, consider an organized river trip out of an hotel. There's a good one offered by **Narai Hotel**, Silom Rd, running from 7 am to 12 noon daily and priced at 270B.

By Car
Cars can be hired at around 600B a day from: **Avis**, 10/1 Sathorn Nua Rd (tel 233–0397); **Dollar**, 272 Soi Chinda Thawin, Si Phraya Rd (tel 234–9770); **Grand Car Rent**, 144 Silom Rd (tel 234–9956); **Hertz**, 987 Phloenchit Rd (tel 253–6251). Consider hiring a hotel limousine with driver (fixed rates)—much safer than driving yourself.

TOURIST INFORMATION
TAT (Tourist Authority of Thailand) main office is at Ratchadamnoen Rd (tel 282 1143–7). Very good at handing out information, pretty poor at handling individual enquiries (just try asking about, say, scuba-diving facilities on Phuket). Beautiful wall-posters on Thailand are sometimes available from the small Distribution Office, round the side of the main building. TAT also has a desk in Don Muang airport arrival lounge.

WHAT TO SEE
Sightseeing in Bangkok takes time and dedication—this is a large city, about the size of London or Paris, and its sights are widely spread. To see everything at leisure, ideally you need two weeks. Most visitors however, allow only 4 or 5 days, and this really puts the pressure on. Enervating heat, snarled traffic, and the barrier of language mean that lightning tours are simply not possible. Independent travellers often have difficulty covering more than one or two sights in a day. The old city is completely camouflaged by modern business blocks, cinemas, shopping centres and hotels, making quick orientation impossible. To make best use of your time, you have to be organized. First, aim to be out and about as early as possible—see as much as you can in the cool of the morning. Second, only use public transport between 10 am and 4 (thus avoiding the rush hours). Third, spend your first free morning or afternoon on the Chao Phya River (cf. Getting Around). Go armed with a good city map (the 35B 'bus' map is adequate) and get a quick overview of the city sights and layout. Fourth, alternate individual sightseeing with organized tours. Many hotels and guest houses offer half/full-day tours by air-con minibus or coach at around 120–220B (50B extra, if booking through a big hotel). These are very useful, if you've a lot to see in a short time. Fifth, don't take on too much—in Bangkok, the visitor must slow down to the Thai pace, or perish. Finally, make a list of the sights you *must* see, and do as much advance preparation for them as possible (e.g. arrange early-morning call, advance-book taxi, check opening and closing times of various sights—they vary greatly). If you need an English-speaking guide, contact **World Travel Service**, 1053 Charoen Krung Rd, Silom (tel 2335900) or the **Professional Guides Association** (tel 2513504). They provide badge-carrying guides at around 1000B a day—quite cheap, if you're in a large group. Freelance guides are in very short supply. I've only ever come across them at the Grand Palace and at Wat Pho. Often, your best bet is to tack onto a package tour—every sight has one, and they always seem to have the best guides.

Wat Arun

Grand Palace and Major Temples
(by river-boat, on foot; full day)

Wat Arun – Wat Po – Grand Palace – Wat Phra Keo – Vivanmek Palace
For this suggested tour, go down to the pier below the Oriental Hotel and take a public express boat up to **Wat Arun**, then across to **Wat Po**. From here, it's a short walk to the **Grand Palace and Wat Phra Keo**, and then a short 20–30B ride by *tuk-tuk*/taxi over to **Vivanmek**. Set out early, and dress reasonably well—you won't be allowed in the Grand Palace in shorts or sleeveless tops.

Wat Arun
Wat Arun, or the Temple of the Dawn, lies on the west (Thonburi) bank of the river, and is perhaps Bangkok's most striking landmark. Formerly a 16th-century temple called Wat Chang, it was repaired for use as a royal temple by King Taksin during the early 1800s. Its main claim to fame is that it once housed the famous Emerald Buddha—in fact, this was the last home of the venerated image before Rama I founded Bangkok across the river, and moved it over to the Grand Palace. He compensated the monks for their loss by instructing his son (later Rama II) to make this wat 'more glorious than the others'. Rama II obliged by elevating the central spire (*prang*) from 15 metres to a staggering height of 79 metres, leaving the four smaller *prangs* around it to be completed by Rama III. All five *prangs* are in the Cambodian style, inviting comparisons with Anghor Wat (the famous Khmer sanctuary in present-day Kampuchea), and their stucco exterior is completely covered with colourful pieces—some whole, some broken—of glazed Chinese porcelain and crockery. Each of the *prangs* is surmounted with Shiva's trident, and each rests on a series of terraces, 'supported' by rows of angels and demons. The lower terrace has four small pavilions, depicting the four main events in Buddha's life: birth, enlightenment, first sermon, and death. The central *prang*—which you can climb for great views of the river and city—has four niches, each with an image of the

58

Hindu god Indra, seated on his three-headed elephant, Erawan. The niches of the smaller *prangs* contain figures of the Moon god, riding a white horse.

Wat Po

Wat Po, a few river-boat stops upriver from Wat Arun, and on the Bangkok side of the Chao Phya, is one of the capital's largest and oldest temples. Built over an older monastery called Wat Potharam, it was begun by Rama I in 1793, and later added to by Ramas III and V. It's open 8 am to 5 pm daily, admission is 10B, and guides can be hired at the entrance (120B for one or two persons). Look out for Guide No 5—a real performer. His tour often starts with an inspection of two giant statues, of Chinese mandarins wearing European dress. 'Hat like Johnny Walker', is his opening gambit, 'They have stick! Look like Johnny Walker . . . a bit!' If you want to wander round on your own, turn right inside the entrance (then left, past a brace of bronze lions) to find the *bot*, which lies in a private courtyard. This enclosure is surrounded by double galleries, containing 394 seated Buddha images. The three-tiered roof of red and yellow tiles is supported by a colonnade of square pillars. The huge teakwood doors at the east and west walls, beautifully inlaid with mother-of-pearl, are examples of superb work-manship. The substructure of the main chapel features bas-relief marble panels—recovered from Ayutthaya's ruins—showing scenes from the *Ramayana* epic. The *bot* itself contains an ancient bronze Buddha and, in the altar, some of Rama I's remains. Moving on, you'll spot the 'Four Great Chedis' in another private courtyard. Rama I built the green *chedi*; Rami II, the white and yellow *chedis*, and Rama IV, the highly elaborate blue one.

Wat Po's main attraction, located in the western courtyard, is its enormous Reclining Buddha. This measures 46 m long and 15 m high, and represents the Buddha entering Nirvana. Built of brick, covered in gold leaf, it was commissioned by Rama I and donated to the monastery by Rama III. The soles of the feet are of special interest—covered with mother-of-pearl. They are inscribed with the 108 'extraordinary signs' by which a true Buddha is recognized.

Wat Po was Thailand's first open university, and today it offers courses in acupunc-ture, herbalism and massage. Its traditional 'medical massages' are famous. They are given in a small hall near the main entrance, last one, glorious hour, and cost 120B. If you're here *just* for the massage, there's no need to pay the 10B entrance to the temple—just slip in the side-door, always left slightly ajar, on the eastern side of the compound. The best time to show up is 7 am—by 10 am, all the masseurs are usually booked. Wat Po also has an amazing night market—fizziest between 7 and 9 pm—with hundreds of foodstalls selling cheap, tasty meals. It's a great place to hang out in the evening.

The Grand Palace

The Grand Palace, a short walk up from Wat Po, and overlooking the river, is a whole square mile of extraordinarily beautiful temples and palaces. A vast, glittering Dis-neyland of gilded spires, colourful mosaics, jewel-encrusted shrines, gargoylish Chinese figures, and landscaped gardens, it's an absolute sensory overload—and not to be missed. As one awestruck traveller remarked, 'If this isn't one of the wonders of the world, it certainly should be!'. Bring your camera or movie camera (8 mm only), and lots of film. Also bring sunglasses—the reflected glare of all this gold and glitter is quite blinding. There are a few guides knocking round, whom you can bargain down to 100B an hour. Otherwise, just wander round in dazed stupefaction like most people do. There's a free guidebook given on admission, which few people can follow. Still, who cares. It's all quite magnificent.

The Grand Palace was built by the early kings of the Chakri dynasty, and was—in Rama I's time—the heart of the capital. Its wide compound of high white walls contained the King's private residence, the Royal Secretariat, the Ministries, the army barracks and the royal elephant stables—also some 50 temples, many covered with dazzling sheets of gold leaf. It was, effectively, a city within a city, which could be defended in times of trouble. Even up until recently, it remained the residence of the king and the governing centre of the country.

Tours of the palace generally start at the **Royal Coins and Medals Pavilion**, just inside the entrance. This is an air-conditioned mini-museum of coins (including Ayutthayan pebble-coins gathered from the sea-shore, polished, and carefully carved on each side), gold-encrusted spittoons, uniforms, photos, and various other royal paraphernalia. Within the compound, track down the two beautiful halls of audience—the **Amarinda Vinichai Hall** (used for coronations) and the traditional Thai-style **Dusit Maha Prasad** which is considered the finest building here. It contains a famous stone 'throne seat' slab hewn by Ramkhamhaeng, King of Sukhothai, in 1292. Both halls date to around 1783, and are closed on weekends. Don't miss the **Chakri Palace**, an impressive structure built in the Italian Renaissance style in 1876.

Wat Phra Keo (The Temple of the Emerald Buddha)

The centrepiece of the Grand Palace—the one thing that everybody comes to see—is **Wat Phra Keo**. This is the king's personal chapel, the only wat situated inside the royal palace itself, and the most important temple in Thailand. It was built by Rama I (completed 1785) to house the country's most sacred object—the **Emerald Buddha**. This tiny image, just two feet high, is made of fine green jade—not emerald at all. It is believed to be over 1000 years old, and to have originated from Ceylon or Northern India. It first came to light in Thailand in 1436, when a large plastered Buddha image in Chiang Mai revealed a crack—and its hidden treasure. It later travelled from one Lao capital to another, depending on the power of each, and came to Vientiane. From there, it was brought to Thonburi by Chakri (later Rama I) in 1778. The present king changes the Buddha's robes three times a year—dressing it in blue for the rainy season, gold for the cool season, and in diamond-studded finery for the hot season. Protocol is very strict at this temple—shoes must be left outside, photographs are not allowed inside, and pointing your feet at the altar is taboo. These preliminaries observed, you can relax and gaze up in awe at the tiny figurine perched up on a high dais, lit by a single spotlight, and enjoy the beautiful friezes running round the walls, which tell the story of Buddha's life.

The Grand Palace and Wat Phra Keo are open 8.30 to 11.30 am, 1 to 3.30 pm daily. The audience rooms are closed on Saturday and Sunday. The 100B admission ticket also includes entrance to Vivanmek Palace. To get your money's worth, see both places the same day—Grand Palace first, Vivanmek second. Doing it the other way round, you'll have to pay twice.

Vivanmek Palace

Located at Uthong Nai Rd (off Rajavithi Rd, next to Dusit Zoo), Vivanmek—or

'Paradise on the Cloud'—is a beautiful L-shaped teakwood palace, built at the turn of the century as the home of Rama V. Packed with royal regalia, period furniture, worldwide *objets d'art*, 'magic' carpets and interesting old photos, it's quite possibly the best sight in Bangkok. Novelty exhibits include the first typewriter used in Thailand, the country's first shower (in the king's bathroom) and a quaint porcelain pig nestling in a velveted black box which was a present from Rama V to a queen born in the year of the pig. Vivanmek is open 9 am to 4 pm daily—though you should arrive at 3 pm at the latest, to catch the last guided tour in English. These tours, which run every hour (on the hour) are excellent. The guide concludes her commentary with 'Now, ladies and gentlemen, you can take photographs at the backside . . .' She's referring to the rear of the palace, which is the **only** place where photography is allowed. Having wound on your camera, enjoy the scenery. Vivanmek lies within beautiful gardens, surrounded by canals, and is the ideal picnic-spot to relax after a hard day's sightseeing. Admission is 50B—but free, if you arrive with a 'combination' ticket from the Grand Palace.

National Museum and More Temples
(by boat, taxi, and on foot; full day)

Wat Benchamabopit – National Museum – National Art Gallery and National Theatre – Wat Mahathat – Wat Suthat – Wat Traimit

Wat Benchamabopit
Wat Benchamabopit, the popular **Marble Temple**, is located on Si Ayutthaya Rd—between Chitralada Palace (sometime residence of King Bhumibol) and the National Assembly building. This beautifully symmetrical temple was built in 1899 by Rama V over a smaller earlier structure called Wat Thai Tong (Wat of Five Peers). Made of Italian Carrara marble, it is considered one of the finest examples of modern Thai architecture. It's certainly far less glitzy and gaudy than most Bangkok temples, and Westerners find its restrained charm and elegance very satisfying. It overlooks a peaceful *klong*, full of fish and turtles, with pretty little bridges guarded by laughing Chinese statues. The white *bot* covered with red glazed tiles (also from China) is flanked by rustic Javanese pavilions, each containing a Buddha image (one in bronze, seated on a *naga*; the other is Burmese, in white alabaster). The chapel interior is very subdued—the walls look papered, and all the decoration is on the ceiling. Behind the *bot*, there's an enclosed courtyard with a gallery of 51 Buddha images—mostly copies—from various styles and periods. This has examples from India, Burma and Japan, and is the perfect place to bone up on Buddhas before doing any serious *wat*-spotting. The resident Buddha image inside the *bot* is itself a copy—being modelled on the Buddha Chinaraj in Phitsanulok.

The Marble Temple is home to some of the Buddhist world's most intellectual monks. If here at the weekends, you'll often witness an ordination ceremony. The best time of day to visit is early morning (around 7–8 am), when the monks are chanting in the chapel. Several monks here speak good English, and enjoy talking to foreigners. Admission to the temple is 10B, and it's open till 5 pm daily.

The National Museum
This lies on the far side of the Pramane Ground (if coming in by river boat, get off at

Grand Palace pier), and is open 9 am to 12 noon, 1 to 4 pm daily—except Monday and Friday. Admission is 20B, and free guided tours in English are given on Tuesday (Thai Art and Culture), Wednesday (Buddhism), and Thursday (Pre-Thai Art). You'll need to leave the Marble Temple at 9 am at the latest to catch them—all tours start at 9.30 am sharp.

The **National Museum**, formerly the Palace of the Front (built 1783 as the residence of the *upraja* or deputy king), is one of the largest and best-presented museums in Asia—it contains over 1000 exhibits ranging from neolithic times up to the present Bangkok period. It is a very extensive complex with several well-stocked exhibition halls, and you'll need the guided tour to cover it comprehensively in under two hours. There are three main galleries—Thai History (to the rear), History of Art and Archaeology, and Minor Art and Metals (in the old palace building). The museum's most famous item is the **Phra Buddha Singh**—one of three such in Thailand—which, next to the Emerald Buddha, is the most venerated Buddha in the country. It originated from Sukhothai, and lives in the small Buddhaisawan chapel, formerly used by the *upraja* for his devotions. Elsewhere, there's a larger collection of Buddhas from various periods (including a lovely 9th-century Padmapani—Bodhissatva—reminiscent of a truncated Venus de Milo), displays of dance masks, puppets and costumes, a weapons room (with elephant war apparel), and—in the Coronation Room—a whole hall of royal funeral chariots, the largest of which is 40 feet high, weighs 20 tons, and took 290 men to move.

The National Theatre

The National Theatre is next to the museum, on Na Phra That Rd. It's a modern building, which stages the most authentic Thai dramas and performances of classical dance in Bangkok (tel 2215861 for programme details). The **National Art Gallery** on Chao Fa Rd, opposite the National Theatre, shows traditional and modern exhibits by Thai artists. Admission is free, and it's open the same times as the museum (tel 2812224 for details of current exhibitions).

Wat Mahathat

Wat Mahathat is a short walk south of the museum, at the Pramane Ground. Also known as the 'temple of the great relic', it's a famous meditation *wat* where instruction classes are given to the public. The unusually austere *bot* is said to be the largest in Bangkok, and contains a sacred relic of the Buddha. Most times of the day, Wat Mahathat is a positive hive of activity—there's a pleasant courtyard here, beautifully laid out, full of students dying to practise English on foreigners, and to show them round their classrooms. At the weekends, the temple has a wonderful vegetable and food market—come in the after-noon, and bring your camera.

Wat Suthat

Wat Suthat, Dinso Rd, is a short 15B *tuk-tuk* ride from Mahathat. Commenced by Rama I (completed by Rama III), this large temple is mainly notable for its fabulous 18th-century murals—witty scenes of animals, nature and everyday life, full of zest and vitality. These are inside the *bot*, which features a unique double-roof and a covered gallery full of seated Buddhas. In the grounds, there's the usual assortment of Chinese ballast figures (mandarins, dogs, lions, etc), also a lot of original stuff you won't find at any other *wat*. Worthy of special mention are the lovely, low-key gardens with bonsai trees and exotic flowers, and the two beautiful pavilions, with majestic standing Buddhas and leaping bronze horses. There's a great atmosphere here too, enhanced by myriad monks, chanting or meditating.

Wat Traimit
Wat Traimit (Temple of the Golden Buddha) is near Hualamphong railway station on Traimit Rd, and is a nice spot to wind up a day's tour. This is a small, modest *wat* with one big attraction—the solid-gold Buddha image, 3 metres high and weighing 5½ tons which resides in a small private chapel. When first discovered upcountry, this 'Golden Buddha' was believed to be just a concrete image. But then, when it was being transferred to Bangkok, it fell from a crane, lost some of its thick plaster coating, and revealed its true nature.

An exceedingly fine piece (in the Sukhothai style, probably 13th century), the Buddha sits in a tacky bathroom-pink room, surrounded by plastic lotuses and fairground paraphernalia. The kitsch donation box with 'the covered cement parts from Golden Buddha' is a masterpiece of tat. Still, there's no denying the simple power and dignity of the image itself. Included on nearly every city tour itinerary, the Golden Buddha is open to view from 8.30 am to 5 pm daily.

Other Sights

Jim Thompson's House – Suan Pakkard Palace – Rose Garden Resort – Kamthieng House – Snake Farm – Floating Market – Ancient City

Jim Thompson's House
Jim Thompson's House (Soi Kasemsong, off Rama I Rd) is a traditional Thai-style dwelling containing one of the finest private collections of Oriental Art in Thailand. The building comprises six old houses, five of which were floated downriver from Ayutthaya. Jim Thompson himself was an American who settled in Thailand after WWII, and who contributed substantially to the revitalization of the Thai silk industry—primarily, by replacing vegetable dyes with colour-fast artificial dyes. He lived in Bangkok until 1967, when he went on holiday in the Cameron Highlands of Malaysia, and disappeared without trace. Jim Thompson was a great collector of (now priceless) antiques, and his house has now been turned into a private museum, of great interest to anyone interested in Thai art. There's an exquisite collection of Sino-Thai *Bencharong* (five-colour) pottery, a wooden palace full of china mice, the front door of a Chinese pawn shop, and all manner of weird and wonderful curiosities. He was also a great interior decorator and you can see the use of his Thai silk fabrics throughout the house. Jim Thompson's is open 9 am to 5 pm, Mon to Sat. Admission is 80B (students under 25, only 30B), and includes a good one-hour guided tour. Photography is not allowed.

Suan Pakkard
Suan Pakkard Palace is near the junction of Sri Ayutthaya and Phayati roads, opposite New Amarin Hotel. This is similar to Jim Thompson's House—i.e. five traditional Thai

63

houses in an attractive garden setting, housing Asian art treasures—but is different enough to make a visit worthwhile. The centrepiece of this palace 'museum'—lovingly assembled by the late Princess Chumbot of Nagar Svarga—is the delightful **Lacquer Pavilion** which she received from her husband on her 50th birthday. It is said to have once graced a royal residence in Ayutthaya, and has been beautifully restored. Elsewhere, look out for bronze geese, Chinese lions, a model of a royal barge, prehistoric Ban Chiang artefacts and huge carp in the pond. The Japanese-style semi-enclosed gardens make a perfect, tranquil retreat from the noise and bustle of the city. Admission to Suan Pakkard is 50B, and it's open from 9 am to 4 pm, Mon to Sat.

Kamthieng House

Kamthieng House at Soi 21 (Asoke) off Sukhumvit Rd is open 9 am to 4 pm, Tues to Sat, admission 25B. This attractive northern-style house has interesting displays of hilltribe costumes and farming implements. From Suriwong, it's a No. 16 bus to Siam Centre—then another bus (Nos. 25, 40, 48 or 71) along Sukhumvit.

Snake Farm

Red Cross Snake Farm on Rama IV Rd (corner of Henri Dunant Rd) is the world's second-largest snake farm, established in 1923 to produce vaccines and sera to treat snake-bites. There's an hour-long 'venom extraction' show daily at 11 am. Admission to the 'farm' is 10B (an extra 10B for camera-users), and it's open 8.30 am to 4 pm, Mon to Fri.

Thonburi Floating Market

The Floating Market at Wat Sai (Thonburi) is now very commercialized. Most of the genuine traders have now moved elsewhere to do business, and the few Thai ladies still paddling around selling their wares are being paid 20B a day (by the mass of souvenir shops here) just to show up. Unless you want to see boatloads of Japanese tourists photographing other tourists, forget it. The best bet for getting to Thonburi floating market is to take one of the tour boats that leave from the Oriental Pier—otherwise you will have to hire your own boat. The alternative floating market, at Damnoen Saduak (100 km west of Bangkok), is also firmly on the tourist map but is still worth a visit—for the time being. Independent travel there from Bangkok is difficult—and many people either go from Nakhon Pathom (see p. 89 for full details) or take a set tour from a hotel.

Rose Garden Resort

Rose Garden Resort is situated some 30 km southwest of Bangkok. This is plastic Thai culture for package tourists—a snippet of a wedding ceremony, a snatch of Thai boxing, a bamboo-pole dance, an elephant trooping up and down collecting rides, and a few women in traditional costumes charging fat fees for photos. Few travellers get much out of this kind of 'instant Thailand'. The long bus journey (3 hours return, minimum) and the stiff admission fee (140B—shows start 3 pm daily) are further deterrents. Rose Garden is best done on a conducted tour, and is only worth doing at all if you haven't time to look for real Thai culture elsewhere.

Ancient City

Ancient City (Muang Boran), 33 km southeast of Bangkok, is 200 acres of land imaginatively landscaped into a map of Thailand and filled with impressive replicas

Floating market

and reconstructions of famous monuments and temples from all over the country. It was built between 1962 and 1967, for the benefit of Thai people who couldn't afford to tour their country or to see its beautiful sights. Since then, it has become a tourist attraction of sorts—though surprisingly few people go there. Ancient City is an excellent way of seeing Thailand in miniature in the shortest possible time. Most of its buildings are half to two-thirds actual size, and include a number of sights that just don't exist any more. A classic example is the reconstructed **Samphet Prasat Palace**, a richly ornate 14th-century Ayutthayan building, the original of which was destroyed two centuries ago. It cost 10 million Baht to build, and was the private donation of just one man. Elsewhere, there are reconstructions of a Thai village (complete with opium shop) and an Ayutthayan floating market. Ancient City is best visited on a set tour, being too far from Bangkok for easy independent travel. Tour operators often combine it with the nearby **Crocodile Farm**, which has 30,000 crocodiles, disco-dancing elephants and so-called 'friendly' tigers ('you can pat them like dogs', joked my guide). Most of the crocs end up as handbags, belts or shoes, or as 'crocodile curry' (the speciality dish here). Admission is 80B.

RECREATION
Bangkok's major hotels offer a wide range of sports and recreational activities, including golf, tennis, bowls, health clubs, massage parlours, gymnasiums and swimming pools. Horse-racing takes places every Saturday (from 12.15 pm) at the **Royal Bangkok Sports Club**, Henri Dunant Rd (tel 250181), and every Sunday (from 12.15 pm) at the **Royal Turf Club of Thailand**, 183 Phitsanulok Rd (823770).

Dance
Thai Classical Dance is best seen at one of the city's Thai-style restaurants, which lay on special shows included in the cost of a set 'traditional Thai' dinner. Two of the best

places are **Baan Thai**, Soi 32 Sukhumvit Rd (tel 3913013) and **Piman**, Soi 49 Sukhumvit Rd (tel 3918107)—both restaurants have dance shows from 7.30 to 9 nightly (250B a head). Other good bets are **Bussaracum** and **Silom Village** in Silom, and **D'Jit Pochana** in Sukhumvit. Some large hotels, like the **Oriental**, the **Indra Regent**, and the **Dusit Thani** (Rama IV Rd), also offer classical dance shows as part of an evening meal. To see professional dance and drama, without the culinary trappings, visit the **National Theatre** (see p. 62). This has shows most days at 10 am to 3 pm.

Thai Boxing

Thai Boxing is an exceptionally popular spectator sport in Bangkok. Unlike Western-style boxing, contestants can use almost any part of their body—even knees and elbows—to inflict damage on their opponents. Each fight is preceded by much bowing, prayer and ritual by both boxers, and a live band (or screeching tannoyed music) whips up the baying crowd to a fever-pitch of excitement. The Thais really get into it, though many Westerners don't—all the preparatory ceremony, plus all the dancing about for the first few rounds, tends to leave bored tourists staring into their popcorn just when the *coup de grace* (often the only kick, or rabbit-punch, of the match) is administered. Quite incredible amounts of money are won and lost at these tournaments, and the audience reaction is correspondingly delirious. Best Thai boxing is at **Ratchadamnoen Stadium**, Ratchadamnoen Ave (next to TAT tourist office). Bouts run from 6 to 10 pm every Monday, Wednesday and Thursday, and from 5 pm on Sundays. **Lumpini Stadium**, on Rama IV Rd is more centrally located. There's boxing here from 6 pm every Tuesday, Friday and Saturday. Seats cost between 80B and 200B. For any atmosphere at all, get a ringside seat.

Thai Massage

Traditional Thai Massage is a marvellous experience. It lasts between one and two hours, costs between 120 and 150B an hour, and totally relaxes you in mind, body and spirit. The spiritual home of Thai massage is **Wat Po**, near Bangkok's Grand Palace. Here you can get a wonderful medicinal massage for 120B an hour, or learn the art yourself. Courses last two and three weeks, and cost between 2000 and 3000B. There are several good places offering ancient massage (i.e. no monkey business) in Bangkok. Try **Marble House**, in the Pizza Hut lane at the Rama IV end of Suriwong Rd (tel 2353519, open 10 am to midnight). Or—for therapeutic Japanese-style massage—**Chiropractic Massage**, Soi 44 Charoen Krung, near Shangri-La Hotel (open 8.30 am to 7 pm, Mon to Sat). For an adventurous 'bath massage'—perfectly safe, and enjoyable for both men and women—try **Takara** on Patpong 2 (6 am to midnight). A very good, cheap going-over (only 80B an hour) is given at the parlour next to New Fuji Hotel, Silom. Genuine massages like this are often found attached to, or near, the better hotels. Beware of 'body' massages offered on the street—these are, as one tout delighted in telling me, 'where lady lie on you and massage your body with hers!' Intrigued, I asked him for his card. It said 'Put yourself in our hands. After this massage, you'll think you're dead and gone to *heaven!*' 'Nuff said?

NIGHTLIFE

Bangkok has the liveliest, least inhibited nightlife in the East. It also has a growing reputation as the 'Brothel of the World'. With an estimated 500,000 of the city's female population now engaged in 'entertainment-related activities', the capital is now being accused of sitting on an AIDS time-bomb. Whether one believes the figures or not (one-third of the three million tourists who visit Thailand each year are said to have spent time with a prostitute) there is no doubt that Bangkok's nightlife is aimed specifically at the unaccompanied male tourist. Prostitution is illegal in Thailand, and AIDS is said not to exist in this country, yet every morning sees a flood of 'ladies of night' pouring out of the city's hotels. And as the target area of prostitution, Patpong, becomes included in more and more package-tour itineraries, worldwide concern is mounting.

Most travellers, of course, have little interest in 'sandwich' massages, painted transvestites, or child prostitutes. They can enjoy various other forms of after-dark entertainment—fun discos and coffee bars, live jazz and Western music etc—and even hit the red-light areas without either losing their dignity or taking home a nasty disease. The trick is to go in a group—far safer and more enjoyable than wandering around on your own—and to look 'poor'. I spent five nights researching Patpong's bars and clubs—the first four nights, I dressed casually and received no hassle whatsoever. The last night however, I wore a smart 400B shirt, and was bodily assaulted within 30 seconds of arrival. It's generally a good idea to have no more than 500B in your pockets—that way, even if you get talked into trouble (bar girls can be *very* persuasive), you won't be able to afford it.

Patpong is the original red-light area of Bangkok, first patronized by American troops on leave from Vietnam, and now kept just as busy by plane-loads of foreign tourists. Named after a Thai-Chinese millionaire who owns most of the district, Patpong divides into four parallel streets—Patpong 1 and 2 (girlie bars), Patpong 3 (gay bars/transvestite shows) and Patpong 4 (Japanese restaurants and massage parlours, which are very selective about who they admit). By day Patpong is mainly a business district; around 6 pm the bars open and the area takes on a whole new face. Dotted between airline offices, travel agents, bookshops and restaurants, are scores of girlie and go-go bars. They're all pretty much the same—thinly-disguised pick-up joints for unattached males, with loud disco music, smiling girls bopping around on a stage wearing numbers, and customers sitting apprehensively in swivel-seats waiting for the inevitable tap on the shoulder and a low, purring 'Herrro Sir, you like me?' A couple of bars have a small dance floor where you can bop around yourself—quite fun in a group—while the go-go dancers look on, applaud or even join in. Western men are often asked to buy colas for the girls (they get 20–30B for every 60–80B drink you buy). To avoid confusion, and possible bill-padding, pay for each round of drinks as it comes. The cost of a beer is 45/50B, and you'll need to make sure there's no cover charge before entering. Many bars have a 'Happy Hour' between 8 and 9 pm, when drinks are somewhat cheaper, occasionally half-price.

Some of the bars have 'live shows'. These are illegal, and are usually held upstairs—giving the performers a chance to vanish when the police arrive. Bizarre props are used in these shows, and visitors quickly learn to expect only the unexpected—feathered darts whistling past their ears, airborne bananas plopping into their drinks, and girls opening Coke bottles and playing mouthorgans in the most unorthodox fashion. Few people find the acts erotic or a turn-on—some even find them boring. Western women and couples need feel no apprehension entering these places—the Thais are a very tolerant lot. Certainly, being inside a bar is often far safer than being on the street, running a gauntlet of persistent touts offering all kinds of 'services'. You're also safe in places like **Book seller**, between Patpong 1 and 2 (a great bookshop, stocking maps, guides, fiction etc), **Trattoria da Roberto** (mellow Italian restaurant) and **Bobby's Arms** (British-type pub) in Patpong 2. Shopping is good at Patpong market—fake watches at knockdown prices of 350B–700B, and novelty gifts of mounted tarantulas.

For a tour of Patpong, start at the cosy **Toby Jug** pub at 185 Silom Rd. This has darts, cheap draught lager, and steak 'n' chips. From here, it's a short stroll down to Patpong 1, where you can drop into the **Safari Bar**, for a quick bop on their small dance-floor. Good sounds here, and minimal hassle. After this, if you're curious to see a show, cross over to **Queen's Castle**, a good 'straight' place with drink prices written on the wall. For something less tame, try **Pussy Alive** ('Happy Pussy Hours 6–9')—the most outrageous bar in Patpong, guaranteed to mist up your spectacles. The **Firecat** is a little more sedate ('We are not just another typical go-go bar—we are Upstairs') and is equally popular. Before the bars close (around 1 am), pop over to the excellent **Rome Club** in Patpong 3. This is a great disco, with a highly professional transvestite cabaret at 12 am nightly, and is a favourite of airline crews. Admission is 100B (1 free drink) from Sunday to Thursday, 200B (2 drinks included) on Friday and Saturday. **King's Lounge**, opposite the Bookseller, is another popular late night disco/pick-up joint, with go-go show at midnight, and there's no cover charge. Downstairs, the **King's Bar** is another good, roomy go-go bar. If you're still raring to go after these places close (around 2–3 am), just hop in a *tuk-tuk* and ask your driver to take you to the nearest late-night hotspot—he'll always know one.

Soi Cowboy, a small bar-street located behind Sois 21/23 Sukhumvit Rd, is 'easy man's Patpong'. None of the bars have girlie shows, and the atmosphere is far less 'hard sell'. Drinks at all bars are around 40–60B, and there's no hassle to buy the girls one. Most places close at 11. Bars come and go, particularly in this area, where many of the bars are slowly dying, but current favourites are **Tilac** (new, Patpong-style), **Jukebox** (professional, pleasant) and **Black and White** (small, friendly). In Soi 23, there's a delightful Dutch-British pub called **Lord Mike O'Henry**. 'I do nothing special', says manager Henk, 'just make food for hungry people.' He does that, and much more. Henk cooks superlative Dutch, European and Thai dishes, stocks some of the best draught beer in Bangkok, and provides bar games, soothing classical music, and even free handrolling tobacco. 'Please don't ask my staff questions,' advises Henk, 'they know less than I do.'

Washington Square between Sois 22 and 24 Sukhumvit Rd, is another pleasant night scene—with a small cluster of bars and restaurants, a couple of cinemas, and lots of cheap foodstalls. There's a definite American flavour to Washington Square—the busy **Bourbon Street** restaurant-bar has New Orleans-style soul food and creole dishes like shrimp and crabmeat gumbo as well as charcoal-grilled burgers and marinated steaks; **Cowboy Bar**, owned by an American Vietnam veteran, is a Texas style bar serving creole food, with good ol' country and western toons to keep your toes tapping. More country music can be heard live every night at the less tame **Traildust** (Soi 31), a re-creation of a latter-day western States watering hole, with Americana wall hangings. This place can get pretty wild. Between Sois 24 and 26, the **Calypso** theatre has professional and very entertaining transvestite shows nightly (at 8.15 and 10—admission

300B). Soi Saracen (north side of Lumpini Park) has a collection of bars with live music, and no hassle from girls. Jazz freaks hang out at the **Brown Sugar**, country and western fans congregate at the **Old West**.

   Discotheques in Bangkok are absolutely amazing. Take, for instance, the **Nasa Spacedrome** at 999 Ramkamhaeng Rd—on a Saturday night, a capacity crowd of 4000 people can be boogying-on-down here—it's the biggest disco in Asia. If the wild atmosphere, giant wall-videos, and laser-lighting fail to impress you, then the 'sci fi show' (where a spaceship emerges to the music from *2001 A Space Odyssey* and showers the dancers with balloons) certainly will. Nasa even has a rest-room, where burnt-out revellers are revitalized with hot face towels and back massages. Admission here is 140B (two free drinks) on weekdays, 180B (three drinks) at weekends. There are many Thai-style discos like this, catering mainly for the very agile Thai youth—average age 19, girls wearing high fashion, guys posing in padded-shoulder jackets and dark shades. The **Mars Party House** disco, Patpong 2, is a huge complex on five floors, attracting a very classy crowd, mainly Thai yuppies, who like to strut their stuff on the top floor, the 'Ozone Layer'. Admission is 80B, one drink included. The fabulous **Paradise** disco, in Arun Amarin Rd (just across the river in Thonburi) is where the classiest Thais go. It's supposed to have the 'sexiest' sound system. Several big hotels have European-style discos, but they're not half as much fun.

SHOPPING

Bangkok's reputation as the Bargain Centre of Asia is well-deserved. The only problem with shopping here is choice—there's too much of it. There are seven main shopping areas used by tourists in the capital. Broadly speaking, there's little difference in price between them—though the range of products does vary from area to area. Thus, Chinatown is known for its gold jewellery, Silom for its silk, Sukhumvit for its leather goods and tailors, Siam Square for its high-fashion, Banglampoo for its hippy hilltribe ware, and markets like Pratunam and the Weekend Market for everything rolled into one. The best general buys in the capital are silk, jewellery and fake designer goods.

Designer Copies

Bangkok is the Capital of Copy, famous for its cheap fake watches, leather goods, clothes and accessories—all expert rip-offs of famous designer names. Unrestrained by Western copyright laws, Thai entrepreneurs produce copies of every luxury product known: fake Rolex Oyster watches (only 500–700B—the real thing costs £1400), imitation Lacoste T-shirts, Gucci leather purses and bags (complete with 'Made in Italy' stamp), and Christian Dior perfumery. All the big brand-names—Ralph Lauren, Hugo Boss, Yves St Laurent, Benetton and Giorgio Armani—are represented, and with prices this low, it takes real willpower to keep your credit card from going over the limit. Hard bargaining will buy you brand-marked underwear and socks for 30B (75p), 100% cotton T-shirts for 120B (£3), 60% cotton T-shirts (they shrink, and the crocodiles fall off) for 60B, designer leather belts from 100B, Louis Vuitton suitcases and briefcases for (respectively) 600B and 800B, and all manner of Cartier, Charles Jourdan and Givenchy copy accessories at very low prices—handbags at 300B, wallets at 120B, cigarette cases and key holders less than 80B. In Bangkok, you can buy an entire new wardrobe for less than £50—three cotton T-shirts (£8), jeans (£3), trousers (£3), sweatshirt (£10), track shoes (£10), underwear (£2) and two pairs of black plimsolls (£7). You should check the quality of every item, but in general all copy goods are of a pretty high standard. Bangkok's vast range of imitations can be found all over the city—primarily in Silom Rd, Sukhumvit Rd, Siam Shopping Centre, and Pratunam Market.

Silk
Thai silk is among the best in the world—strong, lustrous and very durable. It is dyed in rich colours which hold very well and woven in beautiful designs. Thick in texture, light in weight, it is both warm in the winter and cool in the summer. Silk usually comes in bright colours (often *too* bright for Western tastes, though subtler shades are also usually available), and costs anything between 180B and 280B per yard, depending on grade and quality. You can test silk for quality by giving a handful of the material a good, hard squeeze. If it settles quickly back into shape without a wrinkle, you've got top quality silk. The Silom-Surawong area is the best general hunting ground for superior Thai silk at reasonable prices. You can't go wrong at well-established places like **Design Thai**, 304 Silom Rd, or **Jim Thompson's Silk House** on Suriwong Rd. Jim Thompson's sells a lot of original designs not found anywhere else. Thus the high prices—380B for silk ties, 275–320B for scarves, 380–450B a yard for dress/suit material. Two or three times a year though (usually in August and mid-December), there's a clear-out sale in J. T.'s car park—and you can pick up top-quality silk at half the usual retail price. A couple of excellent tailors—**Julie Thai Silk**, 1279 New Rd (tel 2358197), and **Bon 3 Ltd** (opposite Julie's), offer much cheaper silk (180B a yard for dress material) and can make up the latest fashion in dresses (from 2500B), lined men's jackets (from 3000B), trousers (silk 700B; cotton 500B) and silk shirts (from 750B)—all within 24 hours. Also good for readymade or made-to-measure silk is **Thai Silk Shop**, just below Central Department Store, Silom. But if you're into serious silk shopping, get a list of silk factories from your embassy, and do the rounds—factory prices are wholesale, often 20% cheaper (if you buy in bulk) than in the shops.

Tailors
It's generally better to go to a proper, well-established tailor than cheapie places which may produce inferior work. While men are fairly easy to fit out (men's suits made in Bangkok are classic), women should really visit a dressmaker or tailor with a picture of the design they want, or even a whole pattern. That way, they get exactly what they want. People generally buy their suit and shirt material in Silom or Chinatown, and bring it to the tailors of Sukhumvit (concentrated down Sois 4 and 11) for making up. A first-class tailor, like **Raja** in Soi 4, will make silk shirts for 400B, suits for 3500B, and dresses for around 1000B. They speak perfect English and will give you a warm welcome. Many of the city's ex-pats shop here. Lots of places, like **Siam Suits** near The Trocadero Hotel, Silom, will produce a good-quality men's wool suit, along with two shirts and a tie, for £75. However such 'package deals', most commonly offered in the Sukhumvit area, are not necessarily a good thing—the quality of the tailoring often suffers.

Gems and Jewellery
Many of the finest sapphires and rubies mined in Thailand make their way to Bangkok, and are good buys whether of the clear, or star, variety. Jade, star sapphires and rubies

are especially good value. So are the popular 9-stone Princess rings (set with topaz, garnet, zircon, emerald, cat's eye, ruby, sapphire, garnet and diamond), which are worn by Thai classical dancers. The quality of all gems and jewellery is generally excellent. Bangkok is now one of the gem-cutting capitals of the world. Prices are rising fast, but at present a fine-quality ruby can be purchased from between US$200 and US$5000 per carat, depending on size and clarity, while a Grade A sapphire will cost somewhere between US$20 and US$500. Beware of synthetic stones though, peddled by expert con-artists. This cannot be stressed too strongly. Always buy from a reputable, well-established dealer who provides written guarantees with quality stones, and who gives a receipt. There are many such reliable places round Silom-Surawong area (e.g. **Associated Lapidaries**, 5th floor Jal Building, 1 Patpong Rd), and some in Sukhumvit (e.g. **Tawat Gems**, corner of Soi 3 Sukhumvit Rd). Receipts should clearly state the carat, the percentage of precious metal, and the size and weight of stones. If the item was expensive, and the valuation back home doesn't correspond with what's on the receipt, send the details with a photocopy of the receipt to your local TAT tourist office. Gems can be valued at the **Asian Institute of Gemology**, 987 Rama Jewelry Building, 4th-floor, Silom Rd (tel 234930–1). This place also offers an excellent gemology course—just the thing, if you're in Thailand to study or to buy precious stones. To buy top-quality 18K and 22K gold go to **Chinatown**—and be sure to take a Thai or Chinese friend along with you. Gold here is sold by the weight, and the price is pretty standard (currently, around 6000B per 15 grams). It's best to buy it in chain or bracelet form, because you pay only for the gold content—all the workmanship comes free.

Leather
The best bargains in leather are briefcases and large suitcases or bags. Leather boots, shoes and coats have a near-European price—though having them made to order can certainly save you some money. Go to Sukhumvit for leather—this area is famous for its many 'booteries'. Of these, **Chao Phya Bootery** on Soi 11 (another branch at 116 Silom Rd) has the best quality produce, at reasonable prices—pure leather jackets from 3000B, cowboy boots from 1500B, briefcases and handbags from 1000B, women's shoes from 250B to 3000B—you can bargain all these prices down. **Tony Bootery**, opposite Soi 19, also specializes in cowboy boots and ladies' shoes (dyed every colour of the rainbow). **Siam Bootery** at Soi 12 is a useful place, catering for extra-large or extra-small foot sizes. **Anan Shoes**, between Sois 1 and 3, has well-priced leather shoes, boots and jackets—readymade, or made-to-measure in just two days. Cheap leather goods can be found in most street markets—notably Sukhumvit and Pratunam. But be careful—don't be fobbed off with plastic posing as leather. If you're not sure, hold a lighted match to the item. If the dealer snatches it away, then it's plastic (which will burn) rather than leather (which won't).

Antiques and Bronzeware
Some of the best fake antiques and allegedly old Thai bronzes come out of Bangkok. Take great care that you aren't sold inferior merchandise—lots of fake antiques are sold outside temples. Go to a reputable antique dealer, insist they supply the obligatory permit for exporting genuine articles, and don't pay until you've seen the certificate. Old

temple bells and bronze cutlery are popular buys, and you can pick up high-quality Thai art works (pricey, but good investments) at the galleries within the **Oriental** and **Siam Intercontinental Hotel** shopping complexes. The amulet market at **Wat Tachanada**, near Golden Mount, does a nice line in cheap 'lucky charm' souvenirs. Forget about buying antique Buddha heads or *garudas* though—there's a law banning their export for souvenirs. You can apply for an export licence from the Fine Arts Department, but that takes weeks to obtain. Trying to smuggle them out is not a good idea—penalties are particularly stiff.

Woodwork and Bamboo

Beautiful rosewood and teakwood furniture can be found at **Gold Bell Furniture Ltd**, between Sois 28 and 30 Sukhumvit (tel 2586286). Quality buys include elegant Chinese-style dining suites in rosewood, inlaid with mother-of-pearl (40,000B), hand-carved teakwood secretary tables (12,000B), and exquisite Chinese cabinets (from 8000B). Most pieces made here are coated with durable Chinese lacquer—this brings a natural finish to the wood, brings out the best in the grain, and won't scratch or burn. A one-kilo pot of this lacquer costs 1000B—treated furniture is therefore expensive, but made to last. Gold Bell gives a 5% discount on major purchases, and arranges for shipment at an average freight charge of 10,000B. Because it costs little more to send home six items than one, it makes sense to buy big here. **Wamford Antique Furniture**, down Soi 55 Sukhumvit (tel 3900609) makes the same kind of stuff as Gold Bell at half the price, and half the quality. There are some nice Chinese lacquered screens here, and inexpensive blue-and-white china.

For rattan and bamboo furniture, check out **Pippinyo Ltd** on Soi 47, Sukhumvit Rd (tel 2587262). This has delightful patio suites in bamboo—four chairs, chaise longue and coffee table—for under 1000B. There is another factory next door where you can make comparisons in price and quality.

Boutiques, Department Stores and Markets

For jazzy Thai-style clothing (i.e. non-designer outfits), visit the high-fashion boutiques and department stores of Bangkok. If they haven't got what you want in stock, they'll copy it from any design you supply (turn up with a copy of 'Vogue' or 'Elite'), sometimes within hours. They are especially useful for *farangs* with big feet and long legs, who just can't find shoes or trousers to fit in ordinary Thai shops. **Siam Shopping Centre** on Rama IV Rd is 'Boutique City', with four floors of amazing high-fashion clothing, nice jewellery and souvenirs. This is where all the Thai rich kids come—also many backpackers and travellers, determined to buy at least one smart outfit to complement their usual wardrobe of drawstring Banglampoo pants and Samui T-shirts. The nearby **Mah Boohn Krong Centre**, just off Siam Square, on Phyathai Rd, is similar to the shopping centres of Singapore—it has just about everything. Here are clothes, jewellery, hi-fi stuff, 'Dunkin' Doughnut, and a fine exhibition centre.

For readymade clothes, try the 'haute couture' boutiques between 31 and 37 Sukhumvit—some of the most fashionable clothes in Bangkok are sold here. The 43-floor **Baiyoke Building**, behind Indra Regent Hotel, one of the tallest structures in the city, has fashion shopping arcades (floors 1 and 2), a cheap food centre, a cinema, a 24-hour snooker club (floor 4)—and wonderful views from the roof. Below it, the sprawling

Pratunam Market at the corner of Rajaprarob and Phetburi roads, falls into two sections—a huge covered market crammed with stylish, colourful clothes (*very* cheaply priced), and an endless street market selling best-deal Ralph Lauren (Polo) sweatshirts at 200B, and copy designer watches at only 300–500B. Pratunam also has many good tailors and a host of inexpensive *kai yang* and noodle stalls. **Central Department Store**, 306 Silom Rd, is one of the largest and best stores in Bangkok, with smart, casual Thai clothes on the upper floor (where there's nearly always a sale); and an amazing dairy section (fresh yoghurt and Australian cheese) on the ground floor. **Robinson's Department Store**, corner of Silom Rd and Rama IV Rd, has a wide range of ladies' and gents' clothing, and they often have sales where you can pick up shirts and trousers at street market prices. Over at Banglampoo, **New World Department Store** offers similar cheap clothing deals, with sales on the fourth floor. **Banglampoo Market**, off Chakrapong, is a buzzing honeycomb of shops, stalls and boutiques selling everything from gold chains and jewellery (almost as cheap as Chinatown), to colourful shirts (100B), smart trousers (from 150B) and summery cotton-print dresses (150B to 250B). **Ko-Sahn Rd**, also off Chakrapong, is good for hilltribe produce, Burmese wall-hangings, fake antiques, and cheap knick-knacks. The **Weekend Market** at Chatuchak Park, behind the Northern Bus Terminal, sells all this stuff—and much, much more—at really low prices. It takes place every Saturday and Sunday (7 am to 6 pm) and is by far the best general shopping market in Bangkok—with everything from quality leather shoes and arty T-shirts to dismembered tailors' dummies and old car hub-caps. There's even a pet section, where women squat around offering snakes, irridescent green beetles, and strange squirrel-like things on leads (Thai hamsters?) as pets, though the authorities are cracking down on these peddlers. The weekend market is a long way to go for your shopping (an hour from town, on bus Nos. 77 or 112) but worth it. Come on a Sunday, when there's more choice of produce—and less traffic.

Where to Stay and Eating Out

Silom-Surawong

If Bangkok can be said to have a centre at all, this is probably it. Silom-Surawong is the city's most important business and financial district, with many airline offices, banks and travel agencies. The huge **General Post Office** on New Road (actually an old road, built 100 years ago) is a popular meeting-point for travellers—everybody comes here to post parcels or collect mail from home. Conveniently close to the Chao Phya River, Silom is a good base for sightseeing. It also has many shops, restaurants and hotels (including the prestigious Oriental), plus entertainment centres like Patpong and Silom Village. The cost of living is, however, higher here than in other parts of the city.

WHERE TO STAY

Luxury
The Oriental Hotel, 48 Oriental Avenue (tel 2360400: tx 82997 ORIENTL TH) is one of the oldest and best-known hotels in the East. Over a century old, it has elegant rooms (from 3100B single, 3400B double) luxurious fittings and an unparalleled view

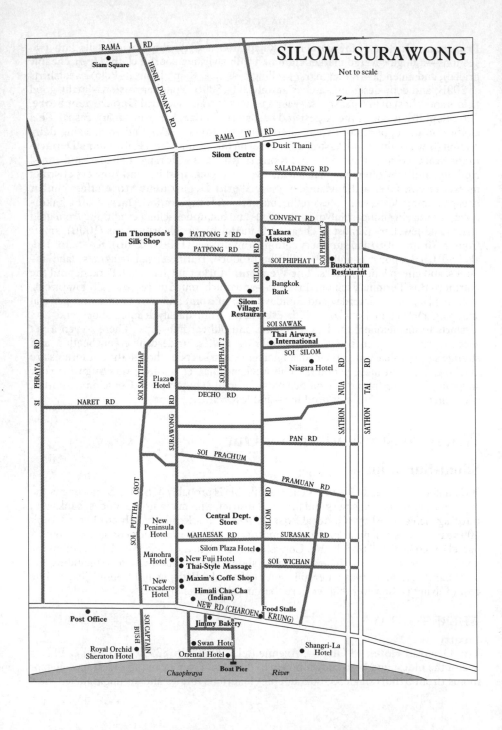

SILOM—SURAWONG

Not to scale

across the river. Even if you can't stay here, it's fun to drop in for evening cocktails on the terrace, and watch the sun going down over the Chao Phya. The Oriental is a place where any traveller would like to spend at least one night. There's a choice of rooms either in the new tower block, or (better) in the stylish old building, with suites named after the rich and famous—Noel Coward, James Michener, Joseph Conrad etc.—who have stayed here. One chap reported spending a sleepless night in Barbara Cartland's bright pink suite for a fee of 11,000B. The hotel's **Sala Rim Naam** restaurant is world-famous. Come here either for the Siamese buffet lunch (12 noon to 2 pm daily, 180B), or for the Siamese Dinner and Dance (7 to 10 nightly, around 500B). Arrive a little early, and go for a leisurely amble through the old building checking out the 'Authors' Lounge', with its Authors' Menu listing the favourite dishes of past literary guests or enjoy the string quartet in the lobby.

The **Shangri-La** at 89 Soi Wat Suan Plu, New Road (tel 2367777; tx 842645 SHANGLA TH) is arguably Bangkok's second best hotel—brand-new and very impressive. The lobby is so vast, that arranging to meet anybody in it is a waste of time. The whole layout of the hotel, on the river's edge, is superb. It's worth paying 45B for a cup of coffe, just to sit here at sunset, listening to the resident pianist or cellist. Sumptuous suites (all overlooking the river) are offered at 5500B. Discounts are available in low season, or if booking through a travel agent. The **Dusit Thani** at 946 Rama IV Rd (tel 2360450; tx 81170 DUSITOTEL TH), flagship of the fleet throughout the country, is extremely elegant, with first-rate service (including Rolls Royce Limousine transport) and sumptuous rooms and decor. Rooms range from 3500B to 6000B, suites 8000–20,000B.

Expensive

The **Manohra** at 412 Suriwongse Rd (tel 2345070; tx 82114 MANOHRA TH) is excellent value for money. Comfortable rooms from 1500B single, 1600B double (best views from 5th floor up), indoor pool, rooftop garden and very convenient location. The nearby **New Fuji** at 299–301 Suriwongse Rd (tel 2345364; tx 84079 PENINHO TH) is another good choice, with several facilities and amenities, bright, spacious rooms (from 1200B–1500B) and personal, cosy atmosphere. Views are best from 3rd-floor rooms and up; guests have use of two swimming pools at nearby associated hotels. You can find sanctuary from sinful Patpong at the **Montien**, 54 Sirawong Rd (tel 2337060). Well-equipped rooms from 3000B, and there's a popular coffee-shop and two restaurants. For the same price and just as comfortable and central are the **Narai**, 222 Silom Rd (tel 233 3350), with Italian pizzeria, and **Silom Plaza**, 320 Silom Rd (tel 236 0333), both within a five minute walk of Silom Village.

Moderate

There's not a wide range of choice in this category around this area. The **New Peninsula**, 295 Suriwong Rd (tel 2343910–7) has seen better days, and better prices. Adequate rooms for around 1000B. Cheaper, but no great bargain (750B), the **Suri-wong**, 31/1 Suriwong Rd (up an alley, tel 2333223), has okay air-con doubles for 750B. It's very popular with gay men, and its restaurant serves high-standard Thai food. You can get nice rooms (from 1000B) at the **Sathorn Inn**, Silom Soi 9 (Soi Suksavitthaya, tel 2344110; reachable either from Sathorn Nua Rd or Silom Rd; a 5–10 minute walk from

Silom village, 10–15 minutes from Patpong). Around the corner, the **Niagara**, 26 Soi Suksavitthaya (tel 2335783) has quite decent air-con rooms for as little as 400B, and there's a small so-so coffee shop.

Inexpensive
The **Swan Hotel** at 31 Customs House Lane (tel 2348594) is central and friendly, just about the best 'budget' buy in Silom. Air-con rooms are 450B–600B, and the quietest ones face into the swimming pool. The Swan also offers a small bar, restaurant and 24-hour coffee shop.

    T. T. Guest House, 138 Soi Watmahaphrutthanam, Sipraya Mahanakorn Rd (tel 2363053) is ideal for shoestring travellers. Run by three friendly brothers, it has clean rooms (from 120B), a cheap dormitory (50B), a snug TV lounge cum restaurant, good noticeboard and information and a warm, relaxing family-style atmosphere. It's my favourite guest house in Thailand—and a great evening hang-out spot. The middle brother, Sukhum, runs sightseeing trips out to Kanchanaburi—and makes superlative popcorn. Come here on a Saturday night, when the small *wat* behind the guest house holds festive film-show parties (plus market). To get to T.T., go down the small *soi* between Sois 37 and 39, New Rd, and follow the signs.

EATING OUT
You're kitted out in your new tailor-made suits and dresses, silk ties and scarves, sparkling Rolex and snakeskin shoes, but where are you going to show them off? At the Oriental, of course. There are five more restaurants in the hotel besides the Sala Rim Naam. For exclusive dining **Normandie** is about as select as Bangkok gets. The river views are enchanting, the decor plush, the chefs are all French, the cuisine exquisite, and the prices astronomical. Two eating *à la carte* won't see much change from 5000B, or 3500–4000B for the *menu fixé*. Another restaurant in the hotel, **Lord Jim**, is done out as a 19th-century steamer, and the nautical theme continues in the menu. The lunch buffet is a seafood orgy, with succulent, gleaming shellfish and fish, and for landlubbers a carvery serving a selection of meats and poultry. Buffet lunch runs to around 600B per person, *à la carte* 1000B.

    For a good night out that won't cost an arm and a leg, go to **Silom Village Trade Centre**, near Central Department Store, Silom Road. This has mid-priced Thai, Chinese, European food and seafood in an attractive outdoor setting. Good handicrafts and shopping mall, and live music with classical Thai dancing nightly. Don't pay 280B for the upmarket dance show upstairs (it's a rip-off). Instead, be seated by 7 downstairs (by the stage) for traditional Thai music at 7.30, followed by dance extracts at 8. No charge for this show, but you're expected to order a meal. A 3-course dinner (nice dishes are Beef Green Curry, Stuffed Baked Pineapple, Spicy King Prawns or Fried Sea Bass) shouldn't come to more than 250B—if it does, check the bill for padding.

    Bussaracum, 35 Soi Pipat 2 (off Convent Rd) offers Thai cuisine at its finest, beautifully presented and served. The service is slick and there is live classical Thai music, and great cocktails. Special dishes include *Kao Tang Na Tang* (crispy rice chips with minced pork and mint dip), *Poo Phim* (deep-fried crab meat and shrimp), *Yum Miang Moo* (minced pork, chicken, prawn, garlic and peanuts seasoned with lemon juice) and delicious *Choo Chee Goong Nang* (thick prawn curry with straw mushrooms). Eat well for around 500B per head. Advance-book this place (tel 2358915)—it's very popular.

Shangari-La (above Silom Village) is a Chinese restaurant well-known for its savoury Shanghai-style food, and frequented by the city's wealthier Chinese residents and visiting businessmen. It can be pricy if you order the exotic fish dishes (around 800B), but you can still eat well and leave satisfied for 150–200B. **The Wall** at Soi Paramote 3, Mahesak Rd (off Silom, near the Holiday Inn) is a New Zealand/Swedish partnership that offers very good western and Scandinavian specialities, including *smorgasbord* for 140B, and draught beers. Cosy, comfortable and air-conditioned, there's also a dart-board and free paperback library.

In the heart of Patpong, **Thai Room** is a very civilized retreat from the girlie bars and busy street-life. It's a poular meeting place, the service is fast and friendly, the food plentiful (with a choice of Thai, Italian, Chinese and Mexican), excellent and reasonably priced (dinner for two, 350B), and mercifully air-conditioned. **Bobby Arms**, Patpong 2 (tel 233 6828—walk up the multi-story carpark ramp to find the entrance) is a British-style pub/restaurant serving traditional British fare for the ex-pats and airline crews. On Friday and Saturday there's live music from guitarist Paul Mendez, and Sunday evening Dixieland music. Dishes are around 80–200B, a bottle of house wine 350B. In the same building **Trattoria da Roberto** (Roberto is 'Bobby') is a popular Italian restaurant, where dinner for two costs around 500B. Look out for **Le Cam-Ly** on the second floor of the Patpong Building, Suriwong Rd. It's an elegant and cosy Vietnamese restaurant, particularly popular with French ex-pats, but it's a little pricy at 600–800B for two.

All Gaengs, 173 Suriwong Rd is an excellent restaurant specializing in all varieties of Thai curries; dinner for two at around 600B. **DK Kitchen**, 109 Suriwong Rd, is for high-brow diners—it's attached to the Patpong University Bookstore, and serves good Thai, Chinese and mediocre European food. Opposite the Tawana Ramada Hotel, you'll find the convenient **One + One**, 119/5-10 Suriwong Rd. Its tacky, plastic cocktail lounge decor is a little off-putting, and the menu over-ambitious, but if you stick to the Thai dishes you're in for a treat, and the live band provides unwitting comic relief, with contorted strains of old 60s' favourites. Dishes are average price (50–80B) and it's open 24 hours. Walk down the lane oppsite the Tawana Ramada, and take the first right to find the recently-opened **Beijing**, Soi Anumanrajathon, Suriwong Rd. Pleasant, if disorganized, service and reasonably-priced Chinese, Japanese and Thai food; it's air-conditioned, and has sparkling clean, red and white decor. Opposite The Trocadero Hotel, **Ismat**, 430 Suriwong Rd, is a favourite dining spot for lovers of Indian, Pakistani and Benghali cuisine; delicious curries and vegetarian dinners for around 200B.

Himali Cha-Cha, off New Road (near Swan Hotel) is another Indian restaurant with a chef who cooks good North Indian food (around 150–200B a head) and who claims to have been the personal cook of Mountbatten in India. **Whole Earth**, 93/3 Soi Lang Suan, Ploenchit Rd (tel 2525574) is a mid-priced, intimate restaurant with mostly vegetarian dishes, and acoustic music upstairs, videos downstairs. **Manfred's Bakery**, at Royal Orchid Sheraton Hotel, Siphaya Rd, makes yummy German-style gateaux, chicken croissants, fancy breads etc.

Sukhumvit

Sukhumvit Road is one of the three longest roads in Thailand, extending right up to the Cambodian border. Only a short stretch of it—from Soi 1 (where it joins Ploenchit Rd) to Soi 63 (the Eastern Bus Terminal)—has really been developed for tourism. Sukhumvit saw its heyday from 1975 to 1982, when it was heavily patronized by oil people on R and R. Since then, the oil crash and the geographical expansion of tourism (mainly to Silom and Siam Square) has led to a swift decline. Today, Sukhumvit is something of a tourist wasteland, occupied mainly by oil-rich Arabs and German businessmen. Noisy and rather impersonal, this area is now geared to the wealthy and powerful, and the lone shoestring traveller may feel out of place. However, very many Western couples and groups have a ball in Sukhumvit—they love its ritzy hotels and restaurants, its fashionable boutiques and tailors, and its raw, vital street action. The busy market between Soi 5 and Soi 7, is a bright, noisy fiesta of food stalls, bars and souvenir shops, and it's fatal to leave your hotel even for a pack of cigarettes—you'll return with a pair of Lacoste underpants instead. Sukhumvit certainly has its seedy site—from Sois 2 to 6 is a maze of massage parlours ('Feeling is Darling'), short-rent condominium apartments ('Cabbages and Condoms'), suggestive bars ('Farang Connection', 'Deep Diggings') and neon-lit brothels—but elsewhere it's quite respectable. Shoppers like this area, but sightseers don't—most of Bangkok's temples are over an hour away by taxi. Best day to visit Sukhumvit is Sunday—when the traffic is less frantic.

WHERE TO STAY

Luxury
High-class hotels in Sukhumvit are remarkably good value for money. A case in point is the well-established **Ambassador**, 171 Sukhumvit Rd (tel 2540444; tx 82910 AMTEL TH) with rooms at 2000–4000B, and no fewer than 7 restaurants and 5 coffee bars. A vast complex of leisure facilities, shopping arcades and food parlours (with low-fat Bulgarian yoghurt): many guests need a guided tour to find their room. The **Flamingo Disco** here is just about the best-value nightspot on a Saturday night—full of young middle-class Thais getting their 150B's worth (admission, plus two free drinks). As a single *farang* man, this one of the few places in Bangkok where you can meet a 'nice' Thai girl (i.e. one who's not there for business).

The new **Landmark**, 138 Sukhumvit Rd (tel 2540404; tx TH 72341) lacks the Ambassador's character, but has bags of style and class, geared to business people mostly, as is evident in their rates: rooms start at 4000B, suites at 6000B. The higher you go (31 floors), the better the views. Numerous facilities (pool, health club, squash courts, sauna, beauty parlour, shopping plaza etc.) and possibly the best Chinese restaurant in town. All this, and the longest escalator in Thailand.

Expensive
The Windsor, Soi 20 Sukhumvit Rd (tel 2580160; tx 82081WINDHTL TH) is a wonderfully peaceful, personal hotel with nice bright rooms at 2000B up. The restaurant offers a superior 200B buffet lunch daily (11 am to 2 pm) and the 70B cocktails are memorable. **The Manhattan**, Soi 15 Sukhumvit Rd (tel 2550166; tx 87272 HOTELMAN TH) is a less expensive alternative, and although it hasn't the glamour of the other hotels, the standards of rooms and service are high. Room rates are 1500–1800B, suites 2800–7000B.

Moderate
Park Hotel, No. 6 Sukhumvit Rd, Soi 7 (tel 2525110; tx 82488 SNJ TH) is a peaceful

European-style haven in the centre of the Arab quarter. Sophisticated too, with polite staff, a select restaurant and plush air-con rooms from 700B. The **Quality Inn II** on Soi 9 (tel 2535393; tx 21145) lives up to its name and is very quiet, with rooms at 900B. **Mermaid's Rest**, down Soi 8 (tel 2533410), is a small, friendly Scandinavian place with decent air-con rooms for 650–900B, a pool and 24-hour coffee shop, and is very conveniently located for shopping. **Miami Hotel**, down Soi 13 (tel 2530369), is good value, with rooms from 220B (fan) to 600B (air-con), a pool, and a 24-hour coffee shop. Very conveniently located for shopping, as is the **Nana**, just off Sukhumvit on Soi 4 (Soi Nana Tai), with air-con doubles from 1000B.

Inexpensive

Crown Hotel, Soi 29 (tel 2580318) is clean, if dilapidated, and has air-con doubles from 400B. The popular coffee shop/bar has a jukebox and offers cheap European-Thai food. **Atlanta**, at the bottom of Soi 2 (tel 2526069), is another budget option, with a nice pool, pretty gardens, and cleanish rooms from 200B (fan single) to 500B (air-con double). Cheaper than that, try **Best Inn**, 75 Soi 3 (Soi Nana Nua, tel 2530573), with fan doubles for around 250B, air-con doubles 400B.

EATING OUT

Sukhumvit is well-known for its international cuisine. The famous **D'Jit Pochana**, 60 Sukhumvit, Soi 20 (tel 279 4990) has changed from Thai cuisine to concentrate on Italian specialities, and is in a pleasant open-air setting. There's a fair choice of German, French and Chilean wines here and also a wide selection of desserts and fruits. Consistently good are **Lemon Grass** on Soi 24, serving mostly southern Thai and **Laikhram** on Soi 49/2—two other good places to enjoy authentic Thai food at under £6 per head. (Laikhram has become so popular that they have opened two more restaurants in the city, in Soi 23, Sukhumvit and in the Thaniya Plaza Bldg, Thaniya Rd, Silom.)

Every visit to Sukhumvit should include a meal at **Ambassador City Food Complex**, Ambassador Hotel. Here you can select from over 30 different vendors selling dishes of every nationality—including Thai, Chinese, Japanese, Italian, Muslim, Vietnamese and Korean. Most dishes are around 30–50B. Look out for the small zoo with flamingoes and mandarin ducks. The upstairs **Bangkapi Terrace** has a choice of 15–20 mid-priced restaurants (dinner for two 350–500B), again offering a wide variety of Asian and international cuisines, but decide before you go which 'country' you want to eat in—window-shopping restaurants can be torture.

Bali, Soi Ruam Rudi, just south of Ploenchit Rd, is widely considered the best Indonesian restaurant in Thailand. Greta, the owner, was resident chef at the Indonesian embassy in Bangkok, and invitations to functions there were highly prized, for her cooking alone. Rijstaafel for 250B, otherwise choose for yourself among the 100 or so dishes. In the same road are **Neil's Tavern**, with the reputation of serving some of the best steaks in town (which you'll pay above the odds for, but well worth it), and **Mandalay**, which describes itself as 'the best Burmese restaurant in Thailand'. As there are, at most, only a handful in the country, it's hard to dispute, but it has a good local reputation; dinner for two around 700B. **Jools**, Soi 4 (or Soi Nana Tai) is a two-storey pub/restaurant serving good traditional British food—pies, stews and roast beef with all the trimmings, and is popular with visitors and residents alike. At weekends they do a

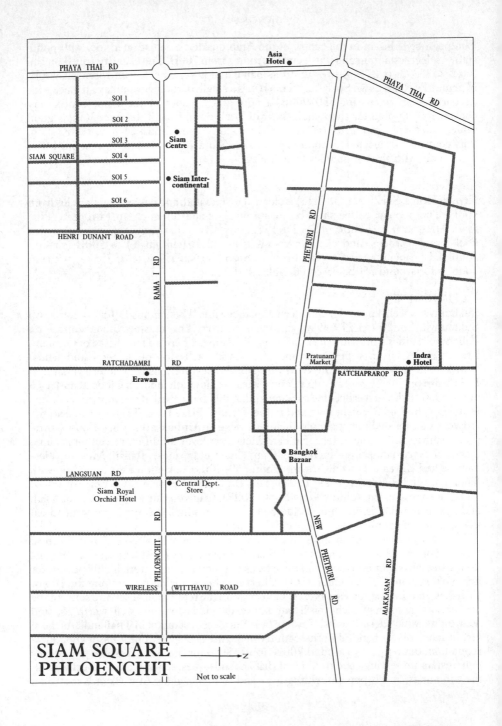

100B buffet, otherwise count on around 300B. Similar fare can be found at **The Huntsman Pub** in the Landmark Hotel, 138 Sukhumvit Rd. It's enormous, but very beautifully done out, with draught beers and live music, though a little expensive.

The in-crowd congregate at **Le Banyan**, 59 Soi 8 (tel 253 5556), an elegantly decorated French restaurant in a painstakingly restored old house. It's very reminiscent of a classy Parisian establishment, with the food to match—including *escargots* and *foie gras*—without paying inflated Paris prices; count on around 1200B for two. **Leena Restaurant** (down Soi 11) is tops for Indian, Pakistani and Arabic food—tasty tandooris at 60B, and very special chicken curries at 55B. If you want to dine well on Thai food and ease your social conscience at the same time, head to **Cabbages and Condoms**, Soi 12, Sukhumvit. Cabbage is only one of the many ingredients in the delicious dishes, and every manner and variety of condoms is on sale. The decor is also far from traditional, with birth-control devices adorning the walls. It's all to help the cause of reducing the spread of AIDS, and raising people's awareness of population control.

New Young Lee, at the corner of Soi 15, is a backpacker favourite—cheap Thai, Chinese and European food, and a novelty menu (Ears Pig Salad, Sour Lost Soup etc). **Nick's Number 1**, Soi 16 is a long-established Hungarian restaurant with lots of goodies from Eastern European kitchens, including the old faithful, goulash. Dinner for two, around 600B. **Wattana Food and Ice Cream Shop**, Soi 19, is hardly like being in Sukhumvit at all—it's totally soundproofed. Good set lunches (Thai/European), continental breakfasts (35B) and ice-cream. **Bei Otto**, Soi 20, is a mid-priced German restaurant, complete with Heidi look-alike waitresses, serving some very good traditional dishes—they also make their own bread and sausages.

Singha Bier Haus, Soi 21, is a Thai imitation of a German beer-hall, straight out of 'The Student Prince', complete with glass yards of draft beer. The food is authentic *bierstube* fare (heaps of meat, sauerkraut and potatoes), but a little expensive. An evening runs to around 800B–1000B for two. **Silom Village Sawatdee**, Soi 23, is the same idea as The Silom Village Trade Centre (see Silom-Surawong, 'Eating Out'), with classical dance shows nightly and exotic seafood dinners for around 500B. Also in Soi 23 you'll find **Lord Mike O'Henry** (see Bangkok 'Nightlife'), a bar/restaurant with a very relaxed atmosphere, good Thai and European dishes, and upstairs a creperie, serving 24 different types of sweet and savoury crepes. **Tiptop Restaurant**, opposite Soi 27, provides a quiet escape from the noisy Sukhumvit traffic, with reliable multi-national cuisine (50–75B per dish) and friendly service.

Town Talk, just beyond Soi 33, is another Indo-Pakistani place with modestly priced set meals (50–90B) and à la carte dishes from 30B. Manager Hassa claims to make the best Tandoori Chicken in Bangkok. **Svensen's** (part of the Pizza Hut cartel), between Sois 51 and 53, is *the* ice-cream palace. It rates high on any ice-cream lover's Richter Scale—'Choose your favourite flavours from this earthshaking extravaganza and rebuild a childhood fantasy!'

Sometime Restaurant, down Soi 55 is delightfully odd—it doubles up as an antique shop. Here you can tuck into Italian pizzas and American burgers, while bargaining for dusty old artefacts and Buddha heads. **Maxim's**, Soi 11, is a haven away from the busy street markets, with a good bakery and cheap breakfasts. **Street food** in Sukhumvit is generally excellent—especially at the **Seafood Market and Restaurant**, 388

Sukhumvit (where you can select your own fresh seafood and veg), and at the *kai yang* and roast duck stalls on Soi 55, and between Sois 2 and 15.

Finally, **Sanguansri**, 59 Wireless Rd, is where wealthy and discerning Thais go to eat, and not for fancy furnishings or to be seen (the decor's plain and tables are crammed together), but for its superb regional cuisine; 150–200B.

Siam-Pratunam

This is Bangkok's biggest and busiest shopping district, with about 10 of the city's largest department stores, countless smaller shops and boutiques, and the famous Pratunam Market. It's a big entertainment centre too, patronized by crowds of young Thais who gather to watch movies (several cinemas here), to chat in bakeries and coffee shops, to eat in dozens of restaurants and cocktail lounges, and to buy the latest fashion clothes. Siam is, however, an expensive place to stay, with few cheap hotels, and many people just drop in for a few hours' shopping.

WHERE TO STAY

Luxury
Hotel Siam Intercontinental, 967 Rama I Rd (tel 2530355; tx 81155 SIAMINT TH), features a spacious 26-acre garden—a perfect retreat from the noisy city. It offers marvellous sports facilities (golf, jogging trail, outdoor gym, *petanque* lawns etc) and low-rise guest quarters, creating an impression of space and freedom. Rooms are 3500–4000B, suites 5000–30,000B, and should be advance-booked in high season. The same goes for another firm favourite, the **Indra Regent** in Rajaprarob Rd (tel 2520111; tx 82723 INDRA TH). This is a palatial 500-room hotel with exotic decor, numerous facilities, and central location. Rooms start at 3000B.

Moderate
All the better inexpensive hotels are situated close together, opposite the National Stadium. Top of the heap is **Krit Thai Mansion**, 931/1 Rama I Rd (tel 2153042; tx 72077 KRIT TH), with immaculate rooms at 1000B, an elegant coffee bar, and free newspapers in the lobby. **Muangphol Building**, 931/8 Rama I Rd (tel 2150033), has 500–700B air-con rooms with *hot* bath, and tight security. The adjoining **Star Hotel** (tel 2150020) is a bit of a knocking shop, but still the best deal in this area. Run by a friendly Thai family, it offers clean air-con rooms from 400–600B.

Inexpensive
There's little to recommend in the way of very cheap accommodation around here. At the **Orchid Guest House**, 21–23 Soi Hasadin, of Ratchaprop Rd (tel 2532437) and **Miami Guest House**, 1629/7 New Phetburi Rd, you can get rooms for 300–500B.

EATING OUT
Hotel Siam Intercontinental has a popular seafood restaurant with special buffet lunch (250B) between 11.30 am and 2.30 pm or order à la carte favourites like the Seafood Basket (feeds three, for 350B). For a big splurge, try the 350B Thai dinner-dance show, commencing 7 pm every Monday and Thursday.

Indra Regent Hotel serves a Thai buffet lunch (in the Garden Bar) from 11.30 am to 2 pm at 350B; the Indra Grill features black pepper steak with a glass of red wine at 250B; and the coffee shop serves 'kao tom buffet' (rice porridge to you) at 70B from 10.30 pm to 2 am. The Indra also does the best hotel-based Thai 'dinner-dance' in Bangkok, recommended by many and a great evening out. It costs 350B if you want dinner (be seated 7.30 latest), and 140B if you're only here for the show.

Lovers of hot, spicy Thai food should go to the Spice Market restaurant in the Regent Hotel, decorated in old Chinese spice-shop style. It's not for the timid; all dishes are infused with exotic spices, many of them unknown to western palates, and most of them hot. Dinner for around 300B makes it a very reasonable dining spot.

Tokyu Food Centre, at the corner of Rama I and Phyathai roads, has a vast eating area on the 6th floor—hundreds of dishes (mainly Thai, Chinese, Japanese, some European) from 25B to 60B. Many travellers end up here—it's pleasantly air-conditioned, and everything is cooked freshly on the spot. Kloster Bier Garden, behind Siam Shopping Centre, is a real party in the evenings, but unfortunately is open only in high season (Nov/Dec); there's seating for a couple of thousand people, draught Kloster beer (35B a glass, 120B a giant flagon), inexpensive Thai dishes, whole suckling pigs roasting on spits, and lots of local atmosphere. Opposite Siam Centre are Pizza Hut, McDonald's and, down a side street, two decent Chinese restaurants, both called Scala.

Nearby, Diva, 1575 New Petchaburi Rd, is aptly named—it looks like a stage set for an opulent Mozart opera, so dress imaginatively—a bouffant powdered wig shouldn't be too hard to find in the City of Angels. The menu is French, and delicious it is too; 600–800B a head. In the same road are some of Bangkok's best seafood restaurants preparing every imaginable fish in the finest Thai and Oriental style.

North of New Phetburi Rd, Tam Nak Thai, 131 Rachadaphisek Rd, is the largest restaurant in *the world*. It's so big that the waiters get around on roller skates. The place is divided up into the regional cuisines of the country, with extensive menus. It is in a very beautiful setting, on a man-made lake in the middle of the city, and is not expensive (around 300B for a full meal). This said, it's more of a 'novelty' place to eat, rather than a memorable culinary experience, and is best visited in a large group.

Banglampoo

This area, near Ratchadamnoen Avenue, started out as a colourful old market: its name derives from its village (*Bang*) origins and the many *lampoo* trees found when the first *klong* was created here. Today, Banglampoo—more particularly, its 'freak street' of Ko-Sahn Rd—is one of the great travellers' centres of the world. This is where most of Bangkok's budget guest houses and cheap flight agencies are concentrated, and it's real backpacker ghetto-land. The main recreations in Koh-Sahn Rd are eating Western food, buying hippy clothes, booking cheap travel, looking out second-hand books and pirated cassettes, checking out guest house noticeboards, watching videos, and meeting other Western travellers. Ko-Sahn certainly isn't Thailand—well, it doesn't pretend to be. It's okay for people with time to hang out, but not really for short-time visitors. After all, if you've only a few days in Bangkok, why spend them sitting with other white faces, eating honey toast, cheese sandwiches and banana pancakes? Still, Banglampoo is cheap, near to the river, just a few minutes' drive from zillions of temples.

WHERE TO STAY
From November to February, Banglampoo's two main guest-house districts—Ko-Sahn Rd and Chakrabongse Rd (Soi Rambutri)—are often packed out. With rooms as cheap as 50B (single) and 80B (double), it's easy to see why. In high season, the best time to look out a room is around 8 am in the morning, when many residents catch early buses out to Samui, Phuket or Chiang Mai.

Moderate
A few upmarket options, with air-con rooms around 600–800B, are **Royal Hotel**, 2 Ratchadamnoen Klang Rd (tel 2229111), **Thai Hotel**, 78 Prachthipatai Rd (tel 2822831) and **Viengtai Hotel** at 42 Tanee Rd (tel 2805392). The Viengtai has a pool and restaurant.

Inexpensive
Places to stay in Ko-Sahn Rd include **Bonny's** (a firm favourite), **Top** (behind Bonny's, quiet and secure), **Good Luck** (the family breaks down and weeps when guests try to leave), **C.H.** (friendly, with sun-roof), **Chart** and **Wally's** (popular, with video), **Hello** (24-hour restaurant and *loud* video—get a top-floor room) and **P.B.** (with snooker hall, manic mascot monkey and a manager who trains Thai kick-boxers). One superior place, the **New Nith Charoen** (tel 2819872) has clean, spacious rooms with bath at 140B. Behind this hotel, down a narrow alleyway, is the **Lek** guest house, with good rooms, laundry service, and baggage deposit, which also offers river trips.

    Siam Guest House ('Our rooms are very cosy and bright cos every room has a window') is located just off Koh-Sahn, at 76 Chakrapong Rd. This has a lovely lady owner and good little restaurant. Pity about the noisy traffic. Over the road, behind the temple, is **New Siam** at 21 Soi Chanasongram, Phra Athit Rd. The best rooms here are the doubles upstairs. Nearby there's **New Apple** (friendly, good roof views), **Ngampit** (quiet, run by friendly family) and **Roof Garden** (the owner, Froggy, is a real travellers' friend). In this area, most travellers favour **Chusri 1 Guest House** (it's the best of the 3 'Chusris') at 61/1–2 Soi Rambutri.

    The new **Youth Hostel**, 25/2 Phitsanulok (tel 2820950) has huge double rooms at 200B, dorm at 50B, a reading room and cafeteria.

EATING OUT
Choose between cheap Thai snacks down at Banglampoo market, or cheap and rather dull Western fare in and around Ko-Sahn Rd. Most guest houses in Ko-Sahn have restaurants and videos. **Suzi's Bar** doesn't have a video—just great food, and the best banana milkshakes (say some) in the world.

Soi Ngam Duphli – Soi Si Bamphen
These two streets—located off Rama IV Rd, opposite Lumpini Stadium—comprise Bangkok's second cheap guest house centre. Handy for foreign embassies, Patpong,

Silom and Siam Square, this area bears many comparisons to Ko-Sahn Rd. It has the same kind of travel agencies, pancake restaurants and hilltribe/hippy clothes, but differs in being noisier (lots of traffic), seedier (drugs, prostitutes etc) and yet more authentically Thai. Many long-stay travellers hang out here.

WHERE TO STAY

Moderate
For comfort, stay at **Malaysia Hotel**, 54 Soi Ngam Duphli (tel 2871457). This has air-con rooms at 220–500B (single), 380–600B (twin), nice pool and coffee shop, friendly staff and a 24-hour video service. You'll want a room at the back of the building, away from the traffic. Once popular as a base for American vets, the Malaysia has recently declined—it seriously needs renovation. **Boston Inn**, Soi Si Bamphen (tel 2861680), has had an overhaul and has new 600B air-con rooms, in addition to the old 200B fan-cooled ones. The Boston has a good pool, with a mysterious sign ('Please do not throw cigarette butts over the other side of the wall'). The nearby **Privacy Hotel** (tel 2862339) has pleasant Thai atmosphere and 350B air-con rooms, but is rather run-down.

Inexpensive
The best cheapie is **Sala Thai** (tel 2871436), a delightful 'daily mansion' with spotless rooms. It's down a small alley off Soi Si Bamphen, and is often full. **Madame**, in the same alley, is a cosy, ramshackle place run by a lovely Thai lady with a heart of gold. Rooms here are 60B to 100B. **Freddy 2**, at 27/40 Soi Sri Bumphen (tel 2866722), is now one of Bangkok's best guest houses with clean rooms (80–120B), an open-air restaurant, sun-roof, novelty T-shirts, an excellent noticeboard, video and good sounds. Freddy himself is a real gentleman. In Soi Ngam Duphli, worthwhile cheapies are **Anna** and **Sweet House Complex**, which has just about everything—crazy but fun staff, bar-restaurant, pool club, travel agency, hilltribe crafts—even a law office. Only the large double rooms are decent though.

EATING OUT
Blue Fox opposite the Malaysia, is a popular air-con restaurant with Western-style food, groovy sounds, a video, and a well-stocked bar. It closes at 11.30 pm, which is a bit of a drag. Over the road, the **Lisboa** offers reasonably priced Mexican food. Next to the Boston Inn, **T.T. Coffee House** has cheap Thai cuisine at around 30–40B per dish. Try *Pla Tod* (tasty fried fish), *Rad Nah* (fried noodle) and *Kao Tom* (chicken rice soup). For a wide choice of 8B curry and rice meals, walk up Soi Ngam Duphli to the pedestrian bridge on Rama IV Rd.

Chinatown

Bangkok's busy and boisterous Chinatown, around Yaowaraj Rd, has been the main centre for trading by the Thai Chinese (the country's largest minority) for the past 200 years. Few people stay here—it's not really a travellers' centre. Most visitors just spend a morning or afternoon enjoyably exploring its numerous narrow alleyways and neon-lit main streets, overhung by high wooden houses, covered in the grime of decades. The **Thieves Market** of Chinatown sells everything imaginable, from Chinese paper lanterns to birds' nests, from motorbike parts to water pumps, but it's antique-hunting and gold-buying that are the main attractions. Chinatown's atmosphere is frenetic, colourful and noisy (the traffic is quite unbelievable) but it's got some of the best street life and tastiest cheap snacks in Bangkok.

WHERE TO STAY

Moderate–Inexpensive
Hotels in this area are few, and not geared to Westerners. The **New Empire**, 572 Yaowaraj Rd (tel 2346990), is a clean, comfy place—very popular with Indians and southern Thais—with smart air-con rooms for 450–750B in the quiet new wing. The **Sineiah** (Somboon) at 415 Yaowaraj Rd (tel 2212327), has clean air-con rooms (350–600B), a cheap Chinese-Thai restaurant, a small tour agency, and a resident astrologer. Of the many murky Chinese-run cheapies in Rong Muang Rd, adjoining Hualamphong Rd, only the **Sri Hualamphong**, with near-adequate rooms at 250B, merits a mention.

GENERAL INFORMATION

Post Office
The GPO on New (Charoen Krung) Rd is open—along with its *Poste Restante* counter—from 8 am to 8.30 pm Mon–Fri, and from 8 am to 1 pm Saturday and Sunday. It has a useful parcel-packing service, open 8.30 am to 4.30 pm Mon–Fri, 8.30 am to 12 noon on Saturday. Next to the main building, there's a 24-hour international phone call service (inside the telex building). The post office at Soi Nana, Sukhumvit/Ploenchit, also has a parcel-packing service.

Bookshops
Good general bookshops, with maps and guides, fiction and non-fiction titles, are **Asia Books**, Sukhumvit Rd Soi 15, and **Bookseller**, 81 Patpong Rd, Silom. **Elite Book House**, 3/6 Sukhumvit Soi 24, has used and second-hand books (rare and multi-language). **Chalermnit**, 2 Erawan Arcade, Erawan Hotel, Ploenchit Rd, offers a vast selection of English, French and German books (new and reduced-price) in addition to an extensive collection of travel guides.

Travel Agents
Most hotels have travel agencies, offering set tours of Bangkok. But for major tour or sightseeing deals, contact **Diethelm Travel**, Kian Gwan Bldg II, 140/1 Wireless Rd (tel 2559150), **DITS Travel** (in the same building) (tel 2559205), **World Travel Service**, 1053 New Charoen Krung Rd (tel 2335900–9), **Exotissimo Travel**, 21 Soi 4 Sukhumvit Rd (tel 2535240) and 755 Silom Rd (tel 2359196), or **Siam Wings** 173 Suriwong Rd (tel 2354757).

Most other arrangements—including visas, cheap flights, cut-price bus/rail travel—are best handled by the bucket-shop agencies of Banglampoo and Soi Ngam Duphli. A typical outfit, like **Ronny's Tour and Travel**, 197 Ko-Sahn Rd (tel 2812556; tx 84482), handles visas (Nepal, Burma and India), cheap bus tickets (Koh Samui, Koh Samet, Phuket and Chiang Mai) and cut-price flights (worldwide). One-way flights from Bangkok are very cheap—to London, £200; to New York, £300; to Bombay, £80; to Kathmandu, £90; to Singapore, £50; to Sydney, £370. Other agencies, like **Gold Travel**, 2/4 Soi Sri Bumphen (tel 2866783), and **Chiangmai First Travel Service** in Ko-Sahn Rd, specialize in cheap domestic bus-tickets—to Samet (and back) for 240B, to Chiang Mai for 160B, to Phuket for 300B, and to Samui for as little as 240B (i.e. 120B cheaper than booking through a hotel). **STA Travel Office**, attached to Thai Hotel, Banglampoo (tel 2815314), is best for rail tickets, travel insurance, and (they'll sell anybody one) student cards.

Useful phone numbers

Directory Assistance	13
Long Distance Service	100
Ambulance	25221715
Tourist Police	22162069
Tourist Assistance	2810372, 2232126
Immigration Division	2867003
Police	191

Part VI

AROUND BANGKOK

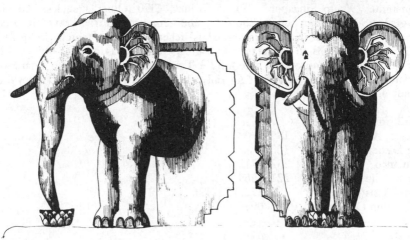

Elephant ruins at Ayutthaya

The central region of Thailand offers a number of interesting excursions from Bangkok—palaces and temples to the north (**Ayutthaya, Bang Pa In** and **Lopburi**), islands and beaches to the east (**Koh Samet, Koh Si Chang**, and **Pattaya**), culture and countryside to the west (**Nakhon Pathom** and **Kanchanaburi**) as well as wildlife to the northeast (**Khao Yai National Park**). All of these places can be seen on their own, or, more rewardingly, in combination with each other.

NAKHON PATHOM

Nakhon Pathom lies 56 km west of Bangkok, and is a convenient stopover on the way to Kanchanaburi. It has two main claims to fame—first, it's believed to be Thailand's oldest city, founded around 150 BC; second, it's here that Buddhism was apparently first introduced to Thailand by Indian missionaries, probably during the 3rd century BC. The city is known to have been the centre of the powerful Dvaravati empire, which ruled over several city-states in this region from the 6th to the 11th century.

GETTING THERE

By Bus
From Bangkok's Southern Terminal, non air-con buses leave for Nakhon Pathom every 10 minutes from 5 am to 9 pm. The one-hour trip costs 13B. Air-con buses leave every 30 minutes from 7 am until 10.30 pm and the fare is 24B.

From Kanchanaburi, there are regular buses (No. 81) to Nakhon Pathom. It's a 1¹/₂-hour journey, and the fare is 16B.

By Rail
There are six trains daily to Nakhon Pathom from Bangkok Noi station, leaving between 9 am and 6.30 pm. The short 1¹/₂-hour hop can be done quite comfortably 3rd class (fare 14B).

WHAT TO SEE
The only real reason for dropping in on this busy, dusty town is to visit the impressive **Phra Pathom Chedi**, said to be the tallest Buddhist monument in the world. Mounted on a circular terrace within a large square park, this landmark *chedi* with a huge bell-shaped dome glittering with orange-glazed tiles from China, rises to a height of 127 metres. The original 6th-century *chedi* (a much smaller effort) built on this site was badly damaged when the Burmese sacked the surrounding town in 1057. It was restored and covered over by the present much larger *chedi*, in the 19th century by Kings Mongkut and Chulalongkorn. At each compass-point in the outer courtyard, you'll find a *viharn* (hall) housing Buddha images in various attitudes—one standing, one reclining, one watched over by the holy serpent, or *naga*, and the last overlooked by a beautiful wall-mural of a Bo tree. A replica of the original Indian-style *stupa* stands to the south of the present *chedi*.

The Phra Pathom is the most venerated *chedi* in Thailand. The constant busy traffic of students, sightseers and pilgrims at this sacred spot gives it a lively, effervescent atmosphere. A leisurely perambulation round the huge base of the *chedi* often turns up all sorts of surprises. On my last visit, I saw a 'Thai Dramatics' show (*lakhon* classical dance-drama) next to a Chinese temple, took part in a Thai action film being shot here, and was given a guided tour by a posse of adolescent monks dying to learn English. If you want to meet monks, this is just the place to do it. Just below the *bot*, there's a little museum. This is open 9 am to 12 noon, 1 to 4 pm, Wed–Sun. Lots of tat here (seashells, stamps, bits of unidentified rock etc.), but also some nice pieces from Ban Chiang and Ayutthaya.

Many independent visitors to Nakhon Pathom are simply passing through—usually to or from Kanchanaburi. To see the *chedi* unhindered by heavy luggage, take a 2B *samlor* to the railway station, and check it in with the stationmaster (he minds bags for free).

Some people stay overnight at Nakhon Pathom, in order to catch the early morning bus out to **Damnoen Saduak Floating Market**, a 40-minute drive south. This is a whole lot better than the much-fêted floating market of Bangkok which is completely ruined by tourism. Buses go to Damnoen Saduak direct from Bangkok's Southern Bus Terminal (No. 78) every 20 minutes starting at 6 am—you'll want one of the first buses out, to be at the market around 8–9 am when it's at its best. From Nakhon Pathom, take a crack-of-dawn bus (6.30 am latest) to Samut Songkhram, asking to be put off at Damnoen Saduak. The two best markets, **Talaat Ton Khem** and **Talaat Hia Kui** are either side of the Damnoen Saduak canal. Alternatively take a water-taxi south to the less commercialized market called **Talaat Khun Phitak**.

WHERE TO STAY AND EATING OUT   (Tel prefix 034)
To stay, choose between **Mittaworn Hotel**, just outside the railway station (tel 243115) with adequate rooms for 180B–300B; and **Nakorn Inn Hotel** (tel 251152), off the northeastern corner of the *chedi* (a 5B *samlor* ride from bus or railway station) with air-con rooms at 380B (single), 650B for a double. This place offers 30% low-season discounts, and 6th and 7th floor rooms have the *chedi* views. The Nakorn Inn is also one of the few places in town to enjoy decent food—the pleasant restaurant-cum-coffee shop has good, mid-priced cuisine, with live music thrown in.

For cheap tasty Thai snacks—*kai yang*, satays, spicy sausages on sticks etc—go to the large, sprawling street market between the *chedi* and the railway station. There are lots of inexpensive Thai-Chinese restaurants in this area too.

KANCHANABURI

Some 130 km west of Bangkok, Kanchanaburi is one of the most beautiful provinces in Thailand. If you want to see some real Thai countryside—forests and waterfalls, rivers and mountains, caves and jungles—and don't want to travel all the way to the far north, this is where to come. Kanchanaburi town has a lot to offer in itself, and is also an excellent base for many interesting day-excursions, notably river-rafting down the River Kwai.

The recent discovery of neolithic burial sites in this region has shown Kanchanaburi to be the site of a very ancient civilization. But the present town is of fairly recent origin, having been founded by Rama III in 1833. It lies at the point where two tributaries—the Khwae Noi and the Khwae Yai—meet to form the Mae Klong River. The old town, founded by Rama I as a frontline defence against Burma, is 18 km away.

Kanchanaburi is best known for its associations with the Second World War. It was from here—during 1942–3—that the Japanese army began constructing the infamous 'Death Railway' leading up to Three Pagodas Pass. The idea was to connect Siam with Burma by rail, providing the Japanese with an alternative to their total reliance on sea transport. To carry out this ambitious project—which involved laying 415 km of track over jungle-covered mountains—they put 69,000 Allied prisoners to work and conscripted 200,000 Asians as forced labourers. By October 1943, when the rail link was completed, an estimated 16,000 prisoners and 49,000 Asians had perished, many of them as the result of fearful atrocities.

Today, many of Kanchanaburi's 'attractions' pay tribute to this terrible page in WW II history. Trains still pass across the 'Bridge over the River Kwai', and run up the Death Railway as far as Nam Tok. A War Museum and various cemeteries keep the memory of the heroic fallen alive, and the town itself stands as something of a living reminder of the pointless waste and tragedy caused by war. But this is only one aspect of Kanchanaburi. It doesn't dwell on the past. Rather, it's an extremely friendly and cheerful place—surrounded by breathtaking scenery—which travellers like so much they stay a week or even longer.

Every year, usually at the end of November/beginning of December, Kanchanaburi celebrates River Kwai Bridge Week, commemorating the Allied bombings on the Death Railway in 1945. This festival features a noisy, colourful Light and Sound Show, with

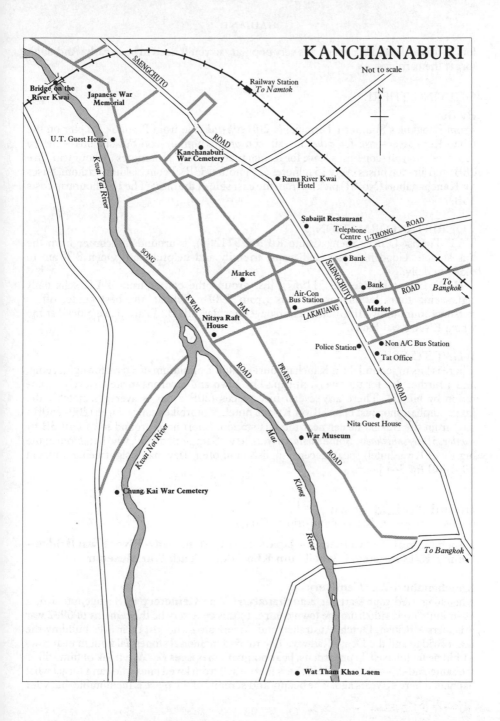

KANCHANABURI

Not to scale

N

Bridge on the River Kwai

Japanese War Memorial

Railway Station
To Namtok

SAENGCHUTO

Kwai Yai River

U.T. Guest House

ROAD

Kanchanaburi War Cemetery

Rama River Kwai Hotel

Sabaijit Restaurant

Telephone Centre

U-THONG

ROAD

Bank

SONG

Market

Bank

To Bangkok

KWAE

Air-Con Bus Station

SAENGCHUTO

ROAD

PAK

LAKMUANG

Market

Nitaya Raft House

ROAD

Police Station

Non A/C Bus Station

Kwai Noi River

PRAEK

Tat Office

ROAD

Nita Guest House

War Museum

Mae

Klong

River

Chung Kai War Cemetery

ROAD

To Bangkok

Wat Tham Khao Laem

lots of fireworks and big bangs. It's very popular, so you'll need to book early. And don't forget the earplugs.

GETTING THERE
By Bus
From Bangkok's Southern Terminal (a 20B *tuk-tuk* ride from Prannok Rd pier on the Chao Rhya river—ask for *either* the air-con *or* the non air-con bus stations—they're separate), non air-con buses leave for Kanchanaburi every 15 minutes (3-hour trip, fare 28B) and air-con buses every 15 minutes (2½ hours, 53B). From Nakhon Pathom, buses for Kanchanaburi (No. 81) pick up from the east side of the *chedi*. The 1½-hour trip costs 16B.

TOURIST INFORMATION
TAT Tourist Office, Saeng Chuto Rd (tel 511200), is around the corner from the bus station. Good handouts and maps, friendly and helpful staff. Open 8.30 am to 4.30 pm daily.

B. T. Guest House (tel 511967), just around the corner from TAT, sells daily sightseeing tours by air-con minibus (from 290B). Titinat, the best guide, offers personal tours (only 100B) on a Thursday—her day off. B. T. also have a desk at the Rama River Kwai Hotel.

WHAT TO SEE
There is lots to see and do in Kanchanaburi—allow a minimum of 3 days for sightseeing, and a further day for the river-raft trip. The town and environs invite leisurely exploration by bicycle. There are several hire places (20B a day is average), notably the Jakkayanphan shop just below River Kwai 2 hotel. Motorbikes can be hired (200–250B a day) from the Suzuki dealer near the bus station. Short hops around town cost 3B by *samlor*, 5B by *songthaew*. Some *samlor* drivers (e.g. 'Samlor Samsun', who hangs out at the big River Kwai hotel) speak decent English, and offer 'lazy man's sightseeing' tours at 80–100B for 3–4 hours.

In and Around Town
(by bicycle/*samlor*, 10 km round-trip, full day)

Kanchanaburi War Cemetery – Japanese War Memorial – River Kwai Bridge – Chung-Kai Cemetery – Wat Thum Khao Pun – Jeath War Museum

Kanchanaburi War Cemetery
This suggested tour starts at **Kanchanaburi War Cemetery** in Saengchuto Rd, a 10-minute cycle ride from the town centre. In this cemetery lie the remains of 6982 war prisoners—British, Dutch, Australian and American—who lost their lives building the Kwai Bridge and the Death Railway. The myriad memorial stones, laid out in neat rows within peaceful, well-kept gardens, bear poignant messages ('. . . We think of him still as the same and say—He is not dead, he is just away') from loved ones who can't forget what happened here 40 years ago. The beauty and serenity of the place is memorable, but your

senses are jarred when reading the tombstones–most of the soldiers buried here died in their early twenties. Light relief is provided by the colourful Chinese cemetery next door.

River Kwai Bridge

Cycling 15 minutes further up Saengchuto Rd, turn left (just before the Bridge) down New Zealand Rd. At the bottom of this is the **Japanese War Memorial**, a rather grim monument erected by the Japanese army to honour the Allied dead. From here, it's only a minute's ride up to the **Bridge over the River Kwai**. This world-famous bridge spanning the Khwae Yai ('large tributary') River, lies some 2 km north of town, and is its main tourist attraction. It's not the original wooden one built by the prisoners which was slightly downstream. This is the later version, assembled from materials brought from Java by the Japanese army (again using POW labour) which had its central spans destroyed by British bombers in 1945. The bridge was rebuilt after the war, and only its curved spans are original. For a real sense of 'atmosphere', be on it when the 10.31 am train passes over on its way to Nam Tok. Post yourself at one of the sentry-points on the bridge, and have your camera at the ready. Listen out for *Colonel Bogey's March*—they sometimes play it on a tinny tannoy as the train passes over. In the evening, return to the bridge for magical sunset views—it really does have a most picturesque location. By the bridge entrance, there's a small Railway Museum, with beautiful old steam engines used during WWII.

Chung Kai Cemetery

From the bridge, take a scenic ride down Patana Rd (parallel to the river) back towards town. Cross the river at the pier below the 'Fitness Park' (a 2B ferry ride), and cycle 15 minutes up the road on the other side—via corn fields and banana plantations—until the **Chung Kai Allied War Cemetery** appears on your left. This smaller, quieter cemetery is built on the site of one of the original POW camps, and is noted for its tranquil, contemplative gardens. Most of the 1750 memorial stones here bear the 'Known to God' inscription for unknown soldiers.

Wat Thum Khao Pun

A kilometre or so above the cemetery—over the railway-line and up the hill—find **Wat Thum Khao Pun**. This is one of many cave temples in the area, and is something of an oddity. On payment of a 5B admission fee, a guide leads you down to a glitzy Buddha image, twinkling with fairy lights, at the cave entrance. This Buddha encloses a much smaller one found on this spot during a visit by Rama V. The cave is a very sacred spot and there are several reports of local devotees hearing 'ghostly voices' and 'heavenly music' here. As you clamber through the labyrinthine recesses of the cave interior, watch out for gold-prospecting Bangkokites. They turn up every weekend, and ferret around in here looking for the large consignment of gold bars the Japanese army left behind during WWII. Outside the cave, chatty monks play endless games of draughts with bottlecaps.

Jeath War Museum

Back across the river, head right—past floating restaurants and up the hill—until you come to the **Jeath War Museum**. Attached to Wat Chaichunphon, this museum is a replica of bamboo-hut dwellings used by Allied POWs in the Kanchanaburi area during

WWII. Inside the huts is a rather crude, amateurish (yet curiously effective) exhibition of watermugs, spades, railway spikes, clothing, photographs and sketches which reconstruct various aspects of prisoners' lives, and which give some idea of the suffering they endured. It's a bit over the top, and needs to be viewed in perspective. Whatever, the 20B admission charge levied is excessive—unless you get one of the monks (a friendly lot) to show you round properly. The name 'Jeath' by the way, is not a misprint for Death. It is made up of the initials of the countries who participated in the building of the Death Railway—Japan, England, America and Australia, Thailand and Holland.

Erawan Waterfall
(by bus; full day)

This is a lovely day-outing, especially between September and November, when the falls are at their best, and the surrounding **Khao Salop National Park** at its most beautiful. Buses go to Erawan every 50 min, between 8 am and 4 pm, from Kanchanaburi bus station (65 km, 17B). The first bus out is best—you'll want to make a full day of it. Also, lots of local tourists show up mid-afternoon, and then it's definitely a case of paradise lost. Last bus back to Kanchanaburi is at 4 pm.

From Erawan bus station, it's $1^1/2$ km (either walk, or hire a taxi—20–30B for up to four people) to the foot of the falls. Have the 5B entrance fee to the National Park ready. Erawan comprises seven levels of falls—the climb to the top takes 2 hours, and the scenery gets better, the higher you go. Among the attractions are glittering ponds and streams, multi-coloured butterflies, and several species of exotic birds. Brind a good pair of walking shoes for this hike—flip flops or sandals won't do. You'll also need a bathing-suit—each of the lower levels of the falls has a 'swimming pool' (September to December only). Some of the Kwai prisoners were brought to these pools—full of nibbling fish—to have their gangrenous wounds 'cleaned out'. The best swimming is at level 2, an idyllic blue lagoon with a delightful mini-waterfall. Stalwarts who climb all the way up to level 7 get a bonus—the best 'jacuzzi' of their lives.

Death Railway – Nam Tok – Kao Phang Waterfall
(by train and bus; full day)

The 'Death Railway' originally ran all the way from Bangkok to Moulmein in Burma. Today, the only section still in use is the short 50 km stretch from Kanchanaburi to Nam Tok. The two-hour train ride along this route is a fascinating, sometimes nerve-wracking, experience. At certain points, the ground literally drops away beneath the train as it passes over yawning chasms on unsupported wooden sleepers. The story goes that the POWs deliberately made the worst possible job of building the railway. Another story is that the 'Death Railway' is so named because it's such a hazard to travel on. This is, of course, not true. Its title derives from the fact that so many people died making it. Every few yards along its length, a wooden cross marks the last resting place of some unknown prisoner. The sobering statistic is that one person died for each sleeper on the track from Bangkok to Nam Tok. Today, the railway is simply an enjoyable ride through beautiful countryside.

The 10.31 am train for Nam Tok leaves from Kanchanaburi railway station daily (fare

17B). The town of **Nam Tok** ('waterfall') is built on the site of a former POW camp called Tarsau, which was the main jungle base for upriver construction camps. From 1943–4, it was also used as a vast primitive hospital, to which tubercular and diseased prisoners were sent by barge from hill camps further up the river. Today, it's a small, sleepy town with nothing worth hanging around for. From Nam Tok station, take a 5B *songthaew* ride (or walk two kilometres) to **Kao Phang Waterfall**. These are very modest falls, nothing to compare with Erawan, but the Thais love it to pieces—splashing about, getting wet etc.

Kao Phang only has enough water to splash about in from June to September. The popular recreation here is to climb up the side of the falls, and make the holy pilgrimage from the top to the elusive **Cave of God**. This cave is a recent archaeological discovery, and is located 2 km behind the falls, down a jungle path. There's a duck up here that's supposed to know the way, but it doesn't. Back on the main road, below the waterfall, you can hitch a bus (15B, 1 hour) all the way back to Kanchanaburi.

River Kwai Raft-trip
(by raft; full day)

This trip is the best thing about Kanchanaburi, and should be booked as you arrive. Several places—including TAT, **Nita Guest House** and **Sunya Rux Restaurant**—offer rafting trips, but they're often heavily subscribed. The best months for river-rafting are November to April, though the season starts as early as September. Trips generally run up and down the Mae Klong River, and include drops at local sightseeing spots. The quality of rafts is very variable, especially if hiring from less reputable places down by the pier. At the time of writing, the best deal is offered by **Sunya Rux**, next to Rama River Kwai Hotel. Sunya offers marvellous one-day trips on his 'houseboat' (actually a 3-section raft—one raft for eating, one for diving, and one for sunbathing) at 200B per person, plus 50B for food. All sorts of fun entertainment is thrown in, including Thai-style water-skiing (i.e. no skis), hula-dancing, rubber-rings, bongo drums, games, songs and lots of laughs. Worthwhile stop-offs include stunning views over rural Thailand from a hilltop Chinese temple and wonderfully tacky fairground animals at an unusual Thai temple. Sunya also offers 500B two-day trips up to the Burmese border, and four-day 'specials' costing 1000–1500B, which include camping in bamboo forests, expeditions to waterfalls, and visits to remote temples.

RECREATION AND SHOPPING

Thai-style **massage**—the perfect way to wind down after a hard day's sightseeing—is provided at the parlour just below Kanchanaburi War Cemetery (look out for the modern-style building, with no sign). Excellent rubdowns are given here, for just 70B an hour.

Best buys in Kanchanaburi are gems—especially blue sapphires from the **Bor Ploy mines** 45 km north of town. Don't shop at the touristy gem shops and jewellers up by the Kwai bridge. Instead, try a reliable backstreet lapidary like **Jumrat Jewellery**, opposite B. T. Travel in the town centre. Blue sapphires sell here from 200B to 20,000B per carat, depending on cut and quality. Cheaper black star-sapphires (around 400B per carat) make attractive necklaces.

WHERE TO STAY
(tel prefix 034)

Moderate
For a touch of luxury, stay at **Rama River Kwai Hotel**, 284/4–6 Saengchuto Rd (tel 511184; tx 78705). This is one of the few places in town with hot water, and has sombre, but nice air-con rooms at 545B single, 641B double. The disco (the 'Raft') is a big Thai scene on Friday and Saturday nights.

Inexpensive
Opposite the River Kwai Hotel, the **V.L. Guest House** is one of the better places to stay in the mid-range bracket. Rooms go for 120–280B, depending on the cooling system, and there's a decent small outdoor restaurant. They also organize raft tours and bike rentals. **Prasopsuk Bungalows**, 677 Saengchuto Rd (tel 511777) is also a good deal, with clean and spacious fan-cooled rooms for 90B, air-con rooms for 200B. Friendly people, good restaurant. **U. T. Guest House**, 25/5 Patana Rd (2 km below the Kwai Bridge) is a pleasant family-style house, with 2–3 bedded rooms at 60B per person, raft tours, motorbike rental, peaceful location and great food (try Briefly Sunny Pork, washed down with Lipton Limited). Close to Jeath Museum, **Nita Guest House** has clean double rooms at 80B and a popular 40B dorm. Nice garden and cheap cycle hire too. The associated **Nita Raft House** offers peaceful 40B river-raft accommodation. So does **Nittaya Raft House**, at the top of Song Khwae Rd. Living on a raft is okay by day—nice views, romantic atmosphere, sunbathing etc.—but at night you really cook. Superior raft-houses like **Kwai Yai Garden Resort** (tel 513611), 2 km from the Kwai Bridge, are pricey—between 600 and 1500B per person. For a full listing of them, contact TAT or B. T. Travel Co.

EATING OUT
The local speciality—*Yeesok* river fish—is best sampled at the **Floating Restaurants** down by the ferry pier. The best of these is **Ruean Ploy** (not 'Rent Boy', as I was first informed), offering mid-priced Thai/Chinese food, amusing live music ('Elvis rip-offs in Thai' was one description) and effusively friendly doll-like waitresses. Our party took 40 minutes to even place an order. The floating restaurants are particularly good places to watch the sunset.

In the town, the travellers' favourite eating place is **Sunya Rux**, next to Rama River Kwai Hotel. Tasty pancakes, great seafood, and cheap breakfasts. The 'Dinner No Spicy' menu offers something called Fried Beef, One Day Light. Sunya is also a cheap guest house, with a mascot monkey who shanghais passers-by in the street. Right next door is **Sabaijit Restaurant**, serving a variety of cheap, palatable Thai-Chinese dishes. Grilled duck and rice, the speciality, is only 10B. The novelty dish is Roast Rib Eye in Sall Crust.

A few people have written in to recommend **Cowboy**, a good little restaurant on the way down to the river from the bus station. Brightly lit and full of Bangkok playboys, it's a popular late-night scene with great live music and phenomenal food and service. Across the road from it, a small Thai food place offers a wide selection of 10B meals, also just about the best seafood in town. **VIP Beer House**, off Patana Rd (1 km below the Bridge), has late-night drinks, a small live band, and a relaxing riverside location. It's the perfect place to round off the evening.

AYUTTHAYA

Just 85 km north of Bangkok lie the stunning ruins of Ayutthaya, Thailand's former capital. Named after the mythical kingdom of Ayodhhya in the Hindu Ramayana epic, Ayutthaya was founded in 1350 by a prince of U Thong (near Suphanburi) who went on to become King Ramatibodi I. Earlier used by the Khmers as a trading outpost, the city's unique situation—on an island at the confluence of three rivers (the Chao Phya, the Lopburi and the Prasak), only 110 km from the sea—soon made it a major trade centre. Over a period of 400 years—from 1350 to 1767—Ayutthaya became one of the greatest and wealthiest cities in Asia. During the 14th and 15th centuries—a period still regarded by the Thais as their Golden Age—the Ayutthayan kings held sway over an empire extending as far north as Vientiane in Laos and as far west as Pegu in Burma. As the capital rapidly outgrew its original 5 × 3 km area, a grid pattern of canals and waterways was dug to enable the incoming armada of boats from China, France, Holland, England, Portugal and Japan to negotiate the city and reach the principal trading points. Astonished European visitors were soon comparing it to Venice. By 1685, when Abbé de Choisy visited with the French embassy, the city walls extended for 10 km and its population exceeded one million. A galaxy of glittering temples had sprung up too, a reflection of the city's burgeoning prosperity. When Glanuis came here in 1682 he found:

> ... Seventeen hundred temples within Ayutthaya, with at least thirty
> thousand priests and more than four thousand images of Buddha, all of
> them gold or gilt ... The spires of the pagodas and temples were so
> gilded that in the sunshine they reflected the light so strongly that they
> disturbed the eyes even from two or three miles away. The King of Siam
> was indeed one of the richest monarchs of the East.

Ayutthaya was ruled by a succession of 33 kings of various dynasties. The earlier ones were particularly strong, using to great effect the new concept of semi-divine kingship borrowed from the Khmer after the Thais destroyed their capital of Angkhor Thom. Two kings in particular were meticulous law-givers. Ramatibodi excluded practically everybody from giving judgement in court, including:

> Infidels, debtors of the parties, slaves of the parties, diseased persons,
> children under seven, old persons over seventy, backbiters, covetous
> persons, professional dancers, homeless persons, the deaf, blind,
> prostitutes, pregnant women, hermaphrodites, impotent persons,
> sorcerers, witches, lunatics, quack doctors, fishermen, bootmakers,
> gamblers, thieves, criminals, and executioners.

And King Trailok (1448–1488) offered death to anyone shaking the king's boat, or allowing stray dogs or love poems into the palace. He went easy on anyone who only kicked the palace door—they just lost a foot. Later Ayutthayan kings were less interested in making laws than in collecting white elephants. The more white elephants they accumulated, the higher they were held in esteem. From 1563–4 there was a 'war of white elephants', when an envious Burmese ruler deprived Chakrapat of Ayutthaya of four of his seven prized elephants. It was the beginning of the end. Naruesan the Great recovered Ayutthaya for the Thais a few years later (1587), but it never regained its

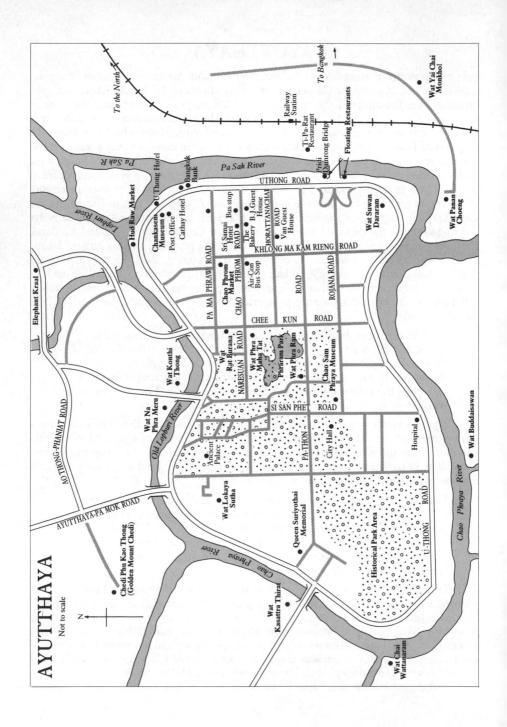

AYUTTHAYA

Not to scale

N

To the North

To Bangkok

Pa Sak R.

Lopburi River

Pa Sak River

Pa Sak River

UTHONG ROAD

Railway Station

Ti-Pa-Rat Restaurant

Pridi Damrong Bridge

Floating Restaurants

Wat Yai Chai Monkhol

Wat Panan Choeng

Wat Suwan Dararam

Hud Raw Market

U Thong Hotel

Bangkok Bank

Chankasem Museum

Post Office

Cathay Hotel

Sri Samai Hotel

Bus stop

The Bakery

B.J.Guest House

Van Guest House

HORATTANACHAI ROAD

KHLONG MA KAM RIENG ROAD

Elephant Kraal

PA MA PHRAW ROAD

Chao Phrom Market

CHAO PHROM

Air-Con Bus Stop

ROAD

ROJANA ROAD

CHEE KUN ROAD

Wat Konthi Thong

AO THONG-PHANIAT ROAD

Old Lopburi River

Wat Na Phra Meru

Wat Rat Burana

NARESUAN ROAD

Wat Phra Maha Tat

Phraram Park

Wat Phra Ram

Chao Sam Phraya Museum

SI SAN PHET ROAD

Ancient Palace

PA-THON

City Hall

Hospital

Wat Buddaisawan

AYUTTHAYA-PA MOK ROAD

Wat Lokaya Sutha

Historical Park Area

U-THONG ROAD

Chao Phraya River

Chedi Phu Kao Thong (Golden Mount Chedi)

Queen Suriyothai Memorial

Chao Phraya River

Wat Kasattra Thirat

Wat Chai Wattanaram

former power and glory. In 1767, following a series of wars with Burma, Cambodia, Luang Prabang and Chiang Mai, the city finally succumbed to its traditional enemy, the Burmese. This time the invaders, determined to destroy Ayutthaya once and for all, razed it to the ground and massacred its inhabitants. When all was done, only 10,000 people were left within its smoke-blackened ruins. The Thais soon regained their independence, but Ayutthaya was never again occupied—its destruction had been so complete.

Ayutthaya today is a small provincial town thinly spread over the vast grid of a once-mighty capital. At one edge lie the temple and the old palace ruins, bleak memorials of a glorious past. A number of temples and towers have been recently renovated, but it's still impossible—surveying the fields of scattered ruins and tumbled buildings—to visualize Ayutthaya's original splendour. Some visitors actually prefer it in its derelict state. 'Ayutthaya was simply *made* to be ruined', is one typical comment, 'you simply can't imagine it being more impressive when it was intact.' Certainly, several of the temples remain majestic in their desolation, and the old city in general exudes a powerful historical atmosphere. This, together with its close proximity to Bangkok, has made Ayutthaya a major tourist magnet.

GETTING THERE

By Bus
From Bangkok's Northern Terminal, non air-con buses leave for Ayutthaya every 10 minutes from 5 am to 7 pm. It's a short 1½-hour journey, costing 17B. Air-con buses leave from an adjacent building and cost 25B. From Ayutthaya, buses go right back into Bangkok city centre—very convenient. Buses also run hourly from Kanchanaburi via Suphanburi.

By Train
From Bangkok's Hualamphong station, trains leave for Ayutthaya at very regular intervals, from 4.30 am to 11.20 pm. A cheap 3rd class seat (15B) should do for this short 1½-hour hop. Some canny travellers make Ayutthaya the very last place they see in Thailand—Don Muang airport is only 40 minutes down the rail line from here. Ideal, if you don't want to revisit Bangkok.

By River
Bangkok's Oriental Hotel offers a de luxe boat tour to Ayutthaya (600B including lunch). Or you can hire a water-taxi (1500B—you'll need a group) from the Oriental pier. In either case, it's a long 3-hour trip upriver, another 3 hours back down, and not much time for sightseeing in between.

WHAT TO SEE
The modern town, overshadowed by its neighbouring ruins, is remarkably dull. The only evidence of its 'gangster' reputation is a marked shortage of cheap accommodation and local transport. The local 'mafia' have a monopoly on *tuk-tuks*, which demand a minimum of 30B for short journeys and 100–150B for a 3-hour tour of the temples. Fortunately, since Ayutthaya is far too large to explore on foot, there are many *songthaews*

99

and *samlors* prepared to take you from point to point for 5–10B. From the railway station, you can take a 50-satang ferry across the Prasak River into town—far cheaper than a *tuk-tuk*. The station is also a good place to pick up good English-speaking guides. Look out for number one guide, Pock (hairy mole on chin, Philip Marlowe fedora on head, 'silver machine' in the forecourt). Along with other members of the local guide association, he meets tourists off the early trains from Bangkok. It's worth hiring your own guide—you see more and pay less (100B hour) than the standard 600B tours running out of Bangkok hotels daily.

Sightseeing in Ayutthaya can be hot, tiring work—the ruins are very spread out, and are best seen in the cool of the early morning. Certain temple areas, take note, charge 20B for admission (half-price with a student card). Ironically, these are often the ones that have been enclosed in landscaped lawns and robbed of their antique character. Regarding what to see, you can afford to be selective. As Ayutthaya was almost completely levelled, after a while, one chipped *chedi* or mutilated Buddha begins to look just like another. To avoid such repetition, content yourself with seeing half a dozen temples at leisure, and avoid places like the Old Palace and Wat Rajburana where you pay 20B to see hardly anything. Visitors not staying overnight in Ayutthaya can leave their bags in the railway station cloakroom (open 5 am to 10 pm)—useful, if you want to carry on to Bangkok, Lopburi or Sukhothai later in the day.

Temple Tour
(by *tuk-tuk*, taxi; 6–8 hours)

Wat Yai Chai Mongkol – Wat Phra Chao Phanom Choeng – Wat Chai Wattanaram – Wat Buddaisawan – Wat Phra Ram – Wat Mahathat – Wat Na-Phra Mane

Wat Yai Chai Mongkol
Wat Yai Chai Mongkol was built in 1384 and houses the remains of the highest *prang* in Ayutthaya. The famous reclining Buddha left of the entrance has recently been restored, like everything else here. Even the temple's resident community of mangy dogs have been 'renovated'—they're all painted pink with antiseptic. Naruesan the Great erected the impressive *prang*, surrounded by 124 mini-Buddhas, in the 16th century. For good views down over the temple complex, climb the low hill. For self-improvement, study the moral messages ('Loving kindness is personal magnet') pinned to nearly every tree.

Wat Chao Phanom Choeng
Wat Phanom Choeng lies on the Chao Phya river southeast of town and is very old—it was built before Ayutthaya was a capital city. The 19-metre-high seated Buddha (covered in gold leaf) is the largest surviving Buddha image in Ayutthaya, and also one of the very few left intact by the Burmese. On view from 8 am to 5 pm daily, it was built in 1324 by the king to atone for a terrible crime. He brought the daughter of the Chinese emperor to Ayutthaya for marriage, but unwisely left her down by the pier (below the present temple) to be escorted into the city by soldiers. Assuming he didn't love her, the beautiful princess stayed put in the boat and committed suicide. Wat Phanom Choeng is consequently very popular with Chinese pilgrims, and does a roaring trade in Chinese

100

fortunes. In my case, not so fortunate—'Buddha say', translated my guide, 'you must get sick … you must lose money … it's not so good, you know!' If you're lucky, you may catch the Khon classical dancers performing here; otherwise, just soak in the moody, meditative, incense-laden atmosphere. High up on the temple walls, armies of tiny bronze Buddhas can be dimly made out, tucked away in little niches.

Wat Chai Wattanaram

From Phanom Choeng, walk down to the river pier. Here you can liberate a caged tortoise for 10B (i.e. make some merit) and call in on the Chinese Shrine dedicated to the ill-fated princess. From the pier, you can hire boats for river-trips right round the city perimeter. For best use of your time, I would recommend a short 1½-hour return trip (300B for one to ten people), dropping in on two riverside temples. Ask first for **Wat Chai Wattanaram**, built in 1630 by King Prasad Thong. Recent renovation has deprived this isolated, rarely visited, temple of some of its earlier overgrown charm—but it still has great atmosphere. The Khmer-style central *prang*, together with various smaller *prangs* in the same style, are strongly reminiscent of Anghor Wat (the famous old Cambodian sanctuary). By way of interesting contrast, the frontal *chedis* are Ceylonese-influenced Lanna Thai-style. This is also one of the few extant temples in Ayutthaya where you can still see fragments of original stucco designs clinging to the walls.

Wat Buddaisawan

Returning downriver to the pier, call in on **Wat Buddaisawan**. Built in 1353, this marks the spot where Ramatibodi I resided before founding Ayutthaya. The inner compound is sometimes closed—if so, ask a novice to open it up. It houses a beautiful Cambodian-style central *prang*, with colourful porcelain pieces embedded in its stucco exterior, much like Wat Arun at Bangkok. Eight sets of double boundary stones ring the main *bot*, denoting a major temple under royal patronage. Also known as the 'temple of mangy dogs', Wat Buddaisawan is full of scabby hounds trooping in and out with 'offerings' of dead owls and mice. There's also a glitzy collection of renovated Buddhas, contrasting violently with the surrounding red-brick ruins.

Wat Phra Ram, Wat Mahathat and Wat Na-Phra Mane

Off the boat, take a *tuk-tuk* over to **Wat Phra Ram** on the west of town. This temple marks the site of Ramatibodi's cremation, and was built by his son in 1369. It has twice since been completely restored. Again, there's a nice ancient atmosphere, and you can climb halfway up the main *prang* (adorned with *naga* snakes, *garuda* birds and Buddhas) for good views. Following Ramatibodi's lead, many of Ayutthaya's nobility have been cremated here. Next, take a short ride into the town centre to visit **Wat Mahathat**, built by Ramesuan in 1384. The main *prang*, destroyed by the Burmese, was later discovered to contain a buried treasure chest and a precious relic of Buddha. Look for the famous Bo tree, just inside the gate—it has a stone Buddha's head ensconced in its roots. Then climb the central *chedi* for fine views over to **Wat Rajburana**'s impressive Khmer *prangs*—this saves you paying 20B to see them close up. Finish off at the old 13th-century Wat Na Phra Mane to the northwest of town, overlooking the Lopburi River. This is a real rarity—the only temple left untouched by the Burmese in 1767. They left it alone because, in a previous encounter, one of their kings blew himself up with a cannon here. Inside, you'll find the most beautiful surviving Buddha figure in Ayutthaya. Richly ornamented, and decked out in royal raiment, it looks every inch a king. Nearby, you'll find a large, very serene, granite-stone Buddha. This one is very ancient—some 1300 years old—and was donated to the Ayutthaya kings by the head of the Buddhist order in Sri Lanka. The temple itself has recently been restored, but the main *bot* still has its original wood-roof, the peristyle of which is decorated with Hindu-style *garuda* and Vishnu motifs.

Museums
For those with any remaining time and energy, Ayutthaya also has two museums—the **Chao Sam Phraya** ('National') museum near the centre of town, which bears a charming resemblance to a 19th-century stately home; and the **Phra Ratchawong Chang Kasem** ('Palace') museum to the northeast of town. Both are open 9 am to 4 pm, Wed–Sun, admission 10B. The Palace museum is the more interesting, and sells a decent 20B map-guide of Ayutthaya. The same guide, issued by the Fine Arts Department, is also sold at Wat Mahathat. All temples sites in Ayutthaya, by the way, are open 8 am to 5 pm daily.

SHOPPING
Fake antiques, synthetic gems and cheap bronze artefacts are peddled (vigorously) outside the temples. If you do want a cheap *garuda* or Kali figure to put up on your mantelpiece back home, don't pay over 40B for it. For something authentically Ayutthayan, visit the bamboo and wickerware shops in Wat Phanom Choeng Square. There's a wide selection of attractive bags and baskets here, well-made and very reasonably priced.

WHERE TO STAY   (tel prefix 035)
Moderate
Second-time visitors to Ayutthaya will be glad to know that it has finally acquired a few good hotels. The **U Thong Inn** on Rotchana Road (tel 242618) is the best in town with rooms averaging 400–600B, more for their luxury rooms and suites. The **Sri Samai** in Chao Phrom Rd (tel 251104) has clean, bright rooms at 180B fan, 400B air-con, and a restaurant which is a pleasure to eat in. All the rooms have Western toilets too.

Inexpensive
The **U Thong** (tel 251136) and the **Cathay** (tel 251562) guest houses on U Thong Rd, by contrast, offer musty, dusty fan rooms at 90B single, 120B double. The U Thong is smellier, the Cathay noisier. At either, *farangs* often end up on the top floor—a wearisome climb after a hard day's *wat*-spotting. **B.J.** at 16/7 Naresuan Rd gets far better mentions; rooms are 120B and it has good food, bike rental and a nice family.

EATING OUT
The civilized **Tevaraj** restaurant down by the railway station is the favourite eating place of local Thais. Food is mid-priced (most dishes around 40 to 60B) and superb. Things to try include *Goong Yai Cao* (grilled freshwater lobster), *Gai Poo Kao Fai* (Chicken in

Volcano) and—the tour de force—*Kai Dum Toon Yajin* (Black-skin Chicken with Chinese Herbs). Eat in pleasant open-air comfort, amid luxuriant palm gardens, and enjoy impromptu live music performed by 'talented' diners. All this, and unbelievable service too. There are a a few **Floating Restaurants**, by the Pridi Damrong Bridge on the Pasak River. These are popular, if overpriced. For quick snacks while waiting for a train, there's **Tip-Pa-Rat Restaurant**, just outside the station. It has an English menu, Western-style fare, and ice-cream. The **Bakery House** in Chao Phrom Rd (opposite Si Samai Hotel) is where to go for continental breakfast and tasty cakes and pastries. For cheap whip-up wok meals, there's either **Hua Raw market** near the Chan Kasem Palace pier, or the **market by the bus-rank** in Chao Phrom Rd.

Bang Pa In

Bang Pa In is a charming little island in the Chao Phya river, just 20 km south of Ayutthaya. The summer residence of Thai kings since Ayutthaya times, it's worth seeing for its exquisite assortment of royal buildings in various architectural styles—Thai, Chinese and European—which together make up the **Bang Pa In Palace**. King Chulalongkorn built this turn-of-the-century summer palace after visiting Europe and falling in love with its architecture. He situated it right by the river, providing him and his queen with easy access when they came visiting by royal barge. Sadly, it was whilst on her way to Bang Pa In that Queen Sunandakumaviratn and her children died so tragically when their boat capsized. Chulalongkorn's touching tribute, expressing his inconsolable grief, can be found in the beautiful palace gardens.

GETTING THERE
By Bus
From Ayutthaya (Chao Phrom Rd bus-stop), minibuses run to Bang Pa In at regular intervals, fare 6B. There are also buses from Bangkok's Northern Bus Terminal, every 20 minutes from 5.40 am to 7.40 pm, fare 13B. This is a one-hour trip.

By Train
From Ayutthaya (3B, 3rd class) and from Bangkok (12B, 3rd class) there are regular trains to Bang Pa In. At the station, you'll need a 2B *songthaew* to the palace.

By River
Boats ply back and forth between Ayutthaya and Bang Pa In every half-hour or so. It's a pleasant 40-minute trip, and the one-way fare is 150B. Boats sing out with kitsch tunes like 'Oh, I wish I wuz in Dixie!' when they're ready to depart.

WHAT TO SEE
If visiting Bang Pa In as a side-trip from Ayutthaya (a common option), note that the Palace is open from 8.30 am to 3.30 pm only, and is closed all day on Monday and Friday. However, if you're only coming for the famous Thai-style pavilion in the middle of the lake—the one depicted on so many postcards and posters—then you can see this, and

patrol the outer grounds too, till 6 daily. Thai picnic people hang out here till late at weekends—buying 8B loaves of bread to feed the 'shadow' fish in the pavilion lake. The larger variety of these fish weigh up to 40 kg, and they're *very* hungry—so don't fall in.

Admission to the palace grounds is 10B. Within, the central attraction is **Phra Thinang Wehat Chamrun**, a Chinese-style building commonly known as the Peking Palace. It's the only building in the compound open to visitors, and is a firm tourist favourite. There's a priceless collection of jade and porcelain (mainly Ming), within, and a twee topiary garden of quaint clipped elephants in the grounds. It's a very romantic spot, much favoured by Thai honeymooning couples. The nearby **Museum** has interesting displays of antiques and ceramics, and is closed on Mondays. Across the river, to the south of the palace grounds, is **Wat Niwega Thamprawat**, a Buddhist temple built in the style of a European Christian church by Rama V. A fascinating blend of English, French and German architecture, this 'church' is situated on a small island, reached by a cable-car ride over the river. Some of the monks give guided tours in English, speaking with pride of their unique *wat*—stained-glass windows, belfry and all. You can swim in the river—at sunset, it's quite a memorable experience.

LOPBURI

Lopburi lies 145 km north of Bangkok, and is one of Thailand's most important historical centres. Recent archaeological finds suggest that the first civilized city here—Lavo—was founded as early as the 4th century AD, though previous to this the area probably received a new Stone Age settlement. The early Dvaravati rulers of Lopburi were replaced in the 10th century by the Khmers, who made it one of their most important capitals. As the old Lavo culture was swept away, the Khmers built an abundance of monuments—the Hindu shrine of Prang Khaek, the Kala Shrine of San Phra Kan, the Triple-spire Shrine of Sam Yot etc—many of which remain near-intact today. In the 13th century, the Sukhothai Thais ousted the Khmers, and the town entered a period of decline. Only 400 years later, when a Dutch naval blockade forced King Narai of Ayutthaya to make Lopburi his second capital (1664), did its fortunes revive. Narai heavily fortified the town, and then brought in French architects to create a beautiful new complex of royal temples, palaces and buildings—in a unique mixture of Thai and European styles. Narai eventually became so enamoured of Lopburi that he spent nine months of every year here and died in the Grand Palace, his finest achievement, in 1688.

Today, Lopburi is rather the 'poor relation' of Thailand's northern temple towns, receiving far fewer visitors than Sukhothai or Ayutthaya. It is not geared to tourism, and people's initial impression of the old fortified town—with its looming Khmer temples employed as traffic islands and its rooftops bristling with TV aerials—is rarely enthusiastic. Nevertheless, it's one of those places which quickly grows on you. Lopburi people are incredibly hospitable and friendly—they'll show you round the sights, they'll point out the best bakeries and ice-cream parlours, and—if you're here in February for the annual 'Beauty Contest for Widows'—they'll probably fix you up with a local bride.

GETTING THERE

By Bus

There are buses to Lopburi every 15 minutes from Ayutthaya, and every 15–20 minutes (between 5 am and 8.30 pm) from Bangkok's Northern Terminal. From Bangkok, it's a 3 hour trip, costing 32B non air-con, 60B air-con. There are also buses to Lopburi from Kanchanaburi, via Suphanburi (3 hours; fare 21B).

By Rail

From Bangkok's Hualamphong station, there are 7 trains daily to Lopburi—one Express (leaving 6 pm, arriving 8.20 pm), four Rapid (leaving 6.40 am, 3, 8 and 10 pm) and two Ordinary (7.05 am and 8.30 am). Basic fares are 111B 1st class, 57B 2nd class, 28B 3rd class. There are also regular trains from Ayutthaya—a 1¹⁄₂-hour journey, costing 13B in 3rd class. If you don't want to stay overnight in Lopburi, come in on an early-morning train from Ayutthaya, look around for a few hours (leave bags in station cloakroom, open 4 am to 9 pm), then hop on a late train (choice of 5.28 and 8.24 pm) up to Chiang Mai (arriving 5.15 am and 7.25 am respectively); or, if carrying on to Sukhothai, choose from the 9.03 am, 9.57 am or 11.33 am trains out to Phitsanulok.

TOURIST INFORMATION

No tourist office, but the **Travellers Drop-in Centre** (cf. Where to Stay) has some maps and printed literature.

WHAT TO SEE

Lopburi divides into the old town, with its Khmer ruins, to the north; and the new town, with its nightclubs and discos (and nothing else) 2 km to the south. *Songthaews* charge 5B for short in-town journeys, and stop running at 8 pm. After that, if you want to take in a club or a restaurant down at Sakeo Circle (in the new town) it's a 20B *tuk-tuk* ride from old Lopburi.

Freelance guides hang about outside the major sights—they're an agreeable lot, who don't want money, just perhaps to share a meal or a drink with you afterwards, and to practise their English. Richard, manager of Travellers Drop-in, is working hard towards a proper guide association, with English-speaking guides capable of providing a professional service to travellers.

What Phra Sri Ratana Mahathat

Not that a guide is essential in Lopburi—its few sights can be seen comfortably in a morning and on foot. If you arrive by train, the very first thing you're likely to see is **Wat Phra Sri Ratana Mahathat**, a large 12th-century Khmer shrine right outside the railway station. Many times restored, it's still the most impressive of Lopburi's ruins, conveying a real sense of ruined splendour. Of the three original laterite *prangs*, only the tall central one now stands. It is decorated with beautiful stucco motifs. To the east of it are the large *viharn* and pavilion added in the reign of King Narai. Scattered round the rest of the compound are several interesting *chedis* and *prangs* of different styles (mainly Sukhothai and Ayutthaya), often with niches housing stucco Buddha images. Surprisingly, the rather haphazard restoration achieved here in recent years has done little to

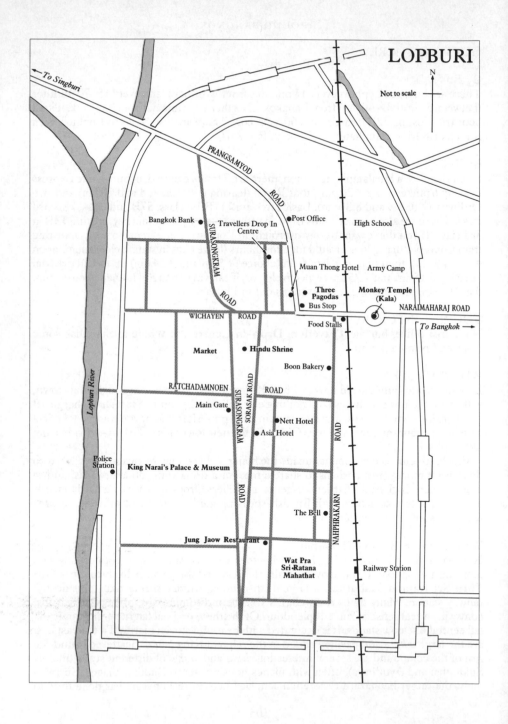

diminish the grandeur of this structure, which was created at the height of Khmer power. This aside, the 20B admission fee levied is steep—many travellers just take photos from the roadside.

Phra Narai Ratchanives
Serious sightseeing should start at **Phra Narai Ratchanives,** or King Narai's Palace. This was built over a period of 12 years (1665 to 1677) and was left deserted shortly after Narai's death in 1688. Though restored by Mongkut in the mid-19th century, time has not been kind to this once-majestic structure. Just past the entrance, to the left, you can just make out the king's elephant stables and royal reception hall. Most other buildings are ruined hulks, and the grounds have been turned into a picnic park. But one section has been set aside for the **Lopburi National Museum,** and this is worth a visit. There's an excellent permanent collection here which describes—via sculpture, art pieces, lintels, votive tablets, etc—the three main cultural periods of Thailand's central plains— Dvaravati (Mon), Khmer (Lopburi-influenced) and Central Plains city-states. All exhibits are well-presented and labelled in English. Outside, there's an odd **open-air museum,** featuring a number of headless and peg-leg Buddhas staked to the lawn and bordered with flowers. Admission to Palace (and museum) is 10B. Opening times are 9 am to 12 noon, 1 to 4 pm, Wed–Sun.

Chao Phraya Wichayen
A short stroll away, **Chao Phraya Wichayen** was built for the first French ambassador to Thailand (Chevalier de Chaumont), and later became famous as the residence of Narai's Greek minister, Constantine Phaulkon. The many brick buildings within its walls—a Roman Catholic chapel to the south, the Thai-European-style ambassador's house to the north—are rather too derelict to merit the 15B admission charge.

The landmark of Lopburi, **Phra Prang Sam Yot** (Three Pagodas), lies only 400 metres from the railway station. Constructed in the Lopburi style, its three laterite/sandstone *prangs*—symbolizing the Hindu trinity of Brahma, Vishnu and Shiva—presently decorate the back of the 500B currency note. Converted to a Buddhist temple in Narai's reign, some Hindu motifs can still be made out on the stucco-decorated spires. For some light relief, finish off across the railway track at **San Phra Kahn,** the Kala (Hindu god of death) shrine famous for its hordes of Samae monkeys. These monkeys are held in high regard by local devotees for their human habit of burying their own dead. No one has yet found a dead monkey at this site.

RECREATION
Lopburi is a well-known centre of classical Thai dance and music. **Nartasin School of Art** attracts students from Ayutthaya, Saraburi and neighbouring provinces, training them for professional careers as dancers in big hotels or tourist 'culture shows'. To visit, take a blue *songthaew* (fare 2B) from Three Pagodas bus-stop down to Sakeo Circle in Lopburi new town. From here, it's a 10-minute walk west to a small bridge, 600 metres past which lies the school. Best time of day to show up is mid-morning—if you don't catch a dance class, you'll certainly hear some good live music. Ask permission to use cameras and tape-recorders.

Below Sakeo Circle (ask your bus to put you off there) is a good outdoor swimming pool. On a hot day, it's well worth the 25B admission. It's open 10 am to 8 pm daily, and women must wear full costumes—and caps. Next to Sakeo Circle bus-stop is **Chao Phraya Nightclub**, with a popular disco on Sunday nights, and good live music every other evening. In the old town, the **Bell** (near station) has a good late-night bar, open till 2.30 am. Behind the Travellers Drop-in Centre, there's a fun snooker club—where smoothie Thais hustle unwary *farangs* at 50B a game.

SHOPPING
There are some good little boutiques, selling fabrics, materials and cheap clothing, opposite the Hindu shrine in Sopasak Rd.

WHERE TO STAY   (tel prefix 036)
Inexpensive
Lopburi is a low-profile tourist centre, and accommodation is thin. In the old town, the **Asia Lopburi** (tel 411892) in Sorasak Rd has fan-rooms from 120B, air-con rooms (with condom dispensers in toilets) at 350B. This is a clean place, geared mainly to Thais. The **Nett Hotel** (tel 411738), in a small *soi* behind the Asia, has slightly better rooms (at the same price) but is not so friendly. There are several cheap and nasty budget places, mainly in Nahphrakarn Rd—the red-light area. The **Muang Thong** (tel 411036), overlooking Three Pagodas, has adequate rooms at 100–140B and interesting roof views. The **Travellers Drop-in Centre** at 34 Wichayen Rd, Soi 3 Muang, is the pick of the bunch. It's run by Richard, a young English teacher, who rents out clean, cosy rooms at 50–80B and lets guests cook their own food. He invites foreign travellers to make friends with his Thai pupils, and to join in English lessons. This is great fun ('What has Frank been doing in Chiang Mai?' asks Richard. 'Frank . . . has . . . been . . . spending . . . a . . . LOT . . . OF . . . MONEY . . . in . . . Chiang Mai!' chorus the perceptive class). Richard is a mine of local information, and his students enjoy taking foreigners out on sightseeing tours.

EATING OUT
To enjoy quality Thai-Chinese food at under 100B a head, try **Jun Jaow** (corner of Ratchadamnoen and Surasongkram roads) or **Anodard** (south of Sakeo circle) restaurants. The friendly **Phikulkaeo** opposite the station is good for cheap, reliable dishes like sweet and sour pork or fried shrimp with cauliflower (both 20B). There are lots of open-air food stalls in Nahphrakarn Rd, and a number of happy-happy disco cafés. The large market north of the palace, just off Ratchadamnoen and Surasongkram roads, is especially good for inexpensive Thai-style snacks. A small indoor market near Travellers Drop-in, behind Nahphrakarn Rd, has a wide selection of 'meals', also an amazing waffle stand. Just above the good Chinese-Thai restaurant at the Asia Hotel, there's a marvellous **Foremost** ice-cream parlour. **Boon Bakery** in Nahphrakarn Rd offers continental breakfasts, nice cakes and soothing sounds.

KHAO YAI NATIONAL PARK

Khao Yai is the biggest and the best of Thailand's national parks. Set up in 1962, it was also the first. *Khao Yai* means 'big mountain', but actually encompasses three major mountains and numerous smaller peaks. Comprising over 2000 sq km of tropical jungle, dense forest, rolling meadows and green hills, it stretches across four provinces at a cool, refreshing elevation of around 800 metres (2500 feet). Khao Yai's vast acreage of deciduous and evergreen jungle-forest supports nearly all of Thailand's 195 species of protected wildlife—including tigers, elephants, deer, monkeys, bears, wild oxen, silver pheasants, woodpeckers, great hornbills and butterflies—as well as innumerable species of wild flowers, orchids, trees and exotic plants. Honeycombed with hiking trails, it's an ideal spot for naturalists or for anyone interested in seeing Thailand's flora and fauna.

Khao Yai is most pleasant between November and February, when the climate is fairly dry and cool. The banyan tree flowers in this season, attracting a lot of monkeys. And elephants are a common sight, coming down to the saltlick north of the forest for water. However, if you want to see an Amazonian-type rain forest in its full, burgeoning splendour, visit Khao Yai during the rainy months of July to September. Try to avoid weekends—the park is only 200 km from Bangkok, and is very popular as a picnic spot for Thais eager to escape the hot, busy capital. Each Friday and Saturday, they arrive in hordes—they occupy every bungalow, they have a jolly party, they stroll down to the nearest waterfall (rarely further) and on Sunday night they go home. During the week (your best time to visit), the park is returned to the animals.

GETTING THERE
From Bangkok's Northern Terminal, two air-con buses (7 am and 9 am) leave daily for Khao Yai. It's a 3-hour trip, costing 74B. Returning to Bangkok, there's often only one bus a day from Khao Yai, departing at 3 pm.

WHAT TO SEE
Because much of Khao Yai is damp, dense jungle you can't—unlike say, the open gameparks of Africa—count on seeing anything here. Yes, there are around 200 wild elephants and 20 tigers in the area (plus many bear, gibbon and deer) but if you spot any of these it'll be a bonus. What there *is* to enjoy is a rich variety of birds and butterflies, and the fascinating sights and sounds of an authentic tropical rain forest.

If you're here to spot animals, or simply want to know more about the park, contact Khao Yai's one and only guide—friendly young Po, who has lived and breathed Khao Yai for the past 17 years. He can be contacted at the **Information Centre**, near the visitors' centre, and charges between 100B and 300B a day for guided tours, the price depending on the size of your party.

But the good thing about Khao Yai is that you don't really need a guide. A series of good trails have been marked (i.e. colour-coded trees, set apart at 20–30 metre intervals) which are all easy to follow. Thus, if you walk over 30 metres and can't find a colour marker, you simply return to the last marked tree and try a different direction. All of the four recommended trails can be done in one to three hours, and can be extended or shortened by crossing over from one coded path to another. Trail 1 (red paint) is 4 km long, plus 2 km down the road back to the visitors' centre, and takes 2–3 hours; trail 2 (blue) is a 3.5 km walk through (mainly) grassland, and takes 2½ hours; trail 4 (yellow) is 2.5 km long and takes around 1½ hours; trail 4 (blue) extends 3.5 km, plus 1 km back down to the visitors' centre, and takes around 2½ hours. The most popular walk starts on trail 1 and loops right onto trail 3. At the junction of these two paths, there's often a group of gibbons high up in the trees—listen out for loud whoops, their way of marking out territory.

An early morning walk is nice and cool, and there are lots of birds to be seen from around 5 am to 9 am. Another good thing about Khao Yai is that several trails lead along the edge of the forest, which makes spotting birdlife quite easy. Gibbons and monkeys are most frisky in the early morning too. A pleasant short outing, if you're staying near the visitors' centre, is down to the small suspension bridge at **Gong Gheow Water-fall**.

Two warnings—*always* keep to the paths, and *never* go off on your own. It's very thick jungle, and people have wandered off in the past and never returned. The trails are best negotiated in small groups of 2–4 people. Walk slowly and quietly, keeping alert to any sounds or movement and you may be rewarded with sightings of wildlife. During the wet season, take precautions against leeches. These little bloodsuckers lurk on the trails and can be very distracting—all too often, hikers spend more time squinting anxiously down at their feet than admiring the wonders of the forest. For near-total protection, apply a liberal coating of insect repellent to feet, socks and shoes—any leeches that get through this barrier, you can just flick off. There's no need for applications of salt or for smouldering cigarette butts.

Most animal life here is nocturnal and your best chance of spotting elephant, tiger and large game is in the cool of the night, when they are most active. The big thing to do at Khao Yai is a night jeep safari. Armed with a powerful spotlight and a trained guide, jeeps set out from both TAT and Gong Gheow bungalows (around 15B per person in a large group; but 250B if on your own) and patrol the saltlicks in search of wild elephants etc. Best views are from the jeep roof—you don't see too much down below.

Not everybody comes to Khao Yai for jungle walks and wildlife-spotting. Some play golf. The park offers Thailand's highest golf course—a superb 18-hole links, with club-house. Green fees are 80B (weekdays) to 140B (weekends). To reserve a game, contact TAT (tel 2825209).

There's a moth-eaten museum down at the visitors' centre, with a few stuffed heads and various things preserved in bottles. It's open 9 am to 5 pm every day except Saturday, when it shows an ancient BBC archive film and stays open till 8.30. The small restaurant nearby does reasonable food.

WHERE TO STAY

Moderate–Inexpensive
All accommodation should be advance-booked (especially for weekends), to avoid disappointment. TAT's **Motor Lodge Bungalows** (tel Bangkok 2825209 for reservations) sleep two people and cost 700B. National Park **Gong Gheow Bungalows** (same tel no.) sleep four, and cost 600–700B. There's also some 4-bedded **dormitory** accommodation at Gong Gheow which, at 100B per person, is the best budget option. In the dry season though, you can sleep out with the animals in cheap (10B) and basic jungle huts. To book, contact Po at the Information Centre.

PATTAYA

In just 20 years, Pattaya has mushroomed from a sleepy fishing village to the premier beach resort in Southeast Asia. Today, this wide crescent bay on the Gulf of Thailand, 147 km from Bangkok, attracts thousands of holidaymakers from home and abroad every week. With its high-class Western hotels and restaurants, its discos and bars, its wide range of water-sports and entertainments—not forgetting its miles of clean beaches and pretty offshore coral islands—Pattaya is totally tuned into the package-holiday market. It's hardly like Thailand at all—more like Blackpool or Surfer's Paradise, with its fast-food houses, kiss-me-quick hats and elephant rides up the beach. But if Pattaya is something of a circus, a lot of people do enjoy the show. Especially single men, who constitute some 70% of tourists here. Pattaya is still an international sex capital, with some two-thirds of its 55,000 female population currently engaged in 'entertainment'-related activities. If you haven't seen any middle-aged businessmen with teenage Thai girls in tow in Bangkok, you'll certainly see them here. If you're a man on your own, expect to be hassled—the one Thai phrase you'll have to learn is 'May ow' or 'I don't want you/it/anything, thanks'. If you're a couple or a family, you could find better places to be. But if you want a European holiday in Thailand—with all Western comforts, top-class seafood, and Benidorm-style entertainments—look no further.

As Thailand's 'Riviera', Pattaya was once very expensive, but now, either because it's secure of its mass tourism, or simply because people in the past refused to pay the inflated prices, costs of food, transport and accommodation are on a par with other resort destinations, and in some cases even cheaper than Bangkok. However, there's still the usual double price-standard on major holidays and long week-ends. Budget travellers often can't afford it.

Pattaya's high season is October to February. It's especially busy over Christmas and New Year, when you'll be lucky to find a sleeping berth on the beach. September and March are quieter, cheaper months—many hotels offer generous low-season discounts.

GETTING THERE

By Bus
From Bangkok's Eastern Terminal, non air-con buses leave for Pattaya every 35 minutes from 5.25 am to 9 pm. The fare is 29B, and it's a $2^1/_2$-hour journey. Air-con buses leave at 40-minute intervals from 6.30 am till 10 pm and cost 50B. Major Bangkok hotels also run air-con buses at regular intervals for 150–200B. Note that buses also run from Bangkok's Northern Terminal every 45 minutes from 5.30 am to 7 pm for 53B. Special transfer buses run direct from Bangkok airport to Pattaya at 9 am, 12 noon, and 7 pm. Tickets are 180B, and are sold at the Thai Limousine desk in Don Muang airport.

From Pattaya (N. Pattaya Rd bus station), there are air-con buses to Bangkok's Eastern Terminal every half-hour (fare 50B), and air-con buses at regular intervals to Bangkok airport (180B). Thai Airways also has a minibus service to the airport throughout the day (180B, more if you book through your hotel).

Buses now run from Pattaya to Chiang Mai (3 and 6 pm, 330B), Chiang Rai (12.30 and 4 pm, 330B) and the North Eastern towns of Khon Khaen and Nong Khai (ordinary bus at 5.30 and 8.30 pm, 143B; air-con bus at 8 and 9 pm, 258B).

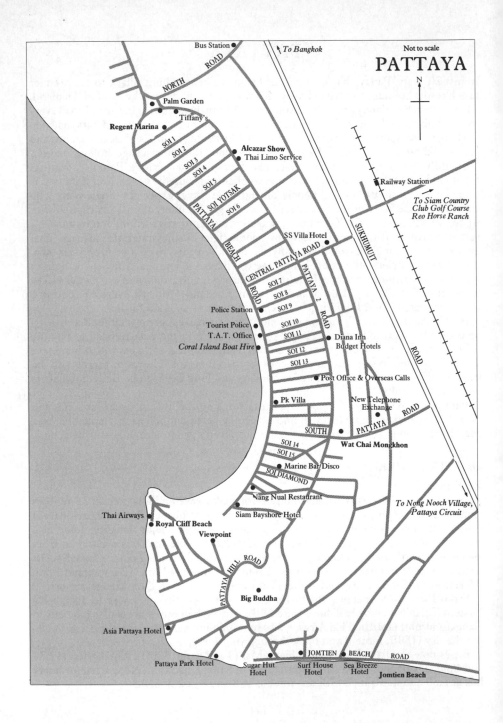

Bus Station ●   ↑ To Bangkok   Not to scale

PATTAYA

NORTH ROAD

● Palm Garden
● Tiffany's
Regent Marina ●

SOI 1
SOI 2
SOI 3
SOI 4
SOI 5
SOI 6

Alcazar Show
● Thai Limo Service

SOI YOTSAK

Railway Station ■

To Siam Country
Club Golf Course
Reo Horse Ranch

SS Villa Hotel ●

PATTAYA BEACH ROAD

CENTRAL PATTAYA ROAD

SUKHUMVIT

PATTAYA 2 ROAD

SOI 7
SOI 8
Police Station ●   SOI 9
Tourist Police ●   SOI 10
T.A.T. Office ●   SOI 11
Coral Island Boat Hire ● SOI 12
SOI 13

● Diana Inn
Budget Hotels

● Post Office & Overseas Calls

● Pk Villa

New Telephone
Exchange

ROAD

SOUTH   PATTAYA

SOI 14
SOI 15
● Marine Bar/Disco
SOI DIAMOND

● Wat Chai Mongkhon

● Nang Nual Restaurant
Siam Bayshore Hotel ●

Thai Airways ●
Royal Cliff Beach ●
Viewpoint ●

To Nong Nooch Village,
Pattaya Circuit

PATTAYA HILL ROAD

● Big Buddha

Asia Pattaya Hotel ●

JOMTIEN ● BEACH ROAD
Pattaya Park Hotel   Sugar Hut   Surf House   Sea Breeze
Hotel   Hotel   Hotel   **Jomtien Beach**

By Train

From Bangkok's Hualamphong station two trains a day go to Pattaya at 6.20 and 11.25 am, and vice versa at 10.50 am and 5.57 pm, with occasionally either a 10-minute delay or change at Chachoengsao. The fare is 29B one way.

By Sea

A daily hydrofoil service operates between Bangkok (from the Menam Hotel, New Road, Yannawa) and Hua Hin, via Pattaya, leaving Bangkok at 7 and 8 am, and arriving in Pattaya at 9.30 and 10.30 m. Check departure details beforehand (2074 Thai Intertransport Building, New Road, Yannawa, tel 2919613).

TOURIST INFORMATION

TAT Tourist Office, 382/1 Beach Rd, S. Pattaya (tel 428750 and 429113) has helpful English-speaking staff, hands out lots of information (including current hotel listings), and issues a fortnightly *Pattaya Tourist Guide* magazine, full of current news and events.

WHAT TO SEE

Pattaya roughly divides into North Pattaya (big hotels, massage parlours, fairly quiet), South Pattaya (mid-range/cheap hotels, bars and restaurants, action-packed), and Jomtien Beach to the far south (expensive resort accommodation, good swimming and water-sports). The cheapest way of getting round are *songthaews*. These make continual counter-clockwise circuits of the main bay area, from Beach Rd round to Pattaya 2 Rd. The standard fare is 5B, but you'll have to bargain very hard to get it. Outside of their 'route', *songthaews* charge more or less what they can get. (Once you're familiar with the town, get on *without* speaking to the driver and press the buzzer overhead when you want to get off—that way you haven't 'chartered' the vehicle and you pay only the standard 5B.) The same goes for air-con taxis. Many people don't bother with local transport, and hire motorbikes (250–500B a day) from hotels. Motorbike taxis also hang around on street corners—10B for a short ride.

Local sights are few. A pleasant motorbike excursion is up **Pattaya Hill** to visit the Buddhist temple at the top. There's a large seated Buddha here—a recent renovation, nothing special—surrounded by seven quaint mini-Buddhas, one for each day of the week. Nearby, there's a small Chinese temple, decorated with garish carnival figures. The hill provides fine views down over the main bay area.

Inland sights are covered by air-con minibus tours, offered by most hotels and travel agents in Pattaya. These are usually full-day excursions, costing around 250—300B per person. Attractions visited include **Wat Yannasangwararam**, a new temple built in a modern style of classic Thai architecture. Meditation courses are held here daily at 6 am and 6 pm. Three km away is **Nong Nooch Village**—a prettily landscaped country resort, 15 km out of Pattaya, with a plastic culture show (tickets can be bought at the office on Central Pattaya Rd, opposite Nipa Lodge Hotel—200B for morning tour, 9–12, 250B afternoon show 1—5.30, which includes a dance and Thai-boxing show). At **Elephant Village**, about 6 km out of town on the road to the Siam Country Club, elephants are decked out in warrior gear, rolling logs and doing tourist tricks (including games of football); contact Novotel Tropicana (tel 428645). **Mini Siam** on Sukhumvit Rd, 3 km from Central Pattaya Rd, has replicas in miniature of Thailand's major temples

113

and sights, together with a few models of European monuments—best left for when you've had your fill of sun, sea, bars or boobs; **Pattaya Park** (near Jomtien beach) has water slides, whirlpools and family-style frolics.

Some 15 km out of Pattaya town on the highway to Rayong is **Bira International Circuit**, a racing track for cars and motorbikes, with events at weekends; you can also hire vehicles to do the circuit if you have an International Driving Licence. For information call 5877448.

An hour's drive out of Pattaya (and 100 km from Bangkok), the town of **Chonburi** holds bi-monthly **Water-Buffalo Racing Competitions**. These are great fun, and well worth going out of your way for. Details and dates aren't well advertised, and you'll need to check with the TAT office, or look for clues in the *Bangkok Post* (though some Pattaya hotels are clued into it, with set tours). Coming from Bangkok, it's a 1½-hour bus trip from the Eastern Terminal. The event usually runs from 9 am to noon, and features live music, cheap eats, a huge open market with fairground, and a real party atmosphere.

If you've got kids in tow, the beach resort of Bang Saen, between Pattaya and Chonburi, has the **Marine Science Aquarium** and **Ocean World** water amusement park. Some 20 km inland from here is **Khao Khiao Open Zoo** in a pretty hillside location. Reckon on a full day if you want to fit in both aquarium and zoo.

Offshore islands are numerous, and are worth visiting for their amazing variety of tropical fish and beautiful live coral formations. Glass-bottom boat trips run out twice daily—at 9.30 and 11.30 am—to the coral island of **Koh Larn**. Tickets are sold for 200B from the booth just below TAT office in Beach Rd, or for 280B from large hotels. The cost of the tour includes a good seafood lunch. The snorkelling equipment provided is poor, so it's best to hire some of your own. The Siren Bar organizes three simple round trips a day to Koh Larn for 50B. There's no accommodation on the island, but there are a number of restaurants and shops. A number of travel agencies offer less touristy trips to offshore islands like **Koh Sak** and **Koh Pai**, a Thai naval zone; daily boat charters work out at an average 1500B per person; overnight and week-end trips are available. Further south, the island of **Koh Khram** is within a restricted naval area and visiting is not allowed.

RECREATION

Pattaya *is* recreation. There's always something going on here—motorsports events, windsurfing competitions, dove-singing contests, game-fishing tournaments or sand-castle free-for-alls. I arrived during the annual Elephant Fashion Show. This included a tipsy tray-waiters' contest, a bellboy luggage-carrying obstacle course, and one hundred chambermaids making the world's largest bed. TAT carries details of all forthcoming events.

Pattaya's wide range of sports and recreational facilities are mostly water-borne. The place to go for water-sports is Jomtien Beach, 2 km south of Pattaya Bay, which proudly describes itself as a 'No Tourist Irritation Area'. Here, you can arrange **Water-Skiing** (800–1000B), **Windsurfing** (150—200B per hour), **Parasailing** (250B), **Catamarans** (300–350B per hour), **Water-Scooters** (205B per hour) and **Laser Sail-boats**—'easy man's windsurfing' (at around 500B an hour). All these prices are low season, and can easily double at weekends. Whenever you go, bargain for discounts.

Scuba-Diving takes place at offshore dive sites, and costs between 900 and 1500B a day. Some reliable outfits are **Seafari Dive Shop** at the Royal Garden Resort, Beach Rd (tel 428126), **Dave's Divers Den**, Soi 6 Yodsak N. Pattaya Beach Rd (tel 423486) and **Steve's Dive Shop**, Beach Rd (tel 428392). These offer tuition up to PADI and NAUI licences. Several big hotels offer free scuba-diving lessons in their swimming pools.

Land-based recreations include **Tennis** at the courts of 20 major hotels (contact TAT for listing) for 200–250B an hour, **Golf** at any of the four good courses in the area (green fees have shot up recently—the average is 500B, 150B extra for caddie—but the most expensive course charges 1600B per person; contact Mike at Caesar's Bar, nr Beach Rd police station, S. Pattaya, or Brian at California Bar, S. Pattaya, to arrange a game); **Bowling and Snooker** at Pattaya Bowl, next to Regent Marina Hotel, N. Pattaya (tel 429466), Palace Bowl (Pattaya–Naklua Rd, tel 428026) and O.D. Bowl (Phra Tamnak Rd, South Pattaya); **Go Kart Racing** at Pattaya Kart Speedway, Pattaya 2 Rd (tel 423062) and **Archery** at Nong Nooch Village. The area round the Regent Marina also has many gyms, saunas and massage parlours.

NIGHTLIFE

After dark, Pattaya offers a different kind of 'recreation' altogether. North Pattaya has two famous nightclubs, presenting extravagant transvestite cabaret shows nightly. Of the two, **Tiffany's**, in Pattaya 2 Rd, is the original outfit—classier and more 'conservative'. The **Alcazar** ('Relief your Tension, and Get Stun to Sensation Spectacular!') offers more racy, topical entertainment. Both clubs charge the same—250B, including one free drink—and have shows at 7, 8.30, 10 pm and (Saturday only) 11.30 pm.

South Pattaya has a raucous, raunchy collection of brightly-lit bars, animal shows, cabarets, discos and restaurants along the 'strip' or 'Golden Mile' in Beach Rd. These places are a drinker's, reveller's and debaucher's dream come true, although no longer are they all-night joints; the police are cracking down as of late and most place have to close by 1 am. This of course means that the partying is more concentrated, not curtailed. I once asked a tourist official if there was anywhere on the strip where a man

Orchids at Nong Nooch

could enjoy a nice quiet drink without being hassled, and he said 'No'. Cruising down the strip at night—dodging giggling girls trying to drag you into bars, fending off gumless crones hawking sugared candies, and tripping over tiny tots selling weight-readings on the pavement—is quite fun. Everybody's very friendly, and you'll only get into trouble if you want to. An Australian resident commented, 'Pattaya is called the Big Shop—you can buy anything here, except a heart.' He was referring to Pattaya's bar-girls, a good-humoured lot with hearts of gold—not for sale at any price. They are far less 'professional' than their counterparts in Bangkok's Patpong. Before you pass any judgement, share a few drinks with them, and get to know something of their lives. Most are here, of course, to support large families living on the breadline in the drought-dry northeast or in the slums of Bangkok, although many are unaware of the real source of their daughter's income.

The club action starts just beyond Soi 14, where the enormous Pattaya Seafood Palace juts out into the bay on a pier. **Sirens Sea** offers the full works—**Thai Boxing** at 8 pm, complete with Elephant Show. Three parallel *sois* off the strip make up 'Pattayaland'; Pattayaland 1 and 2 have a collection of eateries and bars, many run by ex-pats, with names like 'The Kilted Piper', 'The Shamrock Pub', 'London Bridge'; they are more sedate places for people to gather and have a drink before (or after) tackling the 'real' action. Pattayaland 3 has a collection of gay bars with transvestite shows at 11 nightly. Further along, turn into Soi Diamond, and plunge into a vast, heaving complex of go-go bars, discos, seafood restaurants, blaring jukeboxes, and neon-lit street markets. At the 3 **Baby Go-Go** bars, drinks are fixed-price (90B) and off-stage antics are even funnier than the floorshow. Back on the strip, you'll find **Marine Bar and Disco Club**. This is *the* bar in Pattaya. At full capacity, there are up to 1000 girls here, with backdrop entertainments of Thai boxing, snake shows and giant wall videos. Most of the girls are freelance—they get up around 9 pm for breakfast, show up here about midnight, and work till well into the morning. Upstairs is the Marine's disco, the hottest scene in Pattaya. The place really jumps. As one *habitué* remarked, 'If you can't make it here you never will—I once saw an eighty-year-old in a wheel chair leave the place with a girl!' Drinks are 90B, and you're not allowed to stay unless you buy one. Later on, check out the nearby **Plaza**—this is a cheaper disco (drinks only 60B) with a great live band. The **Simon Cabaret** at the southern end of the strip offers the best transvestite show in South Pattaya. You can watch it for free from the opposite side of the road, or pay 50B to watch from the bar, or pay 90B for a front-row seat (and free drink). Showtime is 9.45 nightly, and it's a two-hour cabaret. Near Tiffany's, the **Palladium** disco complex is reportedly the biggest in Asia—it's certainly very popular with Thais and Europeans alike for its superb sound system and nine-frame video screen.

In between all this boogie-on-down, look in at the **C.K. Hotel** in Pattaya Rd 2. Here you'll find Lam Morrison, a brilliant Thai guitarist, heading up just about the best garage band in Thailand. He plays all the heroes of the '60s—like Hendrix, Cream, Free and Chuck Berry—with the same raw energy and nearly as well as the originals. He tunes up about 10.30 pm, and plays on till 1 am, or until one of his strings breaks.

SHOPPING
Apart from Bangkok's Chinatown, Pattaya is probably the best place in Thailand to buy gold. Well, there's such a local demand for it. Walking down the strip, you'll notice many

of the Thai girls wearing high-fashion gold jewellery. This metal matches their skin texture perfectly. If you see a local girl wearing something you like, it's often worth the price of a drink (40B) to find out where she bought it.

Chanthaburi
A lot of Pattaya jewellery is set with stones from **Chanthaburi**, a 2-hour drive east. This world-famous gem-mining centre is noted chiefly for its star-sapphires and rubies and the whole main street is lined with shops polishing, cutting and weighing out precious stones. You can pick up some real bargains here, especially if you can haggle in Thai. After shopping, visit the gem mines and factory (a 10-minute walk out of the new town), and nearby waterfalls. Chanthaburi also has the biggest church in Thailand. Some travel agents in Pattaya offer one-day trips, leaving at 7 am and returning at 6 pm for 750B, lunch included. You can also get here by bus from Ban Phe/Samet (1½ hours) and from Bangkok Eastern Terminal (4 hours).

Fashion boutiques and shops selling clothes, silks, handicrafts, coral and shells, jewellery and gemstones, are mostly in the main street of South Pattaya. Many large hotels have shopping arcades.

WHERE TO STAY (tel prefix 038)
Pattaya has no shortage of high-class accommodation. But in high season, and at weekends, it's a good idea to advance-book—the better hotels quickly fill up. Pattaya has broadened its horizons and no longers caters exclusively to the luxury bracket—you can find rooms from 20000B down to 200B. You'll be lucky if you can find anything under that—budget accommodation is in short supply. Room prices can fluctuate considerably between high and low season, and between weekdays and weekends. Except where otherwise stated, all prices quoted in this section are 'average' tariffs. Large hotels often offer 30% discounts (or more) during the May to September low season, and several cheaper places discount 50% if you stay a week or more. Bargain hard.

Major hotels often offer swimming pools, tennis and squash courts, jogging trails and watersports, bars and nightclubs, shopping arcades and maybe a private beach.

Luxury
Pattaya's most exclusive hotel—actually three hotels in one—is **Royal Cliff Beach Resort**, 175 Wisut-kasat Rd, Pattaya Hill (tel 428513; tx 85907 CLIFFEXTH). Its location is superb, and all of the 700-plus rooms (tariffs start at 1600B) have good views—either of the beach (4th floor), of the coast (from 8th floor), or of the mountains (9th floor and up). The Cliff has a private beach, eight pools, two restaurants (food could be better), and a host of sports and recreational facilities. In North Pattaya, there's the **Dusit Resort** at 240 Pattaya Beach Rd (tel 425611) with a sweeping vista of the bay, two pools and a choice of three restaurants (Chinese, Thai and European dishes), tennis courts, disco and indoor tropical garden. Rooms start at 2700B, suites from 6000B to 25,000B.

Expensive
Near the Royal Cliff, and just as comfortable, the **Asia Pattaya**, 352 Mu 10, Cliff Rd (tel 428602; tx Bangkok 85902 TH), has rooms from 1600B and a lovely pool, popular

nightclub and lots of modern charm. The **Siam Bayshore**, S. Pattaya Rd (tel 428678), is well-located for Pattayaland shopping and nightlife. Rooms here start at 1850B, and the best ones overlook the beautiful gardens. The **Montien Pattaya**, Beach Rd (tel 418155) and the **Regent Marina**, N. Pattaya Rd (tel 428015) both have nice rooms starting at around 1500B and top-notch facilities. The Marina has a very popular discotheque. Down at Jomtien, but no longer on the beach after its relocation, **Sugar Hut**, on Thappraya Rd (tel 421638), offers exquisite Japanese/Thai-style bamboo huts, set in tropical gardens, at 2000B. For a full listing of luxury hotels in and around Pattaya, contact the TAT tourist office.

Moderate

For a luxury hotel at a moderate price, try **P. K. Villa**, Beach Rd, S. Pattaya (tel 429107). This is one of Pattaya's largest villas, with lovely gardens, a fine pool, and relaxed atmosphere. Rooms start from 600B (low season), and most of them have ocean views. The same goes for **Ocean View Hotel**, Beach Rd (tel 418434), a very comfy place, although rooms here start at 1000B. Friendly **Honey Inn**, 529/2 Soi 10, Pattaya 2 Rd (tel 428117), has bright, attractive rooms for 700B, and is so *quiet*. At Jomtien, the **Sea Breeze** (tel 231057) receives consistently good mentions—rooms at around 700B, great food, and very friendly staff.

Inexpensive

Budget hotels are concentrated round Sois 11 and 12, Pattaya 2 Rd. Better ones include **Diana Inn** (tel 429870), with good-value rooms at 200B fan, 350–600B air-con, with a pool, bar and restaurant; **Pattaya II**, on the corner of South Beach Rd and Soi 11 (tel 429239), with rooms at 180–250B fan, 350–500B air-con, a pool, coffee shop, restaurant, car park etc; **Honey House**, down Soi 10 (tel 424396), with spacious rooms for 180B fan, 350B air-con and the use of a pool; and finally, **B. R. Inn**, Soi 12 (tel 429449), with large quiet 350B air-con rooms. Other good bets are **U-Thomporn** (tel 421350), **Drop In** (tel 429803), **Tossaporn** (tel 424943) and **Malibu** (tel 423180). These all have rooms from 150–250B (fan) to 250–350B (air-con).

EATING OUT

Pattaya has some of the choicest seafood in Thailand. It is also one of the most expensive places to eat in Thailand. Still, there's an amazing range of cuisines. Numerous restaurants, coffee shops, steak houses and fast-food emporia cater for every gastronomic taste—European, Indian, Arabic, Japanese, Chinese, Korean and Thai. But the usual cheap street-snack places are in very short supply here.

Much-copied but never equalled, **Dolf Riks** (in Regent Marina complex, N. Pattaya) is an outstanding restaurant, offering superlative continental dishes in a select setting. The à la carte speciality is Indonesian *Rijstaafel* (a special meat curry) at 185B; also try delectable Fried Prawns at 150B. Riks has a set tourist menu for 220B, and is open from 11 am to midnight. Other good European-style places—all on Beach Rd, South Pattaya—are **La Gritta**, an authentic Italian restaurant specializing in seafood cuisine—try the special La Gritta pasta with clams and white wine (85B), and the rock lobster (150B); **Buccaneer Terrace** (in Nipa Lodge Hotel), a rooftop restaurant with great bay views and delicious Escargot in White Wine Sauce at 120B, fillet steak (180B) and mixed grill

(160B); **Mai Kai** (Hotel Tropicana), a Polynesian restaurant also offering quality seafood and European fare. Several large hotels—notably the **Montien**—offer good evening barbecue buffets.

You can enjoy top-quality Thai food at **Dee Proam**, Central Pattaya Rd, with nice gardens and a romantic atmosphere thrown in. Also good are **Somsak** and **Khrua Suthep**, Thai restaurants on Sois 1 and 2, Beach Rd. Somsak is on three levels in an open plan pagoda-style building, surrounded by lush greenery. Service is delightfully efficient and the menu runs for pages, making it difficult to decide which goodies to order. One small criticism of this otherwise lovely restaurant is that the seafood isn't always as fresh as advertised. **PIC Kitchen** on Soi 5 is another favourite. The restaurant consists of four wooden Thai-style pavilions, amid a luxurious tropical garden. Whilst conventional seating is found in three of these structures, in the fourth you must remove your shoes, and sit on cushions on the floor to eat at low tables—lumbago sufferers beware. There's a wide range of Thai cuisine, with a good choice of seafood dishes; for two years running this restaurant has won awards from the city for its high standards of hygiene. Dinner for two is about 400B, and every Wednesday at 7.30 pm they have a classical Thai dance show.

The best places to sample Pattaya's famous seafood are at **Pattaya Seafood Palace**, behind the Siren Bar on the pier at the beginning of the 'strip', where you can tuck into the freshest lobster or fish while taking in the panorama of the bay, particularly attractive at sunset; and at **Nang Nual**, at the very end of South Pattaya Rd, towards the Siam Bayshore Hotel. Here you can deliberate over a vast array of shellfish and fish, and point out what you'd like. There's a choice of dining areas, too; out on the jetty, inside, or upstairs in the air-con dining room. Dinner for two averages 1000B, more if you have a lobster dinner. Across the road, the other part of the restaurant serves meat in much the same manner—just point out what you fancy. Particularly popular are the mammoth 'Big Cowboy' steaks (320B).

The **Green Bottle** on Pattaya 2 Rd, next to Diana Inn, is home from home for westerners down from Bangkok for the weekend. With modern Texas saloon-type decor and snappy American service, the house specials are Lobster Thermidor and steaks. There's a small selection of European wines. Dinner for two costs around 500B, more with wine. A similar place to this is **Le Bistro**, on Pattayaland 3 (above the Cockpit men-only bar with transvestite show nightly at 11); it serves traditional western dishes with a different menu every day (450–550B for two).

Alt Heidelberg, at the southern end of Beach Rd, has German food (including wurst and sauerkraut) and a selection of draft and bottled imported beers.

The **Orient Express** by the Nipa Lodge Hotel on Beach Road offers unusual dining in two railway cars that have been converted and done out in the style of its namesake. The cuisine covers the spectrum of traditional European dishes, though not to the standards of the original—but then you're not paying those prices (around 800–1000B for two).

Of the many hotel restaurants, the **Narissa Orchid**, in the Siam Bayshore, is a popular spot for its wide choice of Thai, Chinese and Japanese specialities in a very pleasant modern-rustic setting (set menu for 320B). For English breakfast, or indeed civilised afternoon tea, drop into **Oliver's Coffee Shop** on the small side street between Pattayaland 1 and 2, with good sandwiches (25–40B), cakes and scones (15–25B).

Oliver, though English, is the acting Swedish consul, and can head you in the right direction in Pattaya.

KOH SI CHANG

The picturesque island of Koh Si Chang nestles off the east coast of the Gulf of Thailand, about 12 km from the Si Racha shore. Little visited by foreigners—except as a short day-outing—it's a wonderfully secluded island, the ideal retreat from the noise and crowds of nearby Bangkok or Pattaya. Koh Si Chang has fresh, clean air and a relaxing Mediterranean flavour. Lovely scenery, quiet beaches and pleasant walks make this a perfect place to just switch off. There's a small local population of fishermen and retired government officials. Apart from them, visitors who wisely decide to stay overnight often have the island all to themselves.

GETTING THERE
From Bangkok's Eastern Terminal, buses leave every 15 minutes for the small fishing town of **Si Racha**, 104 km from Bangkok. Fares are 28B non air-con, 44B air-con, and it's a 2-hour trip. Boats for Si Chang island leave from the pier on Soi 14, Si Racha, at 9 and 11 am, 1, 3 and 6.30 pm daily. Boats back to Si Racha from Si Chang leave at 5, 6.30 and 9 am, 12 noon and 4.30 pm. The crossing takes 40 minutes and the one-way fare is 20B.

WHAT TO SEE
Koh Si Chang is encircled by a narrow ring-road, which you can walk round at leisure in 3–4 hours. If you need local transport, there are unique motorized *samlors* which resemble souped-up dragmobiles. These charge 20B for short hops, 80B for round-trips of the island—rather expensive. To tour the island in style, hire a boat (cf. Where to Stay).

Island Tour
(on foot; half–full day)

Chinese Temple – Hin Klim Beach – Tampang Beach – King's Palace – Wat Asdang Nimitr.
The **Chinese Temple** on Koh Si Chang is one of Thailand's finest. From the pier, walk five minutes up the low hill road until you reach the temple staircase. A stiff climb of over 400 steps leads up to a small old *chedi*, where a charming monk (guarding a sacred footprint of Buddha) doles out iced water to overheated climbers. Beautifully located, the temple offers wonderful views down over the island interior and surrounding coastline. From the foot of the temple, another 10 minutes' walk brings you to the north of the island and to **Hin Klim**. This is popularly known as 'Round Stone' beach—its large rocks having been worn to their smooth, round shape by strong westerly winds. Just past this, there's a massive yellow Buddha seated up on the hill. To share its privileged view of the island, walk up the rickety staircase to the small temple at its base. Back on the road, and a kilometre further on, a sign appears for **Tampang Beach**. This is the best

beach on the island, but the long 30-minute hike there from the main road tends to put off a lot of visitors. It's apparently not a bad spot to camp out.

Staying on the road, another 10 minutes' walk brings you to the western edge of the island, and to the **King's Palace**. This was the old summer palace of Rama V, left to become derelict after the French took temporary occupation of the island in 1893. Little now remains of the extensive structure, except for the dilapidated wooden summerhouse and the rubble-filled swimming pool. The main palace building is now located in Bangkok. Climbing the staircase which once led up to it, you'll find two temples. The one on the left, **Wat Asdang Nimitr**, has a chapel (used by Rama V for meditation) and a pagoda in European architectural style. Also up here is a famous 'bell rock', wrapped in cloth, which produces a bell-like tone when struck with a large stick or stone. The King's Palace area is open from 8 am to 6 pm daily, and there's an admission charge of 4B. It overlooks the small, shallow **Tawang Beach**, a popular Thai picnic spot. Swimming isn't safe here—too many sea-urchins.

In the evening, buy a refreshing pineapple in the town market, and cool off down by the pier. There's a small open-air cinema here, which shows entertaining Thai or Hindi films most nights. Toom, manager of Tiewpai guest house, lets his guests use his schooner to mellow out under the stars.

WHERE TO STAY   (tel prefix 038)
Inexpensive
Koh Si Chang has three guest houses, all within five minutes' walk from the pier. **Tiewpai Guest House** (tel 272987) is the only one which has got its act together. Toom, the friendly manager, speaks good English (a rarity on this island) and is a mine of local information. He has rooms from 120B (fan-cooled, but stuffy) to 300B (air-con, better). He also has just about the best dormitory in Thailand—large, clean and well-aired—40B per person. Toom offers half-day (9 am to 12 noon) boat trips round the island, with stops for fishing and swimming. At 300B, this is worth doing—if there's a group of you to split costs. Tiewpai's small restaurant serves Thai/European cuisine (nice seafood) and has live music nightly. All the local Thai wide-boys gather here for sing-songs and Mekong parties, and it can get *very* noisy. If it gets you down, move to the quieter guest house just above Tiewpai—it's at the top of the hill, to the right. Otherwise, buy some supplies and camp out on one of the beaches. They're quite safe.

Si Racha

Si Racha is well-known for its seafood (especially oysters) and for its spicy home-grown *nam phrik si rachaa* sauce. There's good dining at **Seaside** restaurant on Soi 18 pier, and **Chua Lee** next to Soi 10. Both are pricey—most dishes between 40 and 60B—and have 'yuppie' menus (e.g. Crab on Toast, Fresh Oysters On the Rock) but food is superb. While in Si Racha, take a walk (15 minutes, heading north up Chermchormpol Rd, turning left past the Post Office) over to **Koh Loi**. This is a delightful little island connected to the mainland by a long jetty. The attraction here is a pretty set-piece Thai-Chinese Buddhist temple—bring your camera.

Staying overnight in Si Racha (a rather dismal prospect), choose between two 'hotels' on the waterfront pier, opposite Tessaban 1 Rd. These are **Siwichai** (tel 311212), with clean 100–150B rooms, and **Siriwattana** (tel 311307), with 100B singles (with bath) and 280B doubles (can sleep four) with air-conditioning.

From Si Racha, buses leave for Pattaya (30-minute journey; fare 5B) from Sukhumvit Road highway. The bus-stop is a 15-minute walk from town—take the road directly opposite Soi 14, walk down to the highway, cross over, and head right. Pattaya-bound buses often carry on to Rayong for Koh Samet.

KOH SAMET

Samet Island has beautiful beaches, crystal-clear waters and some of the whitest, squeakiest sand in Thailand. Only three hours by road from Bangkok, it was first discovered by young Thai weekenders seeking a quick getaway from the busy capital. Still mainly a Thai resort, Samet has, to date, escaped the eye of the developers. Unlike Koh Samui or Phuket, which are well on their way to becoming *farang* ghettoes, Samet still has no raucous neon-lit bars or prostitutes to disturb its laidback tranquillity. In the day, people swim, sunbathe and relax. At night, they sit and talk and play music. Boring, say some—but many can't get enough of Samet's simple backwoods charm. How long can this last? Five years ago, there was virtually nothing on the island. Now there's windsurfing, jet skiing, motorboats and videos. The island has long been a national park (you'll have to pay a 5B 'admission' fee once you leave the harbour village of Na Dan) and recent 'green' policies in government mean that strict building restrictions are now in force, making it, for the time being, impossible for a Bangkok developer to move in and throw up a resort.

Accommodation on the island is mainly cheap, basic bungalows around 100–150B for a single/double (twice the price in high season). Huts usually have just a mattress, a mosquito net, and (sometimes) an attached shower. If you're not coming in the cooler months, though, it's wise to get a hut with fan—otherwise you'll cook at night. The island has a water shortage; water is either rationed or switched on only for certain periods of the day. Most bungalows have restaurants. One or two have money-changers and overseas phones (collect calls only). There are no luxury-class hotels on Samet, though a recently-halted building programme has produced a number of new-style bungalows with all mod cons, charging between 350–500B (again, much more in the high season). Visitors can now afford to be selective regarding where to stay. If you don't like one place, move on. The amazing thing about Samet—the one thing everyone comments on—is that every beach has a completely different atmosphere. Some are quiet, some are party-party, one or two are geared to Thais, others have water-sports, some have no electricity and a few are lit up like Christmas trees. Whatever your mood, you'll find something to suit it here. If you're not into bungalows, simply camp out on the beach—the Thais do it all the time, and it's quite safe—except for the mosquitoes. At weekends in high season you may be forced to camp out, so bring a tent in case. You can also camp around the bungalows with the owner's permission, and he'll charge a small fee for use of showers.

Samet's mosquitoes are of the malarial kind. Be grateful to them—they're probably the main reason the island is so pleasantly deserted. But be aware of them too—nearly

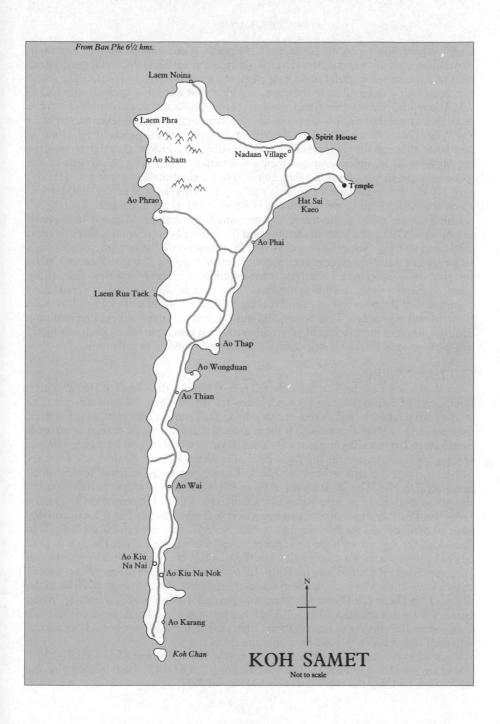

From Ban Phe 6½ kms.

Laem Noina

Laem Phra

Spirit House

Ao Kham

Nadaan Village

Temple

Ao Phrao

Hat Sai Kaeo

Ao Phai

Laem Rua Taek

Ao Thap

Ao Wongduan

Ao Thian

Ao Wai

Ao Kiu Na Nai

Ao Kiu Na Nok

N

Ao Karang

Koh Chan

KOH SAMET

Not to scale

every bungalow-owner on the island has had malaria at one time or another, and there are warning signs all over the place. Even if you're taking malaria tabs, you'll need to take extra precautions—especially after dusk, when malarial mozzies are about. Sleep under a net, cover up with repellent in the open, and have your bungalow sprayed with DDT. While there's no real need for alarm—malaria is pretty difficult to catch and it's been five years since a malarial death—if you do develop symptoms (cramps, fever etc.) contact Sue Wild at Naga Beach bungalows for help or go straight to the public health clinic on the island. Although they only handle simple dressings and the like, they'll ship you off to Rayong hospital for more serious ailments—its malaria clinic gives blood tests on the spot and immediate medication. Bangkok also has a good malaria clinic (cf. 'Health', page 21). But first make sure it *is* malaria you've got—it may only be severe dehydration, which is quickly cured by drinking Coke laced with lots of salt and sugar.

Koh Samet is a useful alternative to Koh Samui. It's rainy in May and June (when Samui is still OK) and it's dry in October and November (when Samui is still subject to winds and storms). Samet is very dry from November to February (the official high season), when water-shortage problems could leave you paying 20B for a shower. On the plus side, dry weather means relatively few mosquitoes. Christmas and New Year is a big scene on Samet—wild, wild beach parties, after which every bungalow verandah is crammed with sleeping bodies. Avoid coming on weekends and national holidays. Koh Samet is still primarily a Thai resort, and gets crowded at these times. I arrived on a Saturday, and ran the gauntlet of seven separate Thai beach parties (at each of which I had to share some Mekong) before finally finding a bungalow to collapse in.

GETTING THERE
From Bangkok's Eastern Terminal, there are 5–6 buses a day direct to Ban Phe pier, from 5 am to 5.30 pm (later on Fridays). Fares are 70B air-con, 40B non air-con. The journey takes 3 hours, and tickets are sold by **D.D. Tours**. (This company, however, does not enjoy a good reputation.) If these are full there are buses at regular intervals from 5 am to 10 pm to **Rayong**, a small town 220 km east of Bangkok. Fares are 38B non air-con, 69B air-con, and the trip takes 2½ hours. From Rayong, minibuses leave every half-hour (from the rank behind the Clock Tower, next to the cinema) for the small hamlet of Ban Phe. The 20-km journey takes 40 minutes, and the fare is 10B. You can also get buses to Ban Phe from Pattaya Bus station for 40B and the trip takes 1½ hours. From Ban Phe Pier, there are regular boats over to Samet Island. The 6.5-km crossing takes 30 minutes, and the one-way fare is 30B. Several companies run boats out of Ban Phe—look for the one with the most people on it: this will be the one that leaves first; otherwise be prepared for a long wait while the boat fills up. If you're in a hurry, you can of course charter the whole boat for 600B. In low season, there are often only a couple of boats a day—then, you just take what you can get. Samet-bound boats go *either* to the village of **Na Daan** (for Diamond, Naga, Ao Phai and Tubtim beaches) *or* to **Ao Wong Duan** (for Tantawan and Ao Tian). All beaches are within walking distance of these two ferry points. Rayong has an Immigration Office, useful for visa extensions. It's a 5B taxi ride from town (ask for *plak nam*), across the river.

Rayong has two decent hotels, with fan rooms for 120B, air-con rooms for 250–350B. These are the **Otani** (tel 611112) and the **Rayong** (tel 611073), both located near the bus station, opposite the clock tower on Sukhumvit Rd.

If you need to stay overnight in Ban Phe (there are no night boats to Samet), try the **Nuannapa Hotel** (rooms 150B fan, 250B air-con) opposite the pier.

WHERE TO STAY   (tel prefix 038)
Moderate–Inexpensive
Samet island is narrow, diamond-shaped and about 6 km long. The best beaches are on the east coast, and the hour-long walk south along it—from Hat Say Kaew to Ao Tian—is just one lovely stretch of white sand after another. Some beaches hire out motorbikes, but the only decent excursion is across to Ao Phrao, the only developed beach on the western coast. Minibuses run from Na Daan as far as Ao Thap Thim.

Hat Say Kaew (Diamond Beach)
A 10-minute walk from Na Daan ferry-landing, this is Samet's nicest beach—and (along with Ao Wong Deuan) the most popular with Thais. It offers silvery-soft sands, calm sea, and (from the promontory at the top of the beach, above the white Buddha) magnificent sunset views. There are several good bungalow operations. **Diamond** is popular, with well-spaced huts with fan and shower for 100–400B. It has the best seafood restaurant on the beach, offering speciality Tuna Steak (50–70B) and agreeable Thai wine, if you've acquired the taste for it. Diamond offers windsurfing (the hourly charge of 120–150B is standard around the island's beaches—but there is little surf till December or January), boat-trips round the island (100B per head—with stops to dive for oysters), snorkelling equipment and rubber rings. **Ploy Thaloy** has immaculate rooms for 100–500B, and a disco on Friday and Saturday. **Toy** is one of the many places around with video. It has nice 100–200B bungalows (with fan and shower) and a good restaurant serving reaonably priced Thai dishes. **Whitesands** is a place to eat, not stay. Try the 'Curry in Pot' dinner—it feeds three people for just 60B. There's also a disco here on Friday and Saturday. Glass-bottom boat trips leave from Whitesands at 1 pm daily—the charge is 200B (20B each, if there are 10 of you). They don't leave at all when the captain has a hangover—very common at weekends.

Naga
Just below Diamond, Naga is a clean secluded cove with a pretty spirit-house and a mermaid on the rocks. Every year, local fishermen turn up with carved wooden phalli for Tuktim, the island goddess, to ensure good luck at sea. Lately, Naga is said to be attracting a lot of graduates and young professionals but I didn't meet any. The beach has two well-run sets of bungalows. **Naga** is run by Sue and Toss—a lovely English-Thai couple—and is famous for its delicious home-made bread, chocolate cake, meat pies and cookies. There's also a shop here—handy for stocking up on mozzie repellent, suncream and basic supplies. Sue is a mine of local information, and has a standard year-round price (80B single, 100B double) for her simple bungalows (no fan). Nearby **Little Hut** has huts at 80–100B, and makes superlative coconut ice-cream and yoghurt. Just past here is the new **Jeppes**, with 8 bungalows for 150–200B and one of the best places to eat on the island, with an extensive menu featuring seafood and Thai dishes, that come in generous portions for 30–60B a dish. Near here is a small gaily-painted ashram, run by a friendly lady, Shawalee, who puts up travellers for a nominal donation.

Ao Phai

This is a small cosy beach, with pebble-sand and some rocks. There are catamarans (300B per hour) and windsurfers (150B per hour) for hire. **Samet Villas** is excellent value; run by a Swiss/Thai couple it offers well-furnished 'chalet' bungalows at high season rates of 300B double; towels are provided and the electricity is on all day, unlike many other places. **Ao Phai** and **Seabreeze** are somewhat cheaper. **Knop's Kitchen** offers great seafood and nightly barbecues (October to January only).

Ao Thap Thim—Ao Nuan

On Ao Thap Thim, a popular spot, stay at **Pudsa**, where the staff are very friendly and accommodation very reasonable. Of the thirty bungalows, 12 are fully equipped with fan and bath. Rates are 100B for basic up to 400B, which sleep four. The restaurant does some very good Thai dishes, and home-made muesli for breakfast. Pudsa is also one of the few places left that does not have nightly videos. Next door **Tuktim** is much larger, with good 300B chalets (fan and bath), 150B chalets (WC and shower only), and spartan 70B huts—be warned that these are way in the back and are high risk for burglaries, so it is best to leave *all* valuables at reception. Ao Nuan is a delightful little cove, down on the rocks below Thap Thim—find it if you can. The single operation here, **Nuan Kitchen**, offers tasteful custom-built bungalows from 100B, also hammocks, mellow sounds and good food (try Chicken with Hot Basil Leaf on Rice—the speciality).

Tantawan (Sunflower Beach)

This is a large, pleasant beach with a pier—handy for boats back to Ban Phe. **Ao Chaw** has 100B huts with fan, shower and mosquito nets—the best budget deal on the island. It also has an overseas telephone (collect calls only—Ban Phe has a proper overseas phone service). **Tantawan** is another good outfit, with comfy huts (100B–180B) and an umbrella-shaded beach restaurant. **Bamboo Restaurant**, set back from the beach, offers boat trips to beautiful **Tha Lu Island** (great for fishing and snorkelling) every Monday and Friday, from October to February, at 120B per person.

Ao Wong Duan (Seahorse Beach)

Ao Wong Duan is a large crescent beach, quickly becoming a yuppie wonderland. Sea views are marred by boats clustered round the pier, and litter clutters the once-virgin white sands. It's all rather tacky, and geared to people with lots of money and no initiative to look elsewhere. The so called 'luxury resort'—**Wong Duan Villas**—charges up to 800B for air-con chalets (especially if you turn up on a Saturday night), 2500B for luxury 'suites', and 15B for a go on its golf course (actually, a 9-hole pitch and putt). It also hires out noisy jet-skis for 500B per hour. Nearby **Malibu** restaurant serves Fish 'n' Chips, Gordon Blue, and Fillet Steak with Bernie's Sauce. Thankfully, there's **Wong Duan Resort**, with nice 300–500B rooms (with toilet rolls), boat-trips to Tha Lu Island, water-sports (windsurfing, scuba, snorkelling), and lovely staff. **Malibu** also has nice bungalows, but at 350–550B they're overpriced.

Ao Thian (Candlelight Beach)

Despite its motto ('Civilization Beach—Free is Now!') this narrow, underdeveloped beach is strictly for ascetics and nature-lovers. Food and accommodation are primitive (bring some food with you), and there's often a shortage of water. **Lung Dum** has the best stretch of beach, and huts are 150–300B.

There's little development below Candlelight—if you want to stay further south, it's often a case of camping out on the beach. At the southern tip of the island, a half-hour walk down from Ao Thian, there's some excellent coral-diving and snorkelling to be had.

Ao Phrao (Coconut Beach or Paradise Beach)
This one is on the western coast—a 20-minute walk across the mainland from the rocks above Ao Phai. Ao Phrao is famous for its amazing sunsets. It's also supposed to be quiet and secluded—though it's anything but at weekends when the Thais arrive. Still, it's a nice spot—with a completely different feel to the east coast. Two good outfits, **Ao Plao** and **Coconut,** offer bungalows from 100B to 300B.

Part VII

THE NORTH

Wat Prasingh Buddha, Chiang Mai

Bordered by Burma and Laos, the North has been the birthplace of many powerful kingdoms—notably Sukhothai (1238) and Chiang Mai (1296)—and today is a fascinating potpourri of different peoples, including the exotic hilltribes of its densely forested highlands, and the quixotic travellers who trek out to meet them. There's a lot to be said for the North. It hasn't been jaded by tourism yet (unlike parts of the South) and its people remain the warmest, friendliest and most 'mellow' Thais around. Their laidback quality has less to do with opium (most of which is now gone) than with their long isolation from the rest of the country. Cut off from Thailand proper until the early 1900s, the North still retains much of its distinctive character and culture, customs and dialect. Folk dances and ethnic handicrafts are two big draws of **Chiang Mai** (the capital), which is also a popular base for hilltribe treks. From here, people trek north to the ancient kingdoms of **Chiang Rai** and **Chiang Saen** (part of the opium-producing **Golden Triangle**), or west to the remote hill regions of **Mae Hong Son, Mae Sariang, Pai** and **Soppong**, which have only recently been cleared of bandits. Alternatively they venture south to visit the historic temple-cities of **Sukhothai, Si Satchanalai** and **Lamphun**. Wherever you go in the North, the people are warm, the climate is cool, and the scenery is beautiful.

CHIANG MAI

Chiang Mai, the 'Rose of the North', is many people's favourite city in Thailand. Beautifully situated in a high valley at the foot of majestic Doi Suthep mountain, it has a refreshingly cool climate and a calm, relaxing atmosphere—the perfect antidote to steamy, frenetic Bangkok, 700 km to the south. A fast-developing tourist centre—famous for its hilltribe treks, ethnic handicrafts, and over 300 temples—Chiang Mai has virtually doubled in size over the past few years, making it Thailand's second-largest city with a population of 150,000. Owing to its mountainous situation, it was virtually cut off from Bangkok until the late 1920s, but is now feeling the full impact of modernization. This is noticeable in the plethora of German beer parlours, European restaurants, trekking agencies and cheap guest houses which have invaded the town centre. Yet Chiang Mai still (somehow) hangs on to its charming 'village' atmosphere, and retains its distinctive culture, customs and cuisine. Wander down any backstreet, and the façade of modern living simply drops away—most of the townsfolk continue to live their lives as in ages past, seemingly unaffected by the bomb of 'progress' exploding around them. They are a happy, easy-going, yet independent people with their own lilting dialect, their own dances and festivals, and (especially in the case of the small hilltribe population) their own colourful costumes and customs. This said, the sight of an Akha girl in full tribal outfit crossing the road (probably on the way home from a Khantoke dinner dance) is today as worthy of comment as, say, a *farang* crossing the same street 20 years ago. Chiang Mai has numerous attractions of its own, but also makes an ideal base for exploring the north of Thailand. It's the kind of place where travellers spend a good deal longer than first planned—or wish they had.

History

Chiang Mai (new city) was built in 1296 by King Mengrai to replace Chiang Rai as the capital of his fast-expanding Lan Na Thai ('One Million Rice Fields') kingdom, which had emerged—along with Mengrai himself—from the old Thai kingdom of Nan Chao in southwest China. From this time on, Chiang Mai remained the principal city of the north, surviving various crises including Burmese occupation and long periods of virtual abandonment. Though the state remained independent for almost 500 years, it was for much of this time vassal to neighbouring powers, such as Ayutthaya, Burma and Luang Prabang.

Every northern Thai kingdom has a legendary background, and Chiang Mai is no exception. Apparently, King Mengrai was out hunting one day, and spotted five mice running down a hole beneath a sacred Bo tree. The appearance of two white sambar deer and two white barking deer clinched it—with three such lucky omens behind him, Mengrai had no real choice but to found a new city. On a more practical level, he needed Chiang Mai as a power-centre to control an empire which was to extend beyond Sukhothai to the south, and as far north as Luang Prabang in Laos. Some 90,000 men working day and night were used to construct the city, and the original walls were completed in just four months. The present siting of the walls and moat, however, date only from the early 19th century—Mengrai's successors altered the city layout and relocated its fortifications on several different occasions.

After Mengrai died in 1317 (reputedly struck by lightning), the kingdom went from strength to strength. It reached the peak of its power and influence under Tiloka Raja (the 'King of the Three Worlds'), whose reigning years—the mid-15th century—are now considered the Golden Age of the Lan Na Thai civilization. In 1556, however, following a period of decline, the kingdom was captured by Burma and became her vassal. For the next 200 years, it was used as a popular base for the Burmese in their wars with the Thais further south. It was only in 1775, in the wake of Ayutthaya's collapse, that King Taksin of Thonburi marched his victorious army north and finally liberated the Lan Na Thai kingdom from its Burmese oppressors. Under the Chakri kings, Chiang Mai remained, at first, semi-autonomous with its own hereditary princes, but then slowly fell under the expanding central control of Bangkok. When the last governor-prince died in 1938, no-one was named to succeed him.

Today, Chiang Mai is two cities in one. The old 13th-century city, with its moat and few remaining sections of thick walls, lies some distance west of the Ping River. The newer city—with its modern hotels and restaurants, rows of shops and handicraft emporiums—is spread all around the old city, between its moat and the river, as well as across the river on the east bank. This area—extending from Ta Pae Gate to Nawarat Bridge—now comprises 'downtown' Chiang Mai. The railway station and the main post office lie on the eastern bank of the river, while the airport is situated to the southwest.

Thanks to its altitude (300 metres above sea level), Chiang Mai is, for much of the year, cooler and less humid than anywhere else in Thailand. Average temperatures are 20°C from October to February (cool season); 30°C from March to May (hot season), and 25°C from June to September (rainy season). For scenery, come in September or October—just after the monsoons—when the valley is at its most beautiful. During December and January, it can get quite cold (an icicle was reported one legendary night) and it's wise to bring a sweater and woolly socks.

Chiang Mai celebrates many joyous festivals—the most notable being the **Flower Carnival** (first weekend of February), the water-throwing festival of **Songkran** (April 13–15) and the candle-floating festival of **Loi Krathong** (Full Moon day of the twelfth lunar month, usually mid-November). They are all exceedingly popular, and it's wise to book transport and accommodation in advance at each celebration.

GETTING THERE

By Air
Thai Airways offer several flights daily to Chiang Mai from Bangkok (standard fare 1650B; it's a one-hour flight). From Chiang Mai, Thai Airways fly to Chiang Rai (420B), Mae Hong Son (345B), Phitsanulok (650B), Khon Kaen (1115B), Phuket (3755B), Surat Thani (2970B), Udorn Thani (2815B), and Hat Yai (4150B). To book flights, contact Thai Airways (Domestic), 240 Prappoklao Rd, Chiang Mai (tel 211044–7), Thai International, Changklang Rd, Chiang Mai (tel 234150), or one of the town's many travel agents. Advance booking is recommended, especially in the winter high season. Chiang Mai airport is only 3 km out of town, a cheap ride by *songthaew* (15–20B), *tuk-tuk* (30–40B) or taxi (50–60B).

By Rail
From Bangkok's Hualamphong station, there are five trains daily to Chiang Mai, four with sleeper facility. The quick, popular Express train leaves Bangkok at 6, and arrives in Chiang Mai at 7.40 am. The Special Express leaves at 7.40 pm, arriving in Chiang Mai at 8.05 am. The (not so) Rapid trains leave at 6.40 am, 3.00 and 10 pm, arriving at 7.15 pm,

5.15 and 11.55 am respectively. Basic fares are 537B 1st class, 255B 2nd class, 121B 3rd class (add 250B per person for 1st-class double cabin). Most people buy a 2nd-class sleeper seat (add 100B upper berth, 150B lower berth for non air-con, 200B upper berth and 250B lower berth for air-con) on the fast Express train (add another 30B). For Rapid trains add another 20B to the basic fare, and for the Special Express 50B.

Lower berth sleeper seats give fine early-morning window views of Chiang Mai valley. Going up to Chiang Mai by train has several advantages—it's safer than the bus, there are great food stops (every station on the way is a bustle of platform vendors running relays of hardboiled eggs, savoury *kai yang*, mango juice and bottled drinks), and, most important, you arrive pleasantly refreshed, after a good night's sleep.

From Chiang Mai, Rapid trains leave for Bangkok at 6.30 am, 3.30 and 8.45 pm, arriving at 8.35 pm, 5.30 and 10.40 am respectively. The Express train leaves daily at 5.15 pm, and the Special Express at 7.30 pm, arriving 6.25 and 8.25 am. All of these trains (except the Special Express) make useful stops at Lamphun, Phitsanulok, Lopburi, Ayutthaya, Bang Pa In and Don Muang International Airport. The Express trains are invariably full, and should be booked 3–4 days in advance. For seat reservations, contact Chiang Mai rail station, Charoenmuang Rd (tel 244795 same-day bookings; 242094 advance bookings). There's a useful baggage deposit (open 6 am to 6 pm) and hotel-booking desk at Chiang Mai rail station. You can also pick up a free city map here.

By Bus

From Bangkok's Northern Terminal, non air-con buses leave for Chiang Mai at regular intervals from 5.25 am to 10 pm (9 hours, fare 133B); four air-con buses leave between 9 and 10 am, eight more between 8 and 9.45 pm (8 hours; fare 242B). Several private bus companies in Bangkok (mainly operating out of travel agencies or guest houses in Banglampoo and Soi Ngam Dupli) and in Chiang Mai (same deal, Moon Muang and Ta Pae roads) offer cheaper tickets, especially for round-trips. Many travellers favour the bus over the train—it's cheaper and quicker. Also, the recent introduction of video cameras on many night buses has greatly reduced the risk of being drugged and robbed—though it's still safer to travel by daylight. Going by night bus, you're not likely to get much sleep. As one couple reported:

> We took the overnight bus to Chiang Mai, and at first couldn't get over
> how civilized it was. As soon as we set off, a smart hostess appeared with
> a food parcel, containing a chicken drumstick, a piece of cake and an
> iced Coke. Minutes later, she returned, this time with free toilet paper!
> This was followed by an issue of paper towels and warm blankets. At the
> unearthly hour of 2 am, 'lunch' arrived—a bowl of rice with hard-boiled
> eggs and dried, sickly-sweet fish. Sleep wasn't easy after this, especially
> when the air-conditioning went into hyperdrive, turning the bus into a
> fridge. Around 5 am, the hostess whipped our blankets away and we
> froze to death. She said she wanted to get 'organized' for the next lot of
> tourists.

Chiang Mai has two bus stations. The **Arcade** terminal (tel 242664) services Bangkok, Chiang Rai, Mae Hong Son, Phitsanulok, Khon Kaen, Udorn Thani, Khorat and all destinations outside the province. The **White Elephant** (Chang Phuak, tel 211586) terminal services Bosang-San Kamphaeng, Lamphun-Pasang, Fang-Tha Ton, and all destinations within Chiang Mai province.

TOURIST INFORMATION

The TAT Tourist Office (tel 248604 and 248607; fax 248605) is at 105 Lamphun Road, 500 metres south of Nawarat Bridge. Staff are very helpful, and hand out a complete 'tourist information pack' (includes maps, bus/train timetables, hotel listings, photocopied sheets on provincial attractions). They also issue the monthly mag *Welcome to Chiang Mai*, and *Chiangmai—What's On . . . Where To Go*, both full of current news and events.

Books

Suriwongse Book Centre at Sridonchai Rd is the biggest bookstore in Chiang Mai, with many guides and background material on the hilltribes. **D. K. Books**, at the moat end of Ta Pae Rd, has a wide selection of art, history, religious and cultural titles. Both shops are open 8.30 am to 8 pm daily. For cheap, second-hand maps, guides and fiction books, visit the small **Library Service** at 21/1 Ratchamanka Soi 2 (off Moon Muang Rd, below Oasis Bar).

Post Office

The main GPO, Charoen Muang Rd (east of Nawarat Bridge) has a handy 24-hour overseas phone/telex service (telegrams, from 11 am to 7 pm only). The small post office, just above Warorot market, is open 8.30 am to 4.30 pm only, but is far more central. Travellers come here to buy stamps/aerogrammes, to send parcels (packing service, 6B a kilo, at the entrance) and to queue up for overseas calls (one booth only, open 8.30 am to 12 noon daily). Domestic calls are best made from Lek House, Moon Muang Rd—using public phones in Chiang Mai is a *very* risky business.

Immigration and Banks

The Immigration Office, for visa-extensions, is off Highway 1141, near the airport (open 8.30 am to 12 noon and 1 to 4 pm; tel 277510). After the banks close, change money at **Krung Thai Exchange**, Ta Pae Rd (open 8.30 am to 8 pm) or Bangkok Bank Exchange at the Night Bazaar 'Plaza' (open 8 am to 10 pm).

GETTING AROUND

Chiang Mai is a compact city—ideal for exploration **by bicycle**. Several places in town hire out bikes (around 20B a day), but give them a short 'test ride' before paying any money. Cycling 11 km back to town from the Crafts Villages on just one pedal is no joke, believe me. For trips further afield (e.g. to Doi Suthep) consider hiring a **motorbike**. Chiang Mai has such a surplus of motorbikes that rates are very cheap (from 100B a day) and getting a trial run before paying is no problem. Some places (unheard of anywhere else in Thailand) even give guarantees against engine failure and breakdowns. There are many hire places along Moon Muang Rd—or you can enquire at your hotel/guest house. For **car/jeep** rental contact **Hertz** at 12/3 Loikroh Rd (tel 275496) and at Chiang Mai Plaza (tel 270040), **Avis** at 14 Huay Kaew Rd (tel 221316) or contact **Suda Travel Service**, 18 Huay Kaew Rd (tel 210030) or **Chiangmai Travel Centre**, Rincome Hotel (tel 221692).

Songthaews (red minibuses) are the cheapest form of local transport. They'll take you anywhere on their (more or less) fixed route for only 5B. But you have to know *exactly* where you're going—if you don't, a passenger who does will always get priority. It sometimes saves time to charter a whole *songthaew* for yourself (20–30B). **Tuk-tuks** are a fairly recent arrival in Chiang Mai. Noisy, but quick, they don't cross the street for less than 20B (which is the average short-hop fare). Man-powered **samlors** are useful for getting to certain places (e.g. the Night Bazaar) denied to motorized transport. Average charge is 10B, but they don't cross the street at all during 'siesta' (i.e. most of the afternoon). Most people can walk faster than a Chiang Mai *samlor*.

For local sightseeing in comfy **air-con buses**, contact well-established travel agents like **Best Tour and Travel**, 3–7 Chareon Muang Rd (tel 242086), **Discovery**, 201/15 Sridonchai Rd (by Chiang Mai Plaza Hotel, tel 276318) and also c/o Chiang Mai Plaza Hotel (tel 221044), **July**, c/o Novotel Suriwongse Hotel (tel 270051) or **World Travel Service**, c/o Rincome Hotel (tel 221692).

If you want something a little more adventurous, contact the **Chiang Mai Motorcycle Touring Club**, 21/1 Ratchamanka Soi 2 (tel 210518). This is a reputable company which organizes motorbike 'treks' for groups of 4–6, on Honda 125cc road or trail bikes; tours are from 1–4 weeks, and itineraries are flexible. An all-in package deal—motorcycle rental, fuel, shared accommodation, breakfast and evening meal—costs 1400B a day.

WHAT TO SEE

You'll need at least a week to 'do' Chiang Mai properly—it has so very much to offer. Set aside one day for shopping (morning, crafts factories; evening, Night Bazaar), 3–5 days for a hilltribe trek, and 2 days for sightseeing. The first thing to do (if you're here for exercise) is to book your trek. While that's coming together, you can slot in the markets and the temples. Save relaxation till the very end. Chiang Mai's general ambience of inertia has grounded many a good traveller.

Most of Chiang Mai's sights are temples—it has an even higher concentration of them than Bangkok. In just one square mile of the old city, there are no fewer than 40 temples, many of them still in use. Chiang Mai Temple architecture is a flamboyant mix of Lanna Thai, Burmese, Sri Lankan and Mon styles. There's enough diversity here to keep your interest alive and your camera clicking. As Chiang Mai is an education centre, several temples have schools or universities attached (great for making friends with Thai student monks). Many also have attractive gardens, full of exotic flowers and plants. But nearly all of Chiang Mai's temples are quiet, spacious and peaceful—a pleasant change from the crowded, touristy *wats* of Bangkok or Sukhothai.

Out-of-town Tour
(by *songthaew*, car, motorbike; full day)

Wat Phrathat (Doi Suthep) – Tribal Research Centre – National Museum – Wat Ched Yod – Wat Umong – Wat Suan Dork

Full marks to anyone completing this tour in just one day—but it *is* possible. Your best bet is to hire a motorbike or a car for the day. Hopping from sight to sight by *songthaew* can work, but it's costly in time and money. There are regular *songthaews* up to Doi

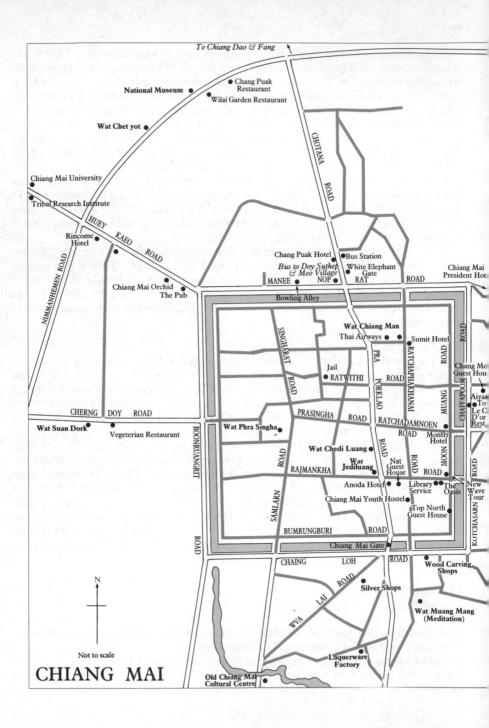

To Chiang Dao & Fang

National Museum
Chang Puak Restaurant
Wilai Garden Restaurant
Wat Chet yot

CHOTANA ROAD

Chiang Mai University
Tribal Research Insitute

HUEY KAEO ROAD

NIMMANHEMEN ROAD

Rincome Hotel

Chang Puak Hotel
Bus Station
Bus to Doy Suthep & Meo Village
White Elephant Gate
Chiang Mai President Hot
MANEE
NOP
RAT
ROAD
Chiang Mai Orchid
The Pub

Bowling Alley

SINGHARAT ROAD

Wat Chiang Man
Thai Airways
Sumit Hotel

PRA
PORKLAO
RATCHAPHAKHNAI ROAD
MUANG ROAD
CHAIYAPOOM
ROAD

Chang Mc Guest Hou

Jail
RATWITHI ROAD

Aiya
To
Le C
D'or
Rest

CHERNG DOY ROAD

PRASINGHA ROAD

RATCHADAMNOEN ROAD

Wat Suan Dork
Vegeterian Restaurant

BOONRUANGRIT

Wat Phra Singha

Montri Hotel

MOON ROAD

KOTCHASARN ROAD

Wat Chedi Luang
Wat Jediluang
Nat. Guest House
RAJMANKHA
Library Service
The Oasis
New Wave Tour
Anoda Hotel
Chiang Mai Youth Hostel

SAMLARN ROAD

Top North Guest House

BUMRUNGBURI ROAD

ROAD

Chiang Mai Gate

CHAING LOH ROAD
Wood Carving Shops

WVA LAI ROAD
Silver Shops

N

Wat Muang Mang (Meditation)

Not to scale

Laquerware Factory

CHIANG MAI

Old Chiang Mai Cultural Centre

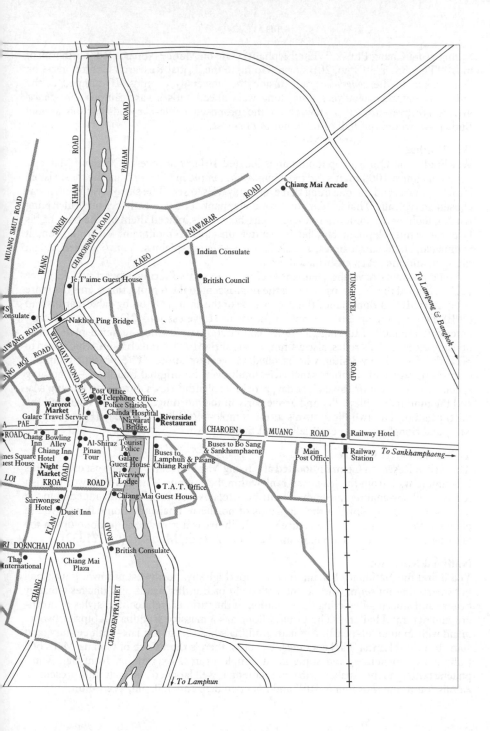

Suthep from Chang Phuak (White Elephant) Gate on Manee Noparat Rd (north wall of moat). The fare is 30B up, 20B down. Going to the Tribal Research Centre, insist on being taken to the *songthaew* rank inside the university campus. If dumped at the university entrance, you've a long, long walk ahead—it's a vast campus. *Songthaew* drivers are presently in a stew about the proposed cable-car construction at Doi Suthep—it would put half of them out of business.

Wat Prathat

Wat Prathat on Doi Suthep mountain is located 16 km northwest of Chiang Mai, at a height of almost 1000 m. It's the most important temple in Chiang Mai, the most visible local landmark, and the one thing that everybody tries to see. The site of Wat Prathat was chosen, in typically Thai fashion, by a royal elephant. The late 14th-century ruler King Ku Na, looking for somewhere to put some holy relics, placed them on the back of his favourite white elephant and let it wander off up the mountain. Near the top, it trumpeted, circled three times, and knelt down—very auspicious. A *chedi* was erected on the spot, and the relics enshrined therein.

Some accounts have the elephant keeling over and suffering a heart attack. Once you've climbed the 306 steps marking the final ascent to the temple, this seems the more likely story. If you don't fancy the exercise, take the short ride up by cable-car instead (10B). Don't show up at the temple in shorts or sleeveless tops ('Dress impolite can't enter this temple'). Entering the inner compound, you'll find the small plated *chedi* housing the Buddha's relics, also a strange little shrine to a sacred chicken, which used to peck the feet of any visitor who strolled in wearing shoes. The present temple—comprising two 16th-century sanctuaries built over the original buildings—is nothing special. But its location, on a clear day, provides splendid views down over Chiang Mai and the mountain valley. Try and arrive early in the morning, before the heat (and the mist) gets up. The two big festivals at the temple—Buddha's birthday (Full Moon in May) and Songkran—are especially good times to visit.

Tribal Research Centre

The Tribal Research Centre is located at Chiang Mai University, 5 km west of town. It's a 5-minute walk from the *songthaew* rank within the campus. The centre is worth a visit for its small, fascinating museum of hilltribe artefacts—an excellent introduction to the various peoples who inhabit the highlands of northern Thailand. Come here if you're planning to go on a trek—the centre's small library is a great place to bone up on the hilltribes. Opening times are 8.30 am–12 noon, 1–4 pm, Mon–Fri (tel 221332).

National Museum

You'll find the National Museum on the Superhighway, northwest of town. It's a small but interesting museum, with a fine collection of Buddha heads and images—mainly bronze and stucco—depicting the evolution of the various architectural styles of northern and central Thailand. The ground floor has a massive Buddha's footprint (wood, inlaid with mother-of-pearl), a goliath Buddha's head from the late-15th century, and some beautiful Lanna Thai ceramics. Upstairs, there's the Prince of Chiang Mai's bed (fully mosquito-netted) and some giant temple drums. Everything, from San Kamphaeng pottery to the smallest tribal implement, is well labelled and tastefully presented. Admission to the museum is 10B, and it's open 8.30 am–4.30 pm, Wed–Sun.

Wat Ched Yod

Wat Ched Yod is a short stroll south of the museum. It was probably built by King Tilokaraja in 1455, and its proper name is Wat Photharam Maha Viharn. The *ched yod* refers to the 'seven spires' of its *chedi*—the unusual design of which derives from the Mahabodhi temple in Bodhgaya, India. There's a spire for each of the seven weeks Buddha spent in Bodhgaya after attaining enlightenment under the Bo tree. One of Chiang Mai's most important temples, Ched Yod is also one of the most striking. Instead of the usual bell-shaped *chedi*, here we have a square edifice with friezes of bejewelled, crosslegged Buddhas (very Hindu) running round the base. Some, notably on the northeast corner of the *chedi*, are completely intact. Beyond them are two Bo trees—both descended (via Sri Lankan saplings) from the 'original'. Nearby, there's a smaller *chedi*, built in 1487 to contain Tiloraja's ashes. This is another square structure, with elements of Sukhothai, Lanna Thai and even Romanesque architectural styles. It has floral Renaissance arches and square Doric pillars, and—like every other monument in the compound—is guarded by temple dogs. I asked a monk why there were so many dogs and he said: 'It's very simple—people donate dogs to the temple, because they know we will feed them. The more dogs we have, the easier it is for us to keep our vows of fasting.' Apart from its dogs and its unique architecture, this temple has great historical importance. It was here that the 8th World Buddhist Council met in 1477 to revise the Tripitaka, or Buddhist teachings.

Wat Umong

Returning south down Nimanhemin Rd, turn east up Cherng Doy (Suthep) Rd. About a kilometre past the canal, a sign for **Wat Umong** appears on the left of the highway. If coming from town (5 km away), it's a 10B *songthaew* ride. Wat Umong was founded by Mengrai in 1296, and is a typical example of a forest *wat*—quiet and secluded, with a mirror-calm lake, several meditative walks, and a large park (open 6 am–6 pm) full of deer, gibbon and exotic birds. The woods are host to a scattering of wooden monks' houses, one of which sells homeopathic medicines (cured my cough!) made from rare plants and herbs grown in the forest. Little remains of the original temple, apart from a large ruined *chedi* with underground chambers where monks once meditated. Some of the niches in the crypt still contain Buddha images. At the top of the steps leading up to the ruins, there's a small pillar—a replica of Emperor Ashoka's pillar in India. Near this is an odd little art gallery full of Dali-esque daubs left behind by monks who've spent time here. For a pleasant woodland walk—and possible wildlife sightings—a path leads off left past the grotesque 'starving Buddha' below the ruined *chedi* to a small gate, giving access to the woods. In the main temple area, all trees have quaint 'moral messages' in Thai, Chinese and English. Some are enigmatic ('Little sacrifice for larger sacrifice is truly dropping a bait'), others are puritan ('A mind without work is most troubled') and one in particular is written for travellers ('To shoulder sufferings, a fool submits himself to the weight of sufferings at the same place. He is seated until his legs become atrophied. He is thus overloaded all his life, being always enslaved by sensual delights'). Every Sunday, between 3 and 5 pm, the head *bhikku* gives lectures at the *wat* (in English) on Buddhist meditation. There's a good 5B guide at the small library/museum.

Wat Suan Dork

Wat Suan Dork appears off Cherng Doy Rd, on the way back to town from Wat Umong.

This 'Flower Garden Temple' was built around 1383 by King Ku Na. It started out as the pleasure gardens of the early Lanna Thai kings, and later became their permanent resting place. Most of the royals of Chiang Mai are buried in the cemetery adjoining the temple—Indonesian-style *chedis* contain their ashes. The central *chedi* contains a Buddha relic which arrived here on the back of a white elephant, after which the city's White Elephant Gate was named. Of the recently restored temple buildings, the main hall is the largest in the North and houses a sitting Buddha and several smaller images. The *bot* holds the famous Chiang Saen-style bronze Buddha, seated and very large. It was constructed in 1504. Just past the main *viharn*, turn right down a small path to find a small house which gives traditional Thai massage (*nuad*) at 100B an hour. Back on the main road, beside the temple, there's an excellent hilltribe craft shop, selling a lot of weavings that you won't find anywhere else. Prices are very reasonable.

In-town Temples
(by bicycle/*songthaew*; half day)

Wat Chedi Luang – Wat Phra Singh – Wat Chang Man
These three temples are all fairly close to each other, within the city walls. You can see them in a morning, and in any order. If, at the end of the day, you want still more temples, just close your eyes and wander down any backstreet to find some.

Wat Chedi Luang
Wat Chedi Luang is on Phra Pokklao Rd, near the intersection with Rajmankha Rd. It has pleasant gardens, several quiescent dogs, and a massive, partially ruined *chedi*—commenced by King Saen Muang Ma in 1401, completed by his queen, and enlarged to a height of 86 metres by King Tilokaraja in 1454. Damaged by an earthquake in 1545, it is only now being considered for restoration. The eastern niche is reputed to have once contained the famous Emerald Buddha. The *bot* has a gleaming gold Buddha (standing) and 32 *jakarta* story panels. The *nagas* flanking the entrance steps are popularly regarded as architectural masterpieces. And there's a great gum tree with an interesting legend—it's said that as long as the tree stands, so will Chiang Mai. Behind the main *wat*, there's a stunning Buddha cut into the hillside—a dramatic sight indeed, when viewed at sunset.

Wat Phra Singh
Wat Phra Singh, at the intersection of Ratchadamnoen and Singharat roads, is one of Chiang Mai's biggest and oldest temples. The large *chedi* was begun in 1345 by King Pha Yu to hold the ashes of his father. The small *viharn* left of the white *stupa* was erected around 1400, to put up an unexpected guest—the important Phra Singh Buddha, which dropped in on its way to Chiang Mai (the chariot carrying it foundered at this spot) and never dropped out again. This is one of three Phra Singh images (the other two are in Bangkok and Nakhon Si Thammarat). It is in the early Chiang Saen style and—despite losing its head in 1922 (the present one is a replica)—still purports to be the 'original' image. Well, so do the other two. The walls of the *viharn* are decorated with peeling murals, interesting for their portrayals of northern dress, customs, and everyday life. The large compound has several interesting buildings, including a university of 700 student monks—many of them delighted to stop for a chat and a photo. To the right of the *viharn*,

there's a small 14th-century scripture repository. Behind this is the *bot* with its large gold Buddha, fine woodcarvings, decorative stucco-work and chandeliers.

Wat Chang Man

Wat Chang Man is on Ratchaphakhinai Rd, near Sumit Hotel. Founded in 1296 by King Mengrai (who used it as his residence while the rest of Chiang Mai was being built), it is the oldest temple in the city. Of the two *viharns* inside the entrance, the one on the right is the more interesting. This houses two venerated Buddha images—one is the tiny Crystal Buddha, said to have been presented to Queen Chamathevi of Haripunchai (modern-day Lamphun) in the 7th century. It is believed to have the power to inspire rain. So does the other image, the diminutive sensuous Buddha Sila (India, 9th century?) which sits alongside it on a raised dais. Outside, the grounds are beautiful—green lawns, tropical fruit trees, oleander and hibiscus bushes etc. This is a real 'farmyard' *wat*, with a twee turtle pond and masses of cats, dogs and chickens. The monks are very friendly—if the *viharns* are closed they'll always be willing to produce a key.

San Kamphaeng and Bo Sang
(by *songthaew*/motorbike; half day)

Chiang Mai is the largest centre for cottage industries in Thailand. The two handicraft villages of **San Kamphaeng** and **Bo Sang**—respectively 13 km and 9 km east of Chiang Mai—produce most of the silk, silver, lacquerware, celadon ceramics, woodcarvings and painted umbrellas found in the street markets of Chiang Mai. Prices aren't necessarily cheaper than in town (indeed, several craft factories are fixed-price) but the quality of goods is generally more reliable—especially silver and lacquerware. Even if you don't intend buying anything, bring your credit card along—you may change your mind. If you don't, there's still much enjoyment to be derived from watching the various craftsmen employing their traditional tools and techniques. Many of the larger factories give interesting English-speaking commentaries, describing the various manufacturing processes. All factories have a showroom (often air-conditioned) and can arrange to send large purchases home for you. There are dozens of craft places lining the famous '13 Kilometre Strip' between Chiang Mai and San Kamphaeng. The places recommended in the sections below are currently those with the best workshop layout, and the best range of fairly priced products.

Don't feel restricted, though—if travellers recommend other good factories, check them out. Buses run up to Bo Sang (4B) and to San Kamphaeng (5B) every 15 minutes or so from Charoen Muang Rd (see map). *Tuk-tuks* can be hired out at 80–100B for a morning—a good option, if there's a group of you. Motorbikes are still the best bet though—very handy for nipping back and forth between the various factories. To save time, it makes sense (as suggested in the order of crafts below) to work your way back to town, having taken the most outlying factory as your starting point.

Silk

Shinawatra Thai Silk, 145/1–2 Chiangmai-Sankamphaeng Rd (tel 331–950; tx 49337 MULBERY TH) is a busy cottage industry where primitive manual handlooms turn out reams of richly coloured silk cloth. The processes of silk production, well illustrated here, are fascinating—first, the silk-worms are gorged on mulberry leaves; later, the cream-yellow thread is drawn from the cast-off cocoons (just one cocoon can produce 1200 metres of silk thread) and bleached white or colour-dyed. A single hand-operated loom, working full-pelt, can produce up to 7 or 8 metres of silk material in one day. All prices at the silk factory are *fixed*. If it's just lengths of silk you're after, you'll probably get them cheaper in Bangkok. However, there are some unique colour-combination patterns here which you simply won't find elsewhere—well worth a little extra expense. Standard 2-ply plain silk (suitable for shirts and blouses) sells at 220B a yard; heavier 4-ply cloth (for suits, bedcovers, furnishings etc) at 290B a yard. There's a good range of silk scarves (250B), hankies (70B), shirts (600B), and patterned kimonos (from 2000B). Silk ties, in rather unexciting colours, are around 150B. For men, the best buy of all are double-breasted suits (lined and interfaced) in heavy black silk at only 3600B (£80)—fitted and made up in just three days. Any other items you want tailored (suits, dresses, shirts etc.) will appear at your hotel within 24 hours. But you may well find what you want in the ready-made section. Ladies can buy smart, fashionable silk jackets, off the peg, for around 1200B (£25)—about one-third of London prices. Shinawatra also has a wide selection of cotton fabrics. Thai cotton is extremely well-tempered and high quality. Prices are cheap too—around 70–100B per yard.

Lacquerware
Laitong Lacquerware is at 80/1 Moo 3, Chiangmai-Sankamphaeng Rd (tel 331178; tx 49324 CAC TH ATT T. SANGCHAK, LAITONG). Thai lacquerware is an ancient craft, which actually originated in Burma. In the past, lacquerwork was used to decorate Thai palaces and temples; today, most products are small items aimed at the tourist trade. Lacquer is a thick black resin extracted from the 'lak' tree of the northern forests. The resin is applied to bamboo or teakwood, to create beautiful bowls, boxes, vases, plates and other decorative pieces. Each item is carefully coated and polished at least seven times (and left to dry for a week between each successive coating) before being finished with eggshell, gold leaf, or handpainted decorations. As with silver, the quality of lacquerware is almost impossible to detect on sight: many lacquer pieces sold in the night market, for example, have only two or three coats. Quality at this factory is however, guaranteed. Nice buys include stylish coffee tables (around 11,000B), handpainted tea-chests (around 16,000B) and gold-leaf trinket boxes (500B). Smaller novelty purchases are lacquer ducks and owls (150–200B) and teak elephants (120B).

Teakwood
For teakwood, visit **Chiangmai Sudaluk Co**, 99/9 Ban Nongkhong, Chiangmai-Sankamphaeng Rd (tel 331489; tx SUDALUK TH). This factory is known to take the best care during its teakwood curing process—a vital consideration. Inferior 'green' teak (which looks exactly the same as seasoned woods to the average shopper) splits within a few months. Northern Thailand used to be a paradise for teak exporters, but the forests have now been sadly depleted and good-quality teak is hard to find. Prices are rising 10% each year—making anything you buy a good future investment. All items are made in perfectly interlocking sections, and are superbly carved. Another good reason for buying 'big' is that it costs more or less the same to insure and ship home one teak cabinet as it does six. Smaller teak items, you can buy more cheaply down at the Night Market.

Silverware
Na Na Phan Silverware, 159/1 Chiangmai-Sankamphaeng Rd (tel 331534) produces high-quality silverware and jewellery. Silver generally comes in three grades: 100%, 80% and plated white bronze. Much of the so-called silver sold in the markets of Chiang Mai is plated bronze, which rapidly tarnishes. Na Na Phan sells the real thing—all 'soft' jewellery (bracelets, rings, earrings etc.) is pure silver; more 'solid' stuff (bowls, teapots etc.) are a mix of 80% silver, 20% copper. Very delicate pieces are produced, cleverly blending modern and traditional designs. Prices are very reasonable—on my last visit, I was offered a 50% discount on everything *before* getting down to hard bargaining. Handbeaten silver bowls (made from old Indian rupees) are offered at a label price of 500B. Silver bracelets go from between 500 and 3000B, necklaces from 1500 to 3000B, and earrings from 250B. If you're into gems, the best purchases are blue sapphires (400B per carat) and turquoise (250B per carat). The factory workshop is a good one, with an interesting new hilltribe jewellery section.

Umbrellas
Bo Sang Umbrella-making Village, 11/2 Opposite of Bosang (tel 331324) started out as a small family collective, but has greatly expanded over the past few years. The craft of umbrella-making, which probably originated in China, was taken up by the Bo Sang villagers some 200 years ago. The gaily-painted parasols they make are usually fashioned from the bark of mulberry trees, which is mashed flat, soaked in a vat of water, and dried (as fine fibres) to form a thin paper called '*sa*'. The wafer-thin sheets of paper are applied in layers to the frame of the umbrella which (astonishingly) is cut and formed from a single piece of cane. The finished product is very strong and very practical. Things to buy are brollies (from 120B), lampshades (from 20B), and fans (from 50B)—all attractive little souvenirs. Umbrellas are best bought at this factory where there's a large selection of sunny designs—rather than in Chiang Mai. Prices in the showroom are fixed—but outside in the workshop, it's a different story. Here cheerful artisans will paint just about anything (cameras, wallets, handbags etc.) for as little as 10–20B per piece. A great idea is to turn up with a yard of plain silk, and to ask Chai—the number one artist—to daub it with a dramatic Chinese dragon or peacock. The result is an amazing silk wall-hanging at a (ridiculous) price of 300B—200B for the silk, 100B for Chai's artistry.

Trekking

Trekking out of Chiang Mai is now the major tourist draw of the North. There are over 30 tour companies in town, offering a multitude of treks from 1 to 10 days, usually a combination of walking, elephant-riding and river-rafting. All trekking has to be organized. While people do wander off into the northern hills on their own, they are advised that this is still a very volatile region—bandits, political insurgents, and even suspicious hilltribe peoples, can regard the lone traveller, unescorted by a local guide, as fair game for theft or worse.

The Hill Tribes

What makes trekking in North Thailand so special? The answer must lie in the 500,000 or so highland peoples, members of six major distinct hilltribes, who now inhabit its mountainous valleys and forests. Most of them are relative newcomers, having only arrived in Thailand over the last century, and substantial numbers are still trickling in from Burma and Laos. The hilltribes of Thailand are descended from Chinese and Tibetan Mongols. There are two main lines of descent; first, the Chinese Lolo and Nosu, who descended into Tibeto and Burmano tribes (the Tibetos subsequently became the Akha, Lisu and Lahu tribes); second, the mainstream Chinese, who descended into the Kuomintang, the famous revolutionaries. The Kuomintang later gave birth to the Meo and the Yao peoples. The sixth major line, the Karen, originated in Burma and began settling in Thailand several centuries ago.

Since the hilltribes are such a fundamental part of trekking, it's worth learning something about them before setting out. A few hours spent browsing in Chiang Mai's Tribal Research Centre library always pays dividends, as does a night out at a Khantoke dinner dance. But the best all-round introduction is Paul and Elaine Lewis' *Peoples of the Golden Triangle* (Thames and Hudson, 1984) which sells at D. K. Book Shop, Chiang Mai, at half its London price. You can also find it at Golden Triangle restaurant, Chiang Rai (even cheaper), which is near to where the authors live. To start you off, here's a short hilltribe primer:

Karen (Kariang, Yan) are the largest of the tribes of northern Thailand (present population 275,000) though most of the Karen people still live in Burma. They settle at low altitudes, generally around 200 metres, and are heavily engaged in shifting cultivation. The four major sub-groups are: White (Skaw), Red (Kayah), Black (Pa-o), and Pwo (or Plong) Karen. The red and white Karen have a unique language—a blend of Latin (taught them by missionaries in Burma) and northern hilltribe dialect. As a whole, the Karen are a fairly straightlaced lot, often dressed in Western clothes, but their women (well-known for their weaving, done on a back-strap loom) are often colourfully attired. Karen girls often wear long white tunics, exchanging them for red ones when they get married. In religion, the Karen are mainly animist, though a few are Christian or Buddhist. The best hilltribe crafts come from this tribe—good things to buy (either on trek, or in Ying Ping Bazaar, Chiang Mai) are hand-embroidered jackets, woven baskets, musical instruments, tobacco pipes and animal bells.

Meo (Hmong or Mong) are the most widespread minority group in southern China. The 80,000 or so who live in Thailand settle mainly at high altitudes (1000 to 1200 metres), ideal for the growing of opium, their main cash crop. The Meo probably grow more opium than any other tribe, but also cultivate dried rice and corn.

In appearance, they look very Chinese or Mongolian (hence 'Mong'); in religion, although animist, they practise various Chinese-based rituals, with a strong emphasis on ancestor-worship. Meo huts usually contain an ancestor shrine and are built, unlike Karen stilt-houses, on ground level. The three sub-groups found in Thailand are: Blue Meo (Mong Njua), whose women wear indigo-dyed pleated skirts and keep their hair up in big, puffy buns; White Meo (Hmong Daw), whose women wear turbans and exchange their regular indigo-dyed trousers for white pleated skirts on ceremonial occasions; and the Gua Mba Meo (Hmong Gua Mba) who are recent arrivals from Laos, mostly confined to refugee camps. The clothing of Meo women is particularly ornate, employing decorative embroidery, appliqué, cutwork, pom-poms and batik cloth. Both men and women usually wear silver necklaces.

142

Lahu (Musuer) probably originated in the Tibetan highlands, and presently number around 60,000 in Thailand. The Lahu divide into four major sub-groups: Black (Lahu Na), Red (Lahu Nyi), Yellow (Lahu Shi) and the Lahu Sheh Leh. The dominant clan, the Lahu Na, have the most interesting traditional dances and have been almost completely converted to Christianity. Partly because opium remains a cash crop, the Lahu are very itinerant. A piece of land on which the opium poppy has grown for four years, is good for nothing. After 20 years, all the land surrounding a village has been exhausted, and the tribe must move on. This is most true of the Lisu (who grow opium for sale) and the Lahu (who both sell it and smoke it). Often, the chieftain or 'shaman' of a tribe will simply drop a raw egg on the ground: whichever direction the albumen flows furthest, the people go. Most Lahu remain strongly animist (despite the Black Lahu defection) and favour swidden agriculture. The women, often heavily adorned with silver medallions, produce unique weaving (notably delicate patchwork trims and fine embroidery) with the pattern appearing on only one side of the cloth. The Lahu are also skilled in basket-weaving and woodwork.

Yao (Yu Mien) are the only tribe to have their own written language. They still use Chinese characters to inscribe Taoist rituals and to keep family records. The Yao are a homogenous group (present population in Thailand 55,000), the only sub-group of their type to migrate to Southeast Asia. Basically animists, with traces of Taoism and ancestor-worship, they tend to settle at opium-producing altitudes. Men traditionally wear black caps. Women often add red-plush collars to their garments. They are noted for their cross-stitch embroidery, and produce richly decorated patchwork clothing. Yao silversmiths are famous for their finely crafted jewellery.

Lisu (Lisaw) divide into two main sub-groups. The Black Lisu (Ha Lisu) live in China and Burma. The Flowery Lisu (Hua Lisu) live mainly in Thailand, and number around 24,000. They have adopted many Chinese cultural influences, but remain firmly animist in their beliefs. Like most hill people, the Lisu are heavily engaged in shifting cultivation and (along with the Meo) grow opium as a principal crop. They wear lots of coin jewellery, colourful cloth outfits trimmed with rows of appliquéd patchwork, tassels and beads, and (at festivals) massive amounts of handcrafted silver ornaments. Of all the tribes, the Lisu are the most visually striking.

Akha (E Kaw, Egor) probably originated in the Tibetan highlands, and currently number around 35,000 in Thailand. The Akha are stubbornly animist, resisting all attempts to convert them to other religions. They place much emphasis on ancestor-worship and erect sacred gates at the entrance to their villages, to safeguard them against evil spirits. The Akha settle at high altitudes and grow opium, in addition to rice and corn. As late settlers, they've had to make do with the poorest land, and are consequently the most desperate to sell crafts to visitors. Poverty makes the Akha a rather cheerless lot (the men are particularly grim), but they have amazing costumes. Especially the married women, who wear elaborate headdresses (*u-cher*) studded with silver rupees, and lots of showy embroidery. The Akha turn out some nice crafts, including lacquer bamboo baskets, silver ornaments, and scarab-beetle necklaces.

Thailand's half a million hilltribe people are presently in a state of crisis. The problem

143

is opium, or rather lack of it. Opium was first brought to China by Arab traders in the 8th century. By the 19th century, it was seen as a miracle crop—successfully used, along with its derivative morphine, as a medicinal aid in both the East and the West. Encouraged by early traders to grow and consume opium, the hilltribe farmers adopted it as an integral part of their traditional way of life—it provided them with both medicine and a stable source of income. Later, when the negative, addictive aspects of opium became apparent, the Thai government—under mounting international pressure—officially outlawed the opium poppy (1959). This threatened the hilltribes' whole way of life, and some of them retreated deep into the jungle to circumvent the ban by producing a new, much deadlier opium derivative—heroin. The impact of heroin (80 times more potent than opium) upon the international narcotic market was awesome. In Thailand alone, where heroin addiction was virtually unknown 20 years ago, the authorities are now treating an estimated 300,000 addicts. In February 1988, the Thai government triumphantly announced the seizure of 1.2 tons of raw heroin, their largest haul to date. But this is as nothing to the estimated 100 tons of the death-dealing drug being illegally produced each year in the infamous 'Golden Triangle' area bordering Thailand, Burma and Laos. The legendary opium warlord Khun Sa, forced to limit operations in Thailand and Burma, is now known to have set up heroin refineries in Laos. Few of the profits of the heroin trade make their way into the hilltribes' pockets—they remain, like the addicts they supply, poor and exploited.

Over the last 10 years, the Thai government has made poppy eradication a major priority. Surprise raids on villages and burning of opium crops have been followed by (moderately successful) crop-substitution programmes. With opium-growing land reduced from 3000 'rai' to less than 15 'rai', only 20 tons of opium were produced in 1988, compared with 200 tons 15 years ago. The general effect of all this on the hilltribes, suddenly deprived of opium and encouraged to settle down and grow kidney beans, potatoes, coffee and cabbages instead, is critical. As they struggle to maintain a traditional lifestyle without the poppy—in the face of a growing population, depleted soil, and increasing poverty—what remains of their culture is being exploited for the benefit of tourists from Chiang Mai. Tourism does of course bring some financial benefits—the highland peoples now have a flourishing market for their craft goods—but many sales are conducted through a middleman, and the workers themselves often see little profit. Once dependent on opium and now dependent on tourism to supplement their incomes, these people of the poppy now face an uncertain future.

Going on Trek

Trekking out of Chiang Mai is neither as cheap nor as straightforward as it used to be. There are still some excellent treks to be had, if you deal with the right people. But to deal with the wrong people is to court disaster. Recently, there have been too many cases of over-trekked areas and inadequate service from trek companies. This produces the following kind of situations:

> All we got to eat for three days were hardboiled eggs—with baby chicks inside them. They were so well-disguised by the sugar coating that we munched quite a few before realizing the truth.

The opium poppy

Our guide was out of his head on opium. The village chief gave him a pipe of peace, and the two of them spent the next 36 hours horizontal. Come to think of it, we hardly ever saw the guide in an upright position—even on an elephant.

Our bamboo raft disintegrated in the middle of the river. Our guide and two old ladies were left dangling out of a tree. The next day, our elephants stampeded off into the jungle.

We arrived in a village to find a party of package tourists already there—all clicking away with Nikons and peering into private family huts. It was like a human zoo!

Good trek companies come and go, and your best recommendations will always come from speaking to other travellers. Still, be prepared to spend a day looking round for the right deal, and maybe another day waiting for the group quota to be reached before departure. Choosing a trek is never easy, so here are a few tips. First and foremost, you'll want a company whose guides are registered with the Tourism Authority (ask them to show their badge). This gives you some comeback should your trek hit a major problem. Ideally, your guide should speak good English, in addition to the northern dialect and a couple of tribal languages. If he can cook as well, you're onto a winner. Secondly, it adds greatly to the enjoyment of your trip if the company takes a genuine interest in the welfare of the villages on its route, and doesn't just use them as a circus for tourists. Thirdly, you'll want a guarantee that you're the *only* group travelling on that particular trek circuit. Don't assume that the further north you go, the more remote it's going to be—most of the north is now overtrekked and very touristy. Most treks from Chiang Mai go north to Chiang Rai and the Golden Triangle (very busy) or west to Pai and Mae Sariang (fairly quiet). The virgin territories to the south and east are still being cautiously opened up by company scouts—if you find a trek blazing trails to these regions, or to the southwest of Chiang Mai, take it. Whatever you do, don't ask any trekking agency if it's the 'best'. I did, and the guide said 'No, we are not best. Two companies are better—first one, finished already; second one, doesn't come yet!'

The average cost of a trek is 300–350B a day—plus another 250–350B for elephants or river-rafting. A typical 3-day, 2-night trek will therefore cost in the region of 1400–1800B. But there's heavy competition between the various companies, and you can often get cheaper deals by shopping around. At the time of writing, recommended low-price operators include **Aiyeret Tours**, 422 Ta Pae Rd (tel 235396), **Exotic Travel Service**, 227 Ta Pae Rd (tel 235515), **Camp of Troppo**, 83/2 Chotana Rd (tel 279360), **Nat Guest House, Folkways** and **Chiang Mai Youth Hostel**. More pricey, but just as good, are **Summit Tours**, 28–30 Ta Pae Rd (tel 233351), **New Wave Service**, c/o Rimping Guest House, Muangsinghkhum Rd (tel 232664), **July Travel**, c/o Novotel Suriwongse Hotel (tel 270051), **Lamthong Tour**, 77 Ta Pae Rd (tel 235448), **Pinan Tour**, 235 Ta Pae Rd (tel 236081), **Top North Tour**, c/o Chiang Mai Plaza Hotel, Sridonchai Rd (tel 252050) and **Galare Travel**, 54–56 Ta Pae Rd (tel 236237).

You won't need to take much on trek—just a change of socks, T-shirts and under-wear, a towel and a swimming costume (for that rare dip in a mountain stream), a water bottle (fill up before departure), sun-oil, sun-hat and mosquito repellent, a camera and lots of sticky plasters, film (plus a flash), toilet paper, and disinfectant, and a small torch. A couple of plastic bags to hold dirty laundry, or to keep clothes dry (i.e. when it's raining, or when you're fording deep rivers) come in very handy. So do a pair of flip flops—you can't wear shoes in hilltribe huts. People often trek in shorts, but a pair of long pants is a good idea for bristly elephants—one person always rides up front, on the elephant's head, as *mahout*. More often than not, the *mahout* ends up in a ditch or a river. The *mahout* always gets very wet. In the cold season, you'll need to take a sleeping bag and some warm top garments. In the rainy season, a waterproof jacket or a plastic sheet is essential. Small presents to give out at the villages take up little room, and are always appreciated. If you feel (as many do) that doling out lollies, cigarettes and money is like visiting the animals in the zoo, stick to practical gifts like embroidery thread and safety pins (for the hilltribe women), pencils and drawing books (for the kids), and antiseptic or fungal creams (for the head man—his village may only see a doctor once in six months). Only take along antibiotics if you're prepared to administer them. Pointing cameras at villagers is very rude—get them to take a photo of you first, or give them a postcard of your home town. Then they'll be far more likely to pose. Regarding money, you won't need to take much—all meals and accommodation should be included in the price of your trek. But one of the villages might have some nice weavings or jewellery for sale (300B should cover this) and you may want to take along a bottle of Mekong for evening sing-songs (another 100B). For a standard 3–4 days' outing, 500B pocket money should be sufficient. The one thing you *must* take along with you (unless booked in a *very* reliable hotel) is your credit card. If it's lost on trek, well at least you know it's gone. There have been too many cases of cards being duplicated by guest houses while their owner is on trek. The duplicate card goes on a spending spree in Bangkok, and the owner returns home to a massive bill.

Trekking is most enjoyable between October and February—especially in February, when the hills are a riot of blossoming flowers. The rainy months of June to September are not recommended—walking is arduous, river-rafting hazardous, and elephants hide a lot under trees. Even in good weather though, you'll need to be fit—walking 4–5 hours a day along unmarked trails, through deep jungles, and up and down hills, can leave people with sedentary life-styles gasping. So, while you're waiting for your trek to come together, hire a bicycle, see some sights, and get some exercise.

RECREATION

Relaxing 'old style' massage is given at **Suan Samoonprai**, 103 Wangsinghkham Rd, just off Soi Sarkakorn. There are several massage parlours in town (some more dubious than others), but at 60B an hour, this one has to be the cheapest. It's open 8 am to 9 pm, and you're wise to ring ahead (tel 252663) to make an appointment. If you want to **learn** massage, go to **Old Medicine Hospital**, south of town near the Old Chiang Mai Cultural Centre. The teacher here was trained at Wat Po in Bangkok, and he offers excellent 10-day courses (with an examination at the end) at 1200B.

There's **golf** at the **Lanna Golf Club**, at Nong Hua, north of the superhighway, 4 km from town and at **Chiang Mai Golf and Country Club** on the superhighway (tel 248321). Green fees are around 400B during the week, 600B at weekends and holidays. **Tennis** is on offer at the Anantasiri Courts, opposite the National Museum, and **darts** and **snooker** at the Black Cat Bar, 25 Moonmuang Rd, Dusit Inn Hotel in Changklan Rd and at the Domino Bar, next to the Top North Center Hotel in Moonmuang Rd. **Anodard Hotel**, 57 Ratchamandkha Rd, **Prince Hotel**, 3 Taiwang Rd, **Rincome Hotel** and **Top North Guest House** have good swimming pools. Admission for non-residents is 30–50B, and you need to bring your own towel. The cine club at the **AUA Auditorium**, 24 Ratchadamnoen Rd, features old movies weekly in English, whilst the **Alliance Française**, 138 Charoenprathet Rd, has regular showings of French screen favourites. If you want to earn money teaching English (a recreation in itself), ask a Thai friend to help you place an ad in a local newspaper. The response is always good, and you stand to earn around 90B an hour.

NIGHTLIFE

After-dark action in Chiang Mai revolves mainly around night clubs, discos, bars, cocktail lounges, coffee shops and open-air restaurants. It's all rather intimate, far less boisterous than raunchy, neon-lit Bangkok. Popular discotheques are **Club 77** in the Chiang Mai Orchid Hotel, **Plaza Disco** in the Chiang Mai Plaza Hotel, **Bubbles** in the Porn Ping Hotel and **Wall Club** in the Chiang Inn Hotel. All are open 9 pm to 2 am nightly; the 100B admission includes one free drink. The Dusit Inn Hotel has the **Music Room**, a fair nightclub with live music for the not so young crowd (open till 1 am, no admission). Headbangers can get their fill at **Early Times**, 53 Kotchasan Rd, where the electric guitarists raise merry hell nightly from 9 pm to 2 am. Two good night-spots are **Oasis Bar** on Moon Muang Rd, and the **Riverside** at 9–11 Jarernrasd Rd, opposite Chinda Hospital. Both have excellent live music—the Riverside is the main haunt of Thai students, and has a great folk, country and blues band. It is one of the few restaurants to stay open past 10.30 pm (it closes at 2 am). The Oasis has a cosy video lounge and a talented girl singer ('Jim') who comes on at midnight.

SHOPPING

Shopping in Chiang Mai centres on the amazing **Night Bazaar** in Chang Klang Rd. This runs from around 6 pm to midnight daily, and is the place to pick up cheap designer goods, ethnic hilltribe handicrafts, and all manner of low-priced souvenirs. The market itself has a pronounced party atmosphere, jollied along by a booming sound system playing songs like *How much is that doggie in the window?* It's quite a joke trying to bargain down a Lacoste briefcase with Elvis moaning *Hound Dog* down your ear. But everybody hums along to Thai disco hits like *Hi Ho, Hi Ho, it's off to work we go.* By 10 pm, the place is really jumping—the coaxing croons of persuasive street-hawkers ('Herrro! You waaant somethink? Special price for yooou!') float enticingly over the jostling bedlam of package tourists fearfully guarding their wallets, backpackers haggling for hippie hill-tribe jackets, and beggars hopefully rattling tin cups from the pavements. Above it all drifts a variety of aromatic, tantalizing smells from sizzling woks and frangipani stalls, overladen with the less aromatic fumes of beaten-up *tuk-tuks*. From elevated hotel balconies, spent-out travellers look down in mild wonderment on one of the last great markets of the East building up to its nightly climax of colour, noise, and excitement.

The night market has two focal points—the **Chiang Mai Plaza**, a large 3-storey covered area in mock northern style, and **Vieng Ping Bazaar**, an old-style covered market set aside for the hilltribes. The Plaza has the monopoly on fashion clothes and shoes (which are the best buys) and has the cheapest leather-bound fake Gucci/Dunhill briefcases (from 500B). Things to look out for are large patchwork shoulder-bags, tartan-style cotton bedspreads and appliqué cushion-covers. The Vieng Ping by contrast, offers a wide range of traditional hilltribe produce—hand-embroidery, chunky silver-jewellery, painted umbrellas, batiks, and musty, dusty 'antiques'. Bargain hard here to get the following prices: Burmese bead-and-embroidery pieces (2 × 2ft size, 500B), opium weights in hand-carved 'pencil boxes' (110B), hippy rucksacks (70B), and beautiful hilltribe jackets (single-sided 250B, double-sided 600 to 100B). Be careful when buying embroidered stuff—some of it is hand-made by villagers and some of it isn't (thinner cloth and bright colours indicate machine-work). For the best bargains, visit the Ying Ping in the early afternoon—this is when the hilltribe folk drop off their best produce.

Outside of the covered markets, there are hundreds of street stalls. Again, bargain hard—for handpainted T-shirts (85B), 'Charles Jourdan' briefcases (1000B), natty 'Gucci' lighters (30B), stylish leather coats (2000B) and jackets (1500B). Don't waste your money on cheap 60B 'Benetton' T-shirts (the only thing that doesn't shrink is the designer label), or regular 35B T-shirts (even large sizes shrink to super-small after one wash). The night market also offers the cheapest pirate cassettes in Thailand (from 20B), and some lovely old-fashioned jewellery—e.g. rough-silver necklaces, studded with jade and semi-precious stones, from only 160B.

Crowded **Warorot Market**, just five minutes' walk above the night bazaar, is where the locals come to shop. The large covered indoor market isn't up to much, but there are clothing bargains to be found in the side-alley behind it—trousers (for short people only) around 120B, summery cotton skirts from 90B etc. A lot of the stuff that turns up at the night market apparently originates from Warorot, though you'll have a job finding it. For clothes that don't fade, shrink, or fall apart, shop at **Tantrapantapea**, north of the moat on Manee Nopparat and its branch in Ta Pae Rd or **Sorkanka** just below Warorot market and **Season Plaza** on Chang Klan Rd south of Sridornchai Rd. These department stores are where young Thai trendies come to buy the latest fashions. The **Central Dept. Store** has now opened at the **Kadsvankaen Complex**, next to the Chiang Mai Orchid Hotel.

Chiang Mai's general stores and supermarkets, centred on Ta Pae Rd, are mostly open from 10 am to 8.30 pm. Silk shops are all over town, but **Kinaree Thai Silk**, 40/3 Moo 6, Tonpaosankampaeng Rd, gets consistently good mentions. So does the tiny silk shop in Ta Pae Rd, next to 'Hello' money-changer. The best tailors are in Ta Pae Road too—they aren't quite as good as their Bangkok counterparts though. A notable exception is **Seiko Tailor**, just over the Nakhon Ping Bridge on Kaeo Nawarat Rd (tell your *tuk-tuk* driver 'Ran tad pa Seiko'). This is the most respected tailor in town, much used by Thais. Seiko can make up trousers for 120B, shirts for 80B, and a whole suit for as little as 600B.

WHERE TO STAY   (tel prefix 053)

Hotels (Expensive)
The best hotel in Chiang Mai, indeed in the north of Thailand, is the **Chiang Mai Orchid**, northwest of town at 100–102 Huay Kaew Rd (tel 222099), with classic Doi Suthep views, extremely helpful staff, a very good restaurant, nightclub, pool, sauna and fitness centre (2600B). Three of Chiang Mai's other good hotels—all with rooms from 1200B—are located at the Night Bazaar. **Dusit Inn**, 112 Chang Klang Rd (tel 281033; tx 251037) is the most comfortable. It's a modern 'international' hotel, with two fine restaurants, nightclub, lifeguards at the pool, and decent views from the 8th floor (and above). The **Novotel Suriwongse Hotel**, 110 Chang Klang Rd (tel 270051; tx 49308 HS TH) is well-established and has lots of style, but shows its age. **Chiang Inn Hotel**, 100 Chang Klang Rd (tel 270070; tx TH 43503) is pleasantly sophisticated, with a popular restaurant/coffee shop and half-decent views from 6th floor and above.

Further afield, the up-and-coming luxury hotel is **Chiang Mai Plaza**, 92 Sridonchai Rd (tel 270036) with doubles from 1500B. Perks here include a smart pool, a swinging disco, and a free American breakfast (10% room discounts too, if booking through Skybird Agency on the first floor). **Chiang Come Hotel**, 7/35 Suthep Rd (tel 281016) is another quiet place, with scenic views. Rooms are very reasonably priced: from 600B double.

Two new hotels in the running for international hotel status are **The Empress** at 199 Chang Klan Rd (tel 272020) with pool, disco, tennis courts and conference facilities (rooms from 2500B) and the **Lanna Palace** at 184 Chang Klan Rd (tel 270722) with similar facilities but cheaper rates—rooms from 1800B.

Guest Houses (Inexpensive)
There are presently some 80 guest houses in Chiang Mai, many of them charging 80–120B for twin-bedded rooms with fan; 160–200B, with attached bathroom. Three 'superior' guest houses, worthy of special mention are **Srisupan** (lovely rooms from 180B) at 92 Wualai Rd (tel 270086); **Galare** (rooms from 220B) at 7–7/1 Charoenprathat Rd (tel 273885); **Top North** (rooms 250–400B) at 15 Moon Muang Soi 2 Rd (tel 278900), and the **River View Lodge** (rooms with river view 500–800B) at 25

Charoenprathat Rd (tel 271110). Galare and River Lodge are both central, with attractive river views, and River View offers river cruises, too. Top North ('We are not fortune tellers, but we know well what you are coming for') is delightfully quiet, with a good restaurant and swimming pool, and has a good travel agency. In the 80–120B range, there's **Nat Guest House**, 7 Prapokklao Rd Soi 6 (tel 212878)—a special place run by a special lady—and the ever-popular **Youth Hostel**, 31 Prapokklao Rd Soi 3 (tel 212863). If these two are full, walk down the small *soi* between them to find friendly **Julie Guest House**, 7/1 Prapokklao Rd with doubles from 80B. Even cheaper places are **Je T'Aime**, 247–9 Charoenrat Rd (tel 241912), with bicycle hire and riverside situation, and **Peter Guest House**, 46/3 Moon Muang Rd, Soi 9 (tel 210617), offering free continental breakfast and toilet paper. Along with Nat and the Youth Hostel, Peter gives excellent service and operates good treks. Travellers have also recommended **Chiangmai Garden**, 82–86 Ratchamaka Rd (tel 210881), and **V.K.** at 22/2 Chang Moi Kao Rd (tel 252559), though everybody I've ever met in Chiang Mai has been able to recommend a different guest house.

EATING OUT
The best introduction to northern food, largely influenced by Burmese recipes and characterized by its spicy curries, is one of Chiang Mai's famous **Khantoke dinners**. *Khan* literally means 'bowl' and *toke* is a small, low table—usually made of rattan or lacquerware—around which diners sit on the floor and share a succession of tasty dishes accompanied with sticky or plain rice. The principal dishes are *Kaeng Han Le* (pork curry with garlic, ginger and other spices), *Nam Prik Ong* (minced pork cooked with tomato, cucumber, onion and chillies), *Kang Kai* (chicken and vegetable curry) and *Larb* (minced meat mixed with chillies). Today, an intrinsic part of Khantoke dinners are traditional northern dance performances. At **Old Chiang Mai Cultural Centre**, 185/3 Wualai Rd (tel 235097), you can enjoy an endless procession of small-bowl dishes while watching a colourful procession of northern Thai folk-dances. Last on the bill is the popular *Ramwong* (circle) dance, where members of the audience are invited to join in. The second part of the show takes place in an adjoining building, and features hilltribe dances. This is an excellent opportunity to see a number of tribes in rotation, and to note differences in appearance and costume. It's also an excellent photo stop, so bring a flash. Khantoke dinner-dances take place between 7 and 10 nightly, and 200B tickets (good value—the same show would be 300B in Bangkok) are sold in hotels, at travel agencies, and on the street.

Similar to the Old Chiang Mai Cultural Centre, but not quite as good is **Khum Kaew Palace**, 252 Phrapokklao Rd (tel 214315; same times and prices as above).

There's a wide range of other places to eat in Chiang Mai. For original Thai cuisine, don't miss **Baan Suan**, 51/3 Chiang Mai-San Kamphaeng Rd (tel 242116) pleasantly set in a typical northern-style teak house. Most dishes are around 60–90B, and include 'specials' like Chiang Mai Sausage, Pork Curry Burmese Style, Grilled Black Fish, Grilled Spare Ribs, and Fried Shrimp with Chilli Paste (hot). There is similar northern-style fare at **Aroon Rai**, 43–45 Kotchasarn Rd (tel 276947). Out of town, the **Galae** restaurant, 65 Suthep Rd (tel 278655) has a romantic atmosphere in a peaceful lakeside setting. Come for the set lunch of spring rolls, pork with honey, chicken satay, shrimp fried rice, chicken in coconut-milk soup, and fresh fruit platter—all for under 200B a head.

China Town Suki, 147/13–16 Chang Klang Rd (tel 274646) does delicious mid-priced Chinese food. If you want to go Indian, **Al-Shiraz**, 123 Chang Klang Rd (tel 274338) serves mouthwatering tandoori, biriani, tikka and kebabs, and you can order half portions if you want. Seafood (and Japanese food) should be sampled at **Nang Nual Seafood**, 27 Koa Klang Rd, Nong Hoi (tel 241771). This is a delightful restaurant in landscaped grounds with a bird garden, waterfall, shopping arcade, and a selection of dining rooms. The fresh crab, shrimp and fish are sold by weight; count on a minimum of 500B per person for dinner. Seafood (and Thai/Chinese fare) is cheaper at **Tangsukjai** restaurant, at 98/7 Sridonchai Rd, near Chiang Mai Plaza Hotel. Run by friendly Poo and sister, this is a real 'Thai-style' hangout. Locals also favour **Takrai**, Soi Wat Phra Singh near the temple. With old Thai-style decor, it specializes in Thai dishes from the north. Service is friendly and efficient, and prices reasonable—500B for two. At the Dusit Inn, the **Jasmine Chinese Restaurant** has a very extensive menu (including bird's nest) and many unidentifiable dishes besides, but the attentive staff will see you through. Arrive hungry though—everything is tempting, and two people can have a complete blow-out meal for 1000–1200B. North of town near the museum, **Chang Puak**, 90/7 Superhighway (tel 272422) has more Thai specialities. It's owned by the chairman of the Chiang Mai Restaurant Club, so standards are high, although not that pricey—500B for two.

For an evening's sophisticated dining, dress up and spoil yourself on excellent traditional European dishes at **Le Pavillon** in the Chiang Mai Orchid Hotel (tel 222099; dinner for two 1500–200B). **Le Coq D'Or**, 68/1 Koa Klang Rd (tel 248251), is also for French and Continental cuisine—fireside meals, served in an old-world setting. As its name implies, steaks and other European staples are the speciality of **Butcher's Shop** at 193 Sridonchai Rd (tel 272493); dining is open-air and prices reasonable (200–300B). **Alt Heidelberg**, Huay Kaew Rd (tel 222034) has authentic German food, strong draught beer, and a homely atmosphere. **Bierstube Rest Bar**, Moon Muang Rd, is a cheaper German-style place, with relaxing ambience and Chicken in the Basket. **Garden Café** (Dusit Inn Hotel) lays on a lunch-time buffet from 11.30 am to 1.30 pm daily—all the European-Chinese food you can eat for 90B. Back on Moon Muang Rd, **Hungry Horse** (near Ta Pae Gate) and **Peacock Coffee House** (Montri Hotel) cater to Western appetites with steaks, grills, pizzas etc. In between them, **Supun House** does a mean 'Chicken on Fire' for 45B. For good home-style food (mainly French), check out the French roof-top restaurant in **Times Square Guest House**, Soi 6 Ta Pae Rd (tel 282448). If you want to impress (or nauseate) your friends back home with stories of how you ate jungle food, **Kaithong Restaurant** at 67 Kotchasarn Rd advertises itself as 'the only restaurant in the world which serves Python Steak, Cobra Steak, Hare Steak and Mixed Jungle Steak'; presumably they also recommend a suitable wine. In the Night Bazaar, find the cheap, **No Name Restaurant** and the **Sala Ice Cream Bar**—two favourite travellers' haunts.

THA TON

Exciting raft or boat trips down the Kok River from Tha Ton—a small village 175 km north of Chiang Mai—are an increasingly popular way of getting to Chiang Rai. The Kok River enters Thailand at Tha Ton from Laos, flowing south past Chiang Rai until it joins with the Mae Khong River in Chiang Saen district. Tha Ton is located just a few kilometres from the Burmese border, and is still used as a (perilous) doorway into Burma.

GETTING THERE
Orange buses (No. 1231) run to Tha Ton regularly from the bus station north of Chang Puak Gate in Chiang Mai. It's a four-hour trip, costing 37B. Alternatively, you could get off at **Fang** (3 hours, 35B) and continue on to Tha Ton (1 hour, 6B) later on.

Fang
Fang is an interesting little 13th-century city, founded by King Mengrai, with a few decent hotels—the **Fang** and the **Metta Wattana** (rooms for 80–100B at both) or the more comfortable **Chok Thani** (180B fan, 330B air-con), a nice Thai-Chinese restaurant near the bus station—the **Koo Charen**, and good treks. Local guides meet tourists off the bus, offering cheap 1- and 2-day walks up to the various tribal villages (mainly Karen and Black/Red Lahu) above Fang town.

WHAT TO SEE AND WHERE TO STAY   (tel prefix 053)
Tha Ton is a scenic little spot, overlooking the Kok River and surrounded by dense jungle and rolling hills. Many colourful hilltribes live in this area, and at the small souvenir shop by the bridge you'll find the cheap, attractive handicrafts which they bring into the village for sale—bright Akha headdresses and anklets, hand-embroidered Karen bags, decorative Lahu ornaments etc. For views down over the winding river and country landscape, climb the steep staircase (just left of the bridge, facing the hills) up to the pretty toybox pagoda, with its huge seated Buddha. At night, the Buddha is eerily illuminated, and the temple compound resounds with strange jungle music, performed by enthusiastic local youths on modern drum-kits. It's quite a party. Another kind of party starts at 4 am every morning, when an immense gong wakes up the monks and everybody else sleeping within a kilometre's radius. If staying overnight here, bring earplugs, especially if staying at **Thip's Travellers House**, which is situated right at the foot of the temple staircase. Thip's is actually the best lodge in town, with clean (if spartan) rooms from 50B a person, a tribe of resident monkeys, lip-smacking chicken curries and banana pancakes, and a relaxing riverside situation. Mrs Thip, the owner, is a bit of an old pirate, but she's red-hot on local information. 'River fed by mountain water', she informs you, 'Good for swimming—no crocodiles!'. While you're thinking about that one, she often dematerializes to watch another Chinese Kung-Fu movie. Her lodge is so popular she has built a new set of bungalows further upriver. If she's full you may have to put up instead at **Jangasem Guest House**, on the far side of the bridge. This isn't half as good as Thip's.

River Trips (Tha Ton – Chiang Rai)
From Tha Ton, you have three choices of river transport to Chiang Rai. First, there's the

public river-boat, which leaves Tha Ton pier at 12.30 pm daily and arrives in Chiang Rai 5 hours later (fare 160B). Second, you can hire longtail speedboats—providing an exhilarating 2½-hour ride through jungle terrain and roaring rapids—from Thip's or Jangasem (160B per head, if you have a group of 10 heads). Third, and most popular, you can go by river-raft. The rafting season runs from September to February and the best months to hit the river are October and November, when water-levels are highest. Mrs Thip has a virtual monopoly on rafting out of Tha Ton—not altogether a good thing. The trips start out fine: you buy your raft (1600B for two, 2500B for eight) and set off on a 3–4 days *Boy's Own* adventure, stopping for side-treks to Akka, Shan and Lisu villages, perhaps even taking in an elephant safari (250B per day extra). But then you hit the rapids. No problem if you've a guide aboard, or if the river is at high-level. But some people do come to grief on the rocks during the dry season. No marks to Mrs Thip for letting them go out unaccompanied in these conditions. No refund either. And of course no chance of re-selling the raft at Chiang Rai—a thriving business—to other travellers wanting to take it on the much safer ride down to Chiang Saen.

Things to do in Tha Ton include swimming, fishing and canoeing in the Kok River, 'adventure walks' into the jungle (use local guides, 150B per day), and boat-trips *up*-river to the Burmese border, calling in on a Shan village (one-hour ride, 30B). For most of these things, it's back—yes, you guessed it—to Mrs Thip.

CHIANG RAI AND THE GOLDEN TRIANGLE

Bordered by Burma and Laos, Chiang Rai is Thailand's northernmost province, a long 785 km from Bangkok. Founded in 1262, it was the first capital of the independent northern Thai kingdom of Lanna Thai. Legend has it that Mengrai decided to build a city here after one of his elephants ran off in a southerly direction, running out of puff at this site on the banks of the Kok River. This auspicious sign (everything a royal elephant did in those days was considered auspicious) encouraged Mengrai to expand his domain south from his previous power centre of Chiang Saen. Later conquered by Burma, Chiang Rai only became Thai territory in 1786, and was created a full-blooded Thai province in 1910. Today, it's a small, relaxed city of mainly two-storeyed concrete shophouses which give little hint of its former importance. But big changes are on the way. Ever since the province was opened to trekking some 10 years ago, Chiang Rai has become the major destination north of Chiang Mai for hilltribe-spotting tourists. It even has a few trek companies of its own—none of which, in the absence of a TAT tourist office in Chiang Rai, have registered guides or guaranteed service. Chiang Rai has a large highland population of tribal peoples—Akha (who only live in this province), Yao, Meo, Lisu, Lahu and Karen—all attracted here by its eminently suitable terrain: 80% forests and mountains, 20% cultivable valleys. Trekking in this area can be very rewarding—if somewhat overcrowded—and the walks here are far easier than at Mae Hong Son or Pai.

Many travellers use Chiang Rai as a jump-off point for the Golden Triangle—the famous opium-producing centre—and the various places of interest along the Burma/Laos border. Generally the best months to visit are September to December, which have the coolest climate and when scenery is at its most beautiful. By January, the

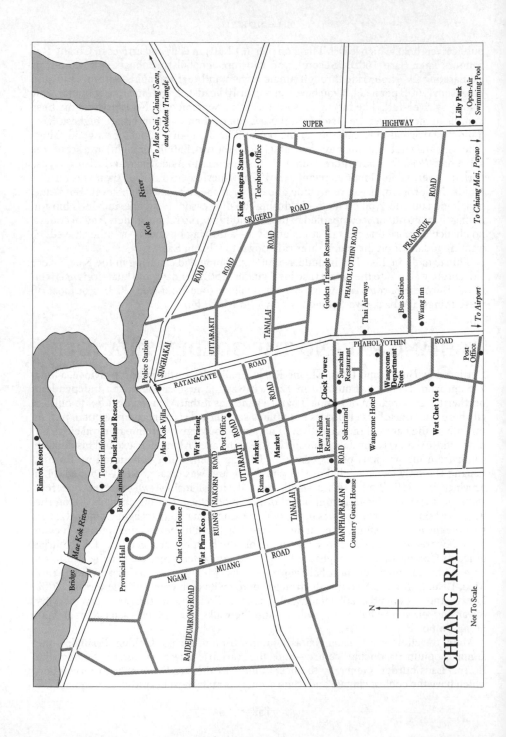

CHIANG RAI

Not To Scale

area gets quite cold (around 12°C), and if going on trek, you'll need warm clothing. From March to May, when summer temperatures climb to 35°C, you'll need your hat. Chiang Rai celebrates its lychee fruit 'harvest festival', complete with parades and beauty contests every May—but few foreigners can take the heat.

GETTING THERE

By Air
Thai Airways flies to Chiang Rai from Chiang Mai at least twice daily (fare 420B; flight time 40 minutes).

By River
Boat/raft trips from Tha Ton are a popular way of going to Chiang Rai (cf. Tha Ton section).

By Bus
There are two routes to Chiang Rai from Chiang Mai. Green buses (no. 148) go every 20–40 minutes from Nawarat Bridge bus-rank in Chiang Mai, and pass through Lampang and Phayao. This trip takes over 5 hours and costs 25B. Buses on the new route (no. 166) leave half-hourly from the Arcade bus station (last air-con bus at 3 pm). The 3½-hour trip costs 47B, or 66B air-con.

From Chiang Rai back to Chiang Mai, buses leave every half-hour from 9 am to 5.30 pm. From Chiang Rai to Bangkok (11 hours), there are five air-con buses between 5 and 7.30 pm (283B) and 10 non air-con buses from 7.30 am to 8 pm 150B) daily. Chat House offers buses to Bangkok too.

TOURIST INFORMATION
The Tourist Information Centre in Singhakhlai Rd (tel 713009) isn't very good. Chat House gives better local information—and a good trek area map.

WHAT TO SEE
Chiang Rai presents a sharp contrast to busy, burgeoning Chiang Mai, 100 km to the south. By day, it's quiet, peaceful and easy to get around. At night, all traffic vanishes off the streets at 10, and it instantly reverts to a sleepy, one-bullock town. To tour around in style, hire a horse and buggy from the Wangcome Hotel. *Samlors* charge 10B, and *songthaews* 5B, for short in-town journeys, but you don't really need them. From the clock in the town centre (the one with four faces, each giving a different time), you can walk to any of Chiang Rai's attractions in under 15 minutes. The provincial capital has a general feel of total inertia, and few people are into heavy sightseeing—most are content to go for a swim, have a massage, wander round the market, and generally relax. Then they hire a motorbike (150–250B a day, from Chat House or Maekok Villa) or hop on a local bus (from the town bus terminal), and travel up to Chiang Saen and the Golden Triangle, or to Mae Chan, Mae Sai and the border areas. Many don't come back for a week—most of these places have far more to offer (especially in terms of atmosphere and scenery) than Chiang Rai.

In and Around Chiang Rai
(on foot, by *samlor*, half day)

This tour is purely optional—Chiang Rai is very thin on 'sights'. The **Morning Market**, overseen by a large Chinese Buddha, is the place to buy mountain food, wild pig, snake and iguana ('You can have dead', chirps a cheerful vendor, 'or you can take home and kill yourself!'). **Wat Phra Keo** used to house the itinerant Emerald Buddha (resident in the temple of the same name in Bangkok) and now only displays a copy. Nearby **Wat Phra Singh** probably dates to the 15th century, and used to contain a precious Theravada Buddha image—but doesn't any more. If you want to see something which hasn't gone somewhere else, visit the **Temple of the Sleeping Buddha**, about 1 km due east of King Mengrai's Statue. This has a 17th-century reclining Buddha in the Burmese style—nothing special, but at least it's original. To finish, walk up the hill to the New Provincial Hall (Government Offices) for nice views down over the Maekok River. Or walk left out of Maekok Villa, left again down a small path and across a bridge, to find a tranquil little park on the riverbank—the ideal spot to watch the sun go down. The **Hilltribe Museum and Handicrafts Centre** on Thanalai Rd has a collection of hilltribe costumes, etc, and a slide show on the customs and culture of the northern tribes.

RECREATION
The ideal antidote to tiring touring is a relaxing massage at **Wangcome Barber**, over the road from Wangcome Hotel. Massages are given upstairs, and from mid-afternoon onwards. If you bargain a rate of 100B an hour (locals pay only 70B), you've done very well. There's good swimming at **Lilly Park** (tell your *samlor* driver 'Sah why nam Lilly Park'). There's a large clean pool here, open 9 am to 6 pm (for a quiet swim, arrive 3–4 pm); admission 25B. An outdoor pool, a kilometre below Lilly Park (and on the same side of the road) charges only 10B admission. For nightlife, check out **Hill Disco** at Wiang Inn Hotel—it's a big scene on a Friday and Saturday night. Admission is 90B men, 70B women (includes one free drink); 'Happy Hour' is from 9 to 10 pm.

WHERE TO STAY (tel prefix 053)
Expensive
Chiang Rai has a wide selection of hotels. The most luxurious of all is **Dusit Island Resort**, 1129 Kraisorasit Rd (tel 715777) which sits on one of the islands in the river and has very spacious grounds and views over the river and surrounding hills; facilities include pool, restaurant, pub and nightclub. Double rooms start at 1700B. North of the island on the other bank of the Mae Kok river stands **Rimkok Resort**, a complex spread out over a wide area surrounded by lovely gardens and pleasant countryside, with pool and restaurants. The drawback, howver, is its distance from town. Double rooms start at 1500B, but there are healthy discounts in the off season. **Wiang Inn**, 893 Phaholyothin Rd (tel 711543), is a quiet, sophisticated hotel with a definite European flavour. Good pool, useful facilities, including a de luxe café and discotheque. Air-con rooms start at 850B, and 50% discounts are given June–September. Similar prices and discounts at **Wangcome Hotel**, 869/90 Pemawibhata Rd (tel 711800). This is a modern, chic place with incredibly helpful staff. South of town, **Little Duck Hotel**, 99 Superhighway (tel 715620) is a modern giant with similar facilities and prices.

Moderate
In the mid-range, the best option is **Golden Triangle Inn**, 590 Phaholyothin Rd (tel

711339), a family-run place where guests come first. It has a garden and pleasant air-con rooms for 500–600B. It also has a very popular café, where on Fridays and Saturdays a live group plays traditional northern folk music. The old-style **Rama Hotel**, 331/4 Trirat Rd (tel 711344) has rooms from 180B (fan) and 400B (air-con); and **Sunknirand**, 424/1 Banphaprakarn Rd (tel 711055), the current Thai favourite (often full), has nice rooms from 200B (fan) to 400B.

Maekok Villa, 445 Singhaklai Rd (tel 711786), has charming bungalow-style rooms (all with bath, hot water, fresh towels daily) at 120–180B. It also has a 30B dormitory, and offers good-value sightseeing tours (e.g. to the Golden Triangle, at 600–900B for one to two people).

Inexpensive
Budget lodges are generally disappointing. The notable exception is **Country Guest House** at 389 Banphraprakarn Rd. Run by a nice English-speaking family, Country is a delightful ranch-house dwelling, with a lawn and a driveway. Rooms are only 60B and have *solid walls* (remember those?), not the usual paper-thin bamboo partitions. Great facilities include hot showers, free bicycles, free rides round town, darts, volleyball and good information. **Chat House**, 1 Trairat Rd, is the place for 'real travellers' run by personable young Chat. He offers safe, clean rooms at 50–80B, also cycle/motorbike rental, trekking, a well-stocked library, information handouts, and an extensive Western-style menu. Chat is a very laidback place, with music, tranquil atmosphere and ethnic decor. It's easy to be laidback here—there's nowhere to sit.

EATING OUT
The best Western-style restaurant is **Golden Triangle**, Phaholythin Rd (see Where to Stay), offering mid-priced cuisine (steaks, grills etc.) at around 90–120B and Thai/Chinese dishes at around 60B. Service is excellent here, and you can eat in air-conditioned comfort while taking in the music. For Thai food, try **Haw Nalika** in Banphaprakan Rd (look for wooden fencing with lights on top). This is where all the locals dine, and the atmosphere is never less than festive. Most dishes cost between 50 and 80B, and specialities include Steamed Fish with Salted Chinese Fruit and Mixed Meat with Cashew Nuts. **Chiang Rai Island Resort**, on the far side of the Maekok River (over the bridge from town) serves delicious Thai food—between 40 and 80B a dish—in a pleasant setting. The **Surachai**, near the clock tower, has inexpensive Thai-Chinese fare and is a big hit with locals. They tuck into 10B bags of crispy locusts, and cram eagerly round trays of dead grubs, beetles and grasshoppers. Most Westerners stick to *kao pat* (fried rice) and Chinese tea. **Bierstube**, near the Wiang Inn on Phaholyothin Rd (tel 714195) is an open-air restaurant with a good name for its German food and homemade breads. Western and Thai food is served at **Cheers Pub** in the Rama Hotel, and they feature a 3-man band playing golden oldies from the 60s. **Chat House** is the place to go for ham 'n' egg breakfasts, yoghurts, fruit salads and muesli. **Mae Korn Coffee Shop** in the Little Duck Hotel has filling buffet breakfasts. The marvellous **Ice Cream Parlour** at Wangcome Hotel offers 24 varieties of Foremost ice-cream and closes at 9.30 pm. There are also lots of tasty cheap-food stalls near the bus station.

The Golden Triangle

(by bus, boat, motorbike; full day)

From Chiang Rai bus station (rank No. 6), public buses leave for **Chiang Saen**—a charming little town on the banks of the Mekong River—every 20 minutes from 6 am. The 40-km trip takes 1½ hours, and costs 15B. Last bus back to Chiang Rai from Chiang Saen is 4.45 pm, so it's best to make an early start. From Chiang Saen, it's a further 10 km along a flat road (okay for motorbikes) to **Ban Sop Ruak**, the point designated as the **'Golden Triangle'**. You can get there by bicycle hired from a riverside guesthouse in Chiang Saen (20–40B, plus possible 500B deposit); *songthaew* (80B return, if on your own; 150–180B total, if in a group); by longtail speedboat (200–300B for the 2½-hour round-trip, cheap if there are six of you) or by public riverboat (80B return). The last method is the most favoured—a very scenic ride up the Mekong and as near as you're likely to get to Burma from here. Public boats allow about an hour for sightseeing at Sop Ruak before returning to Chiang Saen.

Chiang Saen

The once-powerful, fortified city of **Chiang Saen** is now a lively little one-street town, surrounded by ruined temples, crumbling *stupas* and grass-covered walls and ramparts. It's believed to have been built over the ruins of an earlier settlement in 1328 by Phra Chao Saeo Pu, a grandson of King Mengrai—though there's now every indication that the earlier town exercised much power and influence before the 14th century. After the rise of Chiang Mai, Chiang Saen became an associate city ruled over by Lanna Thai princes. Sacked in 1558 by the Burmese, and again in the early 19th century by Rama I, it lay abandoned until rebuilt a century ago by what remained of Chiang Saen's descendants, led by the son of the Prince of Lamphun.

Today, the few skeletal remains of *chedis* scattered around the town are really of interest only to keen archaeological buffs. Many of the old fortifications remain intact, also parts of the old city moat, said to have been scooped out by Naga, the sacred serpent. **Wat Pa Sak**, to the left just before the city walls, is the oldest *chedi* (20B admission) and **Wat Chedi Luang** is the most impressive extant temple, notable for its 58-metre-high octagonal *chedi*. Built around 1390, it is just inside the city walls, to the right. In front of it is the **National Museum**, which houses a fine collection of Chiang Saen artefacts, some dating back to neolithic times. The museum is open 9 am to 4 pm, Wed–Sun (admission 5B), and is primarily of interest for its attractive displays of hilltribe handicrafts and Burmese lacquerware and woodcarvings. Some exhibits (e.g. the 'Wild Cock Trap') have wonderful pseudo-English descriptions. Outside the museum is a bus-stop—handy, if you're on your way back to Chiang Rai.

WHERE TO STAY   (tel prefix 053)
Chiang Saen's lovely setting on the Mae Khong (Mekong) River makes it a popular travellers' haunt, and there are many little guest houses perched on the riverbank looking over to Laos.

Moderate
Out of town, the new **Golden Triangle Resort** (tel 714031) is the luxury place to stay. It

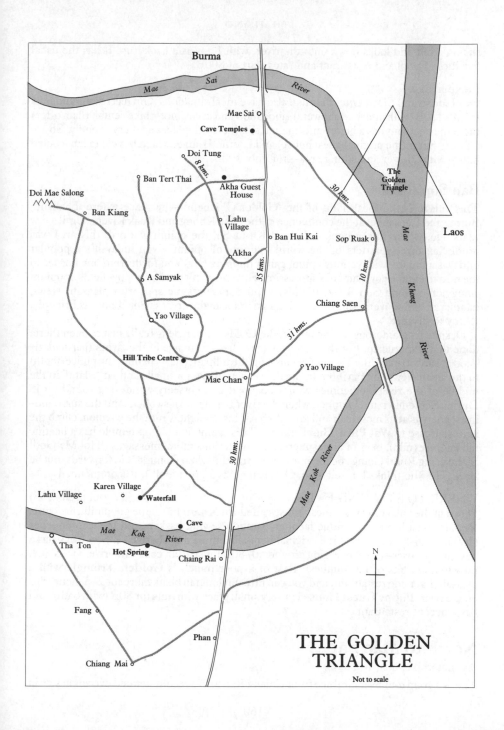

Burma

Mae   Sai   River

Mae Sai

Cave Temples

Doi Tung

8 kms.

Ban Tert Thai

Akha Guest House

The Golden Triangle

Doi Mae Salong

Laos

Ban Kiang

Lahu Village

Ban Hui Kai

Sop Ruak

Akha

30 kms.

Mae

A Samyak

35 kms.

Khong

Yao Village

Chiang Saen

10 kms.

River

Hill Tribe Centre

31 kms.

Mae Chan

Yao Village

30 kms.

Mae Kok River

Lahu Village

Karen Village

Waterfall

Cave

N

Tha Ton

Mae   Kok   River

Hot Spring

Chaing Rai

Fang

Phan

THE GOLDEN TRIANGLE

Chiang Mai

Not to scale

sits on a hill and looks down onto the river, with Laos as a backdrop. It has the usual facilities of pool and restaurant and rates start at 800B.

Inexpensive
Gin House and **Siam Guest House** also have ideal situations. Gin has rooms and huts for 50–120B (with attached showers), good food and cycle/motorbike rental. Siam offers the same deal, but has a better information service. Both places are very friendly. So are **Chiang Saen** (the original guest house) and **Lanna House**, which has clean fan-cooled huts—with shower and sitting area—for only 100B.

Ban Sop Ruak

This village is the focal point of the 'Golden Triangle'—the place where Thailand, Burma and Laos meet at the confluence of the Mae Khong and Ruak Rivers. Until a few years ago, when Thai troops dislodged Khun Sa, the opium warlord, this area was producing three-quarters of the world's supply of opium. Even today it's a popular outlaw sanctuary, with various opium gangs hopping back and forth from one border to the next to escape government suppression. But you won't see any poppy-fields or opium smugglers around Sop Ruak. It's just a quiet, picturesque spot with pleasant views, handicraft and souvenir shops, and a big sign in the main street saying 'Police is Friendly, Ready to Protect'.

Despite its glamorous, exotic image, the Golden Triangle is really just a 'been there, done that' experience. For the best view over the confluence of the rivers (particularly good at sunset) make the 15-minute climb up the hillpath (starts behind the police booth) to the small viewpoint pavilion. In the dry season, there's a small sandbar 'island' in the middle of the river, sometimes with a boatload of sightseers wandering round on it. During September and October, when the river is at its most swollen (and the surrounding scenery is at its most lush and green), this is lost to sight. From the pavilion, climb the *naga* staircase to **Wat Phra Thai Pukhao**. This crumbling hilltop temple has a beatific old *maechee* (nun), bags of atmosphere, and mysterious moral messages ('Ho! My God! Sightseeing Ruin! Goings be memorious, be trustful when Coming. Go forwards, not be Back. He who thinks himself wise, Oh Heaven! is a great fool!'). Recommended.

WHERE TO STAY AND EAT (tel prefix 053)
Down in the village, a small guest house called **Pu Kham** has some good hilltribe crafts for sale. Best buys are antique lacquer-bamboo sewing baskets and tobacco pouches (100 to 150B)—you won't find original items like these anywhere else. Sop Ruak has a few guest houses—most charging around 60–80B for spartan cells with 'river views' (i.e. no windows, lots of mosquitoes). Best of a poor bunch is **Golden Triangle** with a pleasant riverside restaurant, and you can hire out longtail boats there for 2–3-hour trips on the river. **Poppy Guest House** is a very small place with huts for 80B (with bath), and has a decent restaurant.

North to Mae Sai
(by motorbike, bus; 1–2 days)
This is a good tour by motorbike from Chiang Rai, with a recommended overnight stay in

Mae Sai. There are several nice places to stay along the way, however, and many travellers work their way slowly north to Mae Sai (or south back to Chiang Rai) by local bus. Pity about the bad road between Mae Sai and Chiang Saen: the inviting 'triangle' tour (Chiang Rai – Chiang Saen – Mae Sai – Chiang Rai) is presently only negotiable by jeep, not by motorbike.

Mae Sai

Situated right on the border with Burma, 62 km from Chiang Rai, Mae Sai is as far north as Thailand goes. Connected by a concrete bridge to the Burmese village of Tha Khee Lek, it is also the only land-based corridor open between Thailand and Burma. At present, only Thai and Burmese nationals are allowed over the border (from 6 am to 6 pm daily), though from either of the town's two best guest houses, the **Mae Sai** and the **Northern**, you can watch travellers and Burmese braves trying to swim over. Anybody attempting the same thing by raft or boat is politely (but firmly) dissuaded—part of the Sai River belongs to Burma. Most visitors are content with a climb up to **Wat Phra That Doi**, a hilltop temple affording magnificent views down over Mae Sai and the river. The 207-step staircase up to it starts just before Top North Hotel, just off to the left of Phaholyothin Rd.

Mae Sai itself is famous for its strawberries (which bloom in December) and for its jade-cutting factory, which sells high-quality jade far cheaper than at the tourist shops in the main drag. Mae Sai also used to be a great place to pick up rare gems—aquamarine, sapphires and rubies—brought over the border by Burmese traders. But most of the stuff now hawked on the bridge has actually been bought in Thailand, to be sold back to tourists at inflated prices. For authentic, well-priced gems and handicrafts, check out **Meang Lai Antique Shop**—but remember to bargain hard. Good general buys in Mae Sai are sandalwood, Burmese woodcarvings, Chinese herbs and fresh lobsters. Seafood is good here. Try **Rim Nam** restaurant near the bridge—from June to September, it serves up delicious Mekong river-fish at 100B a kilogram. It also has reliable, mid-priced Thai-Chinese cuisine.

A good side-trip from Mae Sai is to nearby **Cheng Dao Cave Temple**, full of Buddha carvings, huge stalactities and dangerous snakes. A little further on, there's a **Monkey Temple** with a host of lively monkeys, and half a kilometre beyond this you can hire a boat (5B) to visit another cave, housing an enormous reclining Buddha. A short distance south, a junction leads the way up to **Doi Tun** (Flag Mountain), the highest peak in northern Thailand. At the top is **Phra That Chedi** (built in 911), with chanting monks, chiming bells and lots of mystical mist. Doi Tung is best approached by motorbike, or by hiring a truck from **Ban Hui Kai**, halfway down the highway between Mae Sai and Mae Chan.

WHERE TO STAY AND EATING OUT   (tel prefix 053)
Moderate
Of the hotels in Mae Sai the **Thai Thong**, 6 Phahonyothin Rd (tel 731975) is the most expensive, if not the best, with air-con rooms for 400–500B. **Top North Hotel** on the same road towards the river is comfortable and slightly cheaper at 350–400B.

Inexpensive

Guest houses around the town include **Mae Sai**, 688 Tambon Wiengpangkam, about a kilometre west of town on the river, with a restaurant and doubles for 80–120B (they also arrange treks and motorbike rentals); **Northern**, also on the river (tel 731537) with rooms and huts for 80–300B and **Mae Sai Plaza**, with a café and simple rooms for 120B. **Frontier Saloon** near the bus terminal sees the only real nightlife, which isn't much.

On the way up the mountain (7 km from the main road), you'll find **Akha Guest House**. This offers spectacular views, cheap bungalow accommodation (50–80B), cosy campfire meals in the evenings, unforgettable sunsets, great hilltribe walks, novelty river-rafting (disintegrating rafts leave people hanging in trees; women travellers get a go on the 'Akha swing' across a ravine, with a choice of potential husbands waiting on the other side), and an eccentric host named Jiad. People hang out here for weeks—it's so good.

Mae Chan

Mae Chan, 34 km south of Mae Sai, is a small trading town used as a supply-point by local hilltribes. There is not much to see here, except a colourful covered market. From Mae Chan, however, you can hire a pick-up truck (30B) to the much-recommended **Laan Tong Lodge**. Run by two charming ladies (Australian-Thai), this place is set on a scenic little creek, surrounded by seven hilltribes and numerous villages. Bungalows are cheap (50–80B) and clean, and every one of them has been constructed in a different hilltribe style. In the evening everyone eats together, and it's good wholesome vegetarian fare. You can walk to at least half a dozen villages (mainly Lisu and Lahu) in under two hours, and enjoy solar-heated showers down by the river. Fishing, swimming, trekking and relaxation—Laan Tong Lodge really does have something for everyone.

Doi Mae Salong

If travelling by motorbike (hire a powerful one: Chat house in Chiang Rai has a couple of nifty 125cc Honda Wings), take a ride up Doi Mae Salong, 36 km northwest of Mae Chan. The scenery along the mountain road is quite spectacular, especially in January when all the flowers are in bloom. Some 20 km out of Mae Chan, you'll pass an interesting Hilltribe Welfare Centre—a good place to pick up handicraft bargains. At the mountain summit, just 3 km from the Burmese border, there's Santi Kiri—a fascinating settlement inhabited by families of the 93rd ('Kuomintang') regiment who fled here from China after the 1949 revolution. Breathtaking views, antique atmosphere (reminiscent of Darjeeling), charming locals and 'gourmet' meals at the highest Chinese restaurant in Thailand—this is another rewarding spot to spend a day or two. Accommodation here includes **Sakura Resort** above the town (air-con rooms for 400B) and **Mae Salong Guest House** (150–200B for room with fan and bath).

LAMPHUN AND PASANG

Lamphun makes a good day-outing, by bus or by motorbike, from Chiang Mai, 26 km to the north. It is the oldest existing city in Thailand, and is said to produce the country's prettiest girls. Both claims to fame derive from the beautiful Mon queen, Chamathevi, who founded the city—then the seat of the Haripunchai kingdom—in the 7th century. She is said to have defeated her main rival, a tribal chieftain with an aggressive desire to marry her, by means of magic picked up from Suthep, the old hermit after whom Doi Suthep is named. Nakorn Haripunchai, as Lamphun was then known, staved off successive attacks from the Khmer and emerged into the 20th century still an independent kingdom. In the process, however, it sustained two major invasions—first by Mengrai, founder of Chiang Mai, later by the Burmese—and little now remains of the original town. One of the few major structures to survive, however, is the beautiful Wat Phra That Haripunchai, a supreme example of classical northern Thai religious architecture.

GETTING THERE
Green buses (No. 181) leave for Lamphun every 15 minutes (6 am to 6 pm) from Nawarat Bridge stop in Chiang Mai. The 40 minute journey costs 8B. From the same stop, white buses (No. 182) go direct to Pasang.

TOURIST INFORMATION
There's a small Thai Airways information desk (oddly situated in a whisky and furniture shop), just round the corner from Lamphun bus stop. Mr Tu, the information officer, goes out of his way to help travellers. He has a small guest house, with a few rooms at 50B, and sometimes takes house-guests out on motorboat excursions down the Ping River, dropping in on Karen tribes. Ask him for directions to **Lamphun Silk Factory**, just below his booth, where special silk is produced for members of the Thai royal family. The weaving processes are worth observing, and there's a small showroom where hand-made ladies' jackets (beautifully embroidered) sell for around 2000B. Stock is limited here—the factory doesn't really deal direct with the public.

Wat Phra That, Lamphun

WHAT TO SEE

Lamphun is a pleasant, airy little town with some nice bakeries and samosa-snack places. If you're here in August, sample the famous local fruit called *lamyai* (longan). Lamphun's lamyai orchards are said to produce the finest kind of this fruit in the country. You pass the orchards on the bus-ride down from Chiang Mai, and a pretty sight they are too.

From Lamphun bus-stop, it's a 2-minute walk up the road to **Wat Phra That Haripunchai**. Open 6 am to 6 pm daily, this is the main attraction of the city and receives a constant stream of pilgrims and visitors. The outstanding soaring golden *chedi* was originally built in 1064 by King Athitayarat (32nd king of Haripunchai) to house precious relics of the Buddha. This *chedi* is 60 metres high and has a 9-tiered umbrella at the top, gilded with 6½ kgs of pure gold. Behind it hangs the largest temple gong in northern Thailand, made at Wat Phra Singh (Chiang Mai) in the 7th century. In olden days, it used to wake up the heavenly gods (and everybody in town) at 6 am every morning. Nearby, in a small chamber, there's a large gold figure of a pot-bellied monk. This is Sangha Jai, the monk who brought the Buddha's relics here from India. The legend goes that he ate himself into this obese condition deliberately, since—when young and handsome—he was so plagued by women he couldn't keep his mind on the Buddha's teachings. To get the full effect of this glorious temple, view it from the front, facing the river. For atmosphere, turn up around 11.30 am or 3 pm—at both times, the temple compound is alive with colourful monks and novices walking to or from classes at the monastic college. Viewed against the background of the gleaming gold *chedi*, their yellow and saffron robes make a beautiful sight.

Opposite the temple entrance, the new **Haripunchai National Museum** houses a small, but well-displayed, collection of Lanna antiques found in the region—mainly engraved stones, temple carvings, weapons and amulets. Admission to the museum is 10B, and it's open 8.30 am to 4 pm, Wed–Sun.

At **Wat Chama Thevi**, a 15-minute stroll north of town (or a 10B *samlor* ride), you'll find the venerated *chedi* containing Queen Chamthevi's ashes. Probably dating from the 8th century, it has been restored many times but retains the architectural style of the Mahabodhi temple in Bodhgaya. The unusual square shape of this *chedi* has given the temple its more common title of Wak Kukut, or 'wat with a topless chedi'. Four-sided, it has tiered niches containing standing images of Buddha, each row smaller than the one below. All of the stucco figures have one hand raised (though most are armless now) in the gesture of dispelling fear.

Pasang

For good shopping, take a *songthaew* on to **Pasang**, a charming little cotton-weaving village 10 km south of Lamphun. The main street here is lined with shops selling cotton products, batiks, wickerware and other local handicrafts. To see the full range of Pasang produce, visit **Nandakwang Laicum** on the right-hand side of the road. This has lovely batik dresses (400–600B), shirts (300B) and cushion-covers (100B), also handwoven cotton placemats (200B) and 8-napkin sets (120B). Prices are a little high, but everything's top quality. Nandakwang has a flair for modern, contemporary designs—you won't find anything like this in Chiang Mai. Over the road, Suchada sells more traditional and cheaper stuff: ready-to-wear dresses and nightshirts (150 to 200B), shirts in cotton batik and printed cotton (70 to 100B) and—the best buy of all—litre bottles of Pasang honey, made from the aromatic Lamyai blossom, for 130B. It's delicious. Walk a few hundred yards above Suchada to find a good little bamboo and wickerware shop selling delightful baskets, handbags and furniture at very reasonable prices.

MAE SARIANG

There are several good reasons for dropping in on Mae Sariang (200 km southwest of Chiang Mai) on the way to Mae Hong Son. Within easy reach of several hilltribe settlements, it's a good base for trekking. And close to the Burmese border, it's also an interesting smuggling centre—especially for teakwood from Burma, for which the local Thais pay in rice, cash or gasoline. The town itself has a very scenic location, surrounded by wooded hills, and has become something of a Thai resort. Coffee shops and video parlours now exist alongside tribal mud-huts; painted transvestites and hip young Thais in Levis now stroll the streets with Karen villagers wearing fedoras over traditional costume; barbers administer 'TV tonsures' in modern salons next door to flaking age-old *chedis*. It's a town of stark contrasts—yet the old and the new blend together surprisingly well. The atmosphere is soothingly calm, though the nightlife is quite a scene.

GETTING THERE
From Chiang Mai Arcade terminal, non air-con buses leave for Mae Sariang (going on to Mae Hong Son) at 6.30, 8, 9 and 11 am, 1, 3, 8 and 9 pm. The fare is 50B, and the picturesque journey takes 4 hours. Air-con buses leave at 9 am and 9 pm, and cost 97B. From Mae Sariang, you can pick up buses for Mae Hong Son at 12.30 pm, 10 am, 12 noon, 3 pm, 5 pm and midnight. This is a rather hairy (but scenic) 4-hour journey, costing 52B.

WHAT TO SEE
Mae Sariang is a small town of few streets—you can walk right round it in 20 minutes. There are two Burmese-Shan temples near the bus station, **Wat Jong Sung** and **Wat Si Boonruang**. The larger *wat* has a couple of semi-interesting *chedis* with ornamental spires, and some pagoda-style monks' residences to the rear. To visit the nearest Karen village, 5 km out of town, you can either hire a (rare) *songthaew* for 5B, or walk it. For any local excursions, it's worth calling on Mae Sariang Guest House, which hands out a half-decent map of the area. This lodge also hires out guides (100B per day) for treks to nearby Red Lahu, Karen, Meo and Lisu villages, plus invigorating walks up into the hills. To see wild elephants at work in the nearby teakwood forests (40 km out of the town), contact Pai Toon—a local man with good English—at 217/2 Panit Rd, near the border police camp. Or ask for him at **Sweet Pub**, behind Mae Sariang Guest House. Lek, manager of the Sweet Pub, handles most trekking in the region. He arranges transport to the two tribal centres of **Mae Sam Lap** and **Mae Kong Ka** on the Burmese border. Mae Sam Lap, 48 km due west of Mae Sariang, is of principal interest for the few Pamalaw or 'long-necked' people who live at the Karen village here. Independent travel there is difficult—the roads are very bad. Lek lays on special cars to Mae Sam Lap and back for 100B per person. He also owns two guest houses in Mae Kong Ka, which is a far more

pleasant ride, with lots of Karen villages to drop into along the way. Mae Kong Ka also has the better shopping—at the village, you can buy beautiful Karen costumes and handicrafts at low prices.

From either Mae Sam Lap or Mae Kong Ka, there are exciting boat trips up or down the Silom River, which separates Thailand from Burma. Going north, you can visit the thriving black-market town of **Joh Ta**, full of smugglers. Here you can buy jade, rubies and sapphires at knock-down prices (haggle hard), and watch water-buffalo and cows being ferried over from Burma. From Mae Sam Lap, boats normally leave around 8 and 9 am, arriving in Joh Ta some 4 hours later. It's best to go early, and in a group—the cost of a boat is around 1000B. But you can get there more quickly and cheaply from Mae Kong Ka, on Lek's boat. The alternative trip, proceeding south down the Silom, brings you to the customs point of **Mae Leh Ta**, where some attempt is made to collect taxes from smugglers. This is a scenic and exciting excursion (the river is very fast) and there's a good chance of seeing elephant-logging along the riverbank.

NIGHTLIFE
There's quite a bit of action in Mae Sariang at night, most of it behind closed doors. Clustered round the small cinema (with its revolving bill of King Kong and Bruce Lee movies) are a plethora of slinky little 'disco cafés' with live music and subterranean lighting. (Some are hostess bars.) **Palace Café** , opposite Mae Sariang Guest House, is the red-light venue after dark—very intimate atmosphere, and twangy live music nightly. Best nightspot is the **Black and White** (inside, all black) opposite the cinema. This has a fun band which invites 'requests' from visiting *farangs*. Whatever you ask for, they play Cliff Richard. Come here in a group—cheap drinks and snacks, lots of laughs. On the way out, watch out for rabid dogs. This town has more mangy, beaten-up and generally done-in dogs than you can shake a stick at.

WHERE TO STAY   (tel prefix 053)
Inexpensive
The **Mitaree**, in the main street (Mae Sariang Rd, tel 611022), is Mae Sariang's only hotel. Scruffy twin-bedded fan rooms are overpriced at 150B, as are air-con rooms in the new building at 350B, the restaurant is mediocre (try 'black rice pudding' for breakfast—it's awful), and the 'English-speaking travel service' comprises one guide, who charges 150B just to see the nearby Karen village. **Mae Sariang Guest House**, near the bus station, is a far better choice—it has comfy fan-rooms at 80B with clean communal showers, fan rooms with bath at 120B, friendly (if eccentric) staff, and a good information service. **B. R. Guest House**, right next to the bus station, is run by a friendly family and is immaculately clean. It has just three rooms. At 80B single, 100B double (with fans and attached bathrooms), they are the best deal in town.

EATING OUT
Inthara Restaurant, just beyond Mitaree Hotel, offers a limited range of Thai/Chinese meals, around 40B a dish. The overrated speciality is Chicken in Hot Basil. Try instead Chicken with Ginger and Onions—it's delicious. Across the road, the civilized **Renu Restaurant** offers superior cuisine at 40–60B a dish, and has an air-conditioned lounge.

The thing to try here is *Tod Mon Phagay*, or local river fish. Western-style fare—including continental breakfasts, cakes and ice-cream—is served at **Sweet Pub**. Best time to catch manager Lek, by the way, is in the evening. During the day, he's often in the forest.

MAE HONG SON

Long isolated from the modern world by rugged mountains, the mist-shrouded valley of Mae Hong Son has only just emerged into the 20th century. As new roads stubbornly push their way through from Chiang Mai, Mae Hong Son is being touted as the last surviving bastion of traditional culture and customs in the north. Situated on the topmost northwestern border with Burma, nearly half of the province's 1500,000 inhabitants are hilltribe people—mainly Karen, Muser, Lisu, Lahu and H'mong. The first settlement was built around an elephant corral site, probably in 1830. The large-scale migrations of tribal clans to and from Burma during the subsequent 40 years led to Mae Hong Son being designated a provincial capital in 1893. Today, while the border to Burma remains closed, the town retains the excitement of a frontier outpost—a modern-day melting pot of old and new civilizations. The surrounding virgin forests and hills—full of caves, waterfalls and hot springs—are a paradise for the nature-lover, especially during December, when the countryside is ablaze with golden *buatong* (sunflower) blossoms. Lying at high elevation, between two mountain ranges, Mae Hong Son valley is shrouded in early-morning mist throughout the year, and is popularly known as 'The Misty City'. It is also referred to, rather less appropriately, as 'Thailand's Shangri-La'. Whatever, enough of the valley has now been cleared of hill-bandits, and its attractions opened to trekking, to pave the way for wide-scale exploration of this beautiful and (as yet) unspoilt province.

Mae Hong Son is at its best—both for trekking and for scenery—from November to February. During these months, the climate is pleasantly dry and cool—cold even, if you're trekking at high altitudes, so take warm clothing and a sleeping bag. In December, the wild sunflowers (*buatong*) and the opium poppies come into blossom. Also in December, the town holds it annual 'Miss Hilltribes Contest'—the aim being to give pretty local widows the chance of attracting a new husband. It's a really big event, with a huge fairground, a lively fête and a market that threatens to engulf the entire town. If visiting Mae Hong Son during the rainy months (i.e. up till November) you'll need to take precautions against malarial mosquitoes—they're whoppers. Even in the dry months, it's wise to sleep under a net.

GETTING THERE

By Air
Thai Airways flies twice daily to Mae Hong Son from Chiang Mai (345B, 35 minutes). There's also one flight daily from Bangkok (1865B), with a change of planes in Chiang Mai. Many travellers take the bus to Mae Hong Son, and return to Chiang Mai by air—the glorious mountain scenery is worth the extra expense. Air tickets out of Mae Hong Son are, however, in heavy demand. You'll need to book in advance at Thai

MAE HONG SON

Not to scale

Labels on map:

To Pai

PANG LO NIKITUM ROAD

SOI 1

Mae Hong Son
Guest House

SOI 3

SOI 5

Wat Panglo

SOI 2

Ban Buatong
Restaurant

● Siam Hotel

● Bus Station

PANETWATTANA ROAD

Airport

Khun Thon
Trading ●

KHUN LUM PRA PAHT ROAD

Mai Tee
Hotel ●

Market

PRA DIT JONG KHAM ROAD

● Bank

RATTHUMPHETUG ROAD

NEE VEAT PEE SAN ROAD

● Thai Airways

Wat Khang Thug ●

SING HA NATBAMLUNG ROAD

To Temple
on the Hill

Telephone ●

● Hospital

Honey House ●

Bank ●

Holiday House ●

UDOM CHOW NEE THET ROAD

Jongkhum Lake

Baiyoke
Chalet ●

● Post Office

CHUM NAN SATHIT ROAD

● Bai Fern

Wat Jong Khum

N

Airways on the airport road, leading out of town, immediately on arrival. Some people play safe, and buy a return air-ticket in Chiang Mai.

By Bus
From Chiang Mai Arcade terminal, buses leave for Mae Hong Son (via Pai and Soppong) at 7, 8.30 and 10.30 am, 12.30 and 2.30 pm, requiring a change of bus at Pai. The fare is 100B, and the journey presently takes around 8 hours. One air-con mini-bus leaves Chiang Mai at 8 am via Pai, cost 75B. When the new road from Chiang Mai to Mae Hong Son is completed the journey time between the two cities will be much shorter. Until then, travel by bus—especially the section between Pai and Mae Hong Son—is a real thrill-a-minute experience. Landslides, floods, yawning chasms, hairpin bends and bulldozers shoving wreckage down the mountain, are all part of the fun. The other route goes via Mae Sariang, and non air-con buses leave the Chiang Mai Arcade bus station at 6.30, 8, 9 and 11 am, 8 and 9 pm. The journey takes 78 hours and costs 97B. Air-con buses leave at 9 am and 9 pm; the fare is 175B.

From Mae Hong Son, there are five non air-con (6 and 8 am, 12.30, 8 and 9 pm) and two air-con buses (10.30 am and 9 pm) daily back to Chiang Mai via Mae Sariang, and via Pai (change again) at 7, 9 and 11 am and 2 pm, with one air-con mini-bus at 8 am.

From Mae Hong Son there are two buses daily to Bangkok—non air-con at 12 pm (199B), air-con at 2.30 pm (358B). The trip takes 18 hours.

WHAT TO SEE
Not everybody cares for Mae Hong Son town. Ever since it began gearing up for tourism, it's become rather dirty and noisy. Still, many enjoy its raw energy and lively atmosphere—and there are a couple of spots set aside for peace-lovers. The prettiest of these is **Jongkhum Lake** at the south of the town, below the post office. This scenic freshwater lake, with its fountains and exotic gardens (Fitness Park), lies in the shadow of a large mountain and is overlooked by two charming monasteries. It's the place to be with your camera in the early morning when mist still clings to the town, or in the warm glow of sunset. One of the twin temples here, **Wat Chong Klang**, definitely merits a visit. It houses the oldest, most revered Buddha in the province, said to have been cast in Burma and recovered from the Pai River. It also has 'paintings on glasses' and 'wood carvings old ancient of Buddha'. The former are brilliantly coloured glass paintings of various *jakarta* (life of Buddha) stories; the latter are a fascinating collection of wooden dolls, depicting princes, paupers, beggars and various ascetics. Both attractions were brought here from Burma in 1857. If they're locked up, ask one of the monks to produce a key. The famous Buddha can only be seen at the annual Songkran Festival (mid-April), when it is taken in procession around the town.

The town's principal monastery, **Wat Prathat Doi Khun Mu**, is known locally as the 'Temple on the Hill'. Built 150 years ago to hold some relics of Buddha from India, it sits atop a 250-metre-high hill offering fine views down over the capital, and the surrounding mountains and valleys. This *wat* is constructed in the Burmese style with ornately carved, many-tiered roofs, and distinctly Burmese features on the main Buddha image. There are two important *chedis* up here, both of them illuminated at night. The temple has its big annual festival at the Full Moon in October. This marks the end of the rainy season, and the end of a long period of fasting for the resident monks. During the rains, they have to stay put in the temple (by order of Buddha), living on meagre rations. The festival marks their descent from the hill, to resume collecting food daily once more. It's a rich, colourful event, with all the local farmers and townsfolk dressed up in traditional costume, providing some excellent opportunities for photography. To get up to the temple, either hire a motorbike (from Mae Hong Son Guest House or Khun Thou Trading) or climb it. The path starts directly opposite the Mai Tee Hotel in town, and you head up it—keeping left all the way—until the temple entrance appears on your right. After this 10-minute stroll, you can either scale the hill head on—via the crumbling old staircase beyond the temple entrance—or take the easy hill-road, which starts as a dirt-track some 50 yards *before* the *wat* entrance. In either case, it's about a further 20-minute climb.

Trekking

Ever since Chiang Rai and the Golden Triangle started to become 'overtrekked', adventure-travellers have been drifting over to Mae Hong Son instead. New companies are springing up all over town, offering interesting hill-walks, elephant safaris and river-rafting trips at an average cost of 200–250B per day. Few of them are well organized—trekking in this region is still very much in the trial-and-error stage—but several people enjoy pioneering unspoilt, sometimes dangerous, trails. Local attractions include **Ban Mai**, a Shan village 3 km south of Mae Hong Son; the **K.M.T.** (Chinese refugee) village at the north frontier, previously the HQ of the opium warlord Khun Sa; the 'Fish Cave' of **Tham Pla**, full of giant catfish and located 18 km out of town; the King's old **Pang Tong Palace** (he still flies in by helicopter every year or two); and the impressive **Pha Sua Falls**, considered by many the best waterfall in the North. Some companies operate longer treks which loop round the Burma border, returning back down the Pai River by raft. Most treks make deliberate detours via opium fields (now very few) and most guides expect you to walk between six and eight hours a day. The scenery is often spectacular, but you have to be fit to enjoy it—the going can get very tough. There's a lot of hill-climbing involved, and the villages visited can sometimes offer only very basic food and acommodation. Even if your trek company provides food, it's wise to bring some supplies of your own. A water-bottle, decent walking shoes, a waterproof (for rainy days) and a sleeping bag (for cold nights) are other useful inclusions.

Independent travel up to the border point of **Mae Aw** isn't as safe as before. Buses no longer run up there (too many have been held up by bandits) and you'll have to hire a jeep. Enquire at the K.M.T. office opposite the old Mae Aw bus-stop in town. Jeep rides cost around 200B return, and you'll need to take a guide along (another 100B) for safety. On the drive up, you can stop off at the King's Palace, the waterfall and an interesting Meo village. At Mae Aw itself, there's a colourful Karen village—but don't go walking about on your own (police and locals aren't always friendly) and keep your camera well out of sight.

The best trek agency in Mae Hong Son is **Don Enterprises**, just up from the post office on the main road. Don were the first team to organize treks to the Burmese border, four years ago, and they've got contacts (even with the Red Karen army) that no-one else has. A very adventurous outfit, they boldly go where other companies fear to tread. Jack, the top guide, knows every village along the border, hardly any of them visited by tourists.

Don's standard, 2-day 3-night treks cost around 700B, and run up from Soppong to visit Yellow Lahu, Red Lahu, Red Karen and other hilltribe settlements near the Burmese borderline. They also offer elephant treks at 500B per day, and river-rafting up to the border (to visit the long-necked Pamalaw people) at 200B per day. Run by three Burmese guys, Don Enterprises enjoy a particularly good relationship with the various local tribes, and are presently trying to set up a 'Hilltribe Culture Show' with them—this should be interesting. Meanwhile, guide David is planning to run out treks to the newly discovered Kaiyo tribe, who live—along with other primitive clans—at the river-side village of **Padong**, right on the border. Padong used to be just inside Burma, but the villagers were moved to the Thai side of the border when it was closed. The area around Padong is virgin trekking territory—hardly any of the tribes (mainly Burmese) have yet seen Westerners. Independent travel there is possible, but pricey. Buses run half-hourly from Mae Hong Son market up to the Boat Station on the Pai River. From here, it's a 2–3 hour longtail boat trip (320B one-way, for one to six people) up-river to Padong. Trouble is, there's a 300B charge to visit the village itself—if you can't afford it, stay in the boat. It works out cheaper (around 600B for the whole 'package') to book the Padong trip in town—by now, both **Don Enterprises** and **S and N Tours** (near Siam Hotel) should be handling it. Two other reliable trek places in town are **Mae Hong Son Guest House** (250B a day, for small 3–4 person groups only; ask for Pang, the best guide) and **Khun Thou Trading**, opposite Mai Tee Hotel. Take note, river-rafting from Mae Hong Son down to Pai is not practical—the water is too shallow.

SHOPPING

Half the school kids in the valley are now busily producing handicrafts for tourists—most of this stuff is attractive and cheap. For authentic hilltribe crafts, try the small shop outside Bangkok Bank in Khunlum Praphat Rd. This has a full range of locally produced crafts, including rough-cotton Burmese jackets (120B), handwoven Karen tunics (180B) and Burmese printed cotton, plaited with gold and silver thread (120B per 6 × 4 ft length). Prices are a little high here, but the quality of workmanship is generally excellent.

The town's morning market is the place to pick up wildflower honey (delicious), beautiful woven sarongs from Burma, and trek supplies and gear. Novelty buys here include bags of crispy fried pigskin (yes, it keeps) and lung-wrenching Burmese cheroots. Lots of good cheap food too. But arrive at the market early—by 9 am it's all over.

WHERE TO STAY   (tel prefix 053)
Moderate
In a tranquil setting on the river 6 km from town, **Mae Hong Son Resort**, 24 Ban Huay Daer (tel 611504), has a small air-conditioned bungalow complex, complete with restaurant. Although a little isolated, you can join their treks to hilltribe villages or raft trips along the river. Rates are 800B, breakfast included.

In town, there are three good hotels in Khunlum Praphat Rd, the main street, offering fan-rooms from 120B, air-con rooms between 300 and 800B. The best is **Siam** at no. 23 (tel 611148)—every room has twin beds, soap and toilet-paper, followed by **Mai Tee** at no. 55 (tel 611141)—less friendly, but clean, and **Baiyoke Chalet** at no. 90 (tel 611486)—the most expensive, with nice, if sombre, rooms; popular with Thais.

Inexpensive

There's a host of cheap guest houses in Mae Hong Son, most charging around 50B for one person, 80–100B for two. Check out **Holiday House** and **Honey House**, both beautifully situated overlooking Jongkhum Lake. The Honey is brand-new, and has a cheap dormitory. Two other goodies are **Mae Hong Son Guest House** and **Galare**, 23 Panglo Nikhom Soi 2 (tel 611150)—both well-advertised (with directions) at the bus station. The Mae Hong Son has a better atmosphere and information service; Galare has better rooms, with decent mosquito-netting and real beds. **Khun Thou Trading** has amazing rooms (a little pricier at 160B for two), great information, a useful restaurant, and gives the best haircut and massage in town. **New Guysorn**, 5 minutes' walk north of the bus-stop, is quiet and clean, and run by friendly people. Pity about the spiders though . . .

EATING OUT

The most stylish place to eat is **Fern Restaurant**, just below the post office. This has wicker easy-chairs, Swiss clocks, exotic plants and bags of period charm. The food's good too—especially Fried Pai River Fish with Pepper and Garlic, Coconut Milk Soup with Chicken and Garlic, and exceptional sweet and sour dishes. Dishes are 40–60B. There's an amazing selection of coffees (including expresso), and the polished-teak bar mixes a terrific Singapore Sling. It also plays Sinatra and jazz. The nearby **Kai Muk** (Pearl) is another good Thai-Chinese restaurant. Nice things on offer are Fried Chicken with Lemon Juice, and Spicy Catfish Salad. Less appetizing items include Frog Salad and Spicy Pig Intestine Salad, but the standard *kai yang* and *som tam* fare is excellent. The **Chalet Café** in the Baiyoke Chalet has a good mix of western and Thai food, and there's live music in the evenings. Dinner for two costs 300–400B.

Cheaper Thai-Chinese eats are available at the popular open-air **Joke** restaurant, just above Kai Muk. Food here is best in the early morning, when it's fresh. The night market is handy for late snacks—mainly omelettes, soups and 15B meals.

Western-style food is provided at the cosy, friendly **Ban Buatong**, opposite Siam Hotel. It's a good evening hang-out spot, with mellow sounds and friendly staff. Tasty local dishes include Chicken with Fried Cashew Nuts and Grilled Pork with Honey. The B.B. is famous for its great breakfasts and fruit salads.

Soppong

The small, sleepy market village of Soppong is a popular stop-off on the mountain road between Pai and Mae Hong Son. On first acquaintance, it's hard to see the attraction. It's even harder when making the 1½-hour ascent up to **Tham Lot Cave** (the main attraction) on foot. Once up there, however, all regrets fade away. The scenery around Tham Lot—one of Thailand's longest-known limestone caves—is quite breathtaking, especially round October and November, when the hills and forests are at their most green and luxuriant. The place to stay is the popular **Cave Lodge**, run by friendly Diu and John, which is within easy walking distance of several intersting hilltribe villages. It is also only five minutes' walk from the cave, and you can hire a guide (50B) plus a lantern (50B) to explore its vast interior, full of fascinating side-chambers and grotesquely-shaped pillars. Be prepared to get wet, though. A stream runs through the cave, and when water-levels are high, the guide often just hands the lantern to the best swimmer and hops it. Travellers also like Cave Lodge for its vegetarian food, its brown bread, and its strawberry and peach wine. All meals are eaten together, so you'll make lots of friends. John himself is an authority on the local hill-peoples, and has written much about Tham Lot and other caves in the region. At present, he only has about 20 rooms for let (40B per person) plus a few 80B two-person bungalows. **Cave Lodge 2**, some 25 km from the present lodge, near a checkpoint on the way to Mae Hong Son, should now be in operation. Check also if they are running river-raft trips between the two lodges.

The tiny café at Soppong bus-stop—now called **So Cheap Guest House**—has a few rooms for 50B per person. Current bus-timings for Pai, Mae Hong Son and Chiang Mai are posted here. So is a map giving directions up to Cave Lodge. Another place to stay is **Lisu Lodge**, a few kilometres east of Soppong in **Ban Namrin**. Buses go right past it, so you can ask to be put off. Run by a homely Lisu family, this place has rooms for 30B, and good, cheap meals.

GETTING THERE
Buses leave Pai for Soppong (40 km, 2 hours) at 7, 9 and 11 am and 1.30 pm daily. From Soppong to Pai, there are buses at 8 and 10 am, 1 and 4.30 pm daily. See Mae Hong Son section for bus-timings via Soppong from Mae Hong Son and Chiang Mai.

PAI

People hang out in Pai for weeks on end, and it's easy to see why. Situated midway between Chiang Mai and Mae Hong Son, this restful little town lies in a charming valley completely ringed by rolling hills and mountains. Unlike so-called outposts like Mae Hong Son, it has a genuine pioneer-town atmosphere, and is within easy walking distance of several interesting hilltribe villages, most of them inhabited by refugees from Burma. Pai also offers better and cheaper trekking at present than anywhere else in the North. Rapid development is only a year or two away—already they are planning the new airstrip here—but for the time being Pai remains a tiny one-horse (actually, two-street) town totally geared to relaxation. The standard greeting in these parts is a lazy *Bai nai?* (where you go?), to which the equally laconic response is *Bai eeway* ... (Oh, just cruising ...) If there's anywhere on earth that invented the word 'laidback', it must be Pai. The only thing that ever ruffles its calm are its dogs. The hounds of Pai are famous. They come out at night and roam around in packs scaring lone pedestrians witless. You can try pretending to pick up a stone (this is how everybody in Asia tends to move their animals), but if that doesn't work, be prepared to leg it.

The name Pai is actually a corruption of the Shan word for 'refugee'. The original settlers in this region were outcasts from the large Shan state in Burma. They first crossed over the Pai River some 150 years ago, founding Old Pai—still a thriving Shan village—a few kilometres west of the present town, which is only 100 years old.

GETTING THERE
Buses run to Pai from Chiang Mai (3½ hours, 50B) and from Mae Hong Son (4½ hours, 50B). For bus timings from these two points, see relevant 'Getting There' sections.

WHAT TO SEE

There are some beautiful walks around Pai for which you need no guide. Some people hire out motorbikes (contact Pai Café, or Duang guest houses), but the dirt-track trails connecting the various hilltribe villages are treacherous. For a safe, relaxing bike tour, contact Joe at Duang Guest House. He'll take you out for a great half-day's sightseeing, including good commentary in English, for only 120B. This way, you can enjoy the scenery, and cover all the local attractions in just a morning.

Pai has some worthwhile temples—there's a nice Burmese-style one above the hospital, and Pai's finest temple just behind the bus station. The most popular, however, is **Wat Mae Yen**—the 'Temple on the Hill'. This is a 30-minute walk (1½ km) east of town—over a bridge, through a Shan village, and up a 350-step staircase. At the top of the shallow steps are a group of three small *chedis*—the central one is the only original thing in the otherwise brand-new temple complex. Twelve years ago, this site was derelict. The present structure—built in mixed architectural style, primarily Lanna Thai—is the work of one persuasive monk, who convinced the town that it was time it made some merit. This little monk, often found seated within the shiny new *bot*, can talk money out of just about anyone. Remember this when he offers you a 'free' banana. The temple has a beautiful situation overlooking a valley—from here you can see across to 'Umbrella Mountain', the highest peak in the province. The views are especially fine around sunset.

The 'road' east out of town, via Kim Guest House, leads to a succession of tribal villages. First, some 3 km from Pai, there's a small K.M.T. settlement. The people here are refugees, forced to flee China after resisting Mao Tse Tung. They only arrived from Burma 10 years ago, and have (a rare phenomenon) converted to Christianity. They did so because missionaries said this was their meal-ticket to Taiwan or Singapore. Discovering that they still need a passport (denied to political refugees) hasn't dampened their new faith in the slightest. Now they pray for a passport. Over the road from this village is a small Lisu settlement—the people here are very poor, and the children really appreciate any small presents you may bring. About 2 km further on, there's the Shan village of **Ban Morepang** (Old Pai), where the people still wear traditional Burmese-style turbans and sarongs. The trail comes to an end at **Morepang Waterfall**, some 7 km (two hours' walk) from Pai town. There's good swimming here from September to November—but *kamikaze* slides down the rocks (the popular local recreation) are *not* recommended.

Another pleasant outing is to Pai's famous **Hot springs**. These are located up in the hills, some 15 km east of town, and are best visited by motorbike (or by cycle—40B day-hire in town). This is a very scenic ride through beautiful woodlands, with the promise of a refreshing mineral-water bath (with a hot tub to soak in) at journey's end.

Trekking

Pai has densely forested hills, deep jungles, green open valleys and an abundance of lovely natural scenery. Unlike Chiang Rai, this area is almost completely untrekked. Unlike Mae Hong Son, which is still getting its act together, Pai has no less than four good English-speaking guides. They are all cheap (around 150B per day, plus an extra 250B per day for elephants or river-rafting) and they all have independent circuits which don't overlap. The result is inexpensive small-group treks to little-visited villages, and no sight of another *farang* from beginning to end. If anything, however, the Pai trails are hillier and harder going than Mae Hong Son, so you'll need good walking shoes and *a lot* of energy. Again, it can get cold at night (especially October to February) and a sleeping bag, even blankets, may be required. In the rainy months, bring a waterproof or plastic sheet. There's no electricity up in the hills, so a good torch with a powerful beam is a real must.

All Pai's trek guides are attached to guest houses in the town. They are Buffalo Bill and Anan (Pai Guest House), Mr Pong (Café), and Jungle Joe (Duang). Of these, the best-known—and the most notorious—is Buffalo Bill. His speciality is the gruelling 7-day trek from Pai up to Mae Hong Son. If you're into walking 6–7 hours a day, and survive days 2 and 3 (a crippling ascent up an 1800-metre mountain), you'll enjoy this one. People trek with B.B. for the 'experience'—wildly eccentric, never less than entertaining, he's a real showman. Of the other guides, only Jungle Joe and Mr Pong are home-grown talents—i.e. born and bred in Pai, with full knowledge of the area. Joe has an especially good relationship with the hilltribes, and is probably the best guide in town—quiet, friendly and reliable. His popular 4-day trek strikes north to visit Lisu, Yellow Lahu, and White Karen villages, and includes an option to river-raft down the Pai River from the Shan village of **Ban Mae Kok** to the Thai settlement of **Sop Kai**. From here, if you don't wish to walk back to Pai, you can take a minibus down to **Mae Malai**, which is only half an hour by bus from Chiang Mai.

Joe also offers a 4-day trek to Soppong's **Cave Lodge**, and (November to February only) 7-day 'adventure' raft trips up the Pai River to Mae Hong Son. The Pai is a narrow, perilous river—non-negotiable before November (too swollen) or after February (too shallow)—but in season, it's an exhilarating experience to travel on it.

SHOPPING
Hilltribe crafts, mainly Karen products, are sold in town at Duang and Café restaurants. Prices are okay—hand-embroidered tunics at 200B, handwoven cotton bedsheets around 300B etc.—but you're generally better off buying direct from the villages on trek.

WHERE TO STAY AND EATING OUT   (tel prefix 053)
Inexpensive
Pai has one 'hotel', the gloomy, Chinese-owned **Wiang Pai**, 26/4 Rungsiyanon Rd (80–120B) and several cheap, basic guest houses. Best of these is **Duang** ('Your Home away from Home'), right opposite the bus-stop. This has large, clean rooms at 50B single, 80B double; also one special twin-bedded room, with a swank bathroom, at 180B. Duang herself is a delightful hostess, welcoming guests with free fruit salads, and giving good local information. Her sister, Kim, teaches classical Thai dance at the local school (worth dropping in to see) and runs **Kim Guest House**, 5 minutes' walk up the road. This is another clean place, with rooms from 40B (decent beds) to 60B (attached bathrooms with hot showers). The back garden is a banana/mango plantation—so more free fruit salads.

Rooms at **Pai** and **Café** guest houses (40–80B) are more basic. Thin bamboo partitions give you intimate knowledge of your neighbour's sleeping habits. Large spiders, and other chummy crawlies, are common co-tenants. Still, the food's good. The

Pai in the Sky (Café's restaurant) serves delicious vegetarian meals and is famous for its yoghurt shakes. Try the 'Hotpot'—a wonderful potpourri of chicken, potatoes, tomatoes, onions, garlic and coconut milk, on a bed of rice. Pai guest house, across the road, is the main freaks' hangout, with psychedelic sounds and wacky staff to match. There's a large stuffed eagle in the lobby (rapidly disintegrating) and the special dinner is Elephant Steak with French Freeze. The elephant steaks are really buffalo, but Buffalo Bill (the resident guide) won't admit it. 'I used to have ten elephants', he says, 'but now I have only one. Tourists eat rest!' Actually, B.B. doesn't have any elephants at all, but it's a good story.

The cosy little **P.O.B. restaurant**, just below Wiang Pai hotel, offers palatable Thai-Chinese cuisine, and is a quiet alternative to the busy Pai in the Sky. It's run by a friendly Thai lady, and has a useful information board. The best up-to-date trek maps of the area, however, are pinned up at Pai Guest House.

SUKHOTHAI

Birthplace of the Thai nation, Sukhothai lies about 440 km north of Bangkok, and is approached by road from Phitsanulok. Wrested from the Khmer by two powerful Thai chieftains, Sukhothai ('Dawn of Happiness') was established in 1238 as the first major independent Thai kingdom.

Though its period of power and influence over the Thai states was short—just 150 years—it produced in that time one remarkable ruler, King Ramkhamhaeng the Great. During his 40-year reign, he conquered many neighbouring territories, began direct negotiations with China, invented the Thai alphabet (1283), promoted religion and culture (actively encouraging Ceylonese Buddhist monks and Chinese artisans into the kingdom), and generally paved the way for classic Sukhothai forms of inspirational religious art and sculpture. The Buddha images created in this period possess a distinctive grace and simplicity, a timeless air of serenity, which help to explain why Sukhothai was the spiritual, as well as the temporal, centre of its time. However, a succession of weak kings after Ramkhamhaeng led to the swift decline of this first Thai capital, and in 1365 it became a vassal state of Ayutthaya, the newly rising star to the south.

An ambitious 10-year project (started 1980) is presently underway, aimed at restoring to their former glory the 70 square kilometres of crumbling brick and stucco ruins comprising Old Sukhothai. Some regret this move, preferring the old walled city in its original derelict state—serene, evocative and lonely. Others cynically remark that the ruins—now renamed 'Sukhothai Historical Park'—are only being restored for the sake of tourism. Most of them have now been made to look as though they were built only last month. The partition of the 'park' into 5 zones—open 6 am–6 pm and to see each of which you have to pay 20B entrance—and the introduction of eyesore barbed-wire fencing (to stop tourists wandering off into restricted areas) can be off-putting. But in the main, the experiment has been successful. The Sukhothai ruins now make far better viewing than those at Lopburi or Ayutthaya. Visited by busloads of package tourists toting video cameras, this ancient city's original grandeur is slowly, meticulously, being reassembled.

The small town of Sukhothai is a short bus or bicycle ride from the Historical Park, and is an excellent base from which to plan sightseeing. It has good little markets, guest houses, coffee shops and ice-cream parlours, and a wonderfully relaxed atmosphere. Best time to visit is October and November for the annual **Loi Krathong Festival**, celebrated in Sukhothai as nowhere else in Thailand. There's a glorious sound and light show, and the river is packed with myriad tiny boats launching decorative candle-lit floats. As Sukhothai's main event, attended by thousands, advance-booking of transport and accommodation is essential during this festival.

GETTING THERE
Sukhothai is reached by bus from Chiang Mai or Phitsanulok, which is connected by plane and train to Bangkok and Chiang Mai. Buses run out to Sukhothai from the centre of Phitsanulok, every half-hour from 4.45 am to 6.15 pm. The fare is 14B, and the journey takes around one hour.

By Air
Thai Airways flies to Phitsanulok from Bangkok (at least twice daily, 920B, flight time 45 minutes) and from Chiang Mai (daily, 650B, flight time 2½ hours—including stopovers). From Phitsanulok airport, it's a 5B *songthaew* ride into town, or 30B by 'limousine' mini-bus.

By Train
From Bangkok's Hualamphong station only three trains leaving at 6.40 am (Rapid), 7.05 and 8.30 am (Ordinary), arrive in Phitsanulok early enough (respectively, at 12.33, 2.55 and 5.25 pm) to carry on to Sukhothai the same day. Basic fares are 292B 1st class, 143B 2nd class, and 69B 3rd class. From Chiang Mai, only the 3.30 pm Rapid arrives in Phitsanulok at a reasonable time (10.55 pm) to find a hotel for the night.

By Bus
From Bangkok's Northern Terminal, there are three air-con buses to Sukhothai daily at

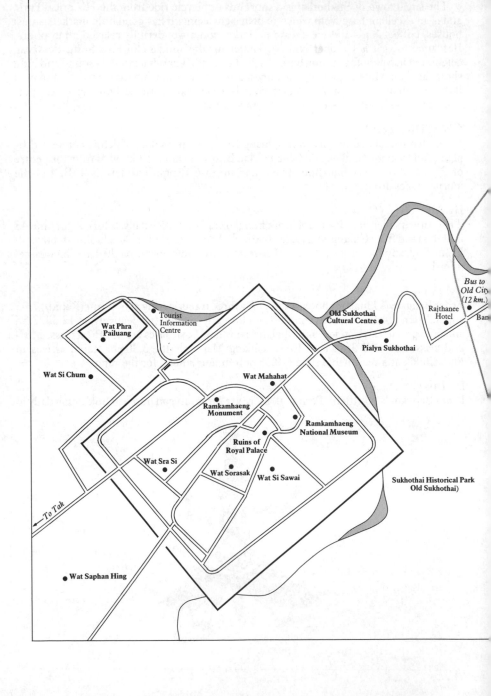

Wat Phra
Pailuang

Tourist
Information
Centre

Old Sukhothai
Cultural Centre

Bus to
Old City
(12 km.)

Rajthanee
Hotel

Ban

Pialyn Sukhothai

Wat Si Chum

Wat Mahahat

Ramkamhaeng
Monument

Ramkamhaeng
National Museum

Ruins of
Royal Palace

Wat Sra Si

Sukhothai Historical Park
Old Sukhothai)

Wat Sorasak

Wat Si Sawai

To Tak

Wat Saphan Hing

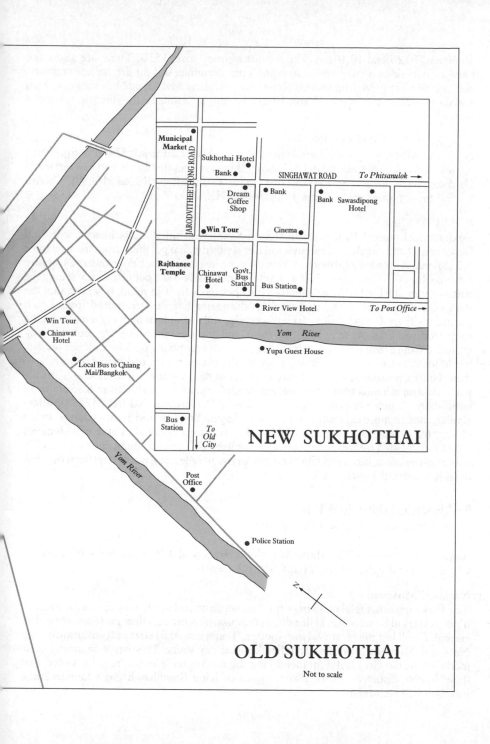

10.40 am, 10.20 and 10.40 pm. The 8-hour journey costs 153B. There are also some cheaper non air-con buses (84B) from the same terminal, but they're far less comfortable. From Chiang Mai, non air-con buses leave Chiang Mai Arcade bus station at 7 am and 3 pm, 72B, air-con at 8.35 and 10 am, 12 and 2.15 pm, 100B—the trip takes five hours.

TOURIST INFORMATION
No tourist office, but good information (and map) from **Chinawat Hotel** in Sukhothai town at 1/3 Nikon Kasem Rd (tel 611385). Chinawat operates an air-con bus service to Bangkok, via Ayutthaya. So do **Win Tours** in Jarodvitheethong Rd (tel 611039). There's a small tourist information centre at Sukhothai Historical Park.

WHAT TO SEE
Sukhothai Historical Park is studded with wonderful old Buddha images, *wats* and *chedis*, moats and canals, and merits a full day's viewing. To get there from the new town (12 km) take a *songthaew* (5B) or bus from the rank just across the bridge (also 5B), or hire a *tuk-tuk* for 50B. Once there, hire a bicycle or motorbike—the popular way of seeing the ruins—from outside the Museum (30–100B per day). Bear in mind, however, that the Park covers a vast area, and that many of the major temples are spaced from 2 to 6 kilometres apart. It can be a long haul by bicycle, and a couple of outlying temples on the suggested route below (e.g. Wat Si Chum, outside the city walls) are probably best excluded from a bike tour. A new **tram** service runs around the park for 20B per person, but it doesn't stop at all the sights. To see all the places mentioned in just a morning— from 100B a person—contact Chinawat Hotel in the new town. This operates worthwhile air-con minibus **tours**, with decent English-speaking guides, from 8.45 am to 12 noon daily. A new company, **Sky Tour**, 28–30 Prasertpong Rd (tel 612236), offers similar, though more expensive excursion packages. You can find guides yourself in the old city (rates around 100B per hour), but they're purely optional. All the main temples now have detailed information boards in English. To see everything at leisure, and in maximum comfort, hire a taxi (500B for one to five people, for a whole day) from the rank outside Chinawat Hotel.

Sukhothai Historical Park
(by tour bus, taxi or bicycle; half/full day)

National Museum – Wat Mahathat – Wat Sri Sawai – Wat Sra Sri – Wat Sri Chum – Wat Saphin Hin – Thai Cultural Centre

National Museum
The Park contains a total of 35 important monuments, all scattered over a wide area, so it's necessary to be selective. Half a dozen temples, plus the excellent museum, should be enough for all but the most avid *wat*-spotter. Tours generally start at **Ramkhamhaeng National Museum**, just inside Old Sukhothai city walls. This has a charming scale model of the old city (useful for identifying the various temples you're going to see, and their relative distances apart), also a replica of King Ramkhamhaeng's famous stone inscription, which reads:

This Muang Sukhothai is good. In the water there are fish, in the field there is rice. The ruler does not levy a tax on the people who travel along the road together ... Whoever wants to trade in elephants, so trades. Whoever wants to trade in horses, so trades. Whoever wants to trade in silver and gold, so trades.

This Thai-style 'Declaration of Independence' was found by King Mongkut in the 19th century. The museum also houses a fine collection of Sukhothai Buddha images in bronze or stucco, most of them in the attitudes of 'subduing Mara' or 'dispelling fear'. Buddha figures of the Sukhothai style are simple and unembellished, with slim torsos, lotus-bud topknots (*usnisha*), long earlobes, Grecian noses, arched eyebrows and uniformly serene expressions. By way of contrast, you'll also find a few Ayutthayan Buddhas: regally attired, heavily bejewelled, haughtily arrogant. Outside in the grounds, there are a couple of surprised-looking elephants emerging from brick walls. Admission to the museum is 20B, and there's a 5B guide for sale at the entrance. There's no photography (and 'no shouting') allowed inside (open 9–4).

Wat Mahathat

From the museum, people generally move on to **Wat Mahathat**, the largest and (for many) the most beautiful temple in Sukhothai. Probably built in the mid-13th century by Sri Indrathit (Ramkhamhaeng's father), it sits amid a tranquil lotus pond and picnic park in fully restored splendour. Enclosed within its low-walled compound is a tightly-packed maze of 98 small *chedis*, parentally surveyed by a large central *chedi* with a bulbous lotus-bud *prang* and unusual friezes of walking monks circumventing its base. Nearby, a huge black-caped Buddha lurks Dracula-like within a high brick enclosure. One of the larger *chedis*, with a large seated Buddha at its base, can be climbed (be careful!) for good bird's-eye views of the whole compound.

Wat Sri Sawai, Wat Sra Sri and Wat Sri Chum

Wat Sri Sawai, a short distance southwest of Wat Mahathat, is another 13th-century shrine, notable for its three Khmer-style *prangs*, surrounded by a low laterite wall. Traces of Hindu sculpture on this structure suggest that it was not always a Buddhist monastery. Renovation has been kind to this temple, adorning it with a pretty lotus pond and colourful flower gardens. **Wat Sra Sri**, north of Wat Mahathat, is another superb temple. This features a round Ceylonese-style *chedi* within a monastery built on an island in the middle of a pond. The large *viharn* to the front contains a stucco Buddha image, while the small one to the south is constructed in the Ceylonese Srivijaya style. Save a photo for the little black Buddha strutting on the lawn—it's outrageously camp. It's also a classic example of the 'walking Buddha' style initiated by the Sukhothai sculptors. To see perhaps their finest creation, head on to **Wat Sri Chum**, just outside the city walls to the northeast. The awesome Buddha here, housed within a deceptively dull square *mondop*, measures 11.3 metres from knee to knee, and is said to have once halted a Burmese invasion. The story goes that the intruding hordes took one look at it and fled in terror. Just inside the entrance, a low, narrow passage leads to the top of the *mondop* for panoramic views over pastoral parklands. The passageway ceiling is lined with slate slabs engraved with various *Jakarta* stories, though only a few of them are illuminated.

Wat Saphin Hin and Thai Cultural Centre

About 2 km west of Wat Sri Chum, and situated on a low hill, **Wat Saphin Hin** is a pleasantly remote place to finish off the day. A rough slate causeway leads to the top, where you'll find a small seated Buddha looking serenely over a picturesque landscape. There's a ruined *viharn* up here too, with a 12.5 metre-high standing Buddha. Refreshingly unrenovated, this *wat* retains its age-old sense of tranquillity—and for once there's no admission charge. Leaving the historical park, about 1 km out of the old city on the road back to Sukhothai town, look out for **Sukhothai Cultural Centre** (tel 611049). This has a mock Thai village in a pleasant semi-jungle setting, a few 250–450B air-con bungalows for rent (book in town), a good restaurant, and live music and dance every evening.

Si Satchanalai
(by bus, then by bicycle; full day)

Si Satch is only 57 km from Sukhothai and was, until absorbed into the Sukhothai kingdom, a powerful political, economic and religious centre in its own right. It also had a reputation for producing quality Thai *celadon* and Sawankhaloke pottery, and there are still bargains to be picked up in the town today. Beautifully set between high hills and the river, Si Satchanalai has lovely old ruins which make a good contrast to the renovated temples of Sukhothai.

Local buses run regularly from Sukhothai to Si Satchanalai for 18B. Chinawat Hotel offers a comprehensive 6-hour minibus tour to Si Satch (150B), taking in the old city, the Ko Noi kiln, and the fabric factories of Hat Sieo. Entering Old Si Satch by bus, **Wat Mahathat** and three other interesting hillside temples appear to the right. Off the bus, cross the bridge over the Yom River, and turn right for the ruins. You'll find bicycles for hire on the way, but you don't need them. The best things about this place are the beautiful walks through the hills and woodlands—besides, several temples are inaccessible by bicycle. Si Satch has fewer 'sights' than Sukhothai, but compensates with beautiful scenery in a peaceful countryside setting. There's also good shopping at **Hat Sieo**, a weaving village in Si Satchanalai district which is famous for its fine handmade cotton. The workers are the Lao-Puan people, who originated in Chiang Kwang and who settled in this area, north of old Si Satchanalai, during the early Bangkok period. Continuing their age-old tradition of fabric-making, they turn out beautiful long Thai sarongs (80B for men, 500B for women) and highly ornate material lengths incorporating designs as intricate (and as stylish) as Arabian carpets.

SHOPPING

You can keep your wallet closed in Sukhothai. A tatty souvenir shop called **Choo's** at the Thai Cultural Centre offers antiques at prices you can't afford. A large house opposite new Sukhothai police station sells 'antique' Buddhas and *garudas* you can't take out of the country. Not much of a choice really.

WHERE TO STAY   (tel prefix 055)

Expensive

Located in an area surrounded by rice fields, 8 km out of town on the way to the historical park, the **Pailyn Sukhothai Hotel**, Jarodvitheethong Rd (tel 613310) has super views of the Khao Luang mountains, a swimming pool, traditional Thai massage, and a restaurant specializing in Thai cuisine. Rates are 800–2500B.

Moderate
The **Rajthanee Hotel**, in Jarodvitheethong Rd, has air-con rooms from 450–1000B, and is friendly and comfortable. But the main travellers' centre is **Chinawat Hotel**, 1–3 Nikorn Kasem Rd (tel 611385). Run by friendly, energetic Lakana ('Slim') and Wijai, it has rooms from 90B in the old building, excellent fan double rooms from 100B and air-con doubles for 250–400B in the better new block. Useful facilities include cycle rental, currency exchange (cash only), travel agency, postal service, overseas phone, and good information handouts.

Inexpensive
The nearby **Sukhothai Hotel** at 15/5 Singhawat Rd (tel 611133) is a reasonable fallback. Rooms here (100B fan, 250B air-con) aren't as clean as at Chinawat, but staff are friendly and guests get a good city map. Travellers also speak well of **Yupa Guest House**, in a *soi* off Prawet Nakhon Rd (tel 612578), a small lodge overlooking the river (cross the bridge, walk left along the riverbank for 400 metres). This has rooms from 80 to 120B, relaxing swingseats and lovely views from the balconies.

EATING OUT
The **Rajthanee Hotel** has a classy restaurant—eat well here for 150B, with live music thrown in. The **Chinawat** has a decent bakery section, but cakes, ice-creams and continental breakfasts are all better at the **Rainbow Bakery**, just round the corner. Near the Chinawat is the very popular **Kho Joeng Hong**, serving good Chinese food for around 60B a dish. **Dream Coffee Shop**, opposite Bangkok Bank in Singhawat Rd, does the best coffee in town, and is the place to make Thai friends (they love this place). It's beautifully decorated in traditional Thai-style. The small night market behind the bus station does incredible 10B vegetarian and mussel omelettes, plus the usual cheap Thai-Chinese curries and snacks. Similar fare—almost as good—is on offer at the municipal market near the town centre.

PHITSANULOK

Sitting on the Nan river, this is a busy, dusty town with not much to recommend it, but you may want (or be forced to) stop off here on your way to or from Bangkok, Chiang Mai or Sukhothai. One thing's for sure—you'll see few *farangs* here, but it's not unpleasant and is a good starting point or base for local trips, including Sukhothai, only one hour away.

GETTING THERE
Phitsanulok is reached by air, train and bus from Bangkok, Chiang Mai and Sukhothai. For details, see 'Getting There' section for Sukhothai.

WHAT TO SEE
There is little to see in the town, apart from **Wat Phra Sri Ratana Mahathat**, housing the much-revered bronze Jinaraj Buddha from the late Sukhothai period. To see this,

you'll need to be in town no later than 5 pm—after that time, all you're likely to find are two locked doors and a compound full of saffron-robed monks wandering round in gumboots. The story surrounding this Buddha has it that on completion of the *wat* King Li Thai wanted three bronze Buddhas to be put in it. Whilst the casting of the second and third images were perfect, repeated castings of the first Buddha were flawed, until the King invoked the assistance of the *devas* (angels), who sent along an old sage dressed in white to supervise the final casting, which then turned out to be perfect. Across the road is the **Folk Museum**, featuring old-fashioned farming and hunting equipment used by northern people in days gone by.

Thanks to the angels, or the industrial revolution, the **Buddha Casting Factory** on Wisut Kasat Rd manages to churn out bronze Buddhas by the score, and visitors are welcome to watch the process, particularly if they buy one on their way out.

From Phitsanulok, buses run hourly to Lom Sak in the east, along Highway 12. This road has a number of waterfalls along the way, between 33 and 80 km from Phitsanulok. **Sakunothayan**, set in botanical gardens, **Keang Song** at the roadside, **Poi** and **Keang-sopa**, both 2 km from the road, and **Si Dit** in **Thung Salaeng Luang National Park**, beyond which is the **war monument and weaponry museum**. This is in honour of the wretched fighting that took place in this area (particularly in Phu Hin Rong Kla National Park to the north) between government forces and student communist insurgents, who took to the hills to wage a campaign of war after the killing of hundreds of Thai students by government troops during an uprising in 1972. The fighting lasted until 1982, during which time the CPT (Communist Party of Thailand) set up a hospital and school on political and military discipline. The Phu Hin Rong Kla Park can be reached by bus from Phitsanulok to Nakornthai, where you change buses.

WHERE TO STAY   (tel prefix 055)

Moderate
There are a few decent hotels in Phitsanulok, despite its apparent lack of tourism. **Pailyn** is the best, on Boromtrailokanart Rd (tel 252411), one block up from the river. It has a pleasant air-conditioned restaurant serving good European and Thai food. Rates start at 900B. Not quite as good is **Ratchapruk**, 99/9 Phra Ong Dam Rd (tel 258788) but it is cheaper, with air-con rooms for 500B, and an okay restaurant. At the back of this hotel is the cheaper guest house belonging to the hotel—ask for their 300B air-con rooms.

Inexpensive
Lower down the scale there's a good choice of budget places—**Pan Sombat** is centrally placed at Sailuthai Rd (tel 258179), with rooms at 150B with fan; on the same road is the slightly cheaper **Sukkit** (tel 258378) and in the southeast of town at 38 Sanambin Rd is the **Youth Hostel** (tel 242060), in a Thai-style house on stilts, where beds in the dormitory cost 50B, double rooms 130B (10B surcharge for non-members).

EATING OUT
Don't be deceived—Phitsanulok has plenty to offer in terms of eateries. Try the houseboat/restaurants on the river; both the **Song Khwae** and **Than Thip** serve excellent Thai-Chinese food. The **Topland** department store has an air-conditioned

restaurant with Thai and European dishes (around 200B per person), and there are restaurants in the bigger hotels. Best fun of all, however, is to be had at the night bazaar by the river, at the southern end of town. Here the speciality is *phak bung loi fha* or morning glory vine, but it's not so much the dish as what the cook does with it—he tosses it into the air to be caught on a plate by an eagle-eyed waiter. This practice has become so popular that tour operators bring their customers here, and the diners are invited to try their skill—from the top of a parked van!

Part VIII

THE NORTHEAST

Rice-workers

Commonly known as *Isaan*, the northeast is the poorest and least-developed part of Thailand. *Isaan* is a derivation of Isana, the old Mon-Khmer kingdom which once flourished in these parts. The name means 'vastness'—which is appropriate, the northeast covering 170,000 square kilometres, or roughly one-third of the country. It also means 'prosperity'—which is far less appropriate. Isaan is a dry and arid plateau which, if lucky, receives only enough rain to produce one crop of rice each year. Recently, successive droughts have triggered off a mass migration of farmers into Bangkok and other major provinces. But if the region is poor in rice, it is rich in history and culture. Folk dances, fairs and festivals go on as in ages past, both delightful and symbolic. Ancient customs and traditions, untouched by the march of progress, continue to charm and fascinate foreign visitors. The northeast is famous for its fine Khmer-style temples, such as those at **Phimai**, and for its *mudmee* silk (much promoted by Queen Sikrit) which is produced at nearby **Pakthongchai**. Further north, the archaeological discoveries made at the small village of **Ban Chiang** suggest that Isaan was the birthplace of the world's oldest Bronze Age civilization. There are some amazing temples—and beautiful cottage industry crafts up at **Nong Khai** on the Laos border, while at more modern towns like **Nakhon Ratchasima** and **Udorn Thani**, traditional Isaan-style food, like *kai yang* (spicy barbecued chicken) and *som tam* (spicy raw papaya salad) can be sampled along with delicious Western-style cakes and pastries.

The main attraction of the northeast is its remoteness. People come here to get off the beaten track and to find 'real' Thailand. They are often successful—Isaan is a land of few sights, and very little spoken English. Here, you have to learn some Thai or starve. Every other traveller I've met in the northeast was doing the same as me—peering into a

186

phrasebook and muttering 'Where is the toilet' or 'I want some food without frog in it' in the local tongue. Getting around is a challenge, but never dull. The pace of life is generally slow and relaxed, the people friendly and hospitable, and the old custom of 'wai-ing' (greeting with a bow) observed even during basketball matches. This is the heart and soul of Thailand—spending a week here, you'll learn more about the Thai people (and their language) than a month anywhere else.

The northeast is a large region, best discovered by rail. There are two routes—one running north via Nakhon Ratchasima (for Phimai and Pakthongchai), Udorn Thani (for Ban Chiang), and Nong Khai; the other running south via Buriram, Surin and Ubon Ratchathani. The southern route is not covered in this guide—partly because it has less to offer the general sightseer, but mainly because ongoing border disputes with Kampuchea make this not the safest place to travel at present.

NAKHON RATCHASIMA (KHORAT)

Only 256 km from Bangkok, Nakhon Ratchasima (better known as Khorat) is the popular and convenient 'gateway' to the northeast. Originally, Khorat was two separate towns, Khorakhapura and Sema, which were merged into one during the reign of King Narai (1656–1688). Today, it still has something of a dual identity—the older, semi-rural eastern half of town contrasting starkly with the busy, commercial section to the west. Khorat is an interesting place in itself, but also makes a good base from which to visit the historic site of **Phimai** and the silk-weaving centre of **Pakthongchai**.

During the 1960s, Khorat was used as a major base for American GIs going into Vietnam. This accounts for all the cinemas, Turkish baths, ex-vet clubs and snooker halls you'll find here, together with the town's veneer of Western sophistication. Walking down the street, you'll often be greeted with a lazy 'Hey man, where you go?' by hip young Thais. And as you tuck into your ham 'n' eggs on rye in an American café, you may hear nostalgic juke-box standards like *Rum Boogie* and even *In the Mood*. Nevertheless, Khorat remains typically Thai. Only during 1987—the Year of Tourism—did the province begin to attract more than a few Western visitors. Today, it's still common to find yourself the only non-Thai in town. There are a few surviving war veterans—but they rarely surface till the evening, when the bars open.

Visit Khorat between January and March, or in October. Avoid the Thai holiday season of November and December, when every hotel is packed out. Rooms are also scarce from August to early September, when the American army (which still has a base outside town) drops in for military exercises. Khorat has a big 15-day festival—commencing 23rd March each year—in honour of 'Lady Mo', a Thai-style Boadicea who ousted an invading Laotian force from the town in 1826. Her real name was Khunying Mo, and she was the wife of the deputy governor of Khorat. Her statue in the town square—the **Thao Suranari Memorial**—attracts a daily procession of pilgrims. Her festival—one of the best in the northeast—is well worth going out of your way to see and has lots of local entertainments, including traditional folk dances, *likhee* theatre, and *luuk tung* (children of the fields) music.

187

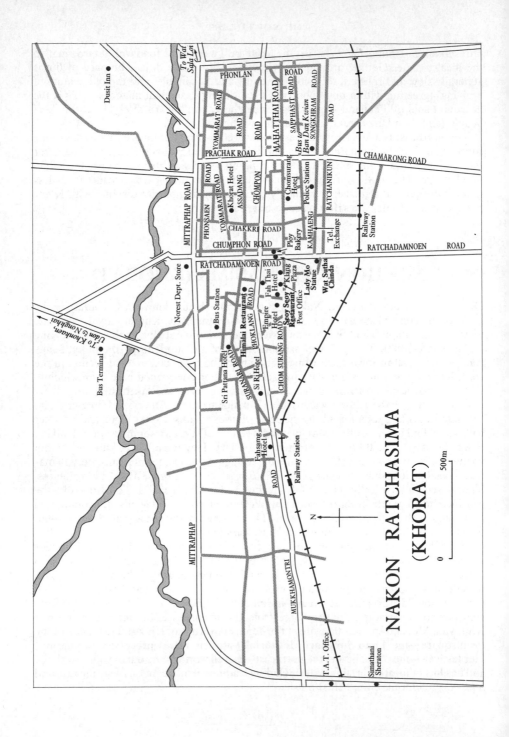

NAKON RATCHASIMA
(KHORAT)

GETTING THERE
By Air
Thai Airways operates one flight daily to Khorat from Bangkok. Flight time is 40 minutes, and the fare is 540B.

By train
From Bangkok's Hualamphong station, there are two convenient early trains to Khorat—the 6.50 am Rapid (arriving 11.46 am) and the 7.15 am Ordinary (arriving 1.58 pm). After these, no more trains leave Bangkok till 3.25 pm. Basic fares are 207B 1st class, 104B 2nd class, 50B 3rd class.

By bus
From Bangkok's Northern Terminal, non air-con buses leave for Khorat every 20 minutes, from 5 am to 9.30 pm; the fare is 51B, and it's a 4½-hour trip. There are also air-con buses every 15 minutes, costing 92B and taking only 4 hours.

Khorat has two bus terminals. In town, on Burin Lane, Terminal I serves Bangkok (every 15–20 minutes throughout the day), Chiang Mai, Chiang Rai, Phitsanulok and local destinations. Terminal II is 1 km north of town on Mittraphap Highway, and buses leave here for Nong Khai (4 per day, 140B), Udorn Thani (hourly from 9 am to midnight, 110B), Pattaya (4 per day, 118B) and other destinations in the northeast.

TOURIST INFORMATION
TAT Tourist office, 2102–2104 Mittraphap Rd (tel 255243) is friendly and helpful, gives out a good town map (with local bus routes) and is open 8.30 am to 4.30 pm daily.

WHAT TO SEE
Khorat is a small, quiet town at its best after dark. Most of the evening action is around **Chumpon Road**, with its lively, atmospheric night market. Elsewhere, school kids play basketball, adolescents do aerobics and drink beer (not necessarily in that order) and everybody in general is out of doors. The place is ideal for leisurely exploration by bicycle—but there's nowhere to hire one. Local transport is bicycle *samlors* and *tuk-tuks*, charging 10B and 20B respectively for short journeys round town. But you'll have to bargain hard (in Thai) to get these prices.

In-town Tour
(by *samlor*, *tuk-tuk*, or on foot; 2–3 hours)

Wat Sala Loi – Maha Mirawong Museum
Located northeast of town, 400 metres off the ring road, **Wat Sala Loi** (Temple of the Floating Pavilion) isn't easy to find on foot—local transport is best. This modern temple is highly unusual—the main *bot* or chapel is built in the shape of a Chinese junk. Constructed from local materials, including famous earthenware tiles from nearby Ban Dan Kwian, the structure has won several architectural prizes. The original temple on this site was built in the time of Khunying Mo, and her ashes are still interred here. Within the *bot*, colourful murals depict key events in the life of the Buddha; outside, a

tiny mini-Buddha faces into the chapel from a charming pavilion over a lotus pond. Wander round the peaceful garden compound—it's full of curiosities.

The **Maha Wirawong Museum**, attached to Wat Sutchachinda on Ratchadamnoen Rd, is rather small and tacky for a 'national museum', but there is some fine Khmer sculpture and art here—notably a huge Ayutthayan door lintel (beautifully carved) and a brace of fierce Singha lions (at the entrance). Lighting is poor, few objects have English labels, and priceless antiques sit propped up on dusty old fruitboxes. Still, it is worth a visit. The modest *wat* outside has a tranquil lake, pretty gardens, and chatty monks. The museum is open daily (9 am to noon, 1 to 4.30 pm), and admission is 10B.

Phimai
(by bus; full day)

Prasat Hin – National Museum – Sai Ngam
Even if you don't like temples, Phimai is a must. Located 60 km northeast of Khorat, buses go there every half-hour from Khorat (Bus No. 1305, fare 14B, journey time $1^1/2$ hours). **Phimai Sanctuary** is open 6 am to 6 pm daily, and admission is 5B for locals, 20B for foreigners. A useful little 10B guide is sold at the entrance. The **Phimai Hotel**, round the corner from the bus-stop, has reasonable fan-rooms from 180B, air-con rooms from 300B.

Phimai has been dubbed the Anghor Wat of Thailand and it certainly bears many similarities to the famous Cambodian sanctuary, and may indeed have been the work of the same architect. If this is so—and nobody knows for sure—then it dates to the reign of King Surijavoraman (1002–1049). It certainly was much added to during the reign of King Jayavoraman VII (1181–1201), but was abandoned in the 13th century when the Khmer empire collapsed. In its heyday, Phimai was evidently of great importance being the largest of the dozen or so sanctuaries erected in the northeast during the 11th and 12th centuries—all of them connected by road to Anghor Wat. Today, it stands as a definitive example of Khmer architecture.

Dominating the extensive ruins is the majestic **Prasat Hin** (Stone Castle) shrine. Destroyed some time in the 17th century it has been lovingly restored by the Fine Arts Department, and is now considered one of the most classic structures in all Thailand. Even though all the pieces don't fit together (so complex was the work of reconstruction), the main *prang* (spire) is a model of simple, elegant symmetry, constructed from massive white sandstone blocks. High up, you'll see the large garuda-bird, carrier of Shiva (most Khmer architecture was Hindu); below this, covering the door lintels, there are powerful friezes depicting scenes from the *Ramayana* epic. Many of the best carvings have been removed to the nearby museum, but some beautiful work remains—exquisite lotus blossom motifs over doorways, and the famous panel of elephant/monkey devotees offering sugar-cane and fruit to Buddha, above a lintel in the central chamber.

The excellent open-air **National Museum** (open 8.30 am to 4.30 pm daily) is a short 10-minute walk left out of the sanctuary. All exhibits here—mainly lintels, pediments, and friezes from Phimai (plus finds from other northeastern sanctuaries)—are well-presented and labelled. A group of ghoulish skeletons dating to round 3000 BC, and described as 'prehistoric remains', live in strange 'chicken-coop' coffins.

About 2 kilometres above the museum, you'll come across a reservoir full of 'petrified' stone herons—some of them stationary, some apparently about to take flight, but all of them eerily lifelike. Here you'll find the **Sai Ngam Banyan Grove**—a single immense banyan tree, covering an area of 15,000 square feet. Its many cool, shady arbours make it a favourite picnic spot for Thai families. Locals revere the grove as a shelter for powerful spirits, and the temple to the rear is a popular spot for buying Chinese fortunes, or for making merit by releasing captive birds or fish.

Ban Than Prasat

Some 42 km from Khorat on the road to Phimai, recent digs have uncovered an **archaeological site** near the village of Ban Prasat. Excavations in three areas have revealed skeletons, ornaments made from animal bones and ancient weapons dated to about 3000 years ago; bronze weapons, painted beads, gold wrist and ankle bracelets from the Dvaravati period (1600–1800 years ago); weapons and pottery from 600 years ago. The site, which sits on a rise and was once encircled by a moat, is believed to date back to prehistory, possibly even farther back than Ban Chiang (see below).

Pakthongchai
(by bus; half day)

Pakthongchai lies 30 km south of Khorat, and produces the best-quality silk in Thailand. The **Silk-Weaving Village** here supplies silk thread for the weaving industry of Bangkok, and is the main supplier of silk lengths and materials to Jim Thompson's. Even if you're not fussed about silk, come to Pakthongchai to see an authentic Thai village, with original wood buildings throughout. The best time to visit is early morning, when all the looms are busily at work and you can see the various silk-weaving processes. Most of the weavers here sell silk direct to the public—it's high-quality stuff, and has unique designs. Opposite the bus-stop, down a side-road, **Praneet Thai Silk** (tel 441173) has a very good range of material. Prices here are fixed, but reasonable: 2-ply silk material is 180B per yard (plain) and 220B per yard (printed); beautiful cushion-covers are 180B each. You'll find many colours and designs here, as well as the bright Eastern colours. Buses leave for Pakthongchai from Khorat bus station (No. 1303; fare 10B) every half-hour. The last bus back to Khorat is at 6 pm.

SHOPPING
You don't have to go to Pakthongchai to find its fabulous silk. Several shops in Khorat sell it too, mainly on Chumpon and Ratchadamnoen roads. Try **Tussanee Thai Silk** (tel 242372), facing Lady Mo's statue in the town square. This is a well-established shop, with a wide selection of designs. Again, cheap prices—plain silk from 160B a yard, patterned silk from 200B a yard.

There's also **Sumon Thai Silk**, 2786 Mitraphab Rd (tel 252113), located on the highway leading out of town. Catch a No. 6 bus from Khorat bus terminal—get off at the Esso station, just before the Pakthongchai turn-off. Sumon stocks silks supplied direct from Pakthongchai, and has a better range of fabrics, furnishings, handicrafts and designs than any shop in town. It also has a weaving factory of its own, producing quality-controlled silk of an extremely soft texture. Prices are a little high—plain silk from 200B a yard, patterned silk from 300B a yard—but the same stuff will cost 30% more at Jim Thompson's in Bangkok (where a lot of Sumon's silk ends up). Ask Samat, the pleasant young manager to recommend the best cheap tailor in Khorat. Another good silk silk shop is **Today Thai Silk**, 724 Ratchadamnoen Rd (tel 251882).

Best general shopping in Khorat town is at **Norest** department store, in Mittraphap Rd, and at the new **Klang Plaza** in Mahatthai Rd.

WHERE TO STAY   (tel prefix 044)

Expensive
By the end of 1992 two big name hotels should be fully operational in Khorat. These are the **Dusit Inn**, northeast of town on Suranarai Rd, and the **Simathani Sheraton**, near the TAT office on Mittraphap Rd. Both should have de luxe accommodation in the 3000–5000B bracket. For the time being, the much-rated **Chomsurang Hotel**, 2701/2 Mahat Thai Rd (tel 257088) is an old hotel trying to look new. Gloomy 600–1500B air-con doubles, grim views and a dinky pool. The modern **Royal Plaza**, 547 Chomsurangyart Rd (tel 254127) is a much better deal. It has a massage parlour, disco and coffeeshop, and rooms are 500–1000B.

Moderate
Far better is the **Sripattana**, 346 Suranari Rd (tel 242944); nice rooms for 500–700B, good pool, and one of the best places for Thai food in town. Another favourite is the **Anajak**, 62 Chomsurangyart Rd (tel 243825). Rooms here are good value at 350–400B air-con double. It has a restaurant, and rather dingy coffeeshop where locals gather till the small hours. The hotel with real character is the **Khorat**, 191 Assadang Rd (tel 242260). Strictly for men, this one—female staff rotate between the lively nightclub and the even livelier massage parlour. The club is a real rage at weekends—admission is 90B; open 9 pm to 1 am. Rooms here are from 300–500B (double air-con). The Khorat has good information at the front desk.

Inexpensive
The inexpensive **Fah Sang Hotel**, 112–114 Mukkhamontri Rd (tel 242143), has large twin-bedded rooms from 200B fan to 450B air-con. This is a friendly place, with an English-speaking owner—a real rarity. In Pho Klang Rd is **Siri**, with fan rooms from 150B, air-con rooms at 350B. The Siri has a 'prepare party place' (a roof with a view) and a bizarre sign in every room, saying it won't accept any guests suffering from 'leprosy or other zymotic diseases'. The **Fah Thai**, 35–39 Pho Klang Rd (tel 242533), is a popular Thai hotel, located near the town square. It is friendly and clean, with rooms for 150–200B fan, 330–400B air-con.

EATING OUT
Khorat has some really *odd* eating houses. Chinese food is best at the **Seoy-Seoy**, 77 Buarong Rd (tel 243180) near the post office. It is famous for its frogs. Here you can have Fried Frog, Sweet Battered Fried Frog, and even Tomato Sauce Baked Frog. Other novelties include Goose Legs in Earthen Pot and Sea Leech Cover Pork (?). Most dishes are around 60B, with very nice specialities like Shark's Fin Soup and Oyster

Platter at 150B. The restaurant in the Sripattana is well worth a visit. They have an extensive Thai-Chinese menu, and an intimate atmosphere, helped by the low-key live music; dinner for two costs around 400B. **Thai Pochana**, at the junction of Mukkhamontri and Chomsurangyart roads, has excellent Thai food at under 60B a head.

The weirdest place to eat in Khorat is the **V.F.W. Restaurant**, adjoining Siri Hotel. It's stuffed with American war memorabilia—dusty cups, trophies, plaques and photos donated by American veterans of the foreign wars—the atmosphere is totally unreal. Apart from the odd war veteran (there are 23 left in town), the place is patronized exclusively by Thais (knocking back Mekong, eating T-bone steaks in snug wooden booths, playing endless games of darts and draughts, etc). Air-conditioned and cheap, the V.F.W. does a wide range of wholesome GI food—burgers, pizzas, spaghetti and Southern Fried Chicken. It's open from 8 am to 10 pm daily (closes earlier on quiet nights, so get there in good time), and the 50B special lunches are recommended.

You'll find **Ploy Bakery** on Chumpon Rd. It's run by a very helpful lady called Nikki, who speaks good English and has cheap Thai, Chinese and Western food. Try the American breakfasts and the marvellous butterscotch ice-cream. Travellers have also spoken well of **Flowers** and **Diamond House**—two more good bakeries, located on Chumphon Road. For cheap Thai/Chinese street food—mainly 15–20B 'whip-up wok' meals—try the night bazaar on Mahatthai Rd.

UDORN THANI AND BAN CHIANG

Udorn Thani, 562 km from Bangkok, is the third-largest province in the northeast. Up until 1893, it was a small village called Ban Markhaeng, but then the prince of Nongkhai moved his HQ here, following Thai-French troubles further north. The village became a province in 1907, by order of Rama V. In more recent times, Udorn Thani became a boom-town when the Americans set up a military base here in the 1960s. The GI influence can still be seen in its many Western-style recreations and entertainments—massage parlours, bakeries, ice-cream parlours and discos. A convenient jump-off point for nearby **Ban Chiang**, Udorn Thani is a busy, modern town with a laidback charm all of its own.

GETTING THERE
By Air
Thai Airways fly to Udorn from Bangkok (via Khon Kaen) once daily, with two flights on Friday and Sunday. Flight time is one hour, and the fare is 1260B.

By Train
From Bangkok's Hualamphong station, there are two Rapid trains daily to Udorn (leaving 6.15 am and 7 pm, arriving 3.56 pm and 5.15 am) and one Express train (leaving 8.30 pm, arriving 6.33 am). Returning to Bangkok, trains leave Udorn at 7.40 am and 6.41 pm (Rapid) and at 7.00 pm (Express) daily. Basic fares are 413B 1st class, 198B 2nd class, and 95B 3rd class.

By Bus
From Bangkok's Northern Terminal, non air-con buses leave for Udorn every hour or

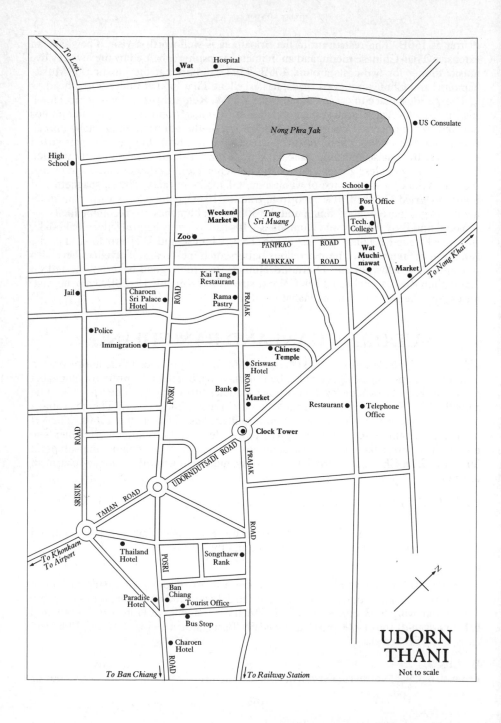

UDORN
THANI

Not to scale

so, from 4.15 am to 11.10 pm. The fare is 106B and the trip is around 12 hours. There are also a few (slightly quicker) air-con buses daily, costing 191B.

From Khorat, non air-con buses leave for Udorn Thani every half-hour; the fare is 60B (110 air-con), and it's a 5-hour journey.

TOURIST INFORMATION
The tourist office (of sorts) is opposite the bus station. You'll probably get better information from the **Charoen Hotel** desk-staff—good handouts, and English-speaking assistance.

WHAT TO SEE
Udorn's few sights can be covered in a morning—either on foot, or by *samlor* (5B for short hops; 20B for round-town tour). There's a popular **Weekend Market** just off Prajak Rd, which sells all sorts of weird and wonderful stuff. Strictly for early birds though—it's liveliest between 3 and 6 am. Close by is the **Zoo** off Posri Road. This is small and nothing special—mid-morning is the best time to find the animals awake. A few quite interesting temples are **Wat Muchimawat** (opposite the Technical College, with rearing naga-snakes guarding the entrance), the **Chinese Temple** off Prajak Rd, and the scenic **shrine** up by the hospital, with a relaxing river setting. Few visitors go out of their way to see sights in Udorn—they often prefer to hang out at the town's yummy bakeries and *kai-yang* stalls.

WHERE TO STAY   (tel prefix 042)
Moderate
Udorn's new **Charoensri Palace Hotel**, 60 Posri Rd (tel 242611), has marvellous air-con rooms at 600B high season, 350B low season. Top-floor suites have the best views. Nice restaurant, coffee shop and pool. Another goodie is the **Charoen**, 549 Posri Rd (tel 248155), with air-con rooms at 400B–900B, depending on the time of year. There's a decent pool (non-residents can use this for a 20B charge), a good information service, and a nightclub called **Ex Calibur** which holds amazing weekend discos (9 pm to 2 am, 100B admission includes one drink). This club is a real scene—cinema usherettes with tiny torches guide guests through the pitch-black gloom to their seats. Single males are instantly joined by a matey Mama-san, who attempts introductions to floppy-eared bunny girls. The best (and safest) night to come is Tuesday—this is 'Ladies Night' and there's a beauty contest.

Inexpensive
The **Paradise Hotel**, 44/29 Posri Rd (tel 221956), has immaculate twin-bedded air-con rooms at 350B a double. There are also a few fan rooms for 180B. Decor is a bit tacky, but it's a friendly place, with a twee heart-shaped pool, where people dance to live music in the evening. The nearby **Thailand**, 4/1-6 Surakorn Rd (tel 221951), doesn't speak English, but does have one regulation in English: 'The guest should not take any disturbing loud noise'. How considerate. Fan-cooled rooms here are 160B, air-con 330B. Best budget hotel is still the **Sawaddiphap**, 264/3 Prajak Road. Friendly family, and large, clean rooms for 100–180B. If full, you may have to stay at the nearby **Tokyo**, 145 Prachak Rd (tel 221349)—pretty gross and dirty but cheap.

EATING OUT

The **Charoensri** Palace does very palatable Thai, Chinese and European food at reasonable prices. Don't confuse it with the similarly-named **Charoen Hotel**, which claims to have the best food in town, but doesn't.

Tasty Isaan-style fare can be found at the top of Prajak Rd—there are three local restaurants here, serving delicious *kai yang* (roast spicy chicken) and *som tam* (grated papaya salad, spiced with garlic, pepper, fish sauce and lime juice). This is eaten with sticky rice, which is moulded into balls with your fingers. These restaurants are open till 10 pm, and the top one has the most going for it: friendly service, a whole barbecued chicken for 40B, and a jukebox which plays the Thai disco version of the *Battle Hymn of the Republic*.

Rama's Pastry, also on Prajak Rd, is a popular air-con bakery and coffee shop. Friendly people, Western-style breakfasts, and exceedingly good cakes and pastries.

Ban Chiang
(by bus, then *samlor*, half/full day)

This sleepy village, 47 km east of Udorn, is now an important centre of Thailand's past—and an emerging tourist attraction. Up until 20 years ago, archaeologists considered Southeast Asia a cultural backwater—they thought its arts and civilization to have been borrowed from India, China and even Europe. Bronze technology, it was believed, only arrived here from the Middle East around 500 BC.

Then, in 1966, a young Harvard sociology graduate, Stephen Young, literally stumbled on a prehistoric burial site here at Ban Chiang. The first fragments of round-topped pots he submitted were carbon-dated to around 4600 BC, and the village became an overnight sensation. Later excavations, by the Fine Arts Department and the University of Pennsylvania, unearthed a rich collection of iron and bronze tools and utensils, buried alongside human skeletons, which proved that prehistoric man settled in this part of northeastern Thailand between around 3600 BC and AD 200. By around 2000 BC, these men had mastered bronze (and later, iron) manufacture, and developed skills in making pottery and glass beads, in weaving techniques and in the cultivation of rice. Ban Chiang is not alone—many other ancient northeastern village sites are now known—but everything points to it having been the major cultural centre in this region. Much more research is still needed—the prehistory of Southeast Asia being still very much a blank page—but if the Thais can prove it, they may soon find themselves the proud possessors of a civilization predating even those of China, India and Egypt.

Ban Chiang may seem an awfully long way to go and see skeletons, but if you have any interest in history (not only of Thailand, but of mankind) it's worth the effort. On arrival, your first question to locals should be *Yuu thii nai phiphinaphan* (where is the museum?). Set up by the Department of Fine Arts, **Ban Chiang Museum** is one of Thailand's finest with smart, well-planned displays and well-labelled exhibits. It's open from 8 am to 4 pm, Wednesday to Sunday, and the 10B admission includes a collection of WOST ('world's oldest socketed tool'), axes, lozenge-shaped infant burial jars, and round-topped burial pots and jars decorated with distinctive burnt-ochre red 'whorl' designs. These pots have become major collector's pieces. Shortly after Ban Chiang became known as the new 'cradle of civilization', large-scale looting took place at the site and, sadly, few intact pots were retained for the museum. The art of faking pottery has become big business here, so be careful if offered 'antiques'. Remember, even if you did come across an original piece, you'd face a stiff fine if you tried taking it out of the country. Best buys here are embroidered linen jackets and cotton materials, both sold (along with the inevitable Ban Chiang T-shirts) at the **Open Museum**, a 10-minute stroll left out of the main museum. This site charges 10B admission, and comprises two of the original ground-level excavation pits—littered with pots, skeletons, supine burials and cord-marked wares. Left exactly as when buried 500 years ago, the skeletons lie face upward, with their heads pointing either northeast or southwest, and their bone arm-ornaments stained green with time. Besides them are placed the weapons and the supply-jars which were to protect and feed them on their journey into the next life.

GETTING THERE
There are two ways you can get to Ban Chiang from Udorn Thani. There are either blue *songthaews* from the rank in Posri Rd, which go all the way to Ban Chiang Museum in 1¹/₂ hours for 20B; or ordinary buses from Udorn's bus station (off Posri Rd), which take you only as far as the highway 6 km out of Ban Chiang. From here to the village is a 15B *samlor* ride. Both buses and *songthaews* leave Udorn regularly. I'd recommend the *songthaew*—great scenery (look out for local fishermen wielding hand-operated Chinese nets in the lush post-monsoon paddy fields) and, if lucky, fascinating co-passengers. I shared a ride with a beaming farmer, proudly holding three muddy bags of fish in the air for everybody to poke and admire, and a young saffron-robed monk in reflecting sunglasses, happily grooving to U2 on his Toshiba ghetto-blaster.

NONG KHAI

This small 'city', 615 km north of Bangkok, has a charming situation on the bank of the Mekong River—right on the border between Thailand and Laos. The town has some delightfully antique wooden houses and buildings of French-Chinese design, and there are some amazing temples and bakeries showing the French-Lao influence. A number of local people in Nong Khai speak fluent French. A popular recreation here is to sit at the restaurant by the pier, and watch boats ferrying folk across the Mekong river into the People's Democratic Republic of Laos. Several travellers entertain notions of crossing over too—the main lure being the famous Lao city of Vientiane, home of the revered Emerald Buddha, which is only 24 km northeast of Nong Khai. You can apply for a visa either at the Immigration Office near the pier, or at the Lao embassy in Bangkok, but it's highly unlikely you'll be granted one. A friend of mine asked an immigration official in Nong Khai. 'Can I go to Laos?' And the official replied, 'Oh yes—but you no come back!'

The province is famous for its flora and fauna, best seen at the end of the rainy season. Many people view it in combination with the popular boat race on the Mekong River, held at Nong Khai during the first week of October. But the two most authentic and colourful of the province's many festivals are the **Nong Khai Show**, held the second

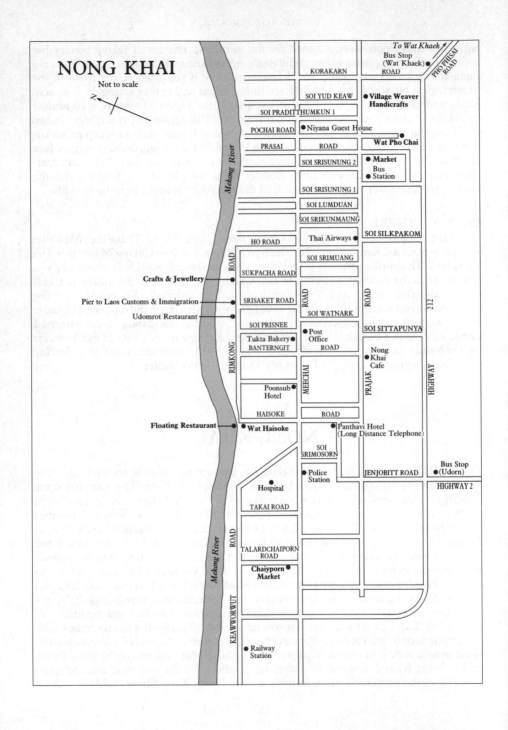

NONG KHAI

Not to scale

Mekong River

KORAKARN

SOI YUD KEAW

SOI PRADITTHUMKUN 1

POCHAI ROAD

● Niyana Guest House

PRASAI

ROAD

SOI SRISUNUNG 2

SOI SRISUNUNG 1

SOI LUMDUAN

SOI SRIKUNMAUNG

HO ROAD

● Thai Airways

SOI SRIMUANG

SUKPACHA ROAD

Crafts & Jewellery

SRISAKET ROAD

Pier to Laos Customs & Immigration

Udomrot Restaurant

SOI PRISNEE

Tukta Bakery ●

BANTERNGIT

Post
Office

ROAD

RIMKONG

ROAD

MEECHAI

Poonsub ●
Hotel

HAISOKE

ROAD

Floating Restaurant

● **Wat Haisoke**

SOI
SRIMOSORN

● Police
Station

● Hospital

TAKAI ROAD

TALARDCHAIPORN
ROAD

Chaiyporn
Market

KEAWWORWUT

ROAD

● Railway
Station

To Wat Khaek

Bus Stop
(Wat Khaek) ●

ROAD

PHO PHISAI ROAD

● **Village Weaver**
Handicrafts

● **Wat Pho Chai**

● **Market**

Bus
Station

SOI SILKPAKOM

ROAD

SOI SITTAPUNYA

Nong
Khai
Cafe

PRAJAK

HIGHWAY

212

● Panthavi Hotel
(Long Distance Telephone)

JENJOBITT ROAD

Bus Stop
● (Udorn)

HIGHWAY 2

week of March, and the annual **Seong Bung Fai** (Rocket Festival), which takes place at Wat Pho temple on full moon day in April.

GETTING THERE

By Rail
From Bangkok's Hualamphong station, trains leave for Nong Khai at 6.15 am and 7 pm (Rapid, arriving 4.50 pm and 6.15 am) and at 8.30 pm (Express, arriving 7.30 am). Basic fares are 450B 1st class, 215B 2nd class, and 103B 3rd class.

By Bus
From Bangkok's Northern Terminal, five non air-con buses leave for Nong Khai between 5.15 am and 8.29 am (plus two late buses at 8.10 and 8.54 pm). The fare is 115B, and it's a long 10-hour journey. Three air-con buses leave daily from the same terminal, at 9 am, 7.15 and 9 pm (fare 209B). These are slightly quicker, but most people still prefer to go by train.

From Udorn Thani, it's a short 1½-hour hop to Nong Khai by non air-con bus every half-hour (fare 20B). You can also get there from Khorat, a longer 6–7 hour trip, by local bus (mid-afternoon to early evening service; fare 75B), or by air-con bus (4 daily) for 140B.

WHAT TO SEE
Nong Khai's quaint old-town atmosphere, scenic river location and weird and wonderful temples make it—for my money—the most interesting centre in the northeast. It's a tiny city of just 25,000 inhabitants, with coffee-shops, bakeries, markets and even a small fairground. Though a pleasant place to stroll around on foot, you'll need two separate day-outings by bus to cover the four major temples in the area (they're worth it). If you're lucky enough to make a local friend—Nong Khai people are *very* friendly—you may find yourself taken everywhere by motorbike, and for free.

Wat Pho Chai – Wat Khaek
(on foot, by bus; half/full day)

Located off Prajak Rd—a short walk to the edge of town—**Wat Pho Chai** houses the major Buddha image of the province, called Luang Pho Phra Sai. Relatively small— 1.5 m high, and with a spread of just one metre across the knees—this beautiful solid-gold figure is believed to have been cast in Lan Chang, and to have spent its early life in Vientiane. The legend is that it came to this spot by 'divine miracle'—General Chakri (later Rama I) was transporting it over the Mekong from Vientiane when the boat sank. But nothing can keep a good Buddha down, and when this one miraculously resurfaced, the *wat* here was built to honour its achievement. The figure receives a personal visit from the King each year, and is taken in glorious procession round the city during the Songkran festival. The *wat* itself has been recently renovated—the gleaming new structure is only 10 years old. All the city's major festivals are held here.

From the sublime to the ridiculous, **Wat Khaek** is a fantastic Disneyland of bizarre and spectacular statues—the highlight of many travellers' northeastern tour. It's located

5 km out of Nong Khai, and buses go there from the stop near Wat Pho. Even if you can't face another temple, Wat Khaek is sure to restore your sense of humour. It's a large open compound of incongruous images—towering, beak-nosed Buddhas, nightmarish *nagas*, eight-armed Kalis, and dogs wielding dinner forks and machine guns—reflecting the eclectic philosophy of a Brahmin *shaman* called Luang Pu. He originally studied in Vietnam, then moved to Laos, and was driven here 12 years ago by the Communists. A highly popular local figure, he certainly gets top marks for verve and imagination—as more and more of these Easter Island-like statues go up (the workers inspired by music and sermons from a blaring tannoy) travellers have been moved to increasingly astonished comment. Whatever your reaction, bring lots of camera film. You'll need it.

At the main building, ask for Bhu Lua—the resident 'master'. He's the guy with the dark shades, often dealing out tarot cards under a mountainous sound system. He'll fix you up with a tour round the shrine—a two-storey building choc-a-bloc with Hindu-Buddhist antiques and photos of Luang Pu. Altogether, one of the weirdest collections of 'art' I've ever come across. Afterwards, you can feed the giant catfish in the nearby lake. Small bags of popcorn are sold for this purpose at the 'picnic' landing—but don't go dropping in large buns. These attract full-grown catfish—the shark-sized variety.

Wat Prathat Bang Phuan – Wat Hin Maak Peng
(by bus; full day)

GETTING THERE
To get to Wat Prathat, 22 km from Nong Khai, take a bus from the town's southern terminal to **Ban Nong Hong Son**. From the junction here, *songthaews* and buses run the final 10 km up to the *wat*. There's a small restaurant at the junction (opposite the *songthaew* rank) which does just about the best *kai yang* and *som tam* meal I've tasted anywhere, and for only 20B.

To reach Wat Hin Maak Peng, 60 km northwest of Nong Khai, you need a bus to Si Chiengmai from the southern bus-stop in town (20B), followed by a *songthaew*, from Si Chiengmai direct to Wat Hin, or to Sang Khom, which is just past it. Buses for Si Chiengmai pass by Wat Prathat, so you can continue on from here to Wat Hin.

Wat Prathat
The sacred site of **Wat Prathat** is one of the most important in the northeast. Monks from India, it's believed, first came here 2000 years ago and they erected the original Indian-style *stupa*. This was covered over by a taller Lao *chedi* in the 16th century. Shortly after this structure was blown over by heavy rains, the Fine Arts Department stepped in and erected a garish new *chedi*, which stands in stark contrast to the crumbling, atmospheric red-brick ruins elsewhere in the compound. Despite this, the site retains a marvellously dilapidated, overgrown charm. There's a fine collection of mainly 16th-century Lao *chedis* and semi-intact Buddhas, and two impressive seated Buddhas housed within corrugated-roof *viharns*. The larger one was constructed by the Lao people, and was probably the model for the main Buddha image at Phra Pathom *chedi* in Nakhon Pathom. The smaller one overlooks a pretty lotus pond. There's an odd little museum to the rear of the compound with some interesting folk handicrafts, stuffed animals, and boundary stones, but most exhibits lie around on the ground like rubble.

Strolling round the compound is fun, but don't sit down—there are a lot of giant ants and crickets around. It's hard to take much in, when you've a three-inch grasshopper up your trouserleg.

Wat Hin Maak Peng

Wat Hin Maak Peng is the most famous meditation temple in Thailand. Set up by an itinerant pilgrim monk called Thet Lang Si, it is known for its ascetic forest-dwelling monks who eat only one meal a day, dress in subdued 'forest-colour' robes made from natural dyes, and don't say a lot. A few monks receive guests, but most are keen meditatives. People accepted for meditation classes at the *wat* get their own little house, and receive a daily group instruction sermon—in Thai. The monastery itself has a wonderfully quiet setting amongst bamboo groves, in a cool forest shelter. Situated at the narrowest point of the Mekong river, you can throw a stone over into Laos during the low-level dry season. On the opposite bank, you'll be able to see a small Lao forest *wat*. The monks of Wat Hin mostly live high up on the cliff above the river, in small cells and huts tucked away between huge boulders. Views up here are spectacular.

SHOPPING

The **Village Weaver Handicrafts** shop, 786 Prajak Rd (tel 411236), is a small self-help project, set up in 1982 by the Good Shepherd Sisters, aimed at giving local villagers a means of supplementing their income—especially young girls who would otherwise be destined for a life of prostitution in Bangkok. Over 200 families now produce goods—mainly high-quality woven fabrics—for the project, which is now making a small yet significant dent in the poverty of the region. Weavers here produce indigo-dyed cotton *matmee* cloth—tie-dyed, mainly with geometric patterns—which is cool, colourfast and very durable. It's an exclusive produce of the northeast, and you can pick it up here at one-third of London prices (the project supplies Oxfam in the UK). Good buys are embroidered jackets, at around 500B; handwoven shirts from 350B, and colourful Cambodian wall-hangings (patterns created in bamboo, then sewn into the cotton cloth) at around 500B. Suvan, the friendly project manager, will discount 10% on most items. All profits go directly to helping the villagers.

WHERE TO STAY   (tel prefix 042)

Moderate
The **Panthavi**, 1241 Haisoke Rd (tel 411568), is Nong Khai's best hotel. It has rooms at 180B (fan) and 450B (air-con), good information, and an overseas telephone—but is not too friendly, and often full.

Inexpensive
Better is the homely **Poonsub**, 843 Meechai Rd (tel 411031)—this has bright, comfortable rooms for 180B with fan, 120B without. Ask for one with a view of the river. Less clean, but with large 150B (fan) and 280B (air-con) rooms, is the **Pongvicht** in Banterngit Rd (tel 411583).

The **Niyana Guest House**, 239 Meechai Rd (tel 412164), warrants a special mention. Basic rooms (80B), but great facilities: a good library (with information/maps), a TV lobby, laundry service, Western-style food (also something called 'Morning Glory Vine Friend in Garlic and Bean Sauce'), motorbike and bicycle rental, sightseeing tours, and heaps of back issues of the *Peace Corps Times*. It also operates longtail boat trips on the Mekong River (200B for one to eight people). Advance-book these at the Niyana between 9 am and 4 pm daily, or contact the Chinese manager of the **Sukaphan Hotel** in town.

EATING OUT
Nong Khai has some lively little eating-houses, often with rib-tickling menus. The **Thipros** restaurant, next to Poonsub Hotel, does exceptional *Kai Lao Dang* (chicken cooked in red wine) for 40B, and a galaxy of novelty dishes. You can start with 'Five Things Soup in Firepan' or 'Stewed Deer Gut', and enjoy 'Fried Frog Cutlets' and 'Lucky Duck' as a main course. Well, why not. Down on the river behind Wat Haisoke, the small **Floating Restaurant** has some oddities of its own. Things like 'Duck Eggs preserved in Potash', 'Three Some', and 'Jerked Pork'. Actually, the food (and coffee) is both cheap and good here. For Western-style food, there's the **Udomrot** next to the customs pier. This is on the river, looking over to Laos, and the speciality is Fried Mekong River Fish ('fish you eat today, slept last night at the bottom of the river') for 45B. Whatever you do, don't miss **Tukta Bakery** on Meechai Rd. This is so good that one guy pigged out on seven cakes, five pastries and four milkshakes—and missed his bus back to Bangkok.

There are several cheap Chinese-Thai restaurants down Banterngit Rd—trouble is, not a lot of the food on offer looks edible. Unless, that is, you're partial to skinned frogs floating about in washing-up bowls. In the evening, check out the **Nong Khai Café**, in Prajak Road. This is open from 11 am to 2 pm, 5.30 pm to 1 am, and serves both food and (pricey) drinks. Here all the young Thai dudes gather to enjoy a nostalgic live band which plays nothing more recent than 1965. The odd *farang* guest is treated to their 'special medley'—Cliff Richard (*The Young Ones*), Neil Sedaka (*Oh Carol*) and the Everly Brothers (*Wake up, Little Suzie*). They're actually rather good.

Part IX

THE SOUTH

Southern Thailand is a long, narrow peninsula, extending through the Kra isthmus from Chumphon (460 km south of Bangkok) to the Thai–Malaysian border. Bounded by the Gulf of Thailand to the east, and by the Indian Ocean to the west, both coastlines are dotted with beautiful islands—ideal for scuba-diving, snorkelling, sailing and fishing. The South is geared to total relaxation—this is where everyone comes at some time or other, to swim, to windsurf and water-ski, to laze on dazzling white beaches, and to dine on some of the most delectable seafood in the East. There's a major development programme due here over the next few years, but some of the islands—**Phuket** and **Koh-Samui** in particular—are pretty developed already. No matter—if you're not into beach videos, discos and nightclubs, there's still a wealth of other islands and beaches with hardly a soul on them. Lovely spots like **Krabi** and **Phi Phi Islands** are only just opening up, and tranquil **Koh Phangan** is still a place for beachcombing backpackers. The attractions of the South are extremely diverse. There are spectacular surreal islands at mysterious **Phang Nga Bay**, great shopping and entertainment at busy **Hat Yai**, tasty seafood at historic old **Songkhla**, and Thai-style beach fun at the seaside resort of **Hua Hin**. Overall, the South has a lazy charm, a peaceful, unhurried way of life, and balmy, tropical scenery which acts as an immediate tonic to the hustle and bustle of Bangkok. Southern Thais have their own dialect (a rapid patter called *pak tai*), and their own cuisine, customs and dress. A lot of Chinese and Muslims (ethnic Malays) live down here, and the further south you go, the more polyglot the mixture of peoples becomes. But they all love the sea (which surrounds them) and they all have a fierce sense of independence. Few southern Thais will own allegiance to the central control of Bangkok, and many will ask you what the frantic, busy capital has to compare with their own calm, idyllic way of life. After a few days here, you can truthfully answer 'Nothing.'

HUA HIN

This small fishing port, 180 km southwest of Bangkok, was Thailand's first beach resort and has been the Thai royal family's summer residence since Rama VII (1925–35) built a palace here called 'Klai Kangwon' or 'place free from worries'. Not the most appropriate choice of name, as it transpired. It was while staying at this palace in 1932 that Rama VII learnt of the coup which transformed him overnight from an absolute to a constitutional monarch. Yet the royal family still come on holiday to Hua Hin every April. And, being so close to Bangkok, it remains the favourite resort of Thais in general. The élite of Thailand like to spend the hot months of March and April here, savouring the period pre-War charm and bracing air of this peaceful old seaside resort. Reminders of the past are everywhere: the royal waiting room at the railway station, the king's palace on the northern edge of town, the old-fashioned deckchairs on the promenade, and the clipped topiary gardens in the stylish ex-Railway Hotel.

GETTING THERE

By Air
Bangkok Airways flies daily to Hua Hin at 2.30 pm; the flight takes 35 minutes.

By Bus
From Bangkok's Southern Terminal, non air-con buses leave for Hua Hin ever half-hour from 5 am to 7 pm (fare 42B). There are also hourly air-con buses, from 5 am to 10 pm (fare 74B). The journey takes 3 1/2 hours.

From Phuket, there are seven non air-con buses to Hua Hin daily, leaving between 6 am and 6.30 pm (fare 129B). Also, one air-con bus (250B) leaving at 3 pm. This is a long 9–10 hour trip, and travelling air-con is a good idea. There are non air-con buses to Surat Thani (for Koh Samui) from Hua Hin mid-morning and late evening, taking about 8 hours, for 89B, and one air-con bus at 10.30 pm for 225B. There are non air-con buses to Krabi at 10 pm and 12 am, taking 10 hours, price 126B, and one air-con bus at 10 pm for 290B, but it's a long haul.

By Rail
From Bangkok's Hualamphong station, there are eight trains daily to Hua Hin—one Ordinary (1.40 pm), four Rapid (12.30, 4, 5.30 and 6.30 pm) and three Express (2, 3.15 and 7.20 pm). Journey time is 3 1/2 to 4 hours. Fares are 182B 1st class, 92B 2nd class, and 44B 3rd class.

By Sea
A hydrofoil service operates from Bangkok (from the Menam Hotel, New Road, Yannawa) via Pattaya to Hua Hin daily at 7 and 8 am, arriving Pattaya at 9.30 and 10.30 am, and Hua Hin at 12 noon and 1 pm. The cost is 450B one way economy class, 550B one way 1st class, but it's best to check beforehand for departure details (2074 Thai Intertransport Building, New Road, Yannawa, tel 2919613).

TOURIST INFORMATION
TAT Tourist Office, corner of Phetkasem Rd and Damnoenkasem Rd (tel 512120), is small and efficient. Very helpful staff, lots of literature. It's open 8 am to 6 pm daily.

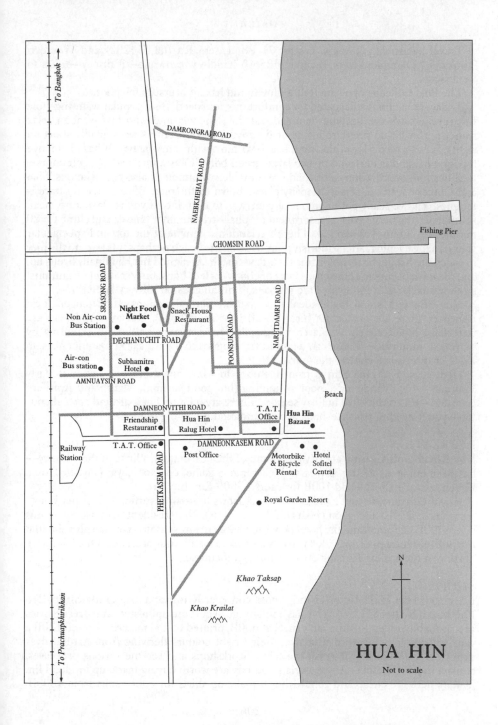

HUA HIN

Not to scale

Travel agents like **Tuck's Tours**, 71 Phetkasem Rd (tel 511202) and **Western Tours**, 11 Damnoenkasem Rd (tel 512560) handle worthwhile—if pricey—tours to local sights.

The Post Office is opposite Ralug Hotel, and has an overseas telephone.

Today, Hua Hin is still geared for comfort, not for speed. It's a popular watering-hole for travellers who've become 'templed-out' in Bangkok, and who just want to relax somewhere with no pressure to see or do anything. Hua Hin is wonderfully short on sights. It has a nice 5 km white-sand beach within a wide, curving bay. It has distinctive topography, and is enclosed by two large green hills. It has a fine 18-hole golf course, facilities for several water-sports, and reasonable swimming. It also has delicious Thai and Chinese seafood, served at many places down by the pier. What it doesn't have is temples. You've really got to go out of your way to find one. If you're desperate, head south down the beach past an assortment of Thai-style summer houses and climb for 20 minutes up **Khao Taksap** hill. There's a Buddhist temple at the top and spectacular views. In the evening, after a touristy pony-ride on the beach perhaps, it's back to the pier to watch the fishing boats unloading their day's catch. At night, Hua Hin finally livens up, and the town becomes a boisterous buzz of chatty coffee shops, busy seafood restaurants, sizzling snack stalls and lively little markets. This all goes on till very late.

Hua Hin is a small town, ideal for leisurely perambulations. If you need local transport, there are *samlors* for hire (10–20B for short hops). Out of town, there are waterfalls, limestone caves, Karen villages and nice scenery—all worth exploring by bicycle or motorbike. These can be hired from opposite the bazaar in Damnoenkasem Rd. For directions, contact the tourist office.

High season at Hua Hin is from October to May, but avoid November to early February—high winds make poor swimming (but good surfing). March and April are crowded—this is the Thai holiday season. There are a lot of Thais around at weekends too—you'll need to advance-book accommodation if coming then.

RECREATION

The **Royal Golf Course** at Hua Hin—one of the best standard links in the country—has been going strong for 60 years. To arrange a game, contact Royal Garden Hotel. Green fees are 150B—add 100B for caddy, 300B for club hire.

Royal Garden Resort handles all water-sports too—windsurfing (150B per hour), parasailing (350B) and sailing boats (250B per hour). Non-residents can use the tennis courts (90B per hour) and the hotel pool (no charge in low season). You can also slip into the **Sofitel Hotel** pool, provided you buy a drink to justify your presence. One kilometre north of a town is an amusing 36-hole mini-golf course.

SHOPPING

Check out Hua Hin's famous handprinted cotton at **Khomapastr Textile Shop**, 218 Phetkasem Rd (tel 511250). This has a full range of curtain, upholstery and dress fabrics at reasonable prices—cotton table mats at 600B, printed cotton material around 120B a yard etc. Designs are very attractive, their bright colours deriving from natural dyes extracted from the sea. To visit the fabric workshops and see the various processes, contact the TAT office. Any materials you buy are worth having made up in Hua Hin. Tailors here are cheap and good—they'll make up shirts for 200B, suits from 1000B.

There's an interesting **night market** running down Phetkasem Rd. This sells a variety of cheaply-priced trinkets—shell jewellery, bone bracelets, bamboo beach-mats etc. It also does a good line in pirated cassettes.

WHERE TO STAY
(tel prefix 032)

Luxury
Hotel Sofitel Central, Damnoenkasem Rd (tel 512–021), is still *the* classic hotel in Hua Hin, very much geared to rich Thais. An extravagant oddity, with colonial-style architecture, immense landscaped gardens, and quaint topiary, it was used to represent Hotel Le Pnom in the film *The Killing Fields*. Rooms here start from 2500B, suites 5000–20,000B. **Royal Garden Resort**, 107/1 Phetkasem Rd (tel 511881) is the big European-style hotel. It has less character than the Sofitel, but has better food, recreation facilities and swimming pool. Nice beach-side location too. Rooms cost from 3000B, suites 9000–12,000B, but (as at Sofitel) 10% discounts are offered in low season. Even better discounts (40–50%) are possible at hotels further down the range.

Expensive
Sailom Hotel, 29 Phetkasem Rd (tel 511890), has a nice pool, tennis courts, and split-rate rooms at 900B (Sunday to Thursday) and 1650B (Friday to Saturday).

Moderate
Supamitra Hotel, 19 Amnuaysin Rd (tel 511208), has rooms at 200B (fan) and 400–700B (air-con) and is a popular mid-range bet. The economical **Hua Hin Ralug Hotel**, 16 Damnoenkasem Rd (tel 511940), is a curiosity—quaint bungalows with *vast* double beds, pet eagles 'minding' the tropical-garden restaurant, and illicit couples creeping around in the dead of night (150–300 fan, 450–700B air-con). On the other side of the road, down from the post office **Jed Pee Nong**, 17 Damnoenkasem Rd (tel 512381) has large rooms with beds to match for 300B fan, 500B air-con.

Inexpensive
Of the crop of new budget cheapies which have appeared in Naretdamri and Dammnoenkasem roads, **Gee Guisine** and **Welcome Place** get the best mentions. They both have seafood restaurants with Western-style menus and charge between 100 and 250B for fan rooms.

EATING OUT
Hua Hin is well-known for its fresh seafood, and for delicious fruits and vegetables like pineapple, sugar-cane and asparagus. For seafood, Thais favour the **Saeng Thai** down by the pier. Specialities here are grilled cuttlefish and fresh lobster, and you can dine well for under 100B. Pity about the sewage floating under the pier which tends to overcome Western appetites. Europeans often prefer to eat at the **Sailom Hotel**—good things to try are kingfish (*pla samlee*), crab (*pu*) and mussels (*maleng phu*). Cheap seafood snacks are widely available down at the main market.

Western-style food is great at **Friendship Restaurant**, 112 Phetkasem Rd. Amazing T-bone steaks (150B), ice-cream sundaes and coffee. This also has the most courteous waiter in Thailand—he bows every time you breathe. It is a good evening hangout spot, with jolly live music and entertainments. **Snack House**, further down Phetkasem Rd has a delightful antique flavour—polished mahogany furniture, framed pics of Louis Armstrong's Five Pennies, a massive buffalo's head, and a fun snooker club. This is the place to come for western breakfasts and evening cocktails. In Naretdamri Rd are some small eating places, popular with Thais and *farangs* alike. **Than Thong** has a good menu of Thai-Chinese dishes at medium price. The **Beergarden** in an outdoor setting, and the **Headrock Café** both serve Thai and western food.

KOH SAMUI

For 15 years or more, the idyllic island of Koh Samui—lying off the western coast of the Gulf of Thailand—was considered the private domain of the shoestring traveller. A tropical paradise of green hills and coconut groves, of towering palms leaning over white-sand beaches, of rustic bungalows serving up delicious seafood, coconut milk-shakes and magic-mushroom omelettes, it was the classic hippy hideaway, far removed from the noisy, expensive package-tourist playgrounds of Pattaya and Phuket.

But all that is rapidly changing. First came electricity, followed inevitably by videos, discos and motorbikes. Today, the major beaches—notably Lamai and Chaweng—have first-class hotels, German beer gardens, and pick-up bars. The final transition from back-pack to Boeing required only the opening of Samui's elusive airport. Not that the brutal thrust of progresss has been altogether a bad thing—there are now well-surfaced roads around the island, slicker transportation to and from Surat Thani (the nearest coastal town), superior accommodation, and international dining facilities. But as this is Thailand's third-largest island—over 250 sq km in area—a few beaches have managed to escape full-scale development for the time being. At present, Koh Samui has something for everyone—which is just as well, since everyone wants to go there.

Samui has periods of bright, sunny weather throughout the year. January to June is dry and hot. July to November is hit-and-miss; sometimes you'll get weeks of perfect weather, other times double-thunderstorms rage and travellers hole up in huts while locals cheerfully wash their cars in the rain. Christmas Day marks the official end of the rainy season, and it's a very big party. Other festivals centre round the island's principal produce—coconuts. Samui's hinterland is one of the largest plantations in the world, and supplies Bangkok alone with millions of coconuts each year. If you're around in mid-October, here's an offer that's hard to refuse:

> The Samui Municipality warmly invite all foreign tourists to watch the yearly monkey competition of the coconuts reaping in the compound of the Customs habitat. We also invite the esteemed tourists to watch the coconut peeling down by islanders in the children's playground near the post office.

GETTING THERE
By Air
Bangkok Airways have seven direct daily flights from Bangkok to Samui island. The

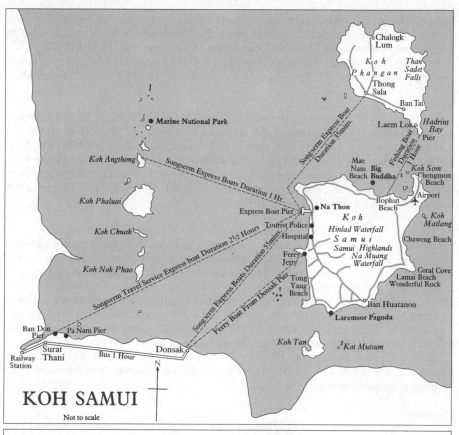

Chalogk
Lum

*Koh
Phangan*

*Than
Sadet
Falls*

Thong
Sala

Ban Tai

Laem Lok

*Hadrint
Bay*

Fishing Boat Duration 1 Hour

Songserm Express Boat Duration 35mins.

● Marine National Park

Koh Angthong

Songserm Express Boats Duration 1 Hr.

Koh Phaluai

Mae
Nam
Beach

**Big
Buddha**

Koh Som

Chengmon
Beach

Airport

Bophut
Beach

*Koh
Matlang*

Express Boat Pier → ● **Na Thon**

Koh

Koh Chuak

Tourist Police ●

Hinlad Waterfall

Samui

Chaweng Beach

Hospital ●

Samui Highlands
Na Muang
Waterfall

Songserm Travel Service Express boat Duration 2½ Hours

Koh Nok Phao

Ferry
Jetty ●

Coral Cove
Lamai Beach
Wonderful Rock

Songserm Express Boats Duration 35mins.

Tong
Yang
Beach

Ferry Boat From Donsak Pier

● Ban Huatanon

● **Laremsor Pagoda**

Ban Don
Pier

Pa Nam Pier

Donsak

Koh Tan

Kot Mutsum

Surat
Thani

Bus 1 Hour

Railway
Station

N

KOH SAMUI

Not to scale

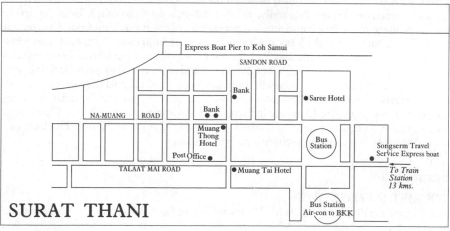

Express Boat Pier to Koh Samui

SANDON ROAD

Bank ●

● Saree Hotel

NA-MUANG   ROAD

Bank
● ●

Muang ●
Thong
Hotel

Post Office ●

Bus
Station

Songserm Travel
Service Express boat

TALAAT MAI ROAD

● Muang Tai Hotel

To Train
Station
13 kms.

SURAT THANI

Bus Station
Air-con to BKK

flight takes one hour and ten minutes and costs 1880B. There are also daily flights from Samui to Phuket (tel Bangkok 253–4014 for further information). An alternative air-link is from Bangkok to Surat Thani on Thai Airways (one hour flight; fare 1710B).

At Surat Thani airport, you can either pay 150B for a combined bus-ferry ticket to Samui (best), or hire a 35B limo down to Ban Don pier, and pay the boat separately.

By Rail

From Bangkok's Hualamphong station, only three trains (the Rapid 5.30 and 6.30 pm, and the Express 7.20 pm) arrive in Surat Thani at convenient times (4.46, 6.03 and 6.34 am) for the early morning ferry over to Koh Samui. Basic fares are 470B 1st class, 224B 2nd class, and 107B 3rd class. Hualamphong's Advance Booking Office sells handy train-bus-ferry combination tickets to Samui—well worth considering. From Surat Thani, trains run back to Bangkok at 5.35, 6.20, 6.52, 7.23 and 10.46 pm (all Rapid), and at 8.12 and 10.01 pm (Express).

By Bus

From Bangkok's Southern Terminal, there are four buses daily to Surat Thani—two air-con (9.15 am and 8.20 pm, 225B) and two non air-con (9.20 am and 11 pm, 125B). There are also two buses direct to Samui island, via the Don Sak ferry—one air-con (8 pm, 288B) and one non air-con (8.45 pm, 172B). Several tour companies, in Bangkok—centred mainly in Koh Sahn Rd or Soi Ngam Dupli—operate private buses direct to Samui too. Shopping around, you can buy a bus-ferry combination ticket from them for as low as 250B. Buses to Surat Thani/Samui usually leave Bangkok early in the morning, or late at night, arriving some 11 or 12 hours later.

There are buses from Surat Thani to Phuket (120B, 6–7 hours), Krabi (120B, 4 hours), Hat Yai (125B, 6–7 hours). From Samui you can book bus/ferry connections to all these places at Songserm, Na Thon.

By Boat

There are two companies operating between the mainland and Koh Samui, Samui Ferry Co and Songserm Travel. Naturally, neither has heard of the other. Boat departure points are therefore a little confusing—at present there are three. From Ban Don pier at Surat Thani, there's a night ferry at 11 which takes six hours and costs 80B. Day-time departures are from either the new Pa Nam pier, 7 km from Surat Thani (boats leave at 8 am, 12.30 and 2.30 pm; the trip takes $2^1/_2$ hours and costs 100B) or from Don Sak pier, two extra boats for Samui leave daily at 9 am and 4 pm. Fare is 120B (less in low season), and the journey takes just $1^1/_2$ hours. Don Sak is an hour by bus, but the ticket includes the air-con bus from Ban Don pier in Surat Thani. Coming back to Surat Thani from Samui, you've a choice of three boats daily—7.15 am, 12 noon and 3 pm. The later two boats offer free bus transfer to Surat's railway station.

Surat Thani

TOURIST INFORMATION

Surat Thani is a pleasant, unremarkable town 650 km from Bangkok. There's little to do here; most people take a walk down by the river and drop in on the several interesting fruit stalls and shops. Don't be fooled by its backwoods charm, though—you'll still be offered 'massage by number one ladeee!' while wandering round after dark.

TAT has an office at 5 Talaat Mai Rd (282828), open 8.30–4.30 daily; it has details of all boat departures to Koh Samui.

If you have to stay overnight here, there's a good choice of decent accommodation in the moderate to inexpensive range. Places to get a good night's sleep are **Wang Tai Hotel**, 1 Talaat Mai Rd (tel 273410) (air-con rooms start at 500B, many facilities) or the cheaper **Muang Tai** on the same road (tel 272367) (fan/air-con rooms at 150–350B). Fifty metres from the bus station is **Thai Thani Hotel**, 442 Talaat Mai Rd (tel 273620), a cavernous place on the 2nd and 3rd floors, where the staff giggle coyly at the sight of a *farang*. Large air-con rooms with bath are a very reasonable 280B, 180B with fan. **Rajthani** on Na Muang Rd (tel 272143) is also centrally placed, and fine for an overnight stop (180B fan, 280B air-con). There are a few cheaper places around the bus station, but check the rooms first, some are far from clean.

Surat Thani has some good places to eat. Twenty metres down from the Thai Thani Hotel, on the corner of Talaat Rd, is an open-air restaurant that locals love. It has no name and no menu—you just walk up to the chef at the counter and point at whatever takes your fancy, but order small portions—the choice is enormous. Two can gorge to the full for 300B. Further down Talaat Rd, **Lucky Restaurant** serves delicious Thai food at reasonable prices (40–70B a dish); the menu is in English and the staff are charming, if a little slow. You can dine out on tasty *kao kai op* (marinated baked chicken and rice) at Kaset Market, just above the bus station; look out for the excellent Chinese restaurant (try the fresh crab and asparagus) 400 m from Phun Phin railway station, walking into town.

Buses run every five minutes from Phun Phin station to Ban Don pier (and back), from 6 am to 8 pm. The fare is 5B.

GETTING AROUND KOH SAMUI

A well-paved 50-km ring-road runs around the island, connecting the town (Na Thon), the beaches, and various inland attractions. *Songthaews* are the main form of local transport—they'll take you anywhere on their route for 15–20B. Trouble is, while *songthaews* cover most places of interest, they don't connect the island's two main beaches—Chaweng and Lamai (20B per person). Half of them ply up the east side of the island, and the other half cover the west side. This means that if you want to go from Chaweng to Lamai, you have to take one *songthaew* into Na Thon, and another one down to Lamai (or vice versa). Another inconvenience is that *songthaews* only run from 6 am to 7 pm—no good at all, if you want to go late-night partying on another beach, or need to get home from a distant disco. Hotel mini-buses wait at the dock to take you to the resorts. This service is free if you are staying at their hotel, otherwise they charge 30–50B per person.

The obvious solution is to arrange your own transport. There are places all over the island that rent out mopeds (150–200B per day), motorbikes (250–500B) and jeeps (600–800B). Insurance is not provided, so it's wise to have a short test-drive before signing any agreement. And always check plugs, brakes, lights, oil and petrol before setting out—few of these machines are well-maintained. Be very careful when driving round Samui—the main ring road is very good, but the gravelly dirt-tracks connecting

211

the various beaches with the road are downright dangerous. The number of people who die from motorcycle injuries is alarming. Your best bet is a good, solid 175cc road-bike which will hold the roads, rather than frail mopeds which won't.

WHAT TO SEE

Samui has much more to offer than beaches. There's some beautiful natural scenery in the interior, worth exploring as a day-tour by motorbike or by *songthaew*. Where you start your tour is up to you (the suggested route begins at Na Thon, but you can pick it up anywhere). Set out early in the morning (coolest) and bring walking shoes (for Samui Highlands), snorkelling equipment (for Coral Cove), sun-oil, bathing costume and towel. If travelling by motorbike (100B's worth of petrol should see you through the day) you'll also need a sun-hat and sunglasses.

Island Tour
(by motorbike/jeep/*songthaew*; full day)

Hin Lad falls – Samui Highlands – Na Muang Falls – Wat Laem Sor – Wonderful Rock – Coral Cove – Big Buddha

From Na Thon, head south down the ring-road until a sign for **Hin Lad Falls** appears, 3 km out of town. From here, it's a 2 km stroll inland to the waterfall. No swimming here, but nice scenery. Many people give it a miss, preferring to save their energy for **Samui Highlands**. This pretty hilltop spot is reached via a steep jungle path, leading off the ring-road about 1 km south of Hin Lad. It's a stiff climb, but encouraging signs ('Don't be lazy! Sure! Samui Highland—UP! UP!') and cool drinks served along the way, make it bearable. At the top, friendly Colum provides refreshments and showers for a 20B 'donation', and there are fantastic views. He puts travellers up overnight in his charming bamboo rest-house for a nominal charge (to book contact him in Na Thon any evening). This lodge has a lovely rock park and flower garden, also a perfect sunset location. Back on the main road, proceed a few kilometres further south (down route 4169) to **Na Muang Falls**. Again, a long 2 km walk inland from the road—though there is access for motorbikes. Na Muang is Samui's best waterfall, especially after the rains when there is great swimming and you can sit beneath the roaring waters and enjoy the best jacuzzi of your life.

Wat Laem Sor is at the southern tip of the island. It's an unusual old pagoda, in a beautiful setting, erected by a venerated monk called Luang Ko Dang. He's dead now, but locals still call his temple a 'very, very magic place'. Stay around until sunset—it really *is* magical then. There's a small beach here, with the bungalow operation **Laem Sor Inn**, run by an English–Thai couple. It's well known for its Thai fruit wine (highly drinkable) and for its superb food.

Wonderful Rock, just below Lamai Bay, is another 'very, very magic place'. it's actually two rocks—nicknamed Grandfather and Grandmother—which reveal themselves in full phallic glory at low tide. Spotting 'Grandfather' is no problem, but there are numerous candidates for 'Grandmother'. The legend here is that if you don't pray to the resident spirits, you'll get sick and go off your food for days.

Coral Cove lies below the headland separating Lamai and Chaweng bays. It's a small

212

beach, with fantastic snorkelling. You need only go waist-deep into the water to be surrounded by coral wonderland.

Coral Cove Bungalows, up on the rocks, hire out snorkelling equipment for 20B an hour. They also serve some of the best food on Samui. Delicious 'No Name Mixed Seafood' (50B), chicken salads and fruit salads. Bungalows are marvellous value—particularly the 300B ones right on the beach (these have comfy chairs, flush loos and vast double beds). The coral itself, and the colourful marine life, need no recommendation. Wear flippers or flip flops in the water, if possible—if you cut your feet on coral or rocks (and this goes for *anywhere* in Samui), you'll have to take strong precautions against infection. Apply antiseptic and a dry dressing immediately—and stay out of the water for at least four days. Why? Well, there's a chemical quality in Samui's waters which badly aggravates open wounds. Swollen feet are a common sight in Na Thon's hospital, open daily 8.30 am to noon, 1 to 5 pm. (You'll also find a number of roadside clinics, which not only handle minor emergencies, but also perform tests for pregnancy and AIDS, an indication of the island's great leap forward.)

Big Buddha lies north of Chaweng bay, up route 4171. This modern Buddha image, 12 metres high and covered with tiny mosaic pieces, sits on a low hill linked by a narrow causeway to the mainland. It makes a beautiful silhouette at sunset—the best time to visit. Below it are seven mini-Buddhas, one for each day of the week. You'll need to dress correctly to visit the temple—the monks are hospitable, but they do turn away people wearing shorts and sarongs.

Ang Thong National Marine Park
(by tour boat; full day)

The beautiful archipelago of Ang Thong ('Golden Tub') lies northwest of Koh Samui, and comprises 40 islands covering 250 square kilometres. Various tour agencies in Na Thon—including Songserm, whose 'big boat' gets there first in the morning—offer good day-trips to the Marine Park. Tickets are 150B, and can be purchased in advance at the major beaches, without having to go all the way into Na Thon.

Ang Thong has several attractions. Tour boats make stops at various coral reefs in the lagoons, where you can go snorkelling. Then there's a longer stop at an island, where you can climb to the top (a gruelling one-hour slog) for panoramic views of hills and cliffs, lakes and islands. You can stay overnight here, if you make advance arrangements. The next day's boat will pick you up. There's a second island on the itinerary, with a crystal-green saltwater lake, fed by a subterranean tunnel. Ang Thong is, for many, the highlight of their Samui experience—but bring your own food. Meals on board the boat are pretty awful.

RECREATION
Samui's beaches offer various water-sports, many of them yet to be properly organized. There is, for instance, no problem finding **windsurf** boards, but there's often no boat to bring you back if you blow out to sea. This said, Samui doesn't get much surf. Apart from windy November, surfers often find themselves standing on mirror-calm waters. Some of them send back to shore for drinks, while waiting for a breeze to blow up. Two affiliated operations handle **Scuba-Diving** and **Water-Skiing**. These are **Samui**

213

Diving School at the Malibu (tel Na Thon 421273) or **Coco Cabana Beach Club** at Thong Yang Bay (tel 251–4801). These offer diving courses (starting every Tuesday) up to PADI standard, and charge 1100B a day (500B a day for non-divers). Dives commonly take place at **Koh Tao**, one of the best undersea locations in Thailand, or at Ang Thong Marine Park. Both companies are fairly reliable, though scuba-diving on Samui is still rather hit and miss. It's still wise to check equipment before paying over any money.

Several bungalows offer **Fishing** trips—at about 50B a head if there's a group of you. Fishing is said to be best in **Ta Ling Ngam Bay**. A small agency called **Southsea**, in the village just south of Na Thon, goes here—their day trips cost 300B (again, cheap in a group) and call in at **Koh Mudsum**, a lovely little offshore island. For snorkelling, I would recommend **Koh Matlang**, located off the top of Chaweng beach. At low tide, this tiny island is actually connected to the mainland, and you can wade across. Head for the island's point, behind which is a rocky beach. Entering the water here, you'll discover a wonderful underwater world of technicolour live coral and marine life. Look out for pike, angel fish, and giant parrot fish (usually nibbling on the coral), and wear flippers or flip flops to prevent cut feet.

The Beaches

Samui's beaches are famous—long curves of crisp white sand that seem to go on for ever and ever. As someone said, 'Tomorrow is a vision, yesterday is a memory, but today is a beach.' Not a lot happens on the beach. Some bungalows lay on volleyball and beach games, but sun-worshipping and swimming are still the main recreations. For many, the only walk of the day is a leisurely stroll along the sands to see which bungalow is showing the best video, which one is offering the best barbecue or beach party or which has the most amusing menu board. 'Special today!' announced my favourite, 'Magic Mushroom and Barbecued Crap!'

There's a wide range of accommodation available, from basic 50B bungalows with bed, mosquito-net, and (sometimes) an attached toilet, to comfortable 250–500B bamboo dwellings with wood-panelling, ceiling fan and an annexe or balcony. Some beaches now have luxury hotels, with air-con rooms and resort facilities for around 1000B. These low-season prices automatically double in November, when Samui's busy period starts, but you can still get good discounts by renting for a week or more. Outside of the big hotels, food on the island is standard beach fare—banana pancakes, chips, coconut milkshakes etc. Most bungalow operations have their own restaurant, and people generally eat at the one showing the best video.

Each beach has its own scene, and attracts its own devotees. Chaweng is big enough to cater for everyone, but is becoming something of a 'couples' beach. Lamai has a lot of action and boogie-on-down, aimed primarily at the singles market. Maenam and Bophut (Big Buddha) are mellow mushroom-lands, popular with peace-lovers. Laem Sor is where people retreat for total seclusion. And Coral Cove is wonderful for underwater enthusiasts. If you have time, tour them all by motorbike before deciding where to stay. Somewhere out there is a beach just right for you. Once settled, buy yourself a hammock (25B), string it up between two trees, and then just switch off.

214

Lamai

This is probably Samui's most popular beach. It's rather rocky, and the sand isn't as clean as it once was, but the water's great for swimming. And if it's entertainment you're after—discos, bars, parties etc.—there's no need to go any further. Unlike Chaweng, where each set of bungalows has its own restaurant, here at Lamai people often eat at the small 'village', with its several bars and eating-houses. At night, they move on to **Flamingo** discotheque, which is presently Samui's main scene. Of late, it's become something of a pick-up point for Thai girls, but 'The joint is jumpin' with the hip-hop happening sounds and that sight-sound synchro that you love so much!' And there's a good DJ, who comes on at midnight. Admission is free, and you get a straw with each (60B) drink. The Flamingo rocks up until 2 am. Next to the Flamingo, **Clip Clop Bar** has a nightly transvestite cabaret show. The **P.P. Paradise Bar** has Thai boxing every evening, followed by a live band. **Mix Pub** has a disco popular with *farangs*. The biggest disco is behind the beach, **Time Spacedrome**, and is always jumping. If you don't want Thai rap music and ZZ Top 'happening' inside your head at this late hour, get a bungalow on the far side of the beach. Light-sleepers find staying in the 'village' area disturbing—all those motorbikes revving up in the small hours, not to mention the merry revellers searching for their beds.

WHERE TO STAY   (tel prefix 077)

Expensive

The 'civilized' end of Lamai begins at **Seabreeze** bungalows and extends north to **Weekender Villa**, around the middle of the bay. Either side of these two operations, accommodation tends to be rather basic. The new **Pavilion Resort** has the poshest and priciest accommodation, and there's a pool and restaurant. Air-con bungalows go for 1800–2500B. Whilst this is a lot to pay, here you feel as if you're in a glossy mag. **Casanova's Resort** (tel 421425) is up on a hill away from the action, and is said to have the largest freshwater pool (complete with jacuzzi) on the island. Bungalows are 800–1200B.

Moderate

Weekender Villa (tel 421428) is near the village, and is run by 'Big Mama'—a large raunchy Thai lady who fusses over all guests like a broody hen. She offers large, modern bungalows at around 200B (fan) up to 800B for smart air-con bungalows, and has an overseas phone and small post office. Similarly-priced operations nearby include **Coconut Beach** and **Best Resort**.

Inexpensive

There are plenty of places in this category, but at some you won't be guaranteed a peaceful night's sleep. Some of the better operations include **Seabreeze** (120B fan, 400 air-con), **Fantasy Villa** (250–450B), **Lamai Inn** (200B–400B; everything good, especially the food) and **Mui** (200B huts with twin beds, fan and shower; seafood is superb). All of these operations command the best stretch of beach. A couple—notably Seabreeze and Mui's—are quieter than others.

Chaweng

The largest beach on the island, this divides into Chaweng Yai (to the north) and

Chaweng Noi (to the south). The larger bay, Chaweng Yai, is itself divided into two parts by a reef. North of the reef, towards Koh Matland, is quiet and unspoilt—many bungalows up here offer hash cookies, magic mushrooms and other psychedelic munchies. Opposite Matlang island, the beach glows green with phosphorescence at night, and it's like walking round in moonboots. South of the reef is the 'original' Chaweng beach. This still has the whitest sand, clearest water and most surf, but is rapidly turning into yuppie resort-land with big hotels and lots of beautiful people posing in dark shades and G-strings. Chaweng Noi, the small southernmost beach, is quiet and good for snorkelling, but is frequented by Thai prostitutes.

The **Chaweng Shop**, set back from the bungalows at the south end of Chaweng Yai, is a useful general store—it saves having to go into Na Thon for supplies, and it has an overseas phone and a Songserm Travel office. Close by, behind the new Imperial Samui Hotel, is **Madonna** discotheque. This is tacky, with Thai-oriented music, but can be fun in a crowd. It's open till 2 am nightly, and there are often novelty videos playing at the bar. We saw the porno cartoon version of *Snow White and the Seven Dwarfs*—unforgettable. Other discos that draw the crowds are **Reggae Pub**, **The Green Mango**, done out in coconut shells, and the neo art-deco **Fiesta**. Party-happy Aussies and Brits seem to like **Fresh Star** and **Chicago**. Drinks at all these places will range from 45–90B. If the disco is not your scene, there are plenty of other watering holes, outdoor places with horseshoe bars overlapping into each other. Take your pick—Kiwis can drop into **Andy's Place**, while Brits might like to have a chat with tattooed Tom from Romford at the **Bulldog Bar**.

If it's serenity and solitude you're after, then choose another beach—if not another island.

WHERE TO STAY (tel prefix 077)

Expensive
The **Imperial Samui Hotel** (tel 421390) caters to 20th-century ideas of desert island paradise. Sprawling over the hills, and looking down onto the southern beach, Chaweng Noi, it's built in a southern Spanish style, with a beautiful pool (but who needs one on the beach?), and all rooms look out to sea (2500–4000B). The **Tropicana Beach Resort** is popular, although the beach itself is a little rocky (1000B up). In the middle of Chaweng Beach, the **Chaweng Beach Resort** (tel 421378) is a similar luxury place with well furnished 2000–2500B air-con bungalows (each with their own safe), pool and good restaurant.

Moderate
At Chaweng Noi, take your pick from: **J.R.** (tel 421402) with a small post office, overseas phone, great breakfasts at **Good Morning Restaurant** and huts for 200B (fan), 500B (air-con) and some 1200B family suites; **Magic Light** (tel 421388) with 250B fan huts and very smart 600B air-con bungalows.

At central Chaweng the **Samui Cabana** (tel 421405) has very comfortable bungalows in an extremely pleasant setting (450B fan, 800B air-con) but it's a little expensive. The restaurant serves delicious fresh fish and western steaks, along with normal Thai cuisine. If this is full, or too expensive, try **Chaweng Palace**, similar idea but not as nice.

Inexpensive
North Chaweng has **Blue Lagoon** (clean 150B huts, small windsurfing/catamaran school), **Moon** (150–200B huts with verandah and toilet, fun staff, lots of laughs), **O.P.** (quiet 150–300B bungalows with fans), **Lucky Mother** and **Venus** (two late-night hangout places with superior food) and **Marine** (*the* place to eat—tuna salads, fresh yoghurt, fruit salads, and famous 'Bungalow Shakes'). South of the reef, places to stay include **Liberty** (at 80–150B, the best budget bungalows on Chaweng); **Royal Inn** (100–180B huts right down on the beach); **First** and **Maew**, where huts are 100–200B.

Bophut (Big Buddha)
This is a smaller beach which is becoming more popular. People come not so much for the sands (which get rather dirty after the rains) but rather for the fishing village, the stunning sunsets and the general air of relaxation. Bophut has a lot of peace and quiet.

WHERE TO STAY
Inexpensive
Places to stay include **Peace** (80B to 250B huts; friendly 'Mama' offers boat trips, windsurfing, volleyball, table-tennis and gourmet seafood—Peace is *the* night scene on Bophut, with good parties); the new **Palm Gardens** (80–100 bungalows right on the beach, great seafood and salads); **Smile House** and **Ziggy Stardust** (200–350B superior shacks—Smile is famous for its beach parties). Eat out at **Ran's** by the pier and enjoy cocktails at the nearby **Oasis** bar, where huts are 80–150B.

Mae Nam
Mae Nam is a quiet sandy 5 km beach with calm, clear water (great for swimming), a few fishing boats, and some nice scenery. Ideal by day, it has no electricity at night. After dark, people light small fires on the beach, and play music and munch mushrooms under the stars. There's a small windsurfing school here, and a pleasant little village. Bungalows are mostly basic, but the average charge for two persons is 80–150B (low season). An entertaining place to stay is **Ubon Villas** ('To service with good food. Electric have 24 hour'). Famous for its coconut curries, hallucinogenic mushrooms and 'steamed crap' (crab!), it has delightfully eccentric staff. Other current favourites include **Friendly** and **Happy** (both live up to their names), **Cleopatra Palace** (good information and views of Koh Phangan), **Phalarn** (upmarket 200–400B bungalows; manager Bo is a gem), and **Rose** and **Rainbow**.

KOH PHANGAN

Ever since Koh Samui began to develop its image as a popular resort, backpackers have been drifting over to Phangan, a short boat-ride away. This is a wonderfully scenic little island, with unspoilt beaches, lovely tropical terrain, and beautiful sunrises and sunsets. Very little development has taken place as yet—the main recreations are coral-diving in the bays and relaxing strolls up into the high forested hills. Most bungalows are simple 30–40B 'dog kennels on stilts', and few of them have electricity, let alone videos. There are only two dirt-track roads on the whole island, and although you can hire motorbikes, there's nowhere of real interest to go.

Koh Phangan is best during November–December (good weather) and March–April (lovely scenery, few tourists). High winds hit the west of the island (including Hadrint) from June to November, and the east (Laem Lok, Thong Sala etc.) from December to June. Swimming and snorkelling are pretty dismal when the wind's up.

GETTING THERE
There are two ways of getting to Phangan from Samui. From Bophut village, there are two boats daily (9.30 am and 3.30 pm) direct to Hadrint Bay. The fare is 50B, and it's a scenic one-hour trip. From Na Thon, there are two boats a day (10.30 am and 3.30 pm) to Thong Sala. The fare is 65B (book from Songserm), and the journey takes 40 minutes. Boats leave Thong Sala for Samui at 6.15 am and 12.30 pm. From Thong Sala, it's a 5B boat-trip down to Hadrint.

WHERE TO STAY   (tel prefix 077)

Inexpensive
Most people stay at **Hadrint Bay**—this has a beautiful long stretch of sand, with clear water and good swimming. The top part of the beach is where, as someone said, 'old hippies go to die'. They mostly hang out at **Paradise** and **Palita** bungalows (well-priced at 150B) and have turned hippie sandcastles—swirly, spirally, dreamy creations—into a fine art. The **Sunrise** has adequate 100B bungalows, and a very psychedelic menu. The nearby **Seaview** has hammocks and good 80B huts right on the beach. **Hadrint Bay** bungalows are acceptable, and **Tommy's** are top-notch. Tommy's is another mushroom place, but gets rave reviews for its 'Full Moon' parties and food. Every morning sees a long queue outside **Palita**, which does marvellous cheese buns (bungalows with bath 150B), and every afternoon there's a crush to get in **Win Bakery** (next to Family House), for its home-made cakes and real Lipton tea (served in earthenware pots). Win is excellent for seafood too.

If Hadrint has the best sunrises, then **Laem Lok**—a short walk across the narrow peninsula—has the best sunsets. There's no beach to speak of here, but there is an amazing coral cove. Laem Lok has two excellent places to stay. The **Lighthouse** has the best location, with bungalows (60–80B) imaginatively staggered up the rocks. Guests get free snorkelling equipment, and spend a lot of time in the restaurant. Well, with Mexican tacos, chip butties, vegetarian food, seafood, cakes and cookies on offer, why not? The other outfit, **Sunset** is just as popular, with a friendly family, great seafood and cheap boat-trips round the island. The bungalows are clean as a whistle.

From Hadrint, two boats go up daily to **Thong Sala**, the main town on the island. This has a post office, a few shops, a Songserm Travel office, and some fairly basic bungalows. The beaches here are nothing to write home about. From Thong Sala, a couple of taxis run out daily to **Ban Tai**. It's at this small village that you can hire out 200B per day roadbikes to visit **Thansadet Waterfall** (only worth it from September to November, after the rains). Bungalow operations here—**Boon, Windy, Laem Thong**—rent huts for 40–60B. If you really want to get away from it all, charter a boat out from Thong Sala to **Koh Tae Nai**, a pretty (and pretty remote) island with a few bungalows for rent.

PHUKET

Popular 'Pearl of the South', the large provincial island of Phuket lies in the Andaman Sea some 891 km south of Bangkok. Once a quiet backwater, development over recent years has turned it into an international resort. Formerly known as Koh Thalang, it used to derive its wealth from tin and rubber. Renamed Phuket—from the Malay word *bukit* (meaning mountain)—it now does just as well out of tourism. The combination of long white beaches, lovely coves and bays, scenic waterfalls and parks, undersea scenery and marine life, superb seafood and resort hotels, calm, clear waters and relaxed tropical atmosphere has made it a natural target for rapid development. A surging tide of tourism is sweeping over Phuket, and the ominous lines of girlie bars are already spreading along the major beaches. 'It's becoming another Pattaya', say some. 'It's not Thailand at all', moan others, 'just an absurdly expensive rip-off'. And it's true that the prophetic rise of 4-storey hotels on the main beaches spells doom to the old cheap bungalows, striking dismay into the heart of the economy traveller. Phuket is going all out to develop its image as an upmarket family-style resort. In a way, this isn't a bad thing. There's now a full range of water-sports, including scuba-diving and surfing; there's high-class European, Chinese, Thai and Islamic cuisine; there are discos, bars and a lively nightlife; and there are well-organized excursions by boat to nearby attractions like Phi Phi islands, Phang Nga and Ao Luk. Phuket has far more diversity than Koh Samui. Also, being connected to the mainland by a causeway, it is far more accessible. There's really little to complain about. Once you're on a motorbike, and away from built-up Patong and Kata beaches, it won't take long to appreciate how unspoilt the rest of Phuket is. This is Thailand's largest island, and only about 10% of it has been directly affected by tourism. There is nothing one-dimensional about Phuket either. In the hour it takes to drive the length of it, through hills and rubber plantations, running down to coconut groves and white beaches, you'll see no bungalow signs (unlike in Koh Samui, where they appear at every bend in the road), only some of the most beautiful inland scenery of any island in the country. So, don't be put off by Phuket's yuppie tag—the locals still fish, they still culture pearls, water buffalo still graze the golf course, and the water is as clear as the glass in your diving mask.

Phuket has its high season from November to May. By December, it's really buzzing, and accommodation prices soar. Christmas and New Year have some of the biggest parties in Thailand. September and October are rainy and windy, but there's some great surf. The nine-day Vegetarian Festival, Phuket's main celebration, usually happens at the end of September. This is when the islanders of Chinese ancestry commit themselves to a vegetarian diet, and undergo various painful austerities like fire-walking, climbing ladders with knife-blade rungs and puncturing themselves with pointed sticks. The last day is the best—joyous street-festivals, and lots of firecrackers and rockets.

GETTING THERE

By Air
Thai Airways fly daily to Phuket from Bangkok (2000B, 1 hour 10 minutes) and from Hat Yai (900B, 30 minutes).

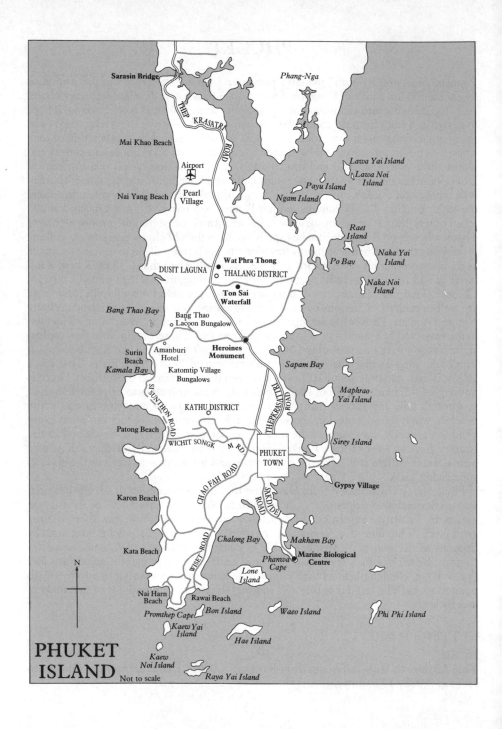

Sarasin Bridge

Phang-Nga

THEP KRASATRI ROAD

Mai Khao Beach

Airport

Nai Yang Beach

Pearl
Village

Lawa Yai Island

*Lawa Noi
Island*

Payu Island

Ngam Island

*Raet
Island*

*Naka Yai
Island*

Po Bay

Wat Phra Thong

DUSIT LAGUNA

THALANG DISTRICT

*Naka Noi
Island*

**Ton Sai
Waterfall**

Bang Thao Bay

Bang Thao
Lacoon Bungalow

**Heroines
Monument**

Surin
Beach

Amanburi
Hotel

Sapam Bay

Kamala Bay

Katomtip Village
Bungalows

*Maphrao
Yai Island*

SI SUNTHON ROAD

KATHU DISTRICT

Patong Beach

WICHIT SONGK

M RD.

Sirey Island

**PHUKET
TOWN**

THEP KRASATRI ROAD

Karon Beach

CHAO FAH ROAD

SAKDIDEJ ROAD

Gypsy Village

Kata Beach

Chalong Bay

Makham Bay

WISET ROAD

*Phanwa
Cape*

**Marine Biological
Centre**

N

Nai Harn
Beach

Rawai Beach

*Lone
Island*

Promthep Cape

Bon Island

Waeo Island

Phi Phi Island

*Kaew Yai
Island*

Hae Island

PHUKET
ISLAND

*Kaew
Noi Island*

Not to scale

Raya Yai Island

By Bus
From Bangkok's Southern Terminal, non air-con buses leave for Phuket throughout the day, from 7.30 am to 10.30 pm (fare 165B). There are also two air-con buses daily, leaving at 6.45 and 6.50 pm (fare 299B). In both cases, it's a long 13–14-hour journey. Several tour agencies in Bangkok and Phuket operate private buses—these cost a little more, but are often quicker and more comfortable.

From Phuket back to Bangkok, there are seven non air-con buses daily (leaving between 6 am to 6.30 pm), also one air-con bus leaving at 3 pm.

From Surat Thani, a few non air-con buses go to Phuket each day. The fare is 120B, and the awesomely slow 6-hour journey is made tolerable only by the magnificent scenery.

TOURIST INFORMATION
TAT Tourist Office, 73–75 Phuket Rd (tel 212213), is located near the bus-station in Phuket town. This should be your first port of call on arrival—lots of useful handouts and information; helpful and efficient staff, open daily 8.30 am–4.30 pm.

GETTING AROUND
From Phuket town, *songthaews* run out to all the major beaches at regular intervals from 8 am to 6 pm. The rank in Ranong Rd (opposite Thai Airways) services Patong, Kata, Karon and Surin beaches (fare 10B), also Kamala and Nai Yang beaches (15B). *Songthaews* for Rawai (10B) and Nai Harn (20B) beaches leave from the circle in Bangkok Rd. A few *songthaews* also go up to the airport, 32 km north of town, for 20B. Taxis and *tuk-tuks* charge a minimum fare of 100B, and at sundown, when they know you want to get out to the action at Patong, up the rate to 150B. Only hire taxis or *tuk-tuks* (100B minimum fare from town to beaches or airport) if there's a group of you. *Songthaews* and *tuk-tuks* patrol around Phuket town itself for a standard 5B charge—but you still need to bargain.

To get around the island itself, consider hiring a motorbike or jeep. These are useful for beach-hopping, exploring the island's hinterland, and for trips into Phuket town. They can be hired, at an average daily rate (low season) of 150B for mopeds, 300B for big police bikes, 500–800B for jeeps, either in town or at the beaches. Hire rates are cheapest at Patong and in Phuket town. As in Koh Samui, there's no insurance provided, but bikes and roads here are in much better condition. A popular outing by bike (or jeep) is north up to the airport, then returning slowly along the coastline, checking out each of the beautiful beaches in turn. There are some especially fine coastal views as you round the headland at Promthep Cape, the southernmost point of the island. But be warned— some of the roads connecting various beaches have been allowed to fall into disrepair. The dirt-tracks between Surin and Patong beaches, and between Promthep and Nai Harn/Rawai, are the main hazards. Tackling these roads by motorbike can be tricky. Casualties should report to **Karon Health Clinic**, located between Kata and Karon beaches. This place gives immediate treatment, and is far better than the hospital in town.

Cars can be rented for about 900B per day without petrol. Contact **Pure Car Rent**, opposite Thavorn Hotel, Rasada Rd, Phuket town (tel 211002); **Avis** at Phuket Cabana Hotel, Patong (tel 321138), Le Meridien, Karon Noi (tel 321480); or **Hertz** at Pearl Village, Nai Yang (tel 311376) and Patong Merlin Hotel, Patong (tel 321070).

Phuket Town

This compact provincial town is becoming rather too touristy for most tastes. The interesting old Sino–Portuguese residences are being swamped by concrete buildings and souvenir shops, and a lot of the town's earlier charm and character has gone with them. For something to do, visit the Provincial Town Hall, used as the French Embassy in the film of *The Killing Fields*. Or take a walk up **Rang Hill** for a nice view down over the town and island interior. If you need to phone or telex overseas, there's a good service at the modern **Telephone Office**, one block up from the Post Office in Montri Rd.

WHERE TO STAY (tel prefix 076)

Accommodation: All prices given in the sections for hotels, except where otherwise stated, are average–high season. Even TAT tourist office, which hands out up-to-date

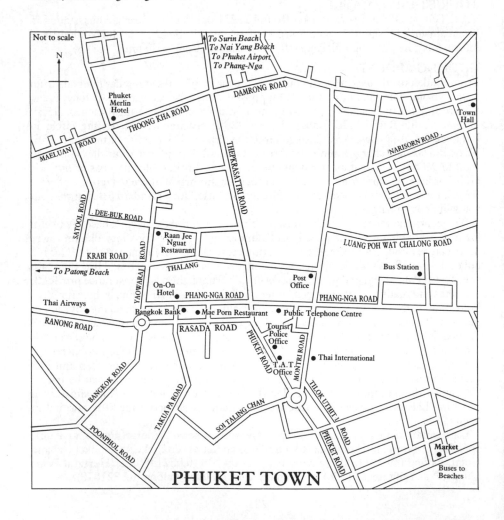

PHUKET TOWN

hotel lists, can't supply fixed tariffs. Prices vary substantially from high to low season. From November to May, tariffs are often double what they are the rest of the year. But it's still worth bargaining for discounts—especially if you're staying for a week or more.

Expensive
Places to stay include **Pearl Hotel**, Montri Rd (tel 211044)—air-con rooms for 1200–1500B, suites 3000–5000B (where Thai dignitaries and celebrities congregate), with pool, restaurant and nightclub; **Phuket Merlin**, 158/1 Yaowara Rd (tel 212866)—air-con rooms from 1000B, with restaurant, nightclub, and 'refrigerator'.

Moderate
A very economical alternative is **Thavorn Hotel**, Rasada Rd (tel 211333), a relaxed, comfy place occupying two large buildings—rooms for 280–500B, with pool, popular disco and coffee shop.

Inexpensive
Centrally placed is **Sintawee**, 81 Phang Nga Rd (tel 212153) with clean, comfortable fan doubles at 200–300B. A little cheaper is **On-On Hotel** (211154,) a little way along on the same road.

EATING OUT
Pearl Rooftop Restaurant (tel 211901) in the Pearl Hotel offers Phuket's most select dining, with a panorama of the town at your feet. The menu is principally Chinese, and prices reflect its exclusive reputation—1200–1500B for two. Opposite the Pearl Hotel, **Laem Tong**, the best Chinese restaurant in town, offers shark's fin soup, birds' nests, and other local favourites. Prices here are standard for an upmarket Chinese restaurant—800–1000B for two. **Mae Porn** at the corner of Phang Nga Rd and Soi Pradit (tel 212106) is a good reliable air-conditioned restaurant with tasty 40–60B Thai dishes and unbelievable service. At the top of Rang Hill the **Tunk-ka Café** has marvellous views, best appreciated with one (or two, who's counting?) of their heady cocktails; the menu is based on seafood, with Japanese *sashimi* and *tempura* dishes as well (1000B for two).

The Beaches
Phuket has beaches to suit every taste and pocket. If you don't like one, hop on a motorbike and check out another. Every one has its own character and clientele, but they all have white sands, lovely sea and (except Patong) lots of space. The bigger beach hotels offer a wide range of recreations, including water-sports, discotheques, massage parlours, swimming pools, bars and clubs. One or two are so large, you can often wander in and use the facilities for free.

RECREATION
Most of Phuket's sports and recreations are water-related. **Swimming** is best from December to April. At other times, strong winds and powerful undercurrents make swimming out of your depth inadvisable. Bathers should take care not to swallow sea-water—some of it is being polluted by non-treated sewage. **Surfing** is *the* sport at Phuket from September to October. During storms, the whole of Nai Harn bay is just one big wall of wave. But most surfers hang out at Kata Noi, or at the point break at the

top of Patong beach. **Boat trips** to offshore islands (for snorkelling, fishing etc) can be arranged with fishermen on the beach. They charge between 500B and 1000B (low/high season) for boatloads of up to 8 people, and will often drop you off on an island, and pick you up later. If you want something very special, take a 3-hour speedboat ride to the **Similian islands**—an enchanting group of nine islands (Similian means 'nine') located to the east of Phuket. It's widely considered, even by Jacques Cousteau, to be one of the three best places in the world for **scuba-diving** and **snorkelling**. Independent travel to the Similians is tricky, but a few people have hitched a ride over from the small coastguard station on Phuket's northwestern coast, and then just camped out on the empty beaches. The trouble is, you'll have to bring your own scuba/snorkelling equipment. The same goes for **Phi Phi Islands**, the second-best undersea location in these parts—equipment rented out here is generally poor. Fortunately, Phuket itself has a couple of reliable deep-sea-diving outfits. These are **Fantasea Divers** in Patong village (tel 321309) and **Marina Sports** in Kata-Karon village (tel 211432). Both offer 4–5 day *PADI* (open-water diving certificate) courses at around 7500B, and make dives out at Phi Phi, the Similians and the west coast. Fantasea is run by two Dutch guys, Jeroen and Maarten, and offers insurance on diving accidents (the only outfit on Phuket to do so). Marina is a friendly German-run company, with a reputation for exciting night-dives, and for going down deeper than anyone else. Both operations are pricey, but offer discounts if you advance-book. In addition to diving, they offer **windsurfing, water-skiing, deep-sea fishing, parasailing** (Marina only) and **catamarans**. All their equipment is top quality.

Landlubbers can take their pick from **horseriding** along Nai Harn beach and surrounding inland trails (contact the Crazy Horse Club); **shooting** at the Phuket Shooting Range, 82 Patak Rd (tel 381667), with both indoor and outdoor ranges; **dance** and **kick-boxing** shows at Phuket Orchid Garden and Thai Village in Phuket town (tel 214860—190B admission).

Nai Yang

Proceeding counterclockwise from Phuket's northern tip, this is the first major beach you'll hit. **Nai Yang** is a secluded half-moon beach with good sand and hardly any people. Set aside as a national park, and fringed by *casuarina* trees, it is short on action and high on relaxation. The Thais like it, and so do retired couples seeking a complete rest. If at a loose end, take a short hike north to **Mai Khao**, which is Phuket's longest beach. Here, between November and February, giant sea-turtles struggle ashore to lay their eggs, though their numbers are dwindling, now that the turtles have become wary of curiosity hungry tourists. The convenience of Nai Yang is that it is only a five-minute drive from the airport.

WHERE TO STAY AND EATING OUT

Luxury

At Nai Yang, **Pearl Village Hotel** (tel 311338) has 80B tents, 500B fan-cooled bungalows, and 2600B luxury air-con rooms and 'cottages'. Located within the Nai Yang National Park, and covering an extensive area, the resort's facilities include horse-riding and cycling, swimming pools with jacuzzi, tennis courts and pitch-and-putt. Rooms have mini-bar and video; also good dining and entertainment. The Pearl offers discounts of up to 50% in the low season. Prices also come down on quiet weekdays, when you can often have the whole beach to yourself.

Surin – Bang Tao – Cape Sing –Kamala

Surin, 25 km from Phuket town, is another nice quiet spot. It has a lovely long beach (poor for swimming though, owing to strong tides), some excellent seafood-snack places, and a popular 9-hole golf course. For a game, contact **Pansea Hotel** (tel 311249).

WHERE TO STAY AND EATING OUT

Luxury
Pansea is a good place to stay—for 3000B, you get a lovely 4-person cottage, with all meals and water-sport facilities thrown in. **Bang Tao Bay**, just above Surin, has **Dusit Laguna Hotel** (tel 311320), part of the Dusit chain with its usual high standards of facilities and service—massage parlour, sauna, pub, disco and four restaurants, serving Thai, Italian and mixed European cuisine. Air-con rooms from 3600B. By the end of 1992 two new luxury places should be in operation—**Pacific Island Club**, a Thai-style Club Med and a **Sheraton**. On the point between Bang Tao and Surin, **Amanpuri Resort** (311394) is one of the best and most exclusive resort hotels on the island, but only the Rolls Royce brigade can afford it. Accommodation is in individual 'pavilions', each with its own sun terrace and dining area. Rates are 6000B for a standard (!), up to 20,000B for a super-super de luxe—sleep well. It has two restaurants, one Thai, **The Terrace**, the other Italian, **Il Ristorante**, which are more affordable. Memorable dining at either will cost 2000B for two.

Expensive
Sing Cape, 1 km south of Surin, is famous for its fantastic rock formations, and you can camp out on the beach. It leads down to **Kamala**, a delightful stretch of the sand with the **Phuket Kamala Resort** (tel 212775) with superior rooms for 15400–2300B.

Inexpensive
Kamala has a good budget bungalow operation, **Kratomtip Village** (low-season rates, 300B a night). The northern end of Kamala beach is suitable for swimming.

Patong
Patong is 15 km from town, and is Phuket's most developed beach. It has a tacky, action-packed 'village' full of bars, clubs, German restaurants and expensive seafood places. The beach itself is nice—if you don't mind being hassled every five minutes to buy fake diamonds, hammocks or massages. But when the navy rolls in, Patong really earns its title of 'Soho on the Beach'. All prices double, and the place is crawling with pubescent Thai hookers. Bars come and go, but the current favourites include **Kangaroo**, **Ex-Pat**, **Doolie's Place**, **Lucky Star**, **Bounty**, **Oasis** and **Diamond Bar** (run by Canadians). After the bars close, the human zoo migrates to the discotheques: **Crocodile Music Hall** is the most popular, with transvestite cabaret three times a week at 1 am. Cover charge is 70B. Others include **Banana** and the new **Hard Rock** with a British DJ, and furnishings to match the best of Bangkok's.

During the day, recreations include water-scooters (400B per hour), jet-skis (1000B per hour), windsurfing (150–200B per hour), snorkelling (100B per hour) and coral-diving over at nearby Freedom and Paradise beaches (500–1000B per day for boat hire).

WHERE TO STAY

Luxury
Other than at the internationally known **Holiday Inn**, Patong's rich kids stay at hotels like **Diamond Cliff Resort** (tel 321501), which sits on high up at the north end of the bay (a 15-minute walk from the action), with beautiful panorama, classy rooms, three restaurants and a live jazz band every night in the cocktail lounge; **Royal Paradise** (tel 321566); **Patong Resort** (tel 321333), **Club Andaman** (tel 321102) and **Patong Merlin**; these are all top notch resort hotels, with full facilities; expect to pay between 3000B and 5000B.

Expensive
There's a lot of choice in this bracket. Three places worth a special mention are **Coral Beach** (tel 321106), at the southern end of the bay (1800B), **Safari Beach** (tel 321230—2000B), and **Seaview** (tel 321103—1500B).

Moderate
For 500–800B you can get decent air-con rooms with bath in **Coconut Villa (tel 321161), Thamdee Inn** (tel 321452) and **Ocean Garden** (tel 321189).

Inexpensive
Budget places are few and pretty dismal. Recommended cheaper hotels, with rooms between 200B and 400B, are **Club Oasis** (tel 321258), **Lobster** (tel 321351) and **Sea Dragon**, with a restaurant outside which does roast duck dinners for 40B.

EATING OUT
Dining out, try seafood at the **No 1** on Beach Rd (speciality is King Lobster, sold by the kilo) or **Patong Seafood** on the sea-front (recommended dishes include Roasted Snapper-Fish with Brandy, 120B, or Roasted Prawns with Brandy, 180B). More expensive but very popular is **Malee**, on Beach Road, again specializing in seafood; arrive early to be sure of a table. European and Thai food is good at **Tums** (the place to go, said one resident, 'when you're fed up of tiger prawns and overpriced steaks'). You can eat well at either place for under 200B. The new **Ban Rim Pa**—'edge of the cliff' (100 Kalim Beach Rd) serves excellent Thai food in a traditional Thai-style teak house on stilts, giving great views, particularly at night, of Patong beach to the south (800–100B for two). **Shalimar** in Soi Post Office is a traditional Indian restaurant serving delicious lamb curries and tandoori dishes—two can eat well for 500B. For pasta and seafood lovers, **Vecchia Venezia**, in Raj Uthit Rd, is a real treat; fresh, home-made *lasagna*, *gnocchi*, *agnolotti*, and many pasta dishes *alla marinara*. If a hearty steak is what you're after, then head for **Buffalo Steak House**, just back from Beach Rd on Bang La Rd.

Karon – Kata
These two long, curving beaches located 20 km out of town are the current favourites.

Karon is the more peaceful option—a good place to go if you're not into crowds. It has better swimming than **Kata**, and there are windsurfers for hire (150B per hour). Fishermen still cast their nets on Karon, and there's lots of good, fresh seafood available. This said, a lot of development has been going on in the last few years and you'll find that the big resort hotels have moved in.

WHERE TO STAY

Luxury
The following are top class places with double rooms or chalets for around 2500–3500B, suites 8000–28,000B: **Phuket Arcadia** (tel 381038); **Le Meridian** (tel 321480); **Karen Villa Royal Wing** (tel 381139—although a little characterless, this place deserves a special mention for its traditional Thai dance shows at 8 nightly: no admission charge, but you're expected to buy a drink); **Karon Beach Resort** (tel 381525) and **Thavorn Palm Beach** (tel 381034).

Expensive
Phuket Island View (tel 381632) and **Karon Inn** (tel 381521) have good facilities, including pools and restaurant. Both have air-con doubles for 1000–1500B.

Moderate–Inexpensive
Marina Cottage is well placed in the 'village' between Karon and Kata, and has basic rooms for 200B, air-con doubles for 600–800B, up to 1500B for fully furnished air-con bungalows. **Phuket Golden Sand Inn** (tel 381493) is another good option, with full facilities and air-con rooms for 800–1200B. Others in this price category include **Sand Resort** (tel 212901) and **Phuket Ocean Resort 1** (tel 381599), which also has cheaper 400B rooms with fan. Cheaper than that, try **Dream Hut** at the north end of the bay, or **Happy Hut** at the southern end, back from the beach. Both have basic accommodation for around 150–200B.

Kata is actually two beaches in one—Kata Yai and Kata Noi. The smaller beach, **Kata Noi**, has bigger waves, better surfing and one notable hotel—the **Kata Thani** (tel 216632) with rooms from 1200B and a perfect location. **Kata Yai** has better swimming and (in September/October) enjoyable body-surfing. The shallow beach is a popular induction spot for beginner scuba-divers. From here, they graduate to offshore **Koh Pu**, known for its beautiful live coral. Kata Yai hires out windsurfers (100–150B per hour) and jet-skiers (500B per hour); in the village, you can rent out surf bodyboards from **Chin Café** from 150B a day.

Ever since Club Med set up shop at Kata, this beach has been going the same way as Patong. There's now a small 'village', between Karon and Kata, with pizza parlours and coffee shops, noisy videos and motorbikes, and a small street bar with monkeys serving the drinks. The village is quite a scene at night.

WHERE TO STAY

Luxury–Expensive
Club Mediterranee (tel 381455) is at the top of Kata Yai, near the village, and

commands a lovely stretch of beach. Rooms start at 2500B, and there's all manner of recreational facilities on offer. In the same bracket are **Kata Beach Resort** (tel 381530) and **Kata Thani** (tel 381417).

Moderate
Kata Guest House (tel 381627) has a good name, with rooms for 500B (fan), 1000B (air-con). **Crystal Beach Hotel** (tel 381580) is even better value, with air-con rooms for 600B. **Kata Noi Riviera** (tel 381726) has fan rooms for 250–500B.

Inexpensive
In the village are **Kata Tropicana** (good-value rooms at 150 to 250B, useful laundry service and restaurant, cheap motorbike rental and sightseeing boat trips), **Kata Villa** (tel 381602—clean rooms for 220B) and **Fantasea Hill** (bungalows at 100–180B). Travellers also recommend the large well-appointed bungalows opposite Sue's Bar—at 70B a night, probably the best deal on Kata.

EATING OUT
If you don't want to splash out on dinner in the big hotels, try **Marina** restaurant (famous 90B steaks and 120B seafood basket meals). The Kata Thani hotel has a fairly good restaurant, **Chom Talay**, where dinner for two (European dishes with wine) costs around 1000B. On the way down to the seedy bar street, there's **Sue's Bar and Restaurant**. This has a pool, darts, hard-rock sounds, and a wild, wild atmosphere. Nearly anything goes at Sue's—except dancing on the tables. After the bars close at midnight, it's time for late-night boogie at the small **Club 44** disco. This is a small, rather ramshackle affair—but drinks are cheap, and (unlike Patong's 'Banana' disco) there's minimal hassle from the girls.

Nai Harn
Viewed from the headland above, Nai Harn—just below Kata Noi—looks just about the prettiest of all Phuket's beaches. Its perfect crescent of white sand is ringed by green hills and embraces an idyllic emerald-green lagoon. Then you spot the ugly **Phuket Yacht Club** staggered up the hillside, and the impression is spoilt. Nai Harn now offers sailing, windsurfing and even tennis (swimming is out between May and October), but if you want to get away from beautiful people and beach umbrellas, stay at the southern end of the sands.

WHERE TO STAY

Luxury
Phuket Yacht Club Hotel (tel 381156) has all mod-cons, reflected in its room rates—3500B up for a double.

Inexpensive
At the southern end of the bay there are two quiet and friendly places—**Nai Harn Bungalow** (Linda Cottage Inn) with cosy huts for 200B, and its own little beach; and **Sunset Bungalows** with basic, but comfortable, huts at 80–100B. You'll find both places off the road leading up to Promthep Point.

Rawai

Rounding Promthep Cape at the southern tip of the island, you'll find **Rawai** beach, 17 km from town. Though one of the first beaches to be developed on Phuket, Rawai today is quiet and neglected. This is much to do with its narrow beach, and general lack of atmosphere. Still, scuba-divers like it (many offshore islands here have spectacular underwater scenery) and so do seafood gourmets.

WHERE TO STAY
Moderate–Inexpensive
Places to stay are limited. Choose between **Rawai Plaza** (tel 381346) at 500–1000B for air-con rooms, **Rawai Resort** (tel 381298), with fan/air-con rooms for 400–600B, **Rawai Garden Resort** (tel 381292) with okay fan rooms for 250–300B and **Pornmae Bungalow**, 58/1 Wiset Rd (upmarket bungalows from 300B).

Chalong

A charming fishing village connects Rawai to **Chalong Bay**. At the pier here, friendly Ruan offers boat-trips over to **Koh Hae** (Coral island), **Koh Lone** and **Koh Hew**. These trips cost 500B (for one to six people), include stops for fishing, snorkelling and coral-diving, and run from 9 am to 4 pm daily. Chalong Bay itself is a pretty spot at high tide, with many boats moored offshore. You can charter these for fishing trips (around 500B a day), or take the regular 9 am boat to Phi Phi islands (500B, includes meagre lunch).

EATING OUT
Chalong Bay is well-known for its seafood restaurants. For around 120B a head, you can eat your fill at **Kaneing 1** or **Kaneing 2**. These offer a mouthwatering range of crab, prawn and fish dishes (steamed or barbecued), also special *tom yum* seafood soup with lemon grass and chilli. **Pan's Lighthouse** is cheaper and almost as good—this is where all the fishermen and boat people hang out in the evening, and is the best place to charter boats. To arrange overnight stays in a schooner off the bay, contact the agent at Kaneing 1 restaurant. He's also the person to see regarding luxury launch trips from the boat club.

Naka Noi

Phuket is world-famous for its fabulous cultured pearls. These come from the small island of **Naka Noi**, off the northwest coast. Several tour agencies in Phuket offer trips there, or you can go independently (30-minute drive up to Po Bay from town, then 20 minutes by boat). Pearls bought at Naka Noi are cheaper even than in the pearl markets of Japan. But don't expect to come away with a pearl necklace. One woman I met has waited 10 years for one of these and still has only 15 matching pearls—she needs 28.

PHANG NGA

Phang Nga lies exactly midway between Phuket and Krabi, and makes a good stop-over from these two more popular resorts. The central attraction here is Phang Nga Bay, an eerie collection of primaeval limestone islands rising out of the sea like grim, forbidding sentinels. The spectacular scenery of this immense bay made it a natural choice of location for the film *The Man with the Golden Gun*. Since then, having captured the public

Ko Tapu, Phang Nga Bay

imagination, it has become a big tourist magnet. Every day, an armada of noisy tour-boats invades from nearby Phuket, and there remains only one way to see Phang Nga in its original, timeless splendour—on your own.

Visit Phang Nga between December and April—then, the skies are clear, there is no rain, and the islands are at their most verdant and beautiful. If you want to avoid the crowds, go in October and November—there's often just enough rain to discourage the tour boats.

GETTING THERE

By Bus
From Phuket's Phang Nga Rd terminal, buses leave for Phang Nga every hour till 6 pm. The 85 km journey takes 1 hour 45 minutes, and the fare is 22B.

From Krabi, there are regular buses to Phuket (181 km, 3 hours, 40B), via Phang Nga (88 km, 1 1/2 hours, 20B). From Phang Nga town, buses leave for Phuket and Krabi every hour, until 5 pm.

By Motorbike
Phang Nga is a popular motorbike outing from both Phuket and Krabi. On a bike, you can really enjoy the scenery.

WHAT TO SEE
The big thing to do here is the spectacular boat-trip round Phang Nga Bay. An enterprising young postman, Sayan Tamtopol, has been offering good, cheap tours for independent travellers over the past seven years. He charges 200B (far less than a tour from Phuket) and throws in a huge seafood supper, overnight accommodation in a

Muslim fishing village, and himself as your personal English-speaking guide. The advantage of booking through Sayan is that, because his village is right at the mouth of the bay, you can have the bay all to yourself for hours if you start out early enough. The tour-boats don't roll in till around 11 am. Another bonus for setting out early are the unforgettable dawn views, rather like Chinese paintings. Sayan's tours usually run from 8 am to 2 pm, and he makes stops for snorkelling and swimming. But the scenery is the main event—so bring your camera and lots of film.

Sayan meets travellers off the bus in Phang Nga town (outside Thai Farmers Bank) between 6 and 8 am daily. This is good if you want free transport to Koh Panyi (the fishing village), but often means a late-start tour. Your best bet is to arrive in town mid-afternoon, and to make your own way to Sayan's place (ring him on 212901–4 ext 089 to let him know you're coming—or just turn up). To get there, cross over from the town bus-stop and hop in a *songthaew* going to Tha Don customs pier. This short 8 km journey often takes as long as 45 minutes. My vehicle crept around town for half an hour before going anywhere. On the way, it picked up sacks of ice and fish, piles of foam mattresses, shrimp nets and sail rigging, a mountain of egg-boxes, six huge Calorgas drums, a cake trolley, and an outboard engine. Oh yes, and 22 passengers. At Tha Don, look out for the Muslim restaurant by the pier (it's the one with the caged bird over the entrance). Beef and green bean curry is the speciality, and it costs just 10B. From Tha Don, it's a 40-minute boat ride over to Koh Panyi—the correct fare is 10B, but you'll have to bargain to get this.

WHERE TO STAY   (tel prefix 076)

Inexpensive
Phang Nga town itself is small, and fairly dull. There are a couple of banks, a semi-interesting Muslim market (opposite the bus-stop) and a few cheap hotels. The **Rak Phangnga**, 98 Phetkasem Rd (tel 411090), has okay 120B–330B double rooms. A blue building signed 'Hotel', a minute's walk below the Rak Phangnga, has simpler rooms for 80B. If you want air-con comfort, choose between the **New Luk Muang** on Highway 4 (on the road into town, just below the mediocre tourist office; live music nightly, nice café, twin-bedded rooms 350B) or the luxury **Phang Nga Bay Resort** near the pier at 20 Tha Don Rd (tel 411067). This has a scenic setting, rooms at 800B double, and there's a little restaurant nearby called the **Jarun**, famous for its cheap, delectable seafood.

Phang Nga Bay
(by boat; 6 hours)

Koh Panyi – Koh Phing Kan – Koh Tapu – Koh Thalu – Koh Hong – Thamlot Cave – Pekinese Rock

Koh Panyi is a fascinating overnight stop. Where else can you stay at a Muslim fishing village built on stilts at the base of a massive limestone island? Koh Panyi means 'flag island', and it was given its name by the first Muslims who arrived here (from Malaysia) over 200 years ago, and planted their flag on its peak. The original settlement of three families is now a thriving township of 1200 people, with its own school, post office and mosque. Colourful exotic birds flutter within wicker cages, cackling elders lull infants to sleep in wooden swing-cribs, the sun sets peacefully against a golden sky, and then everybody vanishes off to prayers in the quaint blue mosque. If staying here, you won't see them again till morning. The evening is spent watching TV soaps and tucking into tasty Muslim pastries with Sayan and his chums. The village generator packs up at midnight and then (provided you've got a mosquito net) it's off to sleep in a comfy bed.

In the early morning, you set off to see the islands. As you approach the centre of the bay, these fan out into a surreal archipelago of tombstone-shaped crags, strongly resembling an ancient stone circle. There are dozens of tiny isles out here, several with interesting shapes which have earned them local soubriquets. **Koh Phing Kan** literally means 'two islands leaning back to back'. Since 007 landed though, it's become more popularly known as James Bond island. The large pillar of rock in its bay looks like a huge nail driven into the sea—thus its name of **Koh Tapu**, or 'nail island'. **Koh Thalu** and **Koh Hong** are two small rock grottos hollowed out in the base of larger islands by the pounding sea—their names derive from the shape of their interiors (Koh 'Hong' resembles a 'room'). **Thamlot Cave** is the largest subterranean cave on the route, with ghoulish limestone fingers dripping down from its vast ceiling. Just beyond this, returning to base, look out for **Pekinese Rock**. This sits on a low crag, overlooking the mouth of the bay, and bears more than a passing resemblance to a pekinese dog.

KRABI

A spectacular blend of vast limestone cliffs, prehistoric islands and serene white-sand beaches, Krabi is the up-and-coming resort on the southwest coast. It's a lot less developed (and much quieter) than Phuket or Samui, and has just as much to offer. Krabi town, 814 km from Bangkok, is for travellers in serious need of relaxation. They come here to enjoy its famous cakes, pastries and ice-creams, to lie back with the locals, and to languish happily in its mellow, late-night bars and restaurants. Later, they move out to one of the many local beaches, or take a boat over to the glorious **Phi Phi Islands**. Most of the islands in this area were, at one time or other, popular smugglers' hideouts. Krabi town itself—situated close to the mouth of the Andaman Sea—was still doing a brisk trade in smuggled whisky and cigarettes (from Malaysia and Singapore) until a couple of years ago, but that's all stopped now. The local population, mainly Muslims, still do a lot of regular trading by sea—rubber and palm oil are the main exports—but smuggling is no longer necessary. Now they have tourism. In and around Krabi, everybody is building like crazy—preparing for the expected tourist boom. It hasn't come yet—the moneyed tourists won't arrive till Krabi gets its airport. Well, it's *got* an airport, and they even opened it. But then they closed it again—the tarmac cracked up.

Krabi province is most pleasant between November and April, the dry months. A bit crowded of late, though. If you don't mind a spot of rain, October is a good month to come—fewer tourists, green and luxuriant flora and fauna.

232

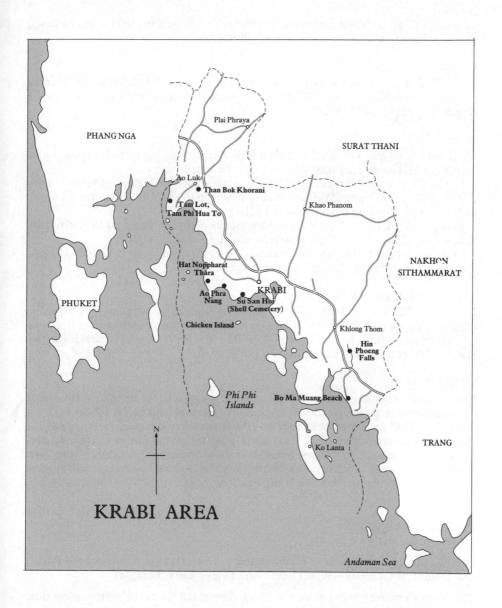

PHANG NGA

Plai Phraya

SURAT THANI

Ao Luk
Than Bok Khorani

Tam Lot,
Tam Phi Hua To

Khao Phanom

NAKHON
SITHAMMARAT

Hat Noppharat
Thara

PHUKET

Ao Phra
Nang

KRABI

Su San Hoi
(Shell Cemetery)

Chicken Island

Khlong Thom

Hin
Phoeng
Falls

Phi Phi
Islands

Bo Ma Muang Beach

N

Ko Lanta

TRANG

KRABI AREA

Andaman Sea

GETTING THERE

By Air
As soon as Krabi airport is completed (which isn't foreseen until 1994 at the earliest), Bangkok Airways will commence operating flights.

By Sea
From Phuket, a number of boats (in season) leave daily for the Phi Phi Islands, continuing on to Krabi. Fare 250B. For further details contact Songserm Travel, 64/2 Rasada Rd, Phuket (tel 216820).

By Bus
All Krabi-bound buses drop off at Talaat Kao village, 5 km out of Krabi town. From here, it's a 5B (20-minute) *songthaew* ride into the town centre.

From Bangkok Southern Terminal, nine buses leave for Krabi daily—five air-con (6, 7, 7.50, 8.30 and 9.30 pm, 290B) and four non-air con (6 and 9.30 pm on the old route, 161B, 7 and 8.30 pm on the new route, 152B).

From Phuket's Phang-Nga Rd terminal, two non air-con buses go to Krabi daily (12.50 and 2.30 pm, 40B). From Hat Yai—see Hat Yai section.

From Krabi (Talaat Kao junction) there are buses every half-hour to Phuket (181 km, 3 hours, 40B) via Phang Nga (88 km, 1¹/₂ hours, 20B).

TOURIST INFORMATION
Krabi town has a small TAT office at the north end of the harbour, with friendly, efficient staff (tel 612740). There is also good English-speaking information from two reliable travel agencies in Krabi town—**Pee Pee Marine Tours** in Uttarakit Rd and **L.R.K. Travel Service**, 11 Khongka Rd (tel 611930).

WHAT TO SEE
Krabi's many attractions require a week or more to appreciate at leisure. Inland sights can be explored by motorbike (hire from Suzuki dealer on Phattana Rd, 180B a day for a small bike, 350B for 250cc) or by tour-bus (book from Pee Pee guest house, 150B). If you want to hit the beaches first, touts meet travellers off the bus in Krabi town and provide free transport to various beach-bungalow operations. Arranging your own transport, you'll need a 15B *songthaew* to **Ao Nang Bay**, followed by a scenic 20B longtail boat ride to **Paiplong** or **Ao Phra Nang** beaches.

Provincial Sights
(by motorbike/tour-bus; full day)

Shell Cemetery – Noppharat Thara Beach – Than Bokkharani National Park and Botanical Gardens – Wat Tham Seua (Tiger Cave Temple)

The **Shell Cemetery** is 19 km west of Krabi Town, and should be visited at low tide. This beach of 75 million-year-old fossilized seashells, forming giant slabs of jutting rock, is a rare phenomenon—something you won't want to miss by turning up when the tide is in. Low tide is also a good time to go shell-hunting on the beach. Though if you're out of luck, a few stalls here sell coral, seashell and mother-of-pearl jewellery, but prices are not cheap.

Noppharat Thara Beach ('Beach of the Nine-Gemmed Stream') is 18 km northwest of Krabi. This lovely 2 km-long stretch of white sands, lined with casuarina trees, is part of a National Marine Park, and there's nothing on it apart from a few private and government bungalows. This is another place to come at low tide—good beachcombing for shells, and you can walk over to a rocky island, about 1 km from the mainland. If you want to make a day of it here (avoid weekends—lots of Thai picnic people), catch one of the regular minibuses from Krabi town. Fare is 20B.

Than Bokkharani National Park lies off Highway 4 between Krabi and Phang Nga. If going there by *songthaew* (15B from Krabi), get off at Ao Luk and walk a short way down Route 4039 to find the park entrance. Ao Luk is 46 km north of Krabi town. **Than Bokkharani** is noted for its magical **Botanical Gardens**, aglow with lush, tropical plants and flowers, and completely enclosed by sheer limestone cliffs. Between November and May, you can swim into an illuminated subterranean cave, leading through to a lagoon fed by a waterfall plummeting down from the mountain. During the rainy season, the gardens are at their most splendid, but the emerald-green waters turn muddy-brown, and swimming can be dangerous. Thais arrive in force at weekends (not a good time to come), but the park is generally quiet during the week.

The jungle hermitage of **Wat Tham Seua** is one of the most famous forest *wats* in South Thailand. Here a community of 120 monks and 130 nuns live a spartan, meditative life in a picturesque setting of ancient caves and dense jungle within a secluded mountain valley. The abbot here, a Thai monk called Achaan Jamnien, was prompted to build this temple by a 'heavenly message' to the effect that Krabi was, in olden times, a self-contained island of great spiritual power. Most of his monks eat just one meal a day. Some don't appear to eat at all. Achaan Jamnien's teaching places great emphasis on fasting and meditation, the aim being to cultivate deep insight into the meaning and workings of life. The bodies of local criminals and road-accident victims make their way to this temple, to help the monks who dissect them gain further 'insights'. The horrid photos of these cadavers are hung all around the *bot* as a grisly reminder to visitors of the consequences of an evil life. The *bot* itself is a low-roofed limestone cave, with a number of tiny grottoes turned into monastic cells (*kutis*). These are very simple affairs, often containing just a sleeping mat, a couple of books, and a light bulb.

Walking down from the main chapel, a steep staircase appears to the left. This leads up to a high ridge overhung by massive limestone crags. Here nuns live in tiny wooden cubicles, while monks sleep out in the open, on pallet beds at the base of the mountain. Past these, a series of caves appears on the left, each wired up with wall switches to enable easy exploration. First there's the famous **Tiger Cave**—named after the stalactite-like projection from the ceiling which resembles a tiger's claw. Beyond this, you'll find **Bow Cave**, with an interior the shape of a stretched bow, and, right next door, **Eel Cave**, where giant eels (with ears) lived till some 10 years ago (low water-levels gradually led to their extinction). The plateau path leads on into the jungle, where hardcore ascetic monks live totally at one with nature in huts buried deep in the rainforest. There are two spectacular 1000-year-old sonpong trees here with massive veined trunks resembling giant ducks' feet. A couple of tips: the monks at this *wat* are not allowed to touch women, or the nuns to touch men. Second, don't embark on the (*very* arduous) climb right to the top of the karst hill (directions on map at foot of the ridge staircase) unless you're fit. It's a killer.

Ao Nang

This is a wide, long bay with clean sands, calm waters and good snorkelling. During October and November, there's even some surf. **Krabi Resort** and **Marine Sports Centre** hire out windsurfers (100B an hour) and snorkelling equipment. Get a group together, and hire out a fishing boat (around 300B per day) to the offshore islands. **Koh Dang** has the best deep-sea coral diving, though you'll also find live coral formations off **Turtle Island** and (behind this) **Chicken Island**. Book your boat in advance—owners tend to hide away their outboard engines at night (so many have been stolen) and often need time to 'find' them again.

WHERE TO STAY   (tel prefix 075)
Expensive
The upmarket **Krabi Resort** (tel 612160), at the top of the beach, has superior bamboo bungalows from 1100B to 1900B (20% discounts from June to September), which you can book at its office in Pattana Rd, Krabi town (tel 611389). Budget travellers favour its marvellous bunk-bed dormitory—for 50B, you get treated just like the rich folks, maid and porter service included. Speciality dishes at the restaurant are Steamed Fish with Soy Sauce (75B), Fillet Mignon Steak (55B) and charcoal-cooked prawns. Don't ask for boiled eggs—one guy did, and got two one-minute eggs, scrambled in a tea-cup before his very eyes. Krabi Resort runs out boat trips (250B for 1–8 people).

Inexpensive
At the bottom of the bay, **Ao Nang Villa** (611129) ('Be with Nature and Simple be with us') has bungalows from 80B (basic), 200B (with bath, shower and towels) and 300B (new luxury jobs, with concrete floors and Western toilets). Boat trips, motorbike rental, and okay restaurant. Boats over to Pai Plong and Ao Phra Nang can be hired here. **Princess Bungalow**, just up the hill-road behind Ao Nang Villa, is a peaceful, laidback operation run by two friendly Westerners, Larry and Phil. They have the best location in the bay and bungalows here (from 80 to 250B) lie in a quiet and natural woodland setting. Good bar cum restaurant, mellow sounds, and bags of atmosphere. Recommended.

Ao Phra Nang

Another nice spot. There are two beaches here, one either side of a tiny promontory circumvented by soaring limestone cliffs. The main beach has **Princess Cave**, a large cleft in the base of one of these mountains. At the start of each fishing season, local men carve wooden *lingams* (phalli) and present them to the resident spirit-goddess. According to legend, this was a heavenly princess who took human form for love of a mortal man. She died giving birth to his child in this cave, and is believed to have protected local

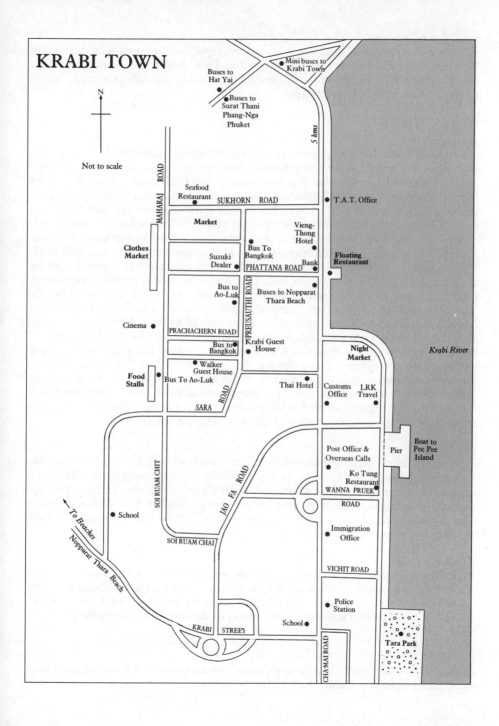

KRABI TOWN

N

Not to scale

Buses to
Hat Yai

Mini buses to
Krabi Town

Buses to
Surat Thani
Phang-Nga
Phuket

5 kms

MAHARAJ ROAD

Seafood
Restaurant

SUKHORN ROAD

T.A.T. Office

Market

Clothes
Market

Vieng-
Thong
Hotel

Bus To
Bangkok

Suzuki
Dealer

PHATTANA ROAD

Bank

Floating
Restaurant

Bus to
Ao-Luk

PREUSAUTHI ROAD

Buses to Nopparat
Thara Beach

Cinema

PRACHACHERN ROAD

Krabi River

Bus to
Bangkok

Krabi Guest
House

Night
Market

Walker
Guest House

Food
Stalls

Bus To Ao-Luk

Thai Hotel

Customs
Office

LRK
Travel

SARA ROAD

SOI RUAM CHIT

JAO FA ROAD

Post Office &
Overseas Calls

Pier

Boat to
Pee Pee
Island

Ko Tung
Restaurant

WANNA PRUEK

ROAD

School

SOI RUAM CHAI

Immigration
Office

To Beaches

Nopparat Thara Beach

VICHIT ROAD

Police
Station

KRABI STREET

School

CHA-MAI ROAD

Tara Park

fishermen ever since. Ao Phra Nang is a very scenic spot, and the crystal-clear waters are excellent for snorkelling. For exercise, try a 1½-hour climb over the mountain (take directions from Cliff Bungalows)—this ends up at a small gully, with a charming inland salt-water lake, prettily ringed by rocks.

WHERE TO STAY

Inexpensive
On the main beach, **Joy Bungalows** have the nicest location, right down by the sea. Like all other operations, accommodation here is pretty simple—a small hut, with mosquito-net, oil-lamp and mattress, for 80B low season, 100–150B high season. Rafi, Joy's friendly manager, has a bar built right into the cliff, and knows all the local island legends. Each island, as he'll tell you, has its own spirit—collectively, they make up a large family (e.g. Phi Phi islands mean 'brother brother'). Behind Joy, in a jungle only cleared of pythons and monkeys three years ago, there's **Cliff Bungalows**. Manager Preecha is a reliable source of information, and does good pancakes and bolognese. Further back is the **Pine** operation, with well-spaced bungalows in a pleasant jungle setting. Food is good and cheap here, and Pine's boat trips to Chicken and Turtle islands (50B per person) are the best value in the bay. They also offer a daily trip over to Phi Phi islands for 100B a head. The other beach bungalow operations, **Phra Nang Place, Phra Nang Village** and **La Cave**, all have huts for 100–250B. **Gift Bungalows**, on the secluded back beach, attract mainly hippies and dopeheads—it's very high on tranquil-lity, and very low on conversation. **Bamboo Pub** regularly has videos and evening barbecues that go on to the early hours. Ao Phra Nang has a few seasonal disad-vantages—vicious sandfleas during the post-monsoon months and severe water shortage in the dry season. It's also under sentence of death, at least as far as the backpacker crowd is concerned. A Bangkok concern has bought up the whole bay and will soon be sweeping away all the cheapie accommodation in favour of a yuppie resort complex.

Pai Plong
This relaxed little cove, a 20-minute walk over the headland from Ao Phra Nang bay, has just one set of bungalows. These lie back off the beach in a shady palm grove, and are run by a friendly family. Basic accommodation (70B), no electricity, but the 25B set dinners—usually fish caught fresh from the sea—get rave reports from the few travellers who've made it here. Pai Plong may be short on action, but the beach is fine—and there are often sightings of dolphin offshore.

RECREATION
Krabi has two cinemas, the **Holiday Theatre** and **Maharaj**, part of which has been converted into a nightclub called the **Mayura**. This club is a scene on a Saturday night (admission 70B, one free drink) and dead as a dodo the rest of the week. Various bars around the night market have live music and dotty dancers—well worth the price of a drink.

SHOPPING
Cheap, bright cotton clothing at the night market, running down Maharaj Rd, and cheap coral/shell jewellery at the nearby **Nid Souvenir Shop**.

WHERE TO STAY   (tel prefix 075)
Moderate–Inexpensive
Krabi town hasn't, as yet, any upmarket accommodation, but it's only a question of time.
What there is, however, is adequate and pocket pleasing. The **Thai Hotel**, 7 Issara Rd
(tel 611122), has fan rooms from 200B, air-con from 400B. It's a clean, comfortable
place with a fair restaurant. The **Vieng Thong**, 155–7 Uttarakit Rd (tel 611288), is a
reasonable fall-back, with rooms for 250B (fan) and 600B (air-con). The **New Hotel**,
Phattana Rd (tel 611545), is an old hotel, with 150B fan-cooled rooms that could do with
a scrub and a lick of paint. **Krabi Guest House**, in Isara Rd, is a reasonable alternative,
with 80B rooms and travel service. The best deal of all though, is **Rong's** at 17 Maharaj
Rd, a short five-minute stroll out of town. 'Absolutely Worth a Walk' is its motto, and it
is. Run by a gentlemanly local science teacher, this is an incredibly clean and relaxing
place, with jungle-setting, twin-bedded rooms from 100B, communal kitchen (you can
cook your own food) and tiled bathroom, free bicycles, and homely family-style atmosphere. Recommended.

EATING OUT
Thai Hotel's **Parkway Café** is tops for Western cuisine (especially the 60B 'Sizzling
Sirloin Steak') and offers soothing live music from 12 noon to 2 pm, from 8 pm to
1.30 am. Near the Thai Hotel **Rim Nam** is a popular little place serving inexpensive
Thai dishes. **Vieng Thong** also has a decent restaurant, with live Thai music nightly.
For seafood, locals rave about **Kotung** restaurant, down by the pier—things to try here
include *tom yam kung*, crab balls, and fresh prawns. Cheap Thai snacks and great fruit are
sold down at the night market. Krabi town is full of 'tourist information centres' which
are really ice-cream parlours or breakfast places. **Walker Pub and Guest House** at
34–36 Ruenruedee Rd (tel 612756), near the Maharaj cinema, is where travellers stay
and gather in the evening to watch videos, or add to the graffiti that adorn the walls. They
serve cheap Thai and western food, and have 150–200B rooms.

KOH PHI PHI

The twin enchanted islands of Phi Phi Don and Phi Phi Ley lie 40 km offshore from
Krabi, in the Andaman Sea. Beautiful beaches, colourful marine life, banks of coral reef
and magnificent scenery combine to make Phi Phi just about the best thing in the south
of Thailand. Gliding in by boat, escorted by schools of flying fish and dolphin, is like
arriving on Treasure island. Phi Phi Don, famous for its stunning white-sand beaches
and excellent snorkelling, is relatively flat. Most of this island is national park territory, so
all bungalow accommodation is centred round Ton Sai and Lo Da Ram, the twin
crescent bays of the narrow isthmus which connect the two main lands. Phi Phi Ley, the
smaller island, is mainly sheer cliffs, inhabited only by the flocks of long-tailed swallows
who live on their heights. A few courageous locals regularly risk death climbing precarious bamboo ladders to collect birds' nests. The nests of Phi Phi Ley are highly prized for
their medicinal qualities, and sell to Chinese restaurants in Thailand, Singapore, Hong
Kong and Europe for quite fantastic prices. The Chinese believe that because Phi Phi

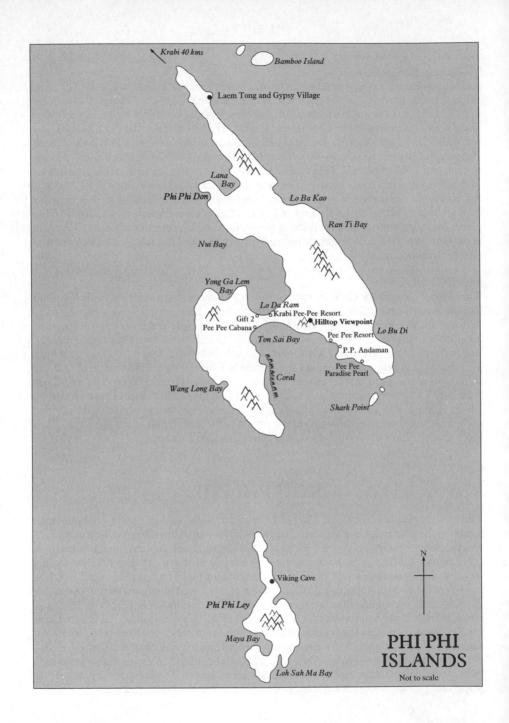

Krabi 40 kms

Bamboo Island

Laem Tong and Gypsy Village

Lana
Bay

Phi Phi Don

Lo Ba Kao

Ran Ti Bay

Nui Bay

*Yong Ga Lem
Bay*

Lo Da Ram
Krabi Pee-Pee Resort

Gift 2
Hilltop Viewpoint

Pee Pee Cabana

Pee Pee Resort

Ton Sai Bay

Lo Bu Di

P.P. Andaman

Pee Pee
Paradise Pearl

Coral

Wang Long Bay

Shark Point

N

Phi Phi Ley

Viking Cave

Maya Bay

PHI PHI
ISLANDS

Not to scale

Loh Sah Ma Bay

swallows live at such high altitudes, they can 'drink water from the sky'. When the birds expel (vomit) this heavenly elixir, it's in the form of near-translucent noodles ('king food' to the Chinese) which hardens when exposed to air, to form the nests. The best nests are made from the high-grade white vomit of young birds (yuk), and sell for up to 10,000B a kilo. Low-grade, or black vomit, nests are collected from old birds, and are very cheap. They are apparently good for little else except curing 'loss of appetite'.

Phi Phi has just been discovered by tourism—new bungalow operations are setting up shop all the time. Every weekend, boatloads of Japanese tourists from Phuket hit the beaches. During the high season (January to March) shortages of food, water and accommodation often mean having to sleep on the beach, bathe in the sea, and live on bananas and coconuts. The best months to come, if you don't mind a little rain, are October and November.

A good alternative to Phi Phi, especially during the overcrowded high season, is nearby **Jum Island**. Good beaches, nice scenery, and, most importantly, hardly any people. The clean, friendly **Jum Island Resort** (tel 611541) has bungalows from 50 to 250B, many of them with scenic views. To book, contact Pee Pee Marine Tours, Krabi town.

GETTING THERE
From Krabi town, boats run out to Phi Phi island from early October through to May. Boats leave between 9 am and 9.30 pm, and at 2.30 pm, depending on the tide. They are often full, so you're well advised to advance-book. The 2½-hour trip costs 100B, and tickets are sold at Krabi Tours and Travel, and Pee Pee Marine Travel. Marine Travel, near Thai Farmers Bank, offers the best deal—they book you onto a larger boat, with life jackets, lots of room, and insurance for all passengers.

From Phi Phi Don, boats back to Krabi leave from the Cabana pier and from Gift 2 bungalows. Boats to Phuket (at least two daily) also leave from the Cabana pier.

WHAT TO SEE
The big thing to do on Phi Phi is the boat-trip round the islands. For many, this is the highlight of their whole Thailand holiday. Various bungalow operations—notably Andaman and Pee Pee Resort—offer half and full-day boat excursions, and charge 70 or 100B per person. Bring your own snorkelling gear for this trip—equipment supplied is poor. You'll also need your camera, and lots of film. The scenery is out of this world.

From the Don, boats go over to Phi Phi Ley and drop in on its **Viking Cave**—a huge indoor amphitheatre of surreal limestone pillars and plateaus. The cave-drawings of 'Viking ships' are actually quite recent daubings of Portuguese galleons and Chinese junks. Knowing this makes it far easier to refuse the 10B 'admission charge' scam operated by local youths. Hugging the base of soaring cliffs, their sheer faces dripping with limestone cascades, boats move on to **Maya Bay**, a beautifully secluded lagoon with excellent live coral. There's a stop for swimming and snorkelling here, then it's back to Phi Phi Don for **Shark Point**—where you can really swim with the shark. Don't worry—these are small black-finned Leopard Shark, which live mainly on crab, not tourists. At the top of the Don, beyond the sea-gypsy village at **Laem Tong**, you'll come to **Bamboo Island**. This is the best undersea location at Phi Phi. The water's so clear here, you need only lean over the side of the boat for a magical introduction to a wonderland of technicolour coral and exotic fish.

241

Back on Don, you can stroll down to the bottom of Tonsai Bay—below Cabana Bungalows—for superb snorkelling. There is over a kilometre of live coral here, running right up to the mouth of the bay. Look out for barracuda, pike, moray eel and (don't touch!) sea-snake. Snorkelling equipment can be hired out from Pee-Pee Cabana or from Mr Jerry just below Pee-Pee Resort. Jerry charges 40B a day for snorkel hire. He also rents out rather tacky scuba equipment at 1500B a day. Better scuba-diving gear is obtainable from the Swedish guy up at Lemhin bungalows, just above Pee-Pee Andaman.

Most people are content with lazing on the silvery sands, and bathing in the calm emerald-green waters. But some wind down with a traditional Thai beach massage. A delightful no-nonsense lady called Suparporn patrols up and down between Andaman and Cabana beaches, offering superior rubdowns for 50B an hour. 'But no Number Ones!', she firmly informs male customers, 'I am respectable married lady!'

A recommended early-morning walk is up to the hilltop **Viewpoint** on the Don mainland. It's an arduous 40-minute climb so you'll need good walking shoes. You're also advised to acquire a local guide—the path up starts from between Andaman and Pee-Pee Resort, but it's easy to get lost. Our bungalow supplied us with a diminutive local lad, wearing enormous wellington boots, who took us up for 5B a head. At the top, enjoy spectacular views down over the twin half-moon bays of the Don. On a clear day, you can see across to Phi Phi Ley, and even over to Phuket.

From the Cabana pier, motorized longboats transport people from beach to beach (15B a trip). Near the Cabana, there's the island's single supply shop—the only place that sells Mekong whisky and mosquito repellent.

WHERE TO STAY AND EATING OUT (tel prefix 075)

Expensive
Pee Pee International Resort (tel 214297) at Cape Laem Thong is one of the latest additions to the island's accommodation. It has 120 luxury rooms for 2000–3500B, pool and restaurant.

242

Moderate–Inexpensive

In Ton Sai bay, **Pee Pee Cabana** (tel 611496) has excellent bungalows (nice 4-person bamboo huts at 550–1200B) but the worst location, right next to the busy, noisy boat jetty. It has a huge restaurant—the **Maya Kitchen**. The Cabana also offers 'choice of Western and oriental toilets' and the food and facilities here are fine.

The back bay, behind Cabana, is less clean than Tonsai, but quieter. Stay here at **Gift 2** (basic 70B sheds) or **Krabi Pee Pee Resort** (tel 612188) with tasteful, well-spaced bungalows at 500–600B.

Further up Ton Sai Bay (a boat-ride from Cabana, or a 15-minute hike east up the beach from the pier) are currently the Don's two best operations. **Pee Pee Resort** is new, clean and friendly, with 200B bungalows (concrete floored) right on the beach, and 100B ones set back from it. **Andaman Inn** is the pioneer outfit, and still owns much of the land on the Don. Bungalows here are 60B to 180B, and face onto a lovely stretch of beach. Andaman has good food and atmosphere, and is extremely popular. Beyond it—a 20-minute walk over the cliffs—there's Long Beach. This has the best swimming on the island—at low tide, it's the only beach where bathers aren't left stranded in the shallows. Stay at **Paradise Pearl** bungalows—these are 150B to 300B and have good bathrooms. The Pearl's restaurant is a favourite evening hangout spot, and does marvellous seafood.

HAT YAI

Hat Yai, the dynamic commercial and entertainment centre of the Deep South, started life as a tiny railway junction a few kilometres inside Thailand from the Malay border. Packed full of nightclubs, restaurants, massage parlours, gambling dens and vibrant bazaars, its cheap shopping and wild nightlife now attract over half a million tourists each year—most of them Malaysians who see Hat Yai as the 'one and only fun town' between Bangkok (1298 km north) and Singapore. The town's border situation makes it a real melting-pot of different peoples—mainly Thai, Malay and Chinese—any one of which will be holding a boisterous, colourful street festival any day of the week. Despite frenetic and noisy traffic, Hat Yai is a clean place with a contagiously optimistic atmosphere. Foreign visitors passing through on their way north from Malaysia, or hopping over the border to nearby Pedang Besar to obtain visa extensions for Thailand, often come for the day—and end up staying a week. Hat Yai is also a useful base from which to jump off to nearby Songkhla (a good day-trip), or to other southern centres such as Krabi, Phuket and Koh Samui.

If you're into spectator sports, time your visit for one of Hat Yai's famous Bullfighting Contests. These take place on the first Sunday of every month—between 10.30 am and 6 pm—at the old Stadium on Suppasarn Rangsan Rd, near the Prince of Songkhla University. This is a fun event, with bull fighting bull (there is no matador involved) until one retires to fight another day. You pay 50B per fight, or 200B to stay all day.

GETTING THERE

By Air

Thai Airways fly to Hat Yai from Bangkok at least four times daily. The fare is 2280B, and the flight time is 1 hour 15 minutes. You can also fly to Hat Yai from Phuket.

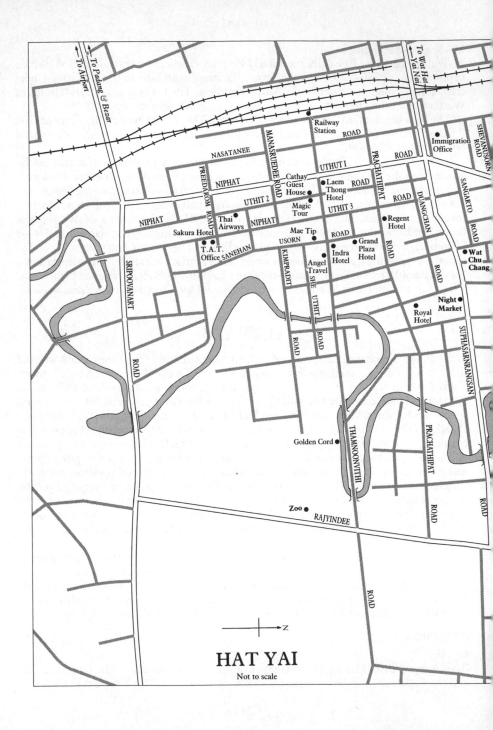

HAT YAI

Not to scale

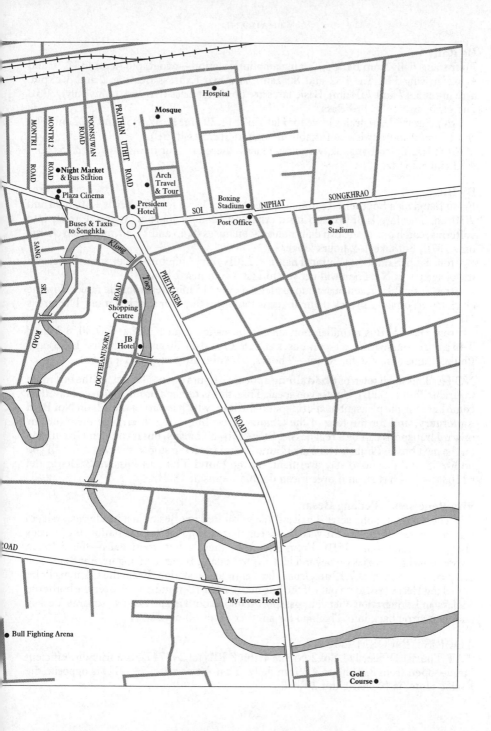

By Rail

Four trains daily from Bangkok's Hualamphong station—two Rapid (leaving 12.30 and 4 pm, arriving Hat Yai 4.32 and 8.50 am), and two Express (leaving 2 and 3.15 pm, arriving at 5.47 and 7.04 am). Basic fares are 664B 1st class (Express trains only), 333B 2nd class, and 169B 3rd class.

From Surat Thani, trains leave for Hat Yai at 11.29 pm, 12.37, 1.52 and 3.22 am. The short 5-hour journey is comfortable enough in 3rd class (75B).

From Hat Yai to Bangkok (via Surat Thani), there are four trains daily, at 2.15, 2.55, 4.53 and 5.15 pm.

By Bus

From Bangkok's Southern Terminal, air-con buses leave for Hat Yai at 4.30, 6.30 and 7.30 pm. The fare is 339B, and it's a crippling 14-hour journey. If you're really into suffering, catch one of the two daily non air-con buses (9.45 and 11.50 pm) which charge only 187B, but take 1–2 hours longer.

From Koh Samui (via Surat Thani), a 220B ferry/minibus ticket from Songserm travel agency in Na Thon will get you to Hat Yai in just 7 hours.

From Songkhla, green buses run to Hat Yai every 15 minutes from the rank below the clock tower; or you can pick them up (taxis too) from the Municipal Market. The fare is 7B.

From Hat Yai Bus terminal, non air-con buses leave for Krabi at 5, 7.30, 8.30 and 9.45 am (6 hours, 75B), air-con buses at 8, 9.30 and 11.30 am (4–5 hours, 125B) and Phuket (same times as for Krabi—9 hours, 91B non air-con, 154B air-con).

NOTE: The small town of **Phattallung** appears 2 hours out of Hat Yai, on the bus route to Krabi/Phuket (22B). Unless you speak Thai, this is rather a problem place. Travellers come here for the pleasant boat-trip round the lake, which is part of the **Thala Noi Bird Sanctuary**, and for the tour of the famous caves, but trying to arrange them (or any onward transport) can be a real hassle. Stop off by all means, but if you don't like it, hop on the next bus to Phuket, Hat Yai or Surat Thani from the stop at the post office. If you do like it, and decide to stay overnight, try the **Hotel Thai**, 14 Dissara-Sakharin (tel 611636)—this has clean if overpriced double rooms at 180B.

Visa Renewals – Pedang Besar

Travellers with double-entry Thailand visas visit Pedang Besar, just inside Malaysia, to start off the second half of the visa. Buses run there from Hat Yai bus station, the journey taking one hour (fare 15B). From Bangkok, there's one train daily—the 3.15 pm Express—which carries on beyond Hat Yai to Pedang Besar, arriving here at 8 am. You can pick this train up at 7.19 am, from Hat Yai Junction station. From the Customs Point at Pedang Besar (ask to be put off the bus here), it's a 10-minute walk over the border to Malaysian Immigration. Get your passport stamped both *in* and *out* (two separate desks), and then stroll back into Thailand for another 30 or 60 days stay.

TOURIST INFORMATION

TAT Tourist Office, 1/1 Soi 2 Niphat Uthit 3 Rd (tel 243747), is a friendly, efficient outfit—open from 8.30 am to 4.30 pm daily. Thai Airways (tel 243711) is opposite the Pacific Hotel in Niphat Uthit 2 Road.

Travel agents—useful for transport to Bangkok, Krabi/Phuket, and Koh Samui, include **Magic Tour**, c/o Cathay Hotel (tel 234535) and **Asia Tours**, 85 Niphat Uthit 2 Rd, opposite the Metro Hotel (tel 232147). Both are reliable, and also help with local sightseeing.

WHAT TO SEE

People come to Hat Yai for shopping and recreation, not to see sights. If the two suggested tours aren't enough, there's a pleasant walk down by the riverside to the south of town. Start at the bridge in Thamnoonvithi Rd, and follow the road looping south-west, until you re-enter town at the bridge leading up Niphat Uthit 3 Road. The river's a bit putrid, but there's much local colour—cows and kids, villages and farms—worth photographing.

Most in-town action, especially at night, centres round Niphat Uthit 1, 2 and 3, and their intersecting roads. Most people get around by foot, but there are *songthaews* if you need them. Their standard charge is 4B.

Wat Hat Yai Nai
(by *songthaew*, 2–3 hours)

This *wat* is located a few kilometres out of town, down Soi 26 Phetkasem Rd. *Songthaews* go there from the town centre for a 5B fare. **Wat Hat Yai Nai** is a real curiosity—there's an enormous reclining Buddha here, which measures 35 metres long, 15 metres high, and 10 metres wide, recently restored and wearing a big ruby-lipped smile. Beneath it is the subterranean mausoleum cum souvenir shop, where a wily old monk lassoes tourists with wrist cords and invites donations. Elsewhere in the compound, there are many other ways of spending money and making merit—including 8B coconuts and 10B tiles for the new *bot* roof (while stocks last). There's a wonderfully tacky 'merry-go-round' of plaster monks with begging bowls, and an ebullient community of real monks who pounce on *farang* visitors with joyful cries of 'Hey, you!' This is a temple with a difference—lots of jollity and good energy.

Thai Southern Cultural Village
(by *songthaew*; half-day)

This is a fairly typical Thai attempt at 'packaged culture', rather similar to Bangkok's Rose Garden Resort. The 'village' is a large picnic park, with a small zoo (disgruntled eagles, green monkeys, exotic birds etc), located some 3 km northeast of Hat Yai. The culture shows run between 4 and 5.30 pm, Wednesday to Sunday, and the cost of admission (140B, bookable from several travel agencies in town) should include transport there and back. If for any reason it doesn't, you'll have to fork out 20B each way for a *songthaew*. The show ties together a number of things—fingernail dances, wedding ceremonies, Thai boxing, sword-fighting etc.—which, if in the south for only a short time, you might not otherwise see. A couple of turns, like the coconut-shell dance and the cock-fighting, are worth getting a front seat for.

NIGHTLIFE

Hat Yai is a city of the night. After dark, the whole town is one huge, bustling bazaar, overladen with the heady aromas of fragrant frangipani, sizzling *kai yang*, and *tuk-tuk* exhaust fumes. Stalls around the Regent Hotel and Uthit 3 Road are still serving the south's most delectable street food at 1 am. Night-time Hat Yai is also a continual round of nightclubs, coffee shops, bars, bowling alleys, video houses and cinemas and discos. Every large hotel has its 'Ancient Massage' parlour, usually packed out with rich Malays. For a good straight massage, you're probably safest at the Indra and Sakura hotels, which charge a reasonable 100B an hour. There are several places offering good live music and early-evening cocktails. The **J.B. Hotel** is a goodie—expensive drinks (100B), but a great disco and restaurant. The **My House Hotel**, on the road leading out to Songkhla, has the best live singers (plus popular cocktail lounge), and the **Washington Café**, attached to King's Hotel, is a good safe place for the unattached male on the loose—with no-hassle hostesses and live music till 1 am. If you can get a group together, make a night of it at the **Hollywood Nightclub**, opposite Angel Travel in Thamnoonvithi Road. This has a large dance floor, exciting laser show, live band (playing good American copy songs) and a hot DJ pumping out the best in current Thai rap music. Drinks are a bit pricey, but it's fun. Like many similar clubs, the Hollywood opens at 9 pm and rocks on until midnight during the week, and until 1 am on Fridays, Saturdays and Sundays.

The **Post Laser Disc**, opposite the Hollywood, provides more sedate entertainment—this is a cosy little video parlour, showing a selection of popular English-language films from 12 noon to 2 am daily. It is a perfect escape from the heat and traffic, and serves beer and snacks. The **Colisium** cinema in Prachatipat Rd has 'original soundtrack rooms' where you can view films in English before they're dubbed over for Thai audiences.

SHOPPING

Full of cheap goods smuggled in from Singapore, Hat Yai has been dubbed the 'poor man's Hong Kong'. At the large **Santisuk Market**, well known as the biggest open black market in Thailand, you can find videos, watches, radios and hi-fi equipment at knock-down prices—e.g. a high-grade portable stereo cassette player, with detachable speakers, for just 1000B. There's also a busy trade in leatherware, batik fabrics, dress materials and numerous other low-priced export or imported goods.

The large shopping area opposite the Chalerm Thai cinema, at the top of Niphat Uthit 2 Rd, is widely considered the best market for fashion clothes in the country—shirts from 90B, summery dresses from 150B—especially if you go hunting amongst the many footpath stalls after dark. For specific electronic bargains—cheap cameras, personal stereos, TVs—try the row of shops alongside the Jomdi Hotel in Niphat Uthit 3. General shopping is good at the **Diana** department store.

WHERE TO STAY   (tel prefix 074)

Expensive

There are dozens of high-class hotels, mostly catering to rich Malaysians and Singaporeans. If coming for the weekend, you'll need to advance-book.

The **J.B. Hotel**, 99 Jootee-Anusorn Rd (tel 234300; tx 62113 JBH TL) is Hat Yai's finest, with all 5-star comforts and air-con rooms for only 800–1200B.

Moderate

Two other good bets in the top range are the **Regency**, 23 Prachathipat Rd (tel 245454;

tx 62195), with plush twin-bedded rooms for 800B, and the **Indra**, 94 Thamnoonvithi Rd (tel 243277), offering rooms from 600B. The Regency has an overseas phone service, and the Indra a popular coffee-house with video and snooker. There are good mentions too, for the **Montien**, 120–124 Niphat Uthit 1 Rd (tel 245399). Rooms here start at 506B. Other good moderately-priced hotels include **King's**, 126–8 Niphat Uthit 1 Rd (tel 243966), **Metro**, 82 Niphat Uthit 2 Rd (tel 244422), **Asian**, 55 Niphat Uthit 3 Rd (tel 245455), **Yong Dee**, 99 Niphat Uthit 3 Rd (tel 234350), **Sakol**, 47–48 Sanehusorn Rd (tel 245256) and **Laemthong**, 46 Thamnoonvithi Rd (tel 244433—which boasts 'the best coffee in Brazil'). All the above have good twin-bedded rooms for around 160–250B (fan) and 350–450B (air-con), and most offer 20% discounts on weekdays, provided you bargain for them. The **Central Sukhonta** on Sanehan Usorn Rd (tel 243999) is excellent value at around 400B for an air-con double, and its **Jade Room** coffee shop and **Zodiac** disco are very popular.

Inexpensive
The old budget favourite, the **Cathay Guest House** at the corner of Thamnoonvithi and Niphat Uthit 2 (tel 243815), has gone into steep decline. It still has a good noticeboard, and still does the cheapest beer and breakfasts in town, but rooms are dirty and way overpriced at 120B single, 180B double. Friendly staff often shout discounts if you walk away (as many do). The nearby **Prince Hotel**, 138/2–3 Thamnoonvithi Rd (tel 243160), is a much better deal—clean rooms here, with bath and balcony, for 150B single, 300B double air-con.

EATING OUT
The local mix of Thai, Chinese, Muslim and Malay peoples results in an exciting and varied cuisine. Hat Yai is close enough to the fishing port of Songkhla to provide some pretty choice seafood too. Western-style food is on offer at numerous coffee shops, fast-food joints, and hotel restaurants.

For seafood, try **Mae Tip II** restaurant, 190 Niphat Uthit 3 Rd. Open from 10.30 am to 10 pm, this has a choice of outdoor garden or indoor air-con dining. Specialities include Songkhla steamed gray mullet with sour plum (60–90B), famous Pomfret fish with chilli, pepper or garlic (100B), and less spicy-hot dishes like roasted clam or prawn, or sweet and sour sea bass (both 40B). At the **Pata Food Centre**, c/o Kosit Hotel, 199 Niphat Uthit 2 Rd, you can select your seafood from the tank. Popular eats here are raw oysters, baked crab claws, shark fin soup and (for less than 60B) the local favourite, a spicy shrimp soup called *tom yam goong*. Also recommended is **South Thai Bird's Nest Restaurant**, diagonally opposite the Sukhonta Hotel in Sanehan Usorn Rd. At this one, you can either play safe with dishes like shark fin soup (200B) or steamed/baked crab, cooked Hong Kong-style (i.e. steamed, then mixed with soya bean sauce, Chinese mushrooms and ginger), or you venture into unknown territory with steamed sea leech ('pure protein!') in red gravy. In a town like Hat Yai, where locals drink cobra blood and eat snake meat, anything goes. The South Thai is also supposed to be one of the best places to sample bird's nest soup. This is mixed in with the dark meat of 'black chicken' (a fowl only found in Hat Yai area), which is supposed to have magical health-giving properties. Diners tend to feel incredibly healthy afterwards or (as soon as they discover what bird's nests are made out of) incredibly ill. A short walk from the J.B. Hotel, **Best**

Kitchen, 53–55 Jootee Anusorn Rd, deserves its name and its many visitors both *farangs* and locals, for its excellent and extensive Thai menu. The speciality is tiger prawns, straight from the tank. A full-blown meal will cost only 300B. **Hong Kong**, in the Lee Gardens Hotel on Lee Pattana Rd, is the best Chinese restaurant in Hat Yai. As in most Chinese restaurants, prices are higher—count on 500B for a full dinner.

Muslim food is good at the **Ruby**, 59/3 Rattakan Rd, serving Malaysian, Pakistani, Indian and Thai favourites. Quickie fare—from hamburgers to Japanese tempura— can be had at the **Noodle Garden**, opposite Odean Shopping Mall in Sanehusorn Rd. The **Boat Bakery**, opposite Kosit Hotel in Niphat Uthit 2, serves quality European-style food at around 150B. All in all, you're not going to starve in Hat Yai.

SONGKHLA

Once a powerful Srivijaya trading port, Songkhla is now a sleepy little resort-town with a large fishing community and a nice beach. Situated on a tiny peninsula between the Gulf of Thailand and a saltwater inland sea called Songkhla Lake, this is a relaxed mini-city (927 km from Bangkok) with Chinese Portuguese-style houses and buildings (a reflection of early settlers), a hybrid cuisine (from the present Thai–Chinese population), a fine National Museum, and some of the best seafood in Thailand.

It's now believed by archaeologists that the area of Songkhla flourished as long ago as the 8th century AD. Both the present centres of southern civilization, Hat Yai and Songkhla, are known to be of very recent origin. The earlier centres, located in the area of Sathing Phra (40 km north of Songkhla), were forced south by commerce. This migration began as early as 1000 years ago, drifting slowly down to the tip of the peninsula at the north side of Songkhla about 150 years ago. At this point, the old town of Songkhla (Singhorat) which had been founded on the Khao Dang Hill at Ko Yo (probably in the early Ayutthaya period by the Muslim Sultan Suleiman) was abandoned.

The prosperity of the province was ushered in by its first governor, a Chinese merchant called Yieng Hoa, who began his career in modest fashion, collecting birds' nests at the offshore islands of Koh Si and Koh Ha. His family held the governorship of 'new' Songkhla city for the next 129 years. During this period, the port shrugged off its earlier disreputable image as a medieval pirate stronghold and became a major trade centre—sending out mainly rubber and tin to China and India, receiving in return beautiful pottery and ceramics. Examples of these, and other priceless art works, are presently housed in Songkhla National Museum.

GETTING THERE
From Hat Yai bus terminal buses leave for Songkhla every 15 minutes or so. The 26 km journey takes 30 minutes, and the fare is 7B. If there's a group of you, it's worth getting a shared taxi (12B per person) from Hat Yai. Buses back to Hat Yai leave from Songkhla's Municipal Market, and also from below the clock tower in Ramwithi Rd.

TOURIST INFORMATION
The nearest tourist office is at Hat Yai. For local information contact staff at the National Museum.

There's a useful travel agency at the Choke Dee Hotel, Vichiangchom Rd. It runs three air-con buses to Bangkok daily—fare 300B, journey time 13 hours.

WHAT TO SEE

Songkhla is a small, quiet and airy town—you can get around by foot, or pay 5B for short-distance cycle-rickshaw rides. Somnolent motorcyclists hang out at the Queen Hotel, offering 50B return trips to the great white *chedi* on **Khao Noi Hill**, but you don't really need them. You can walk up to this ancient *chedi* (reconstructed by Rama V) in 20 minutes from the museum. Nice views at the top. From the pier below the museum, fishing boats put out to **Yoh Island**, where locals collect birds' nests for soup. Ferries also run across the river to the hill-top city of Old Songkhla, with its crumbling Ayutthayan fortress, famous Black Pagoda, and spectacular aerial views of the whole province. If you're going there, take directions from the museum curator—you'll need them.

The pleasant **Samila Beach**, with its casuarina groves and seafood restaurants, is a 10B *songthaew* ride from the town centre. There's a famous mermaid on the point, and from the white-sand beach you can look over to offshore **Cat and Mouse Islands**, named after their respective shapes. Swimming is rather poor, but there are water-skis, sailboats, catamarans and surfboards for hire below the Samili Hotel. Weekends are busy at Samila beach—this is when the Thais come for picnics. Back in town, the **Waterfront** is worth a visit—this is where all the fishing boats unload their catches, and it's a constant hum of activity. The air hums a bit too—visitors don't linger long here. Walking away from the waterfront, down Nakhorn North Rd, there are many old Chinese, Portuguese and Muslim buildings to be seen. This street retains a lot of original Songkhla architecture.

National Museum–Wat Machimawat
(on foot, by *songthaew*; half day)

The entrance to the **National Museum** is opposite the Queen Hotel on Traiburi Rd. Admission is 10B, and it's open 9 am–12 pm and 1–4 pm, Wednesday to Sunday.

Converted from the Old Governor's Palace built in 1878, the museum is an elegant Chinese mansion housing a fabulous collection of Chinese and Thai art treasures—handcarved doors and screens, lacquered furniture (with mother of pearl inlay), Sino-Thai *Bencharong* (five colours) pottery etc. Upstairs, there is King Mongkut's bed, a fine black-stone Vishnu recovered from Sathing Phra, and a Burmese-style Buddha sunning itself on the balcony. Elsewhere, interesting displays of shadow puppets, wooden lintels, abbots' pulpits and garudas. Also, a Dutch cannon, a brace of WWII bicycles (donated by local policemen) and some wooden-dog coconut grinders. The museum has exhibits from all seven provinces of southern Thailand, and is well-labelled in English throughout.

Wat Matchimawat is off Saiburi Rd, to the south of town—a 6B *songthaew* ride from the museum. This is the oldest and the most important *wat* in Songkhla. The *bot* is modelled on that at Wat Phra Keo (Bangkok) and contains beautiful murals, depicting lively scenes of 19th-century Songkhla life and various *jakarta* stories. The venerated marble Buddha within the chapel is 150 years old, and was commissioned by Rama III. If

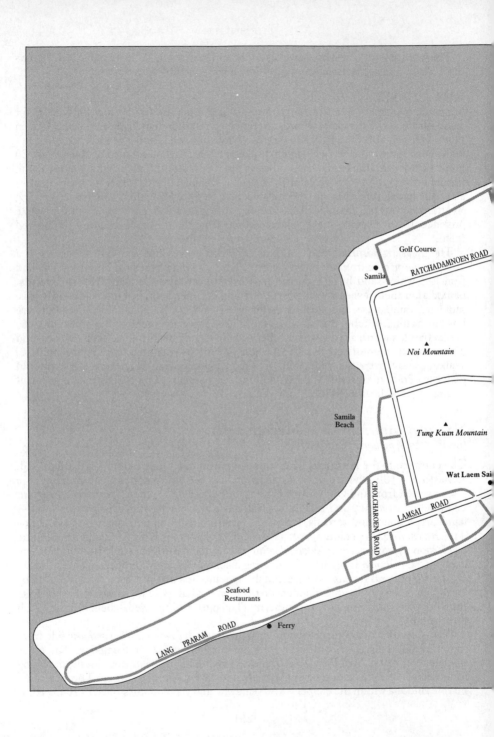

Golf Course

RATCHADAMNOEN ROAD

Samila

Noi Mountain

Samila
Beach

Tung Kuan Mountain

Wat Laem Sai

CHOLCHAROEN ROAD

LAMSAI ROAD

Seafood
Restaurants

LANG PRARAM ROAD

Ferry

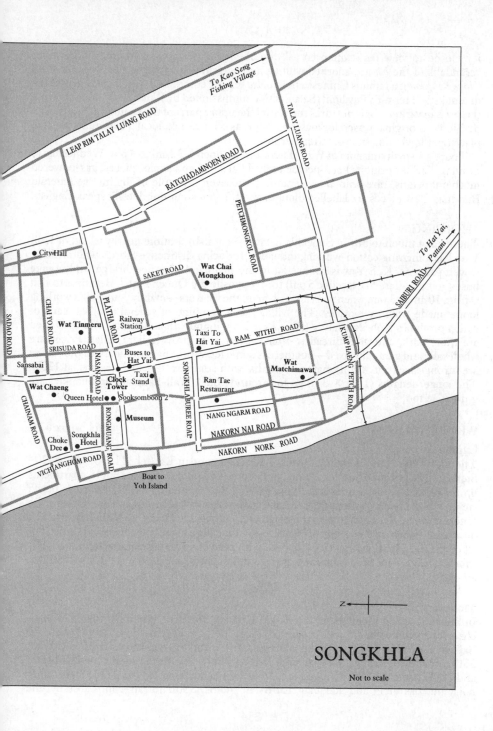

SONGKHLA

Not to scale

it's closed to view (as it often is) ask the abbot for permission to enter. The outer verandahs of the *bot* are adorned with stone bas-reliefs illustrating the *Romance of the Three Kingdoms*, a famous Chinese epic. In the temple compound, you'll come across the quaint little 'Hermit's Pavilion' (Sala Rishi) commissioned by Rama IV. Murals showing the *rishis* in various yogic postures run round the upper parts of the ceiling and walls. The pavilion was originally used for massage. Now, as often as not, local Thai youths use it to play superbowl mini-snooker with marbles.

There's a small museum at Wat Matchimawat, open 8.30 am to 4 pm, Wednesday to Sunday. Various exhibits here include early Thai stone and stucco pieces, gas-powered mechanical fans, rare *bencharong* ceramics, and even a couple of diminutive emerald Buddhas. Few pieces are labelled though, and the monk curator doesn't speak English.

SHOPPING

There's not much to buy in Songkhla itself (except fish), but the nearby island of **Koh Yaw** has a thriving cotton-weaving industry producing distinctive fabrics with intricate woven patterns. Koh Yaw is connected to the mainland by a new bridge, and orange buses go there (fare 5B, last one 5 pm) from opposite the Queen Hotel. Best time to visit is from 10 am to 3 pm, when you can drop in on the weavers—mainly young girls working looms made from ex-bicycles. The 'village' is a combine of several families, each of which produces Koh Yaw fabric (*Phaa Kaw Yaw*) in individual designs. The dyes used are quite dark, and gold thread is often woven in to provide light relief. Prices are wholesale, and generally fixed—but there is some leeway for bargaining. Nice purchases are sarong-size (6 ft × 3 ft) material lengths, with complex 'tapestry' designs, at 120B. The longer lengths (12 ft × 3 ft) go for around 160B. Wall-hangings and hankies are quite nice too.

WHERE TO STAY   (tel prefix 074)

Expensive
The high-class **Samila Beach Hotel**, 1 Ratchadamnoen Rd (tel 311310–4; tx 64204 Samila TH), has good beach location, golf course and pool, rooms for 800B, apartments up to 2000B. Some apartments (Nos. 111–113, 211, and 311–312) have the beach views. Novel topiary gardens ('the result of painstaking tree-bendings') are opposite the hotel entrance. Six kilometres to the north of Songkhla are **Had Gao Villa** (tel 331221), on a lovely beach on the lagoon of Hat Kaew. Come here if you want peace and quiet, but all comforts. The hotel is well equipped, with pool and two restaurants, and the lobby sports a 1920s American limousine. Rates for bungalows are as low as 400B, 1000B for air-con doubles.

Moderate
In this bracket I'd recommend the **Royal Crown**, 38 Chai Namm Rd (tel 312174)—cheerful rooms with TV and fridge for 450B, de luxe at 650–750B; the **Queen**, 20 Saiburi Rd (tel 313072), with fan rooms at 250B, and air-con rooms (with TV) from 350B; or the **Saensabai**, 1 Petchkeree Rd (tel 311106), offering rooms for 250B (fan) and 300B (air-con). The **Choke Dee**, 14–19 Vichiangchom Rd (tel 311158), is rather noisy but has quiet and adequate 150B fan rooms, 350B for air-con. Close by, the

Songkhla, 68–70 Vichiangchom Rd (tel 313505) gives free soap, towel and bottled water with each room (150B fan, 300B air-con) and is friendly. Adjoining it, there's a homely little Thai restaurant with lots of character.

EATING OUT

Try Songkhla's famous seafood up at Samila Beach. Here, there are several beachside restaurants—notably **Nai Wan** which does excellent *tom yum* soup with prawns and curried fried crab, at around 100B a head. **The Seven Sisters** on Rajadamri Rd is no fanciful name—seven sisters run it, and well. They serve imaginatively prepared Thai seafood dishes (60–80B) that will have you smacking your lips. In town, there's the **Raan Ahaan Tae** restaurant on Nang Ngam Rd, serving Songkhla's renowned *yum ma-muang*—a salad made from thin-sliced green mango, blended with dried shrimps and other tangy items. Reliable main courses include spicy fried squid and curried crab claws. In the same road, **Kok Thai** is another Thai favourite, serving, along with its traditional fare, such unusual items as fried frogs and beef tongue. If you want late-night drinks, there's a cheap open-air restaurant—supplying cheap beer and Thai food till midnight—down Jana Rd, near Queen Hotel. During the day, cheap Thai–Chinese–Muslim fare can be found at the large, interesting town market off Vichiangchom Rd.

LANGUAGE

In a country like Thailand, where little English is spoken (except in Bangkok and major tourist centres), it makes sense to pick up some of the local language. With a small stock of Thai phrases under your belt, shopping, bargaining, getting round town, and ordering meals suddenly becomes a lot easier. For their part, the Thais are often keen to learn English—especially young students and monks. Walk into any school or temple-university campus, and you'll soon be joined by someone wanting to share a language lesson. For a crash-course in learning Thai, take a long-distance bus journey to somewhere remote like the Northeast. Local buses and 3rd class trains are excellent places for making Thai friends, and for learning the local lingo. As soon as you begin passing round photos of your family, friends and home-town (the perfect way to overcome the language barrier), you'll find a whole busload of people dying to make your acquaintance. In these circumstances, learning to speak Thai is quick, painless and lots of fun.

The Thai language resembles Chinese in that it is tonal, monosyllabic and uninflected. The spoken language has five different tones (mid, high, low, rising and falling), so that any transcription from Thai into romanized alphabets can only be approximate. The written language is something else again—the general traveller simply won't have time to grapple with its complexities. Most visitors are simply grateful that road signs and restaurant menus are often written in English as well as Thai script.

Acquiring a basic vocabulary of Thai can be surprisingly easy—not only do verbs have no tense, but most of the words that you need comprise just one syllable. Many of them sound the same too (e.g. *mai, bai, yai, chai, sai* and *rai*), and can be strung together to produce simple sentences. To avoid the potential minefield of tonal variations (every syllable, depending on how it's pronounced, can have five different meanings) it's best to say everything in a neutral monotone. The one big exception to this is the word *soway*. Pronounced with rising-tone emphasis (*so-WAY!*), this is a popular compliment meaning 'beautiful'. Saying it with down-tone emphasis however, can go down like a lead balloon—you've just wished someone bad luck.

Polite speech requires the addition of the word *kup* (for men) or *ka* (for women) to the end of every sentence. It shows respect for the listener, and is the commonest way of expressing agreement or understanding. The all-purpose word for 'you' is *khun*, while 'I/me' is *pom* (for men) or *Dee-chan* (for women). The word *khun* can also stand for 'person(s)' or 'Mr' (e.g. *saam khun* = three people; *Khun John* = Mr John).

You'll soon notice, when speaking to Thais, their difficulty pronouncing the letter 'r'. It often comes out as 'l'. Thus, *aroi* often becomes *alloi*, and you may be better understood saying you come from *Anglit* rather than from *Angrit*. Confusing? Oh well, *mai pen rai* (or *lai!*). Whether or not you succeed with Thai, it's great fun trying. You'll know you are getting somewhere when your first intelligible Thai remark meets with amazed silence, followed by an excited jabber of super-fast Thai chit-chat. The only polite way I know of halting this rather one-sided exchange is to quickly interject with *Put Thai nid noi—mai geng*! Which roughly translates as 'I'm only a novice—give me a break!'

256

An important thing to be aware of is regional dialect. The rapid, abbreviated *pak Thai* of the south is miles apart from the clear, more 'correct' speech of Bangkok, and is a completely different language to the relaxed, laidback drawl of the north. This situation can throw many travellers—especially those who arrive in Bangkok from the Deep South, only to find that they've acquired a 'dialect'. Using southern slang like *mabbalai* (*mai pen rai*) or *kup* (*khrap*) simply won't do in Bangkok—here, you'll have to speak proper.

The short vocabulary that follows should be enough to cover most occasions. If however, you're heading into remote provincial areas (e.g. the northeast) where English is hardly spoken at all, Joe Cummings' small *Thai Phrasebook* (Lonely Planet, 1984) is a most useful travelling companion.

VOCABULARY

Hello, goodbye	*Sawadee-kup (ka)*
Good luck, goodbye	*Chock-dee-kup (ka)*
Thank you	*Khop khun kup (ka)*
Pleased to meet you	*Yindee ti-ruja khun*
Sir/Madam	*Khun*
Yes (statement)	*Chai*
Yes (agreement)	*Kup/ka*
No	*Mai* (pronounced 'my')
Good	*Dee*
Bad	*Mai dee*
(Very) beautiful	*SoWAY (maak)*

Conversation

How are you?	*Khun sabai dee rue (OR sabai-dee)*
I'm fine, thanks	*Sabai-dee, khop khun kap (ka)*
What is your name?	*Khun cheu arai*
My name is John	*Pom cheu John*
My name is Cathy	*Dee-chan cheu Cathy*
How old are you?	*Khun ayuu tao rai*
I'm (30) years old	*Pom/dee-chan ayuu (saam-sip) pi*
I'm from England/USA	*Pom/dee-chan khon Angrit/Saharat Amerikaa*
Do you speak English?	*Put Angrit*
I speak Thai (only) little	*Put Thai nid-noi*
Understand?	*Kao chai mai*
I don't understand	*Chan mai kao chai*
Excuse me	*Khaw thot*
Never mind, no problem, you're welcome, why worry	*Mai pen rai*
Where are you going?	*Bai nai*
I'm going to Bangkok	*Chai bai Bangkok*

I like Bangkok	*Pom/dee-chan chawp Bangkok*
I love Thailand	*Pom/dee-chan raak Muang Thai*
Do you have a room ...	*Mee hong mai ...*
for two people?	*song khun*
Do you want (a cigarette)?	*Ao (buri)*
I don't want (it)	*May ao kap (ka)*
I don't have (it)	*May mee kap (ka)*
Do you have a toilet?	*Mee hong-nam mai*
Where is the ...	*Yu thee nai*
bus-station	*sathanee rot meh*
railway station	*sathanee rot fai*
police station	*sathanee tam-ruat*
boat	*reua*
bank	*thanaakhaan*
restaurant	*raan-aahaan*
doctor	*maw*
hospital	*rohng phayaa-baan*

Food and Drink

Rice	*Kao*
Fried rice with ...	*Kao-pat*
chicken/pork/crab/shrimp	*kai/muu/puu/kung*
Spicy fried chicken	*Kai yang*
Spicy papaya salad	*Som-tam*
Noodles	*Kuaytiaw*
Curry	*Kaeng*
Fish	*Pla*
Eggs	*Khai*
Fruit	*Phon-la-mai*
Sugar	*Nam-taan*
Salt	*Kleau*
Water	*Nam*
Milk	*Nom*
Ice	*Nam-khaeng*
Yoghurt	*Nom priaw*
Coffee, no sugar	*Kaafay, mai sai nam-taan*
Tea, with milk	*Nam-cha, sai nom*
Beer	*Bia*
Whisky	*Mekong*
Let's eat	*Kin-kao*
Delicious	*Aroi*
Enough	*Por lao*
I'm full up	*Im lao*
I'm not well	*Pom/dee-chan/mai sabai*
What's your special dish?	*Mee arai phe-set?*
I'm vegetarian	*Pom/dee-chan kin jeh*

Money

How much?	*Tao rai*
How many baht?	*Kee baht*
Too expensive	*Phaeng bai*
Please discount	*Lot noi*
No way, forget it!	*Ma dai!*

Useful Words

Today	*Wan-nee*
Tomorrow	*Pung-nee*
Yesterday	*Meau wan-nee*
Minutes	*Na-thee*
(How many) hours	*(Kee) chua-mohng*
Year	*Pee*
Big	*Yai*
(Too) small	*Lek (bai)*
Hot	*Rawn*
(Very) cold	*Yen (maak)*

Numbers

Zero	*Soon*
One	*Nung*
Two	*Song*
Three	*Saam*
Four	*See*
Five	*Ha*
Six	*Hok*
Seven	*Jet*
Eight	*Paet*
Nine	*Kao*
Ten	*Sip*
Eleven	*Sip-et*
Twelve	*Sip-song*
Thirteen	*Sip-saam*
Twenty	*Yee-sip*
Twenty-one	*Yee-sip-et*
Twenty-two	*Yee-sip-song*
Twenty-five	*Yee-sip-ha*
30	*Saam-sip*
40	*See-sip*
50	*Ha-sip*
60	*Hok-sip*
70	*Jet-sip*
80	*Paet-sip*
90	*Kao-sip*

100	Roi
500	Ha roi
750	Jet roi ha-sip
1000	Nung pan
10,000	Nung Muen
1 million	Laan

INDEX

Note: Page references in *italics* indicate illustrations; references in **bold** indicate maps.

Other Cadogan Guides available from your local bookshop or from UK or USA direct:

From the UK: Cadogan Books, Mercury House, 195 Knightsbridge, London SW7 1RE.
From the US: The Globe Pequot Press, 138 West Main Street, Chester, Connecticut 06412.

Title

Australia .... ☐
Bali .... ☐
Berlin .... ☐
The Caribbean .... ☐
Ecuador, The Galápagos & Colombia .... ☐
Greek Islands .... ☐
India .... ☐
Ireland .... ☐
Italian Islands .... ☐
Italy .... ☐
Mexico .... ☐
Morocco .... ☐
New York .... ☐
Northeast Italy .... ☐
Northwest Italy .... ☐
Portugal .... ☐
Prague .... ☐
Rome .... ☐
Scotland .... ☐
South of France: Provence, Côte d'Azur, Languedoc-Roussillon .... ☐
South Italy .... ☐
Southern Spain: Andalucia & Gibraltar .... ☐
Spain .... ☐
Tunisia .... ☐
Turkey .... ☐
Tuscany, Umbria & The Marches .... ☐
Venice .... ☐

Name ....

Address ....

.... Post Code ....

Date .... Order Number ....

Special Instructions ....

....

General Comments